Advance Praise for ATTENDANT CRUELTIES

"With the dimensions of the American fiasco in the Middle East becoming ever more painfully apparent, and at a time when economic hardships grow for all but the upper echelons of American society, the question of who we are as a people is being asked once again with particular intensity. Patrice Higonnet's thought-provoking historical review of how this question of national identity and purpose has been answered in the past at difficult moments is a page-turner. It holds up a mirror untinted by sentimentalism to help us see how as a people we have arrived at our current condition and what we may do to address the critical challenges that confront us."

–TONY SMITH, Cornelia M. Jackson Professor of Political Science, Tufts University; author of *A Pact with the Devil*

"In this wide-ranging exploration of American history, French-born Patrice Higonnet confronts Americans with the inner contradictions and short-fallings of their highly vaunted democratic republic. From Puritans and Indians to the present war in Iraq, we see how compromised America—and Americans—are by their dual loyalties to a 'Christian America' and a militarized, capitalistic imperialism willing to trample other peoples' rights in the interests of global hegemony. Here, in one compact volume, is the good, the bad, and the ugly of American history."

–HARRY S. STOUT, Jonathan Edwards Professor of American Religious History, Yale University

"*Attendant Cruelties* shows the historical imagination at the height of its power: the power to turn memory into prophecy, and the interpretation of dead experience into our revelation to ourselves. The history of the contest between an exclusive nationalism and an inclusive patriotism in the United States becomes, in Patrice Higonnet's work, a vantage point from which to understand the paradoxes of American life and the troubles of a divided world.

To his generation of historians and to those that will succeed it, Higonnet offers a peerless example of how to combine the outward history of society with the inward history of the heart. To students and their teachers, he provides a way to give intellectual depth and excitement to the study of diversity—and of its acceptance and rejection—in the history of the country.

A good way to begin understanding the United States is to read this book. A good way to begin thinking as a great historian thinks is to master the method of this book."

–ROBERTO MANGABEIRA UNGER, author of *The Self Awakened* and *What Should the Left Propose?*

ATTENDANT

NATION AND NATIONALISM
IN AMERICAN HISTORY

PATRICE HIGONNET CRUELTIES

OTHER PRESS NEW YORK

Production Editor: Robert D. Hack

Text designer: Jeremy Diamond

This book was set in Janson Text by Alpha Graphics of Pittsfield, New Hampshire.

10 9 8 7 6 5 4 3 2 1

Library of Congress Cataloging-in-Publication Data

Higonnet, Patrice L. R.
    Attendant cruelties : nation and nationalism in American history /
Patrice Higonnet.
        p. cm.
    Includes bibliographical references and index.
    ISBN-13: 978-1-59051-235-7
    ISBN-10: 1-59051-235-9
    1. United States–Civilization. 2. National characteristics, American.
    3. Nationalism–United States–History. 4. Nationalism–Religious aspects–
    Christianity. 5. United States–History–Religious aspects–Christianity.
    6. Messianism, Political–United States. 7. Political culture–United States.
    I. Title.
    E169.1.H54 2007
    973.072–dc22

                                                        2006103217

A la mémoire de mon père
René Alphonse Higonnet
inventeur de la photo-composition
citoyen des deux mondes
né à Valence sur Rhône
le 5 avril 1902
mort à Territet, en pays de Vaud,
le 13 octobre 1983

In a fight with savages, where the savages perform deeds of hideous cruelty, a certain proportion of whites are sure to do the same thing. This happened in the warfare with the Indians, with the Kafirs of the Cape and with aborigines in Australia. In each individual instance where the act is "performed" it should be punished with merciless severity; but to withdraw from the contest for civilization because of the fact that there are attendant cruelties, is, in my opinion, utterly unworthy of a great people.

–THEODORE ROOSEVELT, April 1899

CONTENTS

It's graduation day at the most prestigious law school in the United States: a picturesque and typically American ceremony. These one hundred students are a carefully selected group. Most of them, within years or even months, will belong to America's governing elites. Some, in a few weeks, will find places on Wall Street: at the age of twenty-five, they will earn more than do university professors at the end of long and brilliant careers. Others have concerns of a very different kind.

Here are Ethel Tucker Legaré and Margaret Bryan Thurlowe, both brilliant, both beautiful, both from old southern families. I chat with one of them, the daughter of an ambassador, a descendant of Thomas Jefferson and of a seventeenth-century Indian princess, about literature and science; about Oxford and Cambridge; about the Lycée Louis-le-Grand for math, and, for letters, the Lycée Henri IV—of which she has firsthand knowledge; about Harvard and MIT. These young women are, as Boston Brahmins used to say, "perfectly perfect." *L'Amérique est leur patrie.* (America is their homeland.) They introduce me to their friend, Zora Tanner, an African American born in New York City to a single mother. And next to their friend sits this lady, immensely proud, as she might well be: her daughter's success is a fair reward for her lifetime of hard work and sacrifice. *L'Amérique est sa patrie.* (America is her homeland.)

This brings to my mind an incident in Paris that both surprised and shocked me: a *beur*, a young Frenchman of Arab descent, had parked his delivery van in such a way that I couldn't move my own car forward to unload it. We exchanged words, bantering back and forth, our mood gradually more tense: harsher on the one hand, more demanding and ironical on the other. I ask him: "Haven't you noticed that I have the right to drive a car through here, whereas you are parked illegally?" He explodes: "Goddamn France. I could give a shit about your rights." Would an African American speak that way of the United States with an easy conscience? Many would still think "I have a dream"—a dream invariably frustrated but constantly reborn.

Here is Ephrem Immanuel Kaplan, whose philanthropic family has been in the United States for four generations. His branch of the family, to the amazement of their relatives, has just moved to an Israeli settlement in the West Bank. He wears a *kippah* and earlocks. America is one of his two homelands. And here are Zahiaya Banjeree, Srinivas Nehru Kandaswamy, and Alexandros O'Brien Papandrenos: America is their homeland.

I move on to meet John Bouvier Reeves. He's six foot two, with light blond hair and dark blue eyes. He looks like a movie star. His tranquil manner does not conceal a determined certainty. His friends tell me laughingly that he will soon be governor of Iowa, and then, not much later, president of the United States. He smiles, but doesn't deny what they say. America is his homeland.

And here is Victor McMeekin Weinberg, an activist from Oregon, who is planning to work for a pittance at a London-based NGO. America, he believes, will realize itself fully as a nation only when it puts itself at the service of humanity. As he speaks, I hear in his words the echo of the Fourierists and the Kantian Transcendentalists, those American utopians of the nineteenth century who were fired with those same ideals of truth and justice. We chat about Lincoln's Gettysburg Address, that mystical speech of 1863, which Victor knows by heart, and which, more than any other document, explains to America's citizens what their country truly is or should be. Did Lincoln, in a sudden flash of inspiration, spontaneously add those two fateful words, "under God,"[1] words that abruptly made of a self-centered nation engaged in a destructive civil war an "almost chosen people," under the orders of the Lord, a nation whose victories had to be those of good triumphant over evil. Victor is sure of it. I tell him Bismarck's joke about the United States, that there really is a God who protects America, but with that special providence that He reserves for drunkards, idiots, and the American Republic. Victor smiles—one would be hard-pressed to find a group of young people more polite or more affable—but, clearly, Bismarck's cruel joke does not please him. *L'Amérique est sa patrie.*

Patricia Isabel Rivera, Winfield Yu, Akira Yamaguchi, Susan Ju Yoon Li: America is their homeland, as America may be, soon, for Ibrahim ben Salah, here on a scholarship from Ramallah. What American generosity allowed this son of that most frustrated and humiliated of peoples to pay for three years of study in this wealthy, and costly, university?

We say the United States "is," in the singular; but oftentimes we should perhaps say instead (as the early Americans did and as the French still do) that the United States "are." It would be unfair and absurd not to acknowledge and recognize the immense good qualities, and the immense variety, of the American people. This book is often critical. At times, it is quite harsh. That is because its subject is the nature and history of American nationalism, which is a passion that is dark and dangerous. But one could just as well have written a wholly positive history of American philanthropy, American generosity, American medical and scientific research, American universities and museums, American literature and film. And why not, also, a history of American kindness and amiability? Even those Americans whose political ideas are the most violent and ill informed often are, in their private lives, gentle, open, welcoming people. And how could one not admire, and even love, a patriotic and universalist America, which, in spite of everything, is still alive and well?

This book is not intended as a criticism of the day-to-day America as most of us know it experientially: open-minded, welcoming, at the forefront of nearly everything, and, in so many ways, the freest country in the world. Indeed, the book's aim is to praise this libertarian America, but it does certainly also aim to criticize the threat to world peace that is posed by the nationalist, reactionary tradition that is liberal America's darker twin.

Is America today at a turning point for the worse? It often seems so: the gap between an older (and wiser) Europe and an America that carries forward retrograde European religious and economic traditions, which Europe has now left behind, is wide and widening. And so it matters today that all of us, both in America and in the world at large, should be aware of the connections that bind the dark chapters of America's past to its darkening present. George W. Bush's America is a threat to the world and to itself. The enemy of his administration is not just "Old Europe" but the welfare of the American people. A natural link exists (and has always existed) between the progressive America of the Enlightenment, of what Gunnar Myrdal called the American Creed, and forward-minded Europe. (There are in Paris a Rue Lincoln, a Rue Benjamin Franklin, an Avenue du Président Wilson, a massive equestrian statue of George Washington, and a Métro station named for Franklin Roosevelt.) After two disastrous twentieth-century world wars, libertarian and historically informed progressive America, like chastened and historically minded Europe, understands that particularist nationalism is the worst and most disastrous of all public passions. But the United States, or rather its leaders in the administration of George W. Bush, refuses to grasp this basic historical truth. We have to hope that Europe today will be the enemy of Bush's America, but only insofar as Bush is the enemy of America's own libertarian history and of its common sense.

In consequence, the first purpose of this book is to follow, critically, the course of the "American national idea" and its occasional propensity to "attendant cruelties," not just during the adulthood of the United States as a nation since 1776, but also during its earlier Anglo-American "childhood," in a story that stretches from early massacres and enslavement of Native Americans during the 1630s to Bush's preemptive and criminal invasion of Iraq. But the second purpose of this book is also to chart the other, sunny, tradition of inclusion, which has always been the first characteristic of American life. As Walter Lippmann put it in his *Essays in the Public Philosophy* of 1955: "Men can know more than their ancestors did if they start with a knowledge of what their ancestors had already learned." It is with that idea in mind that I write this book.

INTRODUCTION
Patriotism and Imperialism

Americans love their country. They believe it has a mission, as befits, again in Lincoln's words, "an almost chosen people."[1] But less obvious to them (and us) is what their almost divine mission is all about, and why they tend to believe that America's historical experience is an example that every other nation will want to follow or must be made to follow.[2] For many, like Thomas Jefferson in 1800, the message has been that America should be open to the world because it is the best hope of humankind. But others have imagined it instead to be primarily industrious and modernizing, as did Jefferson's contemporary Alexander Hamilton. (Calvin Coolidge surely had that tradition in mind when he said that the business of America was just that: business.) Moreover, these different views align and realign themselves in unexpected ways.[3] Hamilton was opposed to slavery, whereas Jefferson was convinced that African Americans—including, or so we must suppose, the children he had by Sally Hemings, his African-American mistress, slave, and sister-in-law—were hopelessly handicapped from birth. And as regards their national character, many Americans have imagined their nation to be simultaneously pragmatic and idealistic, or generous and fierce, as was their greatest statesman, Abraham Lincoln, during their terrible civil war: typically, Theodore Roosevelt—himself a puzzlingly divided person—described Lincoln as "the great example of sane and temperate radicalism."[4]

From earliest times, however, two themes have structured—and remarkably enough, still structure—this American, and, as shall be seen, divided but durable discursive sense of self, which has proved uniquely impervious to massive material changes of many kinds.

The more consequential of the two has been the importance in American life of religion and of its many derivatives: messianism, moralism, and an often unfocused yearning for transcendence. Today 96 percent of Americans say that they believe in God and 80 percent believe in the existence of the devil. In 2002, more than 20 percent thought that the terrorist attacks of September 11, 2001, had been predicted in the Bible.[5] Most of them go to church at least once a month, and most of them by far claim to have a particular relationship to God. American religion seeps through the entire fabric of "Americanness." It is with good cause that a recent commentator has observed that religion is one of the most pervasive but least understood forces in American history.[6] As Garry Wills writes: "Religion has been at the center of our major political crises, which are always moral crises—the supporting and opposing of wars, of slavery, of corporate power, of civil rights, of sexual codes, of 'the West,' of American separatism and claims of empire."[7] A long list, which could also be extended to include America's understanding of its material success: How could God not want to reward those who are truly worthy? In America, divine providence has been ceaselessly invoked, even when—or perhaps especially when—the nation's blind violence has taken an unusually violent turn, with atomic bombs, agent orange, the Trail of Tears, or Sherman's march to the sea. In the American imagination, materialism, brutality, and a yearning for transcendence have often walked hand in hand. As Karl Marx put it in 1843 (citing Tocqueville), "North America is the preeminent land of religiosity."[8]

Like Proteus, a Greek god who took on many shapes, human or natural, solid or liquid, the deity who is said to protect America's innocence has taken on different guises. In the days of Calvin and the New England Puritans, God was seen as stern and unbendable. Much later, in Lincoln's day, many thoughtful Americans—like Emerson and Lincoln —preferred to think of a more benign providence. And it matters, sadly, that in our own day American Protestant thinking has taken on one of its most dismal colorations: namely, biblical and apocalyptic fundamentalism. This is the sensibility that inspires George W. Bush, who sees himself as the archangel of sacralized democracy, engaged in a life-and-death struggle between the forces of good and evil.

The second central theme in the evolution of America's sense of self—one that feeds both left and right—has been a deep concern for the individualization of property and social life with its various correlatives: an unrelenting suspicion of the State, a deep devotion to self-improvement and self-government, a deep respect for the dignity of every person's labor, a belief in ever-renewed economic opportunity, a dedication to the legal rights of the accused and to the idea of self-becoming. Don Quixote, literature's most famous wanderer, preferred the road to the inn, and so it is, for example, that among the classic topoi of American literature is the road novel (as in Emerson's "everything good is on the highway"). As is the invention—or more particularly, the Augustinian reinvention—of the self. In the words of Jimmy Carter's favorite hymn, "Amazing Grace": "How sweet the sound . . . I once was lost but now am found." Sojourner Truth: what a wonderful American name! In their imagined Eden, Americans, from first to last, have assumed that it was they and God who had created their society, rather than the other way around. "Men make their history," said Marx, "but they do not make it as they please." That is *not* the way Americans have imagined their society and their history.

To be sure, communitarian traditions have also been strong in America, though more so perhaps in fiction than in fact. Tocqueville, for example, was struck in 1831 by the new—and even in America—unprecedented importance of associationism in American life, of town meetings, or religious communities, political parties, and so on, a quality that reminded him, no doubt, of the corporate (and aristocratic) loyalties that had structured pre-Revolutionary France and now—in his country—were no more.

Nonetheless, America's communitarian transcendentalism (which was largely religious before 1750, and was then secularized in the nineteenth century—as in the case of Jane Addams—and which is often today once again expressed in strictly religious terms) has had clear limits. In the end, in America, a sense of community has ordinarily been the handmaiden rather than the rival or the enemy of individuated and even self-seeking passion. Here, we can conjure the image of American pioneers in the movies, and perhaps in real life as well, circling their covered wagons to face and defeat their ruthless and cruel Indian enemies. The point of those uplifting stories, however, is that after a drastic emergency of this kind, the pioneers will soon separate and find their private paths to some empty, inviting, western, promised, and enriching land. In the American historical experience, universalist republicanism and political liberalism have always had to be mindful of economic individualism: Americans are indeed "a nation of joiners," but Schopenhauer's images of porcupines also come to mind here, of animals that fear being alone and cold, but also fear the pointed, wounding nature of each other's quills.[9]

In the imagination of Americans, material progress, democracy, and individual liberty do occasionally—but only occasionally—require the communitarian regularization of institutions. "It was not the policy of the liberal system," wrote a mid-nineteenth-century Massachusetts publicist, "to abstain from all regulations whatever, upon the notion that the present private interest is in all cases coincident with that of the public."[10] The first national plan for the rationalization of America's economic life was (unsuccessfully) proposed to Congress by Albert Gallatin in 1808. Americans, especially when they are rich, like to receive governmental subsidies and grants-in-aid. But they are all individualists in the end.

Americans are awed by the universalizing and sublime majesty of nature, a trait which is common to all human beings, but they yearn also to dominate this selfsame nature, to use it for their private purposes, and even to destroy it for no reason at all. As Leo Marx explained, the myth of American nature, "in its simplest most archetypal form . . . affirms that Europeans experience a regeneration in the New World. They become new, better, happier men."[11] America's parks and garden are indeed a communitarian paradise but one that is marred by many a destructive snowmobile. Economic individualism in America is not a force that can be trifled with.

A mixed heritage, then, but, curiously, an extraordinarily stable one. Of course, other national images have been durable as well: consider the place of romanticized nature in German culture, of aristocratized elegance and cold lucidity for the French, of rugged, yeoman self-government for the British. These national conceptualizations too have had a long shelf life. Indeed, it often happens that a nation will loop back upon itself and find it impossible to break out of its inherited legacies. Some Alamos are all too easily remembered: on the eve of the Great War, for example, the French, however democratic and pacific they may have been, found it impossible to forget their lost eastern provinces, Alsace and Lorraine, which Germany had annexed in 1871. Likewise, Tocqueville's first theme in his *Ancien Régime* of 1856 was precisely to point out that the French were the victims of ancient ways: try as they might and republican as they might be, they could not shake off the habits of centuries of centralized monarchic rule. Napoleon's authoritarian rule was for Tocqueville no accident of modern French history, but, on the contrary, a mere remake of pre-1789 centralized government, where new Napoleonic authoritarian prefects had simply slipped into the shoes, now restyled, of the old royal "intendants."

In a different and more republican mode, it is also evident that the prestige today at home and abroad of the French model of citizenship—which denies the relevance of ethnicity just as it denied the relevance of class in the nineteenth century—has more to do with the weight of French legacies than with the model's contemporary efficaciousness.

Nonetheless, the stability of America's creation myths does stand out from what holds true for most other nations, and above all else, for what holds true of other *modern* nations. As Judith Shklar explained, "The longevity of the ideology that goes under the entirely appropriate title of 'the American Dream' is indeed an extraordinary phenomenon."[12] It is a striking fact that a hyperindustrialized and ethnically hybrid country like the United States should rule itself today through an inadequate and even paralyzing constitution that was created when its inhabitants were in their overwhelming majority white, Protestant, and still protected from the rest of the world by tyrannous distances—by Governor Winthrop's "vast and furious ocean." National American income in 1787 (if translated into dollars adjusted for their value in 2000) was four billion dollars, whereas in the year 2000, American national income was in the order of ten thousand billion dollars, or 2,500 times the earlier sum. But that ancient constitution, like America's earliest myths, is still cherished today, and often absurdly so, to the point that learned legal experts —grown men!—struggle to resolve highly contemporary technical problems by referring to what the Founding Fathers might think of today's technological wizardry.

It is striking also that most Americans are unaware of what is at stake in their perpetuation of their country's ancient image of itself. They too live at times in the past, but nevertheless they are sure they are living their future at this moment. As a well-known student of America's self-image put it half a century ago: "A people unaware of its myths is likely to continue living by them, though the world around that people may change and demand changes in their psychology, their world view, their ethics, and their institutions."[13]

So it is that America's constant dedication to these ancient images of its larger sense of self (as God's chosen nation, as the enlightened homeland of individuated freedom, and as the site also of the American economic dream) is sui generis and unusually durable. "Enlightenment," in the words of Aleida Assmann, "means a break with tradition," to which we would add, in all societies but one.[14]

Indeed, these same broad and inherited constructs, simultaneously divergent and convergent, are oftentimes determining for what happens from day to day as well. One example among many of that quotidian compulsion will perhaps suffice: it concerns Theodore Roosevelt and his comments in 1901 on some press reports of American atrocities in distant lands. These imperial incidents, he patiently explained, while blamable in themselves, had to be set in a larger frame. The larger point that was at stake (namely defeating and civilizing the Filipino rebels) was not negotiable. That work had to be done. Moreover, Roosevelt thought that America's historical experience in the West showed the way in the Philippines as well because the Americans of his day would easily overwhelm Aguinaldo's rebels just as their forefathers had easily defeated the Indians. What had worked against Sioux and Apaches would work in Manila also.

(*On this same subject of continuities and the Philippines, of the thirty American generals who served there at the time, twenty-seven had also fought in the western United States.*[15] *And it is also suggestive that the principles of war that these officers first used in the West and then reused in the Philippines had been developed at the time of the Civil War. During that conflict, reminisced General Sheridan in a letter to General Sherman in 1873, "did any one hesitate to attack a village or town occupied by the enemy because women or children were within its limits? . . . if a village is attacked and women and children killed, the responsibility is not with the soldiers but with the people whose crimes necessitated the attack."*[16] *History does have a way of sounding familiar.*)

"In a fight with savages," quote Theodore Roosevelt once again, "where the savages perform deeds of hideous cruelty, a certain proportion of whites are sure to do the same thing . . . In each individual instance where the act is 'performed' it should be punished with merciless severity; but to withdraw from the contest for civilization because of the fact that there are attendant cruelties, is, in my opinion, utterly unworthy of a great people."[17] This was a view of life that the Puritans would have understood in the 1630s. It is also George W. Bush's understanding of America's situation in the world today.

*****

Of course, we would like to be able to theorize about the genesis and development of the American national idea and of its nationalist excrescence. Here, however, the basic point is that most of the paradigms that social scientists have evolved to think about nationalism in general only serve to underscore the irreducibility and "exceptionalism" of the American experience.

The collapse of European colonial empires in the 1950s, followed in 1989 by the death of what Ronald Reagan had labeled "the Evil Empire," led, around the world, to a blossoming of those local, nationalist passions that domineering empires had previously forbidden.

Eager to explain these surprising developments, many political scientists and some historians—many of whom as private persons had also been affected and saddened by the decline of Marxism as a system of analysis—labored to theorize what they had observed. Some of this literature does bear (tangential) relevance to the American case. It is interesting, for example, to distinguish—as has often been done—the historical experience of societies (like America and France) whose sense of national self has since their eighteenth-century revolutions emphasized abstract values largely derived from the eighteenth-century Enlightenment. Clearly, these two nations with their republican traditions are far removed from societies like Germany, Russia, or Japan, whose nationalism has laid greater emphasis on ethnic, religious, or racial concerns. Jürgen Habermas has suggested that just as feelings can legitimize institutions, so can institutions generate sentiment, and this idea has some relevance to those nationalisms that emphasize abstract, non-territorial principle. As Rousseau put it, "National institutions mold the genius, the character, and the taste of a people . . . They inspire in that people an ardent love of their homeland" (that is, of their patrie)."[18]

Also of some relevance to the American case is Elie Kedourie's analysis of African and Asian nationalism: here the emphasis is on the specificity and power of *ideological* motivations. Nationalism in this view often begins as a kind of "children's crusade." (In 1776 Jefferson, Madison, Monroe—and Lafayette—were in their twenties or early thirties; Washington, at forty-four, was for them a kind of elder statesman.) In this Kedourian frame, national sentiment is a messianic promise that appeals to "marginal" young men fascinated by the (destructive) power of their xenophobic ideology—a view that has to be of interest to those students of American life who emphasize the quasi-religious nature of American nationalism.[19]

Other interpretations of nationalism have been equally plausible and variably applicable to the American scene: Karl Deutsch focused on communication networks, and Ernest Gellner, in his admirable work of the 1960s, emphasized instead the functional importance of economic concerns to nation building. In that view, the invention of nationalism was mandated by economic need. To thrive, burgeoning capitalism and industrialism required the nation as a sociological form so as to guarantee the existence of its material prerequisites: namely, an educated workforce, a capital market, internal free trade. Industrialism required the existence of the nation, which in turn made of industrialization a national imperative.[20] (National industry attracted to the city deracinated peasants to whom nationalism seemed a self-evident value.) But this view of life is of limited relevance to the United States, whose roots as a nation antedate industrialism by nearly two centuries.

Theories of nationalism as an "imagined community" are, up to a point, of greater relevance. Here, the reasoning is that nations are constructed as a reintegrative force, often in response to an external colonizing might. Where community no longer exists, and especially where it is thought to have been destroyed by colonializing outsiders, national community has to be "imagined" anew, in Benedict Anderson's now famous formula. In this view, resentful colonials—or ex-colonials— imagine themselves as partners in a quest or journey of self-assertion whose ingredients (such as the assertion of a national language or some particular historical experience) will grow and change over time. The work of John Breuilly and Anthony Giddens is also set in this mode, but at times with paradoxical consequence. So is it for example that Breuilly argues that the American War of Independence cannot be considered a national rebellion because Americans lacked "an explicit and peculiar character"[21] that set them apart from their British rulers—a view of that situation that will puzzle many historians of the period.

Equally suggestive but in the end similarly peripheral are the highly interesting historicizing observations of Eric Hobsbawm on "the invention of tradition." Here the argument will be that bourgeois states—

oftentimes imperializing bourgeois states—will legitimate their own existence, or their oppression of others, by developing a vast ceremonial panoply of rites, rituals, memorials, and the like. This idea is by no means irrelevant to American life. Statues of Abraham Lincoln do indeed abound in the northern states, many of them nearly as ostentatious as those dedicated in the southern states to Robert E. Lee and the "lost cause." Schoolbooks (Noah Webster's dictionary), popular entertainment (Buffalo Bill), parades and conventions, the myth of a classical golden age (varyingly set in 1776, 1865, or 1944–1945): all have their place as the supports of durable American memories and mythologies. But although very numerous, such artifacts of memory (often imperially conceived on the theme of landed conquest, as in Pilgrim ships at Plymouth, or, again, the Alamo), though not irrelevant to the development of American patriotic life, are nonetheless incidental to it. They are there to express and embellish a sentiment that would have existed— and thrived—without their support.

On balance, then, theorizations of nationalism have had little to say about the American case, and, one is tempted to write, almost inevitably so, because most historians of this "nature of nationality problem" have been basically concerned to show how nationality has come into being, that is to say how and why "pre-modern" societies have managed—or have failed to manage—their transition to modern democracy, be it formal democracy (with sham elections) or "constitutional" democracy (with the rule of law). Most developmental theories of nation have focused on the *rise* of contemporary nationalisms, many of them motivated either by the exemplary rise at the end of the nineteenth century of Zionism in Europe as a gesture of self-defense against the ambient anti-Semitism of European nationalisms, or (often) by the rise in the second half of the twentieth century of anti-Zionist or anti-European Arab and Asian nationalisms. These works are therefore focused on the often sudden and unprecedented *appearance* of national consciousnesses.[22]

By stunning contrast, the most conspicuous—and as of now, incompletely theorized—aspects of American nationalism have been, not its inception, but its ability to subsist and its ability to develop by accretion rather than by renunciation. Historically, what has mattered in America's growing and unchallenged self-perception has been not innovation but constancy. So it is, for example, that "the distrust of power, generated deep within the ideological origins of the Revolution, [runs] through the entire course of American History and is as potent an element in our national life today . . . as it was two hundred years ago,"[23] and this judgment by Bernard Bailyn, one of the leading twentieth-century historians of America's colonial period, could be duplicated for many other themes and moments of American history. "America," wrote Walt Whitman grandly in 1855, "does not repel the past or what it has produced under its forms or amid other politics or the idea of castes or the old religions. [America] accepts the lessons with calmness [and] is not so impatient as has been supposed. [America] still sticks to opinions and manners and literature while the life which served its requirements has passed into the new life of new forms."[24] More humbly but just as tellingly perhaps, a study of Muncie, Indiana, in 1979 showed that opinions in that archetypal town of Middle America had not changed much since first studied in 1924. "In or about December 1910," wrote Virginia Woolf, "human character changed (and) when human relations change, there is at the same time a change in religion, conduct, politics and literature." That may well have been true for the modernist elite of western Europe, but her remark has very little bearing on mainstream American life, either as it was in 1910 or as it is today.[25]

The genesis and development of America's national consciousness obviously deserve close attention. But, again, its most striking trait—in our view—is its ability to move through time as a consistent amalgamation of layered themes that can be either complementary or antithetical, as in the conjunction of communitarian religiosity and economic individualism, or again, of universalist Enlightenment values and the sense of America as a divinely elected place. "The United States," concluded Octavio Paz, "is a society that wants to realize its ideals, has no wish to exchange them for others, and is confident of surviving, no matter how dark the future may appear."[26]

*****

The persistence of its central values, then, has been the most striking (and, as it were, vertical) aspect of America's national and universalist, democratic and religious consciousness. The second (and, as it were, horizontal) characteristic of "The Creed" has been the ability of this American self-image to secure deep—and indeed overwhelming—support at home, and, at least in former times, abroad as well. Americans—and this really does bear repetition!—love their country. Political conflict (like violence) is as American as apple pie, but America's endless quarrels and debates about what is right and proper have not proved inconsistent with the forging of a broad consensus on the larger meaning(s) of Americanism. As Paz put it, again, one finds in the United States "a criticism [that] is valuable and forthright, of a sort not often heard in the countries to the south . . . But it is a criticism that respects the existing systems and never touches the roots."[27] Indeed, it may be because they agree on so many fundamental issues that Americans can afford to quarrel ceaselessly about which legalistic procedure will best give substance to their imagined sense of self.

We can gauge the overall strength of American patriotism and nationalism in many ways, but most clearly perhaps in the juxtaposition of American unanimity about America's exceptional destiny with European divisions over what their nations were about. We could point to nineteenth-century Westernizing ideologues in Russia who urged their divided countrymen to move toward Western models and to renounce their debilitating Slavic roots. Likewise, at the other end of that older continent, we could juxtapose America's nationalism to the internationalism of the embattled twentieth-century French labor movement, which after 1871 turned away from its indigenous, syndicalist, and Proudhonist roots; embraced Marxist ideology; and in 1905 labeled itself "The French Section of the Workers' International." From the 1930s to the 1950s, the Soviet Union was the true homeland of most French workers. These were unthinkable situations in the United States. In America, strikingly different regionalisms are seen as amusingly different aspects of one vast national sameness: in Italy, by contrast, regionalism today is an often embittered denial of national union.

Why this broad and striking resonance in America of ongoing national values? A basic answer has to be that unquestioned American patriotism has made a great deal of sense to millions of migrants who have found in their new homeland two things that matter to them: an improvement in their material life and the freedom to be themselves. These were the goals of English Congregationalists in New England in the seventeenth century, as they were also of late nineteenth-century Jews and Italians in America's major cities, as they will surely be tomorrow of today's migrants and refugees from Latin America, Africa, or the Middle East. In that context of American opportunity and broad tolerance, it is easy to understand why Muslim migrants feel more at ease in the United States than they do in western Europe, where their right to exist has been loudly (but also vainly) proclaimed by states and constitutions. The core of "America from day to day" is in the satisfying conjunction of individualism, diversity, and pluralism, a union that found its letters of nobility in Walt Whitman's verse, in the pragmatism of William James, and in John Dewey's Instrumentalism.

For tens of millions, then, the American dream of personal and libertarian betterment has been a "patriotized" reality that became normative first because it really did prove, in actual fact, not to be "an impossible dream" at all, and, second, because so many of those who failed to realize that dream were subjected to a cruel discourse of Calvinist origin that cast failure and poverty as sinful pathologies. Millions of defeated Americans were made to feel that they had only themselves to blame because "the system" was not at fault, a cruel self-deception that has been a persistent theme of American culture and literature since Nathaniel Hawthorne and Herman Melville. In the United States, the plight of the defeated has merely strengthened the happy optimism of the victors.

It was in the United States—and Argentina, where immigrants were also supposed to find effortless happiness—that Freudian psychiatry (which neglects the relevance of economic context) found its largest audience. Americans fear, as Wallace Stevens observed, "that dreams and defeats are one." Optimism and tragedy in their country are never far apart, but most Americans do not like to be reminded of this, and it is well nigh impossible for them to grasp that, in the words of the historian Scott Sandage, "failure is not the dark side of the American Dream; it is the foundation of it."[28]

So it has been that the achievements of the successful ones and the melancholic self-doubt and self-exclusion of the others have fed the idea that more than any other has defined America for Americans, and often for foreigners as well. Worldwide, America has been seen as "a shining city on a hill" (one of Ronald Reagan's favorite locutions), as a model society and a second Israel. "The chief circumstance which has favored the establishment and maintenance of a democratic system in the United States," concluded a historian of this issue some time ago, is Americans' belief that "their ancestors gave them the love of equality and of freedom; but God Himself gave them the means of remaining equal and free by placing them upon a boundless continent."[29]

Unprecedented individual and communitarian freedom facilitated by unrivaled material betterment in a society sanctioned by divine Providence: moved as they were by this satisfying amalgamation of the practical and the mystical, American patriots have been by instinct nation-proud. Uninformed about and as a rule uninterested in the world beyond their borders, they have all too easily and all too often fallen into stances of tranquil superiority, an attitude that, incidentally, has been a source of exasperation for non-Americans in Europe and Latin America, and especially for those non-Americans who were—by their own lights at least—better educated, more cultured, and in a word, more civilized than the rich and boorish North Americans across the Atlantic or north of the Rio Grande.

But to Americans themselves, looking inward to the state of their union, a patriotic devotion to country has always seemed to make sense, as it also has when they have compared their country with its rivals. It used to be that America's American neighbors to the north and the south were colonized and weak, that European powers were at least one ocean removed, and that distant Asian neighbors were of no consequence to Americans at all. From its location alone, America was born triumphant and a model for the whole of humankind: "The bias of Americans," writes Roberto Unger, "is that the rest of the world must either languish in poverty and despotism or become more like them."[30] So determining is this conviction that American foreign policy has often been conducted in a state of dense mental fog (President McKinley, for example, knew literally nothing about the Philippines, and had "to study a globe to determine the location of the 'darned islands'").[31] Moreover, such mental fogs and ignorance are held by most Americans to be of no durable consequence: for McKinley—and for most of his compatriots—understanding the American experience was enough. Surely the principles that had prevailed in Republican Ohio would sooner or later prevail in Manila as well.

History—or so most Americans have assumed—has confirmed their sense of superiority. And it is a fact that no other polity on any continent has ever experienced anything like the spectacular development of American society, and in so short a time, from the extreme frailty of the European colonies in the early 1600s, to an "American century" that began in 1898, and to global dominance today (from the title in 1941 of an essay by Henry Luce, "The American Century," which cited as the basis of America's international purpose "America as the dynamic center of ever widening spheres of enterprise, America as the training center of skillful servants of mankind, America as the Good Samaritan, really believing again that it is more blessed to give than to receive, and America as the powerhouse of the ideals of Freedom and Justice"). Britain, it is true, also moved from relative insignificance on the edge of Europe in the late 1600s to world dominance in 1815, but nineteenth- and twentieth-century Britain was no more than a *primus inter pares*, unable to defeat the French at Waterloo without the help of the Prussians, or the Russians in the Crimea without the help of the French, or the Germans in two world wars without the help of the United States. For continental Europe, the end point of Napoleonic or Hitlerian policies of national aggrandizement has been extreme and legendary defeat. But America's victorious trajectory has been a happy Pilgrim's progress through seemingly boundless space, from one ocean to the other in the nineteenth century, and in seemingly open-ended time as well: Americans are very reluctant to think that their empire, like all other empires, will one day fail.

In brief, then, for America, we have progress without end in three successfully waged twentieth-century world wars that in one way or another have proved disastrous for all the other states that they engulfed. For many Americans, the question has been not "Why be an American nationalist?" but instead "Why *not* be one?" In America, nation, nationalism, and imperialism have usually been paying propositions.

*****

Nation and patriotism, then, on the one hand, but also, on the other, national*ism*: Should we think of these two strands of America's self-definition as one and the same thing? Yes and no. No, as a first response, and the argument of this book is that these two forces are indeed very different, but also yes, because they are in their origin very close, and in a fashion that is unique in the world.

In many important ways, American nationality and American nationalism are indeed one and the same thing: even in those moments when America has been most divided, some underlying ground has been shared by all Americans. Franklin Roosevelt's New Deal was certainly much detested by many American plutocrats (many of them his peers by birth and at Harvard College), but his acceptance of capitalism as a way of life meant that the gap between his friends and his enemies was not as great as it might seem. In 1860 Southerners dramatically rejected the Northerners' view of what Americanness ought to be, but the Stars and Bars were in many key respects very much like the Stars and Stripes: in 1858, two years before secession, Jefferson Davis declared: "This great country will continue united." That same year he told an audience in the state of Maine: "The whole [United States] is my country and to the innermost fibers of my heart I love it all, and every part." And Southerners, in many ways, were not at all as unlike their northern enemies as was believed both north and south of the Mason-Dixon Line. Southerners, like Northerners, were God-fearing (rural) democratic capitalists. Their favored justification of slavery was that its presence would make for a better white democracy. Besides, as Edmund Morgan remarked about colonial Virginians, southern whites "may have had a special appreciation of the freedom dear to Republicans, because they saw every day what life was like without it."[32]

And yet—and critical to the argument of this book—these common, shared, and national American values have seldom been expressed by a single voice. American patriotism and American nationalism, at once close and very far apart, have to be understood in conceptual terms that are particular to the United States. European social categories are largely irrelevant to the specificity of life in the United States.

In order to sort out the differences between Europe's classic patterns and America's originality, a first step is to define and distinguish these two ways of understanding the meaning of the term "homeland." What indeed is a nation, a *patrie*? What is patriotism? A useful starting point for understanding the European situation is the classic text of Ernest Renan, "What Is a Nation?," of 1882.

Written by a philosopher who, to his embarrassment, had been philo-German before France's defeat in 1871, this text defines peace-loving patriotism as a sentiment that arises from the shared recollection of happy events and symbolic figures—in the case of France, like Joan of Arc or the achievements of 1789. But although the patriot does remember some things very well, he is also an amnesiac who does *not* remember many other unhappy and divisive moments. For the French, this meant that all would choose to forget the massacres of Protestants by Catholics in 1572 or the execution of royalists by republicans (and vice versa) during France's revolutionary decade.

In this same context of the importance of memory for state building, one could also cite, for example, the emblem of the Province of Quebec— French and royal fleurs-de-lis, with, as a legend: "*Je me souviens*" (I remember). Here, French Canada chooses to remember its brand of Frenchness rather than its place as an orphaned province abandoned by its mother-nation. "Nationalism and national identity," writes Thomas Bender, "are founded largely on a sense of shared memories"[33]—but shared forgetfulness as well.

By contrast, Renan went on, the Germans cherished a false definition of nation, one that—perversely, he thought—emphasized race and also language, which Germans (wrongly) took to be the deeply rooted expression of some primal racial affinity. Thus, in Renan's view, German-speaking Alsatians should have been allowed to remain French because Alsace shared with other French provinces the universalist memory of 1789. Germany, in his view again, had had no right to annex this province in 1871. To the contrary, Prussia, the land of Immanuel Kant, had a moral obligation to respect Alsace's Francophile and libertarian wishes. In brief, Renan contrasted a constructed and historicized French "civilisation" against a more natural and sentient, German and emotion-laden "Kultur."

This is a useful starting point for understanding nationality since it opposes race—a category that excludes—to inclusive, diverse, libertarian, and fraternal patriotic remembrance. A patriot feels warmly about his country because, ideally, his homeland respects the equal rights and hopes of all its citizens. Patriotism, ideally, again, guarantees every citizen's fair right to public space. It works for the common good but it also respects social, ethnic, religious, and philosophical diversities. (One could cite here the legend on the crest of the Swiss canton of Vaud: "*liberté et patrie.*") It also works to create the material circumstances that give these rights practical and civic significance. In foreign affairs, it is pacific. Domestically, it works to preserve good government. In Renan's words, patriotism is a "daily plebiscite."

Nationalists, by contrast and by instinct, lean to exclusion: of countries other than their own in international affairs, and of some of their fellow citizens at home, where, in George Orwell's celebrated phrase, all are equal but some are more equal than others. "Patriotism," writes John Lukacs, "is defensive; nationalism is aggressive. Patriotism is the love of a particular land, with its particular traditions; nationalism is the love of something less tangible, of the myth of a people, justifying many things, a political and ideological substitute for religion."[34] Paradoxically (as patriotism is localized and practical, where nationalism claims to be more abstract and ideologized), inward-looking, seemingly narrow-minded patriotisms are in the end more universalist than are nationalist particularisms, which, again, on the surface of things, may seem to be more broadly conceived. Alain Touraine, France's leading sociologist, has described this selfsame tension philosophically:

> It does happen that [libertarian] social movements decay to such a degree as to become the reverse of what they were. They lapse into communitarian assertion, into the rejection of "foreignness" and difference, into violence against minorities or what are then labeled as heresy or schism. This change occurs when collective action begins to define itself by reference to what it is, or to what it holds, rather than by reference to what is universal. And the first precondition of a universalizing reference is that the historical agent or combatant be able to recognize *in others* the drive toward universalism which he feels within himself. When a drive for national liberation becomes nationalism, when a class struggle decays into the defense of corporate rights, when feminism limits itself to the suppression of inequalities between men and women, these struggles cease to be social movements and succumb to the obsessive assertion of their own identity.

Or, in the words of Ian Angus, "particularity is not the opposite of universality but its condition, as universality is not the transcendence of particularity but its articulation."[35]

American patriotism and nationalism can be imagined in this same doubled context of practical affection for one's country and unthinking aggression directed toward other nations and often toward one's own compatriots as well: governments that are kind to their own people tend to be kinder to neighboring states also, and vice versa.

But another key to understanding the history of American nationalism is that although, in America, the forces of inclusive patriotism and exclusionary nationalism are very much as Renan described them, their *relation* to each other has been wholly different from what has been true elsewhere, especially in continental Europe, a critical distinction that Renan neglected. The basic issue is that the origins of American nationalism and imperialism are also those of America's opposing tradition, namely, American decency: as Anders Stephanson has written in his insightful essay on America's Manifest Destiny, American nationalism is both prophetic and universal, which is to say that American imperialism does not as a rule start from traditions that it does not share with a more pacific and universalist American patriotism.[36] The contrast is self-evident here between the United States and, let us say, Germany, where nationalism has its roots in organicist exclusion and anti-parliamentarianism, or France, where French nationalism has (or at least had) medieval Catholic and monarchic authoritarian roots, whereas French patriotism and universalism sprang from the Rights of Man as defined in 1789.

We can likewise contrast here the purpose of the American Constitution of 1787, which, in the words of Gouverneur Morris, was "to form a more perfect union" for all, to the constitutions drafted in these same years by French Revolutionaries. As Lynn Hunt reminded us, the French Constitution of 1791 was differently (and, as events were to show, very divisively) understood, as was prefigured in its first paragraph:

The representatives of the French people, constituted in a National Assembly, considering that ignorance, neglect or disdain for the rights of man are the only cause of public discontent and of the corruption of governments, have resolved to expose, in a solemn declaration, the natural inalienable and sacred rights of man, so that this declaration, constantly present to all members of the social body, will remind them without cease of their rights and their duties; so that the acts of legislative power and those of executive power can be at every instant compared with the goal of all political institutions.[37]

In brief, this meant that in the French scheme of things after 1789, some citizens were more enlightened than others, whereas in the American system (after some initial complaints), all soon rallied to what was to all a self-evidently desirable federal republic respectful of local variants.

Restated again, in a larger and more conceptualized perspective, the point might be that we cannot judge or even understand American nationalism if we consider the reality of American life in terms of the categories that have been developed over the centuries by European historians. In the Old World, patriotism and nationalism have been clearly distinct: the one pacific and the other warlike. In the very particular case of the United States, the two strands—which have a common origin—have been much closer, and in consequence the temptation to move from the one to the other has been stronger in the United States than in other countries.

European historical categories will not work, then, to understand America's sense of self at once united and diverse, but religious ones— and especially those that apply to Judaism and Calvinist Protestantism— will work quite well instead. In the words of Slavoj Žižek, it is a mistake to see in Judaism two divergent traditions, with "the 'good' Levinasian Judaism of justice respect for and responsibility towards the other . . . against the 'bad' tradition of Jehovah, his fits of vengeance and genocidal violence against . . . neighboring people." The two are in a dialectical situation where again and again the one emerges triumphantly from the other. The two, Žižek, goes on, "are identical and simultaneously absolutely incompatible."[38] For the Spanish philosopher Unamuno, Don Quixote and Sancho Panza were not even like the two halves of a single orange. They were the two interwoven parts of a single person. That is the context in which we have to imagine America's warring traditions.

But however the themes of inclusion and exclusion are to be understood abstractly, their convergence in American life is, on the ground, everywhere visible. In his classic text on American foreign policy at the turn of the nineteenth century, Robert Osgood observed that Teddy Roosevelt and his influential advisor, Alfred Thayer Mahan, were not so very different from their internationalist antagonists:

> Few who embraced expansionism as a kind of nationalistic orgy comprehended the practical results of their ambition. In general, ultranationalists were not more burdened than the extreme idealists with the facts of world politics as they impinged on American security. America's egoistic and altruistic impulses were equally free of a sense of limitation prescribed by the realities of world politics. Accordingly, national self-assertiveness and national idealism displayed the same propensity for extravagance; and one impulse was as fickle as the other.[39]

In that frame of proximity, Senator John Kerry's (in)famous statement about George W. Bush's war in Iraq, "I voted for it before I voted against it," is no more than the comic—or even buffoonish—restatement of a profound structural given.

Americans today who dislike recourse to "hard power" are neither humanists nor isolationists: they are cultural imperialists who prefer to guarantee the assertion of America's imperial presence abroad through the pacific power of "culture," sentiment, and influence. This stand is certainly preferable to the use of force, but it is not ideal.

*****

In America the origins of patriotism and nationalism, as well as their proximity, have been very specific to that country's history, and, in consequence, so has been the relationship of the one to the other. In Europe, nationalism and internationalism have ordinarily been at odds, in large part, again, because they are widely removed in their inspiration.

By contrast, American history shows us that Americans, as individuals and as a people, have frequently moved from nation to nationalism without real understanding. What should we make, for example, of Woodrow Wilson when he proclaimed that the message of America's Declaration of Independence should henceforth be applied to the world at large? Was he then an American patriot or an American imperialist and the "bipartisan" herald of the "American century"? Patriotic or nationalistic?

Time and again history has shown that in response to what is collectively perceived as an unjust denial of America's right to moral supremacy, even a peace-loving American progressive can suddenly veer toward aggressive imperialist demands: a nationalist Mr. Hyde from a patriotic Dr. Jekyll, so to speak. Half a century ago John Foster Dulles, then secretary of state, wrote that U.S. foreign policy was set around two "significant facts": "[The] first is that our policies have developed as a reflection of deeply ingrained national characteristics. The second is that our policies have been influenced and modified by changing world conditions."[40] Sometimes for the good but not always for the better! As the jocose saying goes, in America, "a conservative is a liberal who's been mugged." America, wrote Randolph Bourne in his "Trans-National America" of 1916, "is a unique sociological fabric, and it bespeaks poverty of the imagination not to be thrilled by the incalculable potentialities of so novel a union of men. To seek no other goal than the weary old nationalism, belligerent, exclusive, inbreeding, the poison of which we are witnessing now in Europe, is to make patriotism a hollow sham, and to declare that, in spite of our boasting, America must ever be a follower and not a leader of nations."[41] Very true, to be sure, but the imperialist drift of American policy has nonetheless often been a fact of life in American politics.

A complex relationship, then, and complicated historically because American nationalism has often had its origins on the left, and especially so when America's national enemy has anchored itself on the right (as did Britain with its monarchic constitution in 1776, or Southern particularism with slavery in 1861, or the Japanese in 1941 with dictatorial militarism). At those moments, even conservative American nationalists will momentarily rally to what were originally patriotic or even leftist causes. Universalism is after all a part of America's heritage, even in the eyes of those who prefer to think in terms of (a positive) "realism" and (a negative) "idealism"[42] and, ordinarily, to ignore the latter. To love the Constitution—as do all "strict constructionists"—is also to accept the Bill of Rights.

Lines of battle are seldom clear in America. Many of the isolationists who opposed U.S. entry into the First World War were genuine democrats who claimed to be aware of their country's democratic role in the world: in the Senate, George Norris, a progressive, opposed President Wilson's interventionist Mexican policy before he opposed U.S. membership in the League of Nations. The Midwestern "progressive Republicans" of the 1930s were New Dealers who steadfastly refused to be concerned with the international fate of world democracy.[43] American liberals and conservatives are seldom all of a piece.

This shared background of Americanness, which binds exclusionary nationalism to inclusive patriotism (or in Robert Osgood's terms, egoism and altruism), is one of the most distinguishing characteristics of American history. As Abraham Lincoln amusingly and wisely pointed out, you can not only fool some people all the time, you can also fool all the people some of the time. The second of these is the more important fact, and it is also important for us to have in mind the specific events or decisions—the catalysts—that have so often propelled all Americans from patriotic restraint to imperialist, brutal, and destructive adventurism. The deportation of the Cherokee people, for example, was a cruel and unnecessary brutality, but most Americans accepted it. Much the same can be said about the cruel and unnecessary decision to drop the atomic bomb on an exhausted and defeated enemy in 1945, or the generalized use of torture in Iraq today, or the bombing of Iran tomorrow.

Four structuring assumptions, then, for our argument: (1) the ambiguous but persistent nature of America's religious and material sense of self; (2) the broad acceptance of these patriotic self-definitions; (3) the proximity in America of the two variants that have expressed this durable self-definition—patriotism (which is an ethic of peace and *inclusion*) and nationalism (which pretends to be about democratic inclusion but is in fact an ethic of war and *exclusion*); with, most critically, (4) a concern for the ways and means that have brought America's silent majorities to line up on behalf of nationalist exclusion—ways and means of various kinds, incidents which, historically, have followed one another other in an often bewildering "nonpattern" of happenstance. Who would have supposed under the presidency of McKinley in 1900 that in 1917 another American president would become the hope of left-wing democrats throughout the world?

The first and simplest task of these pages will therefore be to trace these themes through the different phases of America's history, which run from a time when America's enfranchised citizens were white and Protestant in their near unanimity to today's America, which is, as Peter Schuck has remarked, "probably the most diverse society on earth—certainly the most diverse industrial one."[44]

Here the essay charts the development of America's self-image and chronicles its continuities as this imagined view of itself was—inevitably—affected by the transformations of American society.

At times, the argument will emphasize the ways in which ongoing, secular inherited definitions of Americanness bore down on political choices: Why was George W. Bush elected at all? At other times, it considers the ways in which ongoing social and cultural ideas have been suddenly transformed by wars and political events, as in 1860–1865.

There is no standard rule. Thus, the idea of opting for a state-directed economy has always run counter to America's ongoing cultural traditions, and this negative apprehension has always limited the range of possibilities available to those who have wanted to build social democracy in America. But it also matters that this ancient and permanent American suspicion of the state makes more organizational and technical sense today in our post-industrial and very complex society than it did a hundred years ago in what was still a recently industrialized America.

In brief, ideological tradition matters critically, but changing circumstance cannot be ignored, if only because the inflections of America's sense of its place in the world have also reflected the turn of its domestic structures. Quite obviously, a small and peripheral nation of 3 million (as Americans numbered in 1776) will not have the same foreign policy goals as a hegemonic nation of 300 million (as America numbers today). At times what matters more is the changing and dramatically adverse, material circumstance—as during the depression of 1893 or of 1929, or again during the war in Vietnam and perhaps also today, with a losing war in Iraq. On balance, however, in America, principle—of exclusion or inclusion, and often of ancient and unspoken religious origin —matters more. Thus, America's resolve to achieve independence in 1776 bore the mark of its religious past as a nation chosen by God and bound to Him by covenant. In 1865, it was economic might that enabled the North to crush the South, but it was not the industrialization that made civil war unavoidable. Moreover, material *dysfunction* is more critical in American life than mere material change: America's imperialism during the late 1890s and her imperial pursuits today have had little to do with the demands of American capitalism. They are instead the direct effect of antiquated cultural atavisms whose survival depends on the tolerance of abusive political and fiscal disorder.

To make matters more complex, America's political choices have also depended on cabals of insiders, on manipulation of the press, on the duplicity of those who are in charge, and on the biased will, especially, of revered presidents. As the leader of a chosen people, every American president is in some sense divinely ordained. Lincoln's hallowed fate is there to prove it. Cardinals elect their pope, and Americans elect a president who, like the head of the Roman Church, is there to preserve a doctrine. "I am charged with being a preacher," Theodore Roosevelt once mused. "Well I suppose I am. I have such a bully pulpit."[45] Much depends on what these leaders do and say. Critically—and this may be the cardinal point of America's political history—the plasticity of American politics and the proximity of its warring traditions have allowed America's presidents to play a strangely determining role in matters of war and peace, and matters of war especially.

Presidents matter immensely, and it is not surprising that much of America's political history has often been recounted by its most gifted historians as a succession of presidential moments. By instinct, we often feel when we read about Washington, Jefferson, or Lincoln, and perhaps also, alas, when we read about George W. Bush, that the contingent lives and sensibilities of American presidents matter more than does the nature of their times.

In that quasi-religious context, sadly reminiscent of Europe's Middle Ages (in which many French political leaders—among them Charlemagne, Saint-Louis, Joan of Arc—were canonized by the Church), we can easily see that those choices (patriotic or nationalistic) that Americans have been led to accept have often critically depended on the decisions and mind-sets of their presidents.

In 1834, for example, nationalism prevailed because President Jackson was in his own way a war criminal, sadistically intent on destroying Native Americans, one of whom, incidentally, had saved his life. Polk did not have to declare war on Mexico in 1847. McKinley did not have to declare war on Spain in 1898. Lyndon Johnson in the 1960s was not compelled to involve America in the war in Vietnam. George W. Bush need not have invaded Iraq and did so illegally, without a United Nations mandate and without the morally binding approval of most democracies. His was instead a deliberate, inhumane, unprovoked, violent choice that, in our view, also makes him a war criminal, albeit as had been said, in a minor register: for good or for evil, there is nothing grand about this C-student.

After 9/11, George W. Bush did have a choice: to militarize America through a war without end in order to rule through fear, as he chose to do, or, as Kofi Annan immediately suggested, to take the lead in a U.N.-sponsored international police action aimed to destroy an international and criminal conspiracy. Americans would have followed their president in that decision also.

In his office, in his times, a man of good will could have become a great and patriotic president. But as Goethe reminded us, character is fate, and in this moment of crisis, George W. Bush was bound to fail as a statesman, just as he had failed everywhere and always as a (failing) student, a (truant) soldier, and a (bankrupt) businessman. To paraphrase the Scriptures, never has America had a president so unworthy of its republican greatness, its extraordinary power, and its democratic glory.

* * * * *

Religious and economic individualism combined with the sense of being God's chosen people: these are at the heart of a persistent central core of values, of America's "civil religion,"[46] that has grown through emendation and "amendation" but has never been rejected. And with this, a divided impulse either to turn inward toward "benevolent" (patriotic, inclusive, and comprehensive) self-improvement, or, inversely, brutally to aggress against neighbors close and far in the exclusionary name of America's core principles, but oftentimes for shameless profit. These are the basic "problematics" of America's historical becoming. They are the ones we will follow in this essay as the constituent parts of an American ideal, at once steadfast and changing.

Strikingly, we find many of these themes present at America's creation in the early seventeenth century: it would seem that in both private and public life trajectories, the first act is often the most important. Here, in the 1620s and 1630s, typically, it matters that Anglo-America's first New England Protestants were not just conquerors but also universalist preachers of a welcoming and ingathering Christian creed. Indeed, seventeenth-century Boston imagined itself to be, first, a universalizing model for Europe as a whole, and second, the agent of the natives' religious rebirth: some of these autochthonous people—the "praying Indians" —were even enrolled in the newly created Harvard College, then a seminary for local preachers. The contrast is striking between the approach of the Puritans and that of the Spaniards, who also converted Native Americans but did so the better to enslave them as mineworkers or even to exterminate them, as happened in the Caribbean islands. The new Bostonians' first project was to create some kind of theocracy that would be open to all believers. In that important sense, theirs was a universalist theodicy. *Limpieza de sangue* (purity of blood) was not their first concern.

But soon afterward, and perhaps inevitably, relations between the settlers and the locals hardened. In 1675, exasperated by what they took to be the threats of the Wampanoag people, the Puritans decided to do away with this Indian nation, which in 1630 numbered one hundred thousand people. After this final round—which was a final solution also—only ten thousand of the Puritans' enemies survived.

In the later seventeenth century the Puritans—who had already become Yankees—changed their ways. Simultaneously religious and brutally aggressive, communitarian and economically individuated (where religious togetherness made up for the increasingly capitalist organization of their colony), these second- and third-generation New Englanders now moved into another phase of collective consciousness, a phase we might call "pre-Americanness."

Between 1688 and 1765 these Anglo-Americans—not yet Americans but no longer properly English—became fierce British patriots, and now imagined their Anglo-American sense of self to be completely compatible with nascent *English* nationalism. They were deeply hostile to Roman Catholicism, which they took to be a tyrannous ideology that served the tyrannous politics of their primary enemies, the French in

Canada. Servility was the first characteristic of these foes, but they, the children of the Puritans, were freeborn Englishmen, and as such, carriers of political liberty, a universalist value that was admired the world over.

The heart of this new American sensibility was in the individuating message of Locke, but also in the political world view that was known in Britain as that of the "Country Whigs," who imagined themselves to be yeomen forever threatened in their rights by the court, the king, and the rampant corruption of urban life. Ideologically, these pro-British, Anglo-American patriots gradually drifted to the notion that politics, both in England and in their own transatlantic part of the British Empire, opposed the king of England, with his corrupt and detested satraps, to traditional rural and libertarian innocence.

(*Looking forward, we can add that the most famous spokesman of this composite ethic would soon be, in the next phase of American life, Thomas Paine, an English-born corset maker and former customs official who arrived in Philadelphia in 1774 and became instantly famous in January 1776 as the author of a pamphlet,* Common Sense, *which sold 120,000 copies in a nation of three million.*)

A broad vision, then, but, this new "pre-American" national feeling also found expression in the nationalistic domination, destitution, and gradual elimination of Native Americans in the Northeast, as well as the destruction of the French colonial empire during the French and Indian War of 1756–1763. The expulsion of the Acadians (Longfellow's *Evangeline* among them) is the best-known incident of that Canadian saga.

After these two early moments of America's history came the creation of an American republic. In 1760 Americans were immensely proud of being British. A mere fifteen years later they had become a nation whose first enemy was Britain. True, in 1775–1776, America's patriotic rebels were for the most part still caught up in progressive Protestantism and in their American legacies of individualism and self-rule. But with this older pre-national image they now blended Enlightenment themes and values, such as citizenship and an American republic. Montesquieu and

Beccaria were their most favored authors. (In the margin of his copy of Rousseau's *Discourse on Equality*, where the Genevan apologist for primitive communitarianism praised "savages" for the "calmness of their passions and their ignorance of vice," an indignant John Adams scribbled: "Calmness of the passions of savages! ha! ha! ha!")[47]

At the same time, however, and on another shore, they also availed themselves of their newly found independence to destroy what remained of the Indian nations to the east of the Mississippi River and to the north of the Ohio. For Native Americans, the War of American Independence, hailed by much of the world as a critical step in the emancipation of western man, was an irremediable catastrophe.

Did the new American state turn against Native Americans as a mere side effect of its war against the allies of its British enemies? Or was it that the libertarian principles of the new republic, in this new world order (*"novus ordo seculorum"*—from Virgil—as it is to this day inscribed on American one-dollar bills), served to legitimize a deep yearning to dispossess and even exterminate Native Americans?

This first period of a specifically American national consciousness also includes the acquisition of the Louisiana territory in 1803. With this move, the expansion of the United States took on an air of nationalist and continental inevitability. Many of Jefferson's contemporaries had assumed that North America would indeed some day be completely settled by Europeans, mainly of British extraction. But they had likewise assumed that this might result in the creation of many distinct American republics.

Henceforth, however, it would seem obvious to all that there could only be one such American state, and a powerful one at that, far removed —ostensibly at least—from the ideals of the Country Whigs that had been broadly assumed a generation before.

The history of Americanness in the following epoch, which runs from 1830 to 1865, centers on the democratization of national mores and institutions. But the country's older principles were not forgotten: the theme of American innocence remained very strong, as did the

Country Whigs' suspicion of the state, and the founders' noble dedication to republican and libertarian ideals.

Nor was the seventeenth-century idea of divine election set aside: Herman Melville, the author of the archetypal American novel *Moby-Dick* of 1851, put it nicely in his *White Jacket* of 1850: "We Americans are the peculiar, chosen people—the Israel of our time; we bear the ark of the liberties of the world . . . God has predestined, mankind expects, great things from our race; and great things we feel in our souls. The rest of the nations must soon be in our rear . . . Long enough have we been skeptics with regard to ourselves, and doubted whether indeed, the political Messiah had come. But he has come in *us*."[48] (*In all likelihood, George W. Bush has not read Melville's novels, but we can assume that this passage would seem to him to be very apt, should someone choose to call it to his attention.*)

Moreover, mid-nineteenth-century America went beyond these memories and now became a nobler, grander, democratic project. As a sign of the times, it was in these years that the men who had been known as either fathers or forefathers of the republic—and whom Jefferson, who was one of them, had immodestly called "an assembly of demigods"—were now ennobled as the "Founding Fathers" of the American system.[49]

Newly aware of their democratic nature, Americans—before 1860, but especially after the Civil War—now understood their nation's purpose in a more noble way. Of this new-found pride, antislavery was surely Exhibit A.

Hand in hand with their new sense of self also came a greater disdain for "Old Europe," and an even more strongly stated disdain for those inside or outside their territory (Native Americans at home and Mexicans abroad) whom they saw as unproductive, incapable of self-government, and in any case, hostile to America's cherished institutions. From 1864–1865, to love a democratic and universalist America meant having to pay a frightful price to destroy southern particularism and its "peculiar institution." But it had also meant carving up Mexico, whose inhabitants, after all, had done nothing useful with their northern territories. And it also meant destroying the even more unproductive Native Americans: the West for Lincoln's contemporaries had become, in Tocqueville's words, "an empty continent, a deserted land waiting for inhabitants,"[50] or in contemporary parlance, a land without a people for a people who needed ever more land to till.

So many legacies and innovations, of which America's greatest president, Abraham Lincoln, became the classic embodiment. From his earliest years, this young man was desperately eager to discover, learn, and understand the many values that were treasured by his fellow citizens. As a Whig, Lincoln could claim descent from Hamilton's belief in moneyed progress. (Sean Wilentz has described his early years as those of a "Whig party hack.")[51] His ruthlessness in the management of the Civil War likewise reminds us of Jackson's nationalistic pride. But these particularistic twists did not preclude his wholly sincere and existential endorsement of the universalist principles that had been so eloquently stated in America's and Jefferson's Declaration of Independence. In 1860 the dissolution of the Union and of the Constitution of 1787 seemed to Lincoln utterly unthinkable: that is why he accepted the possibility of civil war. But he also looked to the future extension of America's early libertarian promise, which had been so clearly stated in 1776: "I am exceedingly anxious," he wrote, "that that thing which they struggled for, that something even more than National Independence, that something that held out a great promise to all the people of the world to all time to come—I am exceedingly anxious that this Union, this Constitution, and the liberty of the people shall be perpetuated in accordance with the original idea for which that struggle was made."[52]

Universalist and democratic inclusion, then, with the rebirth of an American democracy now made responsive to all white, Protestant men, but nationalistic and imperialist exclusion also. Not all American democrats were intent on conquest: Thoreau's name comes to mind here. On balance, however, for Jacksonians in 1828 and for Lincoln's electorate in 1865, American idealism and imperialism did somehow travel hand in hand.

With 1877 as one of the most damaging turning points in American history. In that year, northern abolitionists gave up on their newly freed black compatriots and handed over the conquered southern states to the South's old planter elite. In 1865 a victorious and democratic Union could have brought into being a southern black peasantry who would have dominated southern politics for a century. The reverse happened instead: African Americans were excluded from the national consensus, a step that was to hobble American democracy for a century, and even, perhaps, forever.

And unsurprisingly, it was at that very moment that America's nationalistic overseas imperialism began to take shape. From 1607 in Virginia to 1865, America's imperial progress had taken place locally, as it were, moving westward from one community to the next, but never far from home. Now, however, the United States began its imperial march to the world domination it enjoys today.

Once more, as often before, particularistic Hamiltonians who believed in wealth joined forces with nationalist Jacksonians who believed in force. But now, aligned against them was a renewed, neo-Jeffersonian current of thought, which, for want of a better term, we will call universalizing social democracy.

Of course, ideological quarrels were nothing new in America. Every universalist message has had to face at every step a particularist response, and vice versa. Though in broad accord on what their country was basically about, Americans have forever quarreled over the form they should give to their intuition. Even in colonial times, bitter rivalries opposed Appalachia to Tidewater, with the former favoring debt and easy paper money whereas the latter yearned for fiscal and military prudence. Likewise, in the 1770s, tens of thousands of Loyalists preferred exile to independence, which, in John Adams's famous formulation, was favored by one American in three while another third opposed it,[53] leaving one last third to line up in the end on the victor's side: in proportion to overall population, more people fled the American Revolution than the French one. And of course, the Civil War, in proportion to overall population again, was the bloodiest of all American wars, with 620,000 dead in a nation of 30 million.

What distinguished American politics in the twentieth century from what had happened before, then, was not the existence or the intensity of political rivalry but the duration of the rivalry that opposed inclusion to exclusion. On one side was the inclusive Wilsonianism (Progressivism having been its prolegomenon) with, after Wilson, Franklin Roosevelt, Truman, and Carter, as well as Eisenhower, a moderate Republican, and so, on balance, an "including" rather than "excluding" figure. Aligned against these were McKinley in 1898, followed by Hoover, Nixon, Reagan, and the Bushes, *père et fils*. (*From this perspective Bill and Hillary Clinton would be collaborationist and transitional figures whose purpose was in the main to abandon social democrats on their left in order to recenter the Democratic party toward the right.*)

The historical significance in 2004 of George W. Bush's reelection (or as his foes have it, his first legitimate election) would be to close a very long parenthesis: only half a century runs from the first equilibrium in 1825 of the new republic, to the settlement of 1877. The rise, agony, and fall of inclusive American social democracy, by contrast, lasted nearly a century.

*****

I hope it will be clear by now that this essay does not aim to be a chronological or overall account of America's historical experience. Its first dynamic is to describe the shuttling back and forth from patriotism and national inclusion to nationalism and nationalistic exclusion, as regards both domestic and international affairs.

(*In the American scheme of things, the distinction between domestic and foreign concerns is quite hard to define. So it is, for example, that the relations between the federal government and Native Americans have been set by the contents of "treaties" between the United States and "Indian nations." Likewise, the American Civil War did not merely oppose two factions of a single country as did, say, the French Vendéan rebellion in 1793–1794, or the Russian Civil War in 1919–1920. It was also, inter alia, a war between two continental states.)*

These pages are therefore intended to be a work of historical analysis, but mine also is a presentist agenda, which is the second dynamic of this essay. Once the conflicting but neighboring strands of American passions have been described and their genesis explained, it will then perhaps be easier to show why some malevolent American presidents have been able to push their country away from its republican and universalist mission toward exclusion, aggression, and conquest.

Although George W. Bush may well go down in history as the worst president of the United States, he is not, alas, the first to have chosen war over peace, or lies over truth, or exclusion over inclusion. We can understand him better if we understand what came before him. Some traditions brought him forward. Hitler was a madman, but even he did not become chancellor of the German Reich just because he was a madman.

The cost of this approach, as has been said, is that in some ways this book starts from a chronicle of America's misdeeds. And yet, it is also written from a deep admiration of America's libertarian genius.

PART I: 1630-1825

CHAPTER 1
An Almost Chosen People

English America's messianic religion and its unfettered economic individualism are at the origins of the benevolent tyranny that the United
States currently exerts over the entire planet. American "exceptionalism"
flows directly from these two sources, whose conjunction has no analog
in any other polity.

The durability of America's strange collage of materialism and transcendence is historically incongruous: though they are unaware of it, of
all the peoples of the North Atlantic world, Americans today are without a doubt the most marked by their ancient ideological heritage. For
Europe, the two world wars were material and moral catastrophes, which
forced Europeans completely to rethink their past and present. In Germany, 1945 was *"Stunde null"* (zero hour). But these same twentieth-
century conflicts were a sign of hope and glory for the United States.
For today's Americans, D-Day in June 1944 is the consecration of their
triumphant history. In their memory, in their films and TV shows, they
see that triumphant day as proof that their country should go on as it
always has. What nation, they ask, has a nobler past?

America sees itself as the most advanced and innovative civilization
in the world, and such it often is, but it has always labored in its new
fields under the sign of ancient ways of thinking. Many Europeans stub-
bornly continue to see the United States as an artificial and even virtual society, but they are wrong. America's ancient traditions have been
successively overlaid over the centuries, but the first colors of this palimpsest have never vanished. They form the country's ongoing collective unconscious. Pragmatism—or in any instance its debased
cousin, practicality—is without a doubt America's characteristic way of

thinking, and innovation is a characteristic way of doing in a country that has been constantly renewed by immigration and by technological advances: American society exists today—and always has existed—in a constant state of ferment. But its frenetic pace has been, and to this day still is, firmly situated in an ideological framework whose first premises existed long before the United States became a nation. (*In that context, it is striking that the apostles of Frenchness [for which there is no word in French] have so often harnessed their hopes to the existence of a centralized and oppressive state, to a rigid educational system, and to the action of a tentacular bureaucracy. By eloquent contrast, the institutions of Americanness have ordinarily been informal or even nonexistent. In America, the vehicles of national consciousness are far more deeply embedded in civil society than they are in other polities.*)

For Hegel in the 1820s, history was born in the Near East, passed its childhood in Greece, and attained adulthood in Europe. He thought history might one day become American, but to him, because it had no long past behind it, the America of his time was outside history. (Marx, we might add, saw America in much the same light, if for entirely different reasons.)

But this approach is—and always was—hopelessly parochial. America has always carried its past forward. Unlike all other current polities, however, it has never seen any good need or reason to reshape its myths in response to exterior constraints. America's idea of what an American nation ought to be has persisted in spite of the material and geopolitical transformations that have marked it over time.

The Jewish and the Christian God gives fierce and uncompromising judgments from on high. Greek gods are by contrast forever involved in ordinary daily life with its triumphs, defeats, and infidelities. America's political culture combines these two ways of being, lofty and immediate: it is both metahistorical *and* in the moment, outside time and inside time at once, both grand and silly, as in the political conventions by which American parties (ostensibly) choose their presidential candidates. America has certainly borne the changing marks of the moment, but these should not hide the permanence of its noble, higher self.

4

But few Americans and fewer Europeans understand America's debt to its past. For millions of its inhabitants, America is indeed a country that renews itself constantly, and most Americans have imagined their country to be immanent in both space and time. But that is an illusion: no doubt it is *the* grand historical illusion of American life, and the one that today most distinguishes America from Europe. Although the construction of a unified Europe will no doubt attenuate this feeling over time, the slaughter at Verdun in 1916, Vichy's shame, the horror of the concentration camps in 1939–1945, the crimes of fascism and communism have brought to "Old Europe" a still painful sense of rupture with the past. America has never experienced such a break. "Paradise lost": Europeans are resigned to that fate. "Paradise absent": Americans cannot begin to envisage such a thing.

*****

To understand America, therefore, we begin with its past, strangely present and distant all at once. Its religious roots matter still, and not just for those who still think religiously; more critically, they still matter for those Americans who are no longer religious in any obvious sense. It is in America's religious past that we find the origins of that yearning for transcendence that has always been so characteristic of American becoming. And that quasi-religious permanence is easily explained: European social modernity was often constructed in opposition to religion and the Church. America by contrast was defined by seventeenth-century colonists and nineteenth-century immigrants who thirsted for religion, from Scottish Calvinists to Irish Catholics and Eastern European Jews. America today is still marked by that thirst. American politicians think about religion the way an alcoholic thinks about his drinking needs: ceaselessly.

In order to understand this longing for neo-religious transcendence —this *idée mère*, or "mother idea," as Tocqueville liked to call it—we begin with the English Reformation of the sixteenth and seventeenth centuries.

Generated and imposed by the Tudor monarchs for their own often sordid ends, English Protestantism became modestly Calvinized in the second half of the sixteenth century and the first decades of the seventeenth. For some Anglicans, like Archbishop Laud, soon to be executed, this was too much. For others, however, this did not suffice. To find more freedom to worship as they pleased, some radical Calvinists braved the extreme discomforts and the dangers of a long voyage to the New World.

To be sure, this English immigration to America involved few people, but these were ardent souls whose principles were representative of the Calvinist ideal in its purest form, an ideal that had been redefined around 1640 at the University of Cambridge in England, and then immediately taken up in Cambridge, Massachusetts.

At stake in these two academies was a new synthesis of ordinary Calvinism with an apocalyptic vision of history derived from the Book of Revelation, a vision that made of the wars of religion that were racking Europe, as well as the conflict in England between the Puritans and the Stuart princes, the latest acts in an eternal struggle. First had come Satan and the angels in Paradise lost; then had come the Jews against the Philistines; and now had come a struggle against the British crown that would soon end on the battlefield of Armageddon. (Armageddon, described in some detail in apocalyptic texts, is in the everyday vocabulary of many Americans. It is, however, ignored by the ubiquitous *Petit Larousse*, and is a term that is all but unknown in France.)

Critically, then, we must remember that the Puritans did not journey to America on some parochial quest. Theirs was a universalizing purpose. The intent of these first, messianic Anglo-Americans was not to abandon Europe but, quite the contrary, to inspire it by saintly example. We understand instinctively that any explanation of communism after 1917 in any country (in France let us say, or in Germany) must take into account both Lenin and the Bolshevik internationalist revolution, since—in the Trotskyite version of things, at least—the Bolshevik revolution was merely the first step in a worldwide revolution. One must approach the Puritans in the same way. They, too, situated their actions in a larger context, that of a "Protestant International," if you will.

It is appropriate, then, that the landing at Plymouth in 1620 should have been exactly contemporaneous with the battle of the White Mountain near Prague and the crushing of Czech Protestantism by the Habsburgs, a critical moment in the history of the Reformation in Central Europe. One might imagine that Plymouth Rock was very far removed from Central Europe, but for those involved in its foundation, Protestantism, like the house of their Lord, had many mansions. The creation of their new Plymouth, they were sure, would strengthen the hopes of a threatened messianic Protestantism everywhere. For the Pilgrims, a direct chain of events connected the massacres of Protestants by Catholics, as happened in Paris on St. Bartholomew's Day in 1572, with their own vengeful determination, which made true pilgrims of these English zealots on the shores of a new world: Plymouth Rock in 1620, and then Boston in 1630, the very year when Gustavus Adolphus, the Protestant king of Sweden—a champion of the Reformers and (paradoxically) an ally of Cardinal Richelieu in France—landed in Germany. D'Artagnan, the three Musketeers, and D'Artagnan's treacherous beloved Milady de Winter were no doubt intimately acquainted with these geo-politico-religious strategies.

The "Pilgrim fathers" wished to set their Pascalian example of saintly withdrawal in 1620 at Plymouth by simply retreating from a European worldliness that had become unbearable to them. However, their "un-American" disinvolvement from the real world doomed their colony to stagnation, and Plymouth managed to subsist only by agreeing in 1691 to subordinate itself to the more expansive Boston Puritans, who had landed sixty miles to the north.

In Boston, life was differently organized: there the goal was not to flee the world but to offer it—and maybe one day even to impose upon it—a new model of faith and society from Scotland to Transylvania, by way of the Huguenot France of La Rochelle and Montauban. It is difficult to overestimate the importance of millenarian beliefs in this migration. To arrive on the banks of the Charles River from English Norfolk, to go from Cambridge near London to Cambridge across the river from Boston, was, in 1640, to depart for a new Israel. The grandiloquent words of John Winthrop, a proto-American Moses and the first governor of Massachusetts, are evidence of this frame of mind. In his famous declaration aboard the *Arabella* in 1630, Winthrop explained that the matter at hand was not to rebuild English society, definitively corrupted as it was, in the new world, but rather to construct a more perfect society. "For wee must Consider," Winthrop said, "that wee shall be as a Citty upon a Hill, the eies of all people are uppon us." The well-known Boston pastor William Stoughton told his compatriots in 1668 that God had chosen them among the most pure: "This we must know, that the Lord's promises and expectations of great things have singled out New England, and all sorts and ranks amongst us, above any nation or people in the world . . . The Lord hath said of New England, 'Surely they are my people.'"[1] The exemplariness of American life, which matters so much to our contemporary neoconservative thinkers and to George W. Bush, a fundamentalist Christian, has deep historical roots of which its proponents are rarely aware.

Boston, then (unlike Jamestown, settled in 1607), was no ordinary commercial venture. Like America today, like the America of Jefferson and Lincoln, it was intended to be a cultural beacon for the whole world, for the land the immigrants had left and also for the inhabitants of the land that was now their own.

Initially, the Bostonians and the Native Americans they confronted got along cordially: the Narragansett Indians were invited to the first Thanksgiving feast, in gratitude, we are told, for the agricultural advice they gave to the colonists. (The Indian societies encountered by the European settlers were themselves in a state of evolution: political confederations may be found as early as 1450. Certain autochthonous villages had populations well into the hundreds, which meant that the Indian tribes were, in a sense, more urbanized than were their new neighbors.) In brief, the Indians were not seen, at least at the beginning, as an irreconcilable Other, as the Aztecs and their human sacrifices were for Cortez and his conquistadores.

Quite the contrary, in fact. In the theology of Massachusetts Protestants, the Lord's grace—whose existence was at the fundamental and Augustinian source of Calvinism—could touch each and every settler, or, alas, maybe none of them. Nothing in this domain was certain: a blue-blooded Englishman could choose to continue along his banal, Godless primrose path. An Indian, elected by God and touched by his grace, could, on the other hand, be totally reborn (as, during the French Revolution, a nobleman could be "regenerated by liberty"). These conversions were rare but not unheard of, and two Puritan ministers were particularly attached to the cause of native Christianization.

One of them, Thomas Mayhew, devoted his life to converting the Indians of the island of Martha's Vineyard, and certain Indians who lived there did find a Christian faith without having to change their traditional way of life. In 1657, quite proud of his work, Mayhew set sail for England with his most gifted student, who had himself become a minister. Their ship, it is very sad to say, sank with her crew and passengers. No trace of them was ever found.

John Eliot's career in Roxbury, now a depressed suburb of Boston, was also agitated, if in a different way. Mayhew went about his work peaceably, but the Boston authorities, though supportive of Eliot's methods, were now more exigent: in 1646 they decided, for example, that any questioning of Calvinist dogma by the Indians (as well as by those colonists who had not chosen the right path) would be severely punished, if necessary with death.

But in spite of the severity of this doctrinal stand, Eliot did not lose hope: he even composed an Algonquin grammar book, and an Algonquin translation of the Bible, called *Mamusse wunneetupanatamwe Up-Biblum God naneeswe Nukkone Testament kah wonk Wusku Testament. Ne quoshkinnumuk nashpe Wuttinneumoh Christ noh asoowesit.* Whereas Mayhew met his converts halfway, Eliot was more demanding: his new Christians would have to adopt European comportment in all aspects of their lives, economic and social as well as religious. Conversions now required a total cultural uprooting: "It is absolutely necessary" he said, "to combine religion and manners."[2] Converts were therefore required to leave their villages and establish themselves in a "praying town" that was overseen by autochthonous officials. (Several of these villages survived into the next century.) Had not the apostles left everything behind to follow Christ? Eliot also encouraged his flock to carefully delimit their personal property, and to produce baskets and brooms in the winter and fruits, vegetables, and fish in the summer, in exchange for which they received both shovels and pickaxes. A society of missionaries created by the British parliament aided the converts' efforts, and Harvard offered to train their preachers. Young Indians enrolled in the university to learn Latin, Greek, and Hebrew.

The Puritans' universalism, then, was no shy thing: it was seriously intended and Janus-faced, looking as it did toward the native inhabitants of their new land and toward the Calvinists and other Europeans they had left behind. But in what would prove to be a typically American response to this double focus, their frail universalism soon broke down. Eager at first to be kind, the Puritans quickly drifted toward particularist (and prenationalist) exclusion and revenge: we can see here an ominous precedent to so many instances of nationalist ambivalence in which American policy dramatically moved to exclude and destroy.

From good will to massacres, the Bostonians' path was surprisingly short and swift—though not surprising in a way, since the Puritans, once they had fallen into a dark mood, had at their fingertips many repressive models that Britain had worked out elsewhere to justify barbaric acts. The fate of the Catholic Irish under Presbyterian rule, for example, was for them an instructive precedent. There, Cromwell's policy had simply been to eliminate the native Irish Catholic population as best he could in order to replace it with a Scottish Presbyterian population, a way of dealing with local people that was easily adaptable to Puritan America: "I am persuaded," wrote Cromwell about the notorious massacre of the Irish garrison and civilians of Drogheda in 1649, "that this is the righteous

Judgement of God upon those Barbarous wretches who have so imbrued their hands in so much innocent blood, and that it will tend to prevent the effusion of blood for the future, which are the satisfactory grounds to such Actions, which otherwise cannot but work remorse and regret." Here was an argument that would be used for two and a half centuries to justify the massacre of one Native American tribe after another.[3]

(*The current conflict in Northern Ireland goes back to this same Cromwellian period, and that region's tradition of violence was to have enduring consequences in America when hundreds of thousands of Scotch-Irish migrants later brought with them to the New World the violent, militaristic attitude to life that was best embodied in the nineteenth century by Andrew Jackson, the archenemy of the Cherokee peoples. Some of these same traditions, we should add, are alive today in the states that once composed the Confederacy, and that now constitute a large part of George W. Bush's most favored constituency.*)

Unpleasant incidents occurred with increasing frequency. To the Native American population, confrontations were justifiable measures of self-defense as more and more settlers encroached on their hunting grounds. To the Puritan newcomers, these same incidents were an attack on their natural and self-evident right to settle a land that was almost wholly unused. Indians resisted punitive expeditions, of course, and their resistance justified still greater repression. (Some historians see the first hints of genocidal tactics in this cycle of violence.) In April 1637 a first pitched battle was fought, with two Englishmen killed and twenty others injured. Between four hundred and seven hundred Indians, mostly women and children, were then massacred. "It was a fearful sight," wrote William Bradford, who was Plymouth's governor at the time, "to see them thus frying in the fire, and the streams of blood quenching the same, and the horrible scent thereof; but the victory seemed a sweet sacrifice, and they [the colonists] gave the praise thereof to God, who had wrought so wonderfully for them thus to enclose their enemies in their hands and give them so speedy a victory over so proud and insulting an enemy."[4] (It is suggestive to compare this incident to the infamous Nazi massacre in 1944 of French villagers at Oradour-sur-Glane, in which 697 people were machine-gunned and burned to death.) A few days after the battle, two hundred more Indians were captured. The men among them were immediately killed, some by drowning, and the women and children sent to live with allied tribes. (When Congress finally accorded legal recognition to this tribe in 1892, it then consisted of only twenty-two members.)[5]

And this was just a prelude. In the four decades that followed, relations continued to deteriorate between the Native Americans and the ever-more-numerous colonists (whose population doubled every twenty years and whose life expectancy was greater than that of nineteenth-century Americans). With the death in 1660 of Massassoit, the generally peaceful chief of the Wampanoags, both sides began to prepare for Armageddon. An uneasy peace persisted for fifteen more years, but in 1675 war broke out between the Wampanoags, led by Massassoit's grandson Metacomet (also known as King Philip), and the colonists.

The war was just as merciless as had been the previous battles. By its end around twenty English townships had been destroyed and a thousand colonists killed, about 6 percent of the colony. In 1676 the colonists, this time allied with the Mohawk tribe and with Uncas, chief of the Mohicans, leveled the Wampanoags' villages. Although a fortunate few managed to flee to Canada, most of the Wampanoags who had not been executed were enslaved and sent to the Caribbean. Philip's captured wife and son were sold into Bermudan servitude. John Eliot, mentor to the "praying Indians," voiced disapproval, but Increase Mather, one of the colony's best-known ministers, praised the punishment as one that would devastate the enemy leader: "It must be bitter as death for him . . . for the Indians are marvellously fond and affectionate to their children."[6] Trapped by his Native American enemies, King Philip was decapitated and his head was exhibited on a pike. English preachers spoke of the triumph of God's chosen people.

On one side now were the people of the Lord, on the other, the Native Americans, creatures against whom all forms of violence were permitted. Were not the Indians savages, as the future governor of Plymouth said in 1620, in a savage land? Even before their departure for America, in a strangely detailed piece of writing, Bradford had tried to warn his flock that when they arrived in the New World, they would find

> some of those vast and unpeopled countries of America, which are fruitful and fit for habitation, being devoid of all civil inhabitants, where there are only savage and brutish men which range up and down, little otherwise than the wild beasts . . . savage people, who are cruel, barbarous and most treacherous, being most furious in their rage and merciless when they overcome; not being content only to kill and take away life, but delight to torment men in the most bloody manner . . . flaying some alive with the shells of fishes, cutting off members and joints of others by piecemeal, and broiling on the coals, eat the collops of their flesh in their sight whilst they live, with other cruelties horrible to be related.[7]

Armed with the covenant that bound them to the Almighty (and the Almighty to them in typical American contractual reciprocity) the Puritans, and their successors—Anglo-Americans in 1776 or Jacksonians in 1834—instinctively viewed their differences with their enemies as a conflict between Good and Evil (as in "an Axis of Evil"), between their own God-sanctioned justice and some detested and inscrutable Other.

The Great War made banal the hate and violence of war in Europe: Nazi barbarism was born in the trenches facing Verdun and the Somme. And the pitiless wars that the European colonists waged against their Native American enemies in the seventeenth century are likewise at the origin of an American cult of violence and force, strangely countervailed by an equally strong belief in due process.

But from then on and forevermore, brutality and resentment would be part of the American way of making war. When the English became America's enemies after 1776, even Benjamin Franklin—a gentle man who had spent some happy youthful years in a printing shop in London and had given some thought to moving there altogether—said of his former compatriots that they were so cruel a people that Americans would never forgive them for what they had done during the War of Independence. In the 1940s, America's war against Japan was widely considered "a war without mercy," and Hans-Ulrich Wehler has linked America's oft-repeated demand that its enemies should surrender unconditionally (as Roosevelt announced at Casablanca in January 1943 without consulting Churchill) to the equally unconditional wars that the Puritans waged centuries before against Native Americans, those "children of Satan."[8]

Concerned about individual rights within their own society, Americans, marked as they have been by religious conviction and respect for law and for human rights, seldom kill outright: during the American Revolution, for example, there were almost no death sentences given out for strictly political reasons. The Terror and the guillotine in France disfigured the Revolution of 1789. But nothing like this occurred in America.

At the same time, however, the Americans' sense of their own rectitude has allowed them to destroy shamelessly. In the war in Korea, in which 34,000 American soldiers died, one million Korean civilians were killed. In Vietnam, the ratio of Vietnamese civilian deaths to American military deaths was eight to one. The war in Iraq will in all likelihood produce similar statistics. On March 9, 1945, 325 war planes dropped 1,167 tons of incendiary bombs on the city of Tokyo: 83,793 charred bodies were found in the smoking rubble, and it may be supposed that, since the conquests of Genghis Khan, never in any country and at any time had so many civilians been killed in a single day.[9] The cult of violence, of firearms (40 percent of American households own a gun today) and the idea that war can be not only just at times but justifiable nearly always if it involves the United States, have been troubling undercurrents in American culture since colonial times.[10]

The history of quasi-theocratic New England, to restate the issue, had two poles: on the one hand, universalism, and on the other, the brutal affirmation of a superior economic and productive power (in this instance, agricultural) based on an equally superior military technology (in this case, the colonists' muskets). Inclusion and exclusion.

Typically, these two extremes of force and religion were, in fact, two sides of a single coin: as God's (almost) chosen people, the colonists were charged with bringing Christ's message to everyone, even to the Indians. But as God's (almost) chosen people, the colonists thus also had the right to repel—and even to exterminate—those who chose not to hear the message.

*****

Why choose to concentrate on the destiny of New England alone? Each region, North, South, and Center, had its specificities, which all have echoes—negative and positive—in the American national character of today. Thanks to its Quaker founder, Philadelphia soon became a haven of religious and social tolerance. Chance had the same effect in New York City: from its inception, even in its days as a Dutch colony before 1664, New York was a cosmopolitan and polyglot society. (In 1650 one could count there eighteen different languages spoken by residents from at least six different countries).[11]

But New England matters more. The purpose of aristocratic cavalry, it was joked in stylish nineteenth-century British military circles, was to give tone (as in the useless charge of the Light Brigade) to what would otherwise have been a series of vulgar brawls. And likewise, if much more seriously, the determining purpose of New England religiosity in the domain of land grabbing was to ennoble and ideologize what would otherwise have manifestly been theft, plain and simple.

And revealingly, the cause of civil disturbances in northern and southern colonies was from the first quite different: Bacon's Rebellion of 1676 in Virginia may be taken as an example. There the issue, once again, was war. For the original Anglo-American settlers and their descendants, whose place and estates in the new land had long been secured, war against the Indians meant more taxation. For the newcomers, still poor, and still in search of their place in colonial society, war meant more cheap land.

By contrast, most of the divisions that tore at the Massachusetts colony from its very beginnings (and up until the end of the seventeenth century, when England's mercantilist grip on the colony rendered internal quarrels obsolete) were religious, or even theological in nature, whether the matter at hand was the Fundamental Articles in Connecticut, which were the most pre-democratic of the colonial charters; or Rhode Island's audacious rejection of any allegiance to the Anglican church; or the "antinomianism" of Anne Hutchinson, the wife of a Boston merchant. For her, only those who had been truly chosen and had experienced a sincere conversion or rebirth could be full members of the community. (*This was yet another theme that was to resurface frequently in the history of the United States, as it did for nineteenth-century Evangelicals and more recently for George W. Bush, once upon a time addicted to alcohol, but now born again to grace.*) For her, what mattered was not land but ideology, as it did for the judges who banished her from the Massachusetts Bay colony. When Hutchinson died, scalped—along with five of her six children—by the Indians, one of her former judges saw in their fate the hand of God.[12]

Massacres by Indians and massacres of Indians, then, were everywhere in all of the colonies. After the Pequods had come King Philip in New England; but there was also a massacre of one hundred and ten Indians, widely known to be peaceful, near New Amsterdam in 1642. Some of them were disemboweled; others, once their limbs had been cut off and their entrails slashed out, were beheaded, and their heads tossed about from one soldier to another.[13]

Ideology more than murder was what set New England apart and later gave to the cultural life of all the American colonies a special tone. The intensity of New England's religiosity was what mattered, as did from the first the weight of its preeminent cultural institutions. (Harvard College, now Harvard University, was founded in 1636.)

Paradoxically, Boston is today the American city that most resembles its European counterparts, and yet more of the American national idea originated there than in any other colonial city. Whether in the religion, the democracy of manners, or the republican idealism of Americans, wrote Tocqueville, "it is in the English colonies of the North, better known as the New England states, that we find the two or three principal ideas which are the basis of social theory in the United States. These principles . . . state by state, reached even those furthest away, and ended, if I may put it thus, by permeating the entire confederation. They now exercise their influence beyond these limits, over the entire American people."[14]

Ernest Gellner asked himself if nations, unlike Adam and Eve, had navels. Was their origin lost in time and divinely ordained somehow? Or did they have a birth date? It is hard to sort that out, but we certainly can surmise that if the United States of America does have a navel, it lies in its New England heritage.

Of course, for enterprise and business, it was not Boston but New York and Philadelphia that would become the principal centers of American trade and industry. But in terms of world view, culture, and religion, Boston remained critical to Americans' understanding of their larger self. Both directly (in the westward migration of New Englanders) and indirectly (in their ideological contribution to America's sense of self), the early ideals of Massachusetts became the foundation of America's raison d'être.

A single example of the persistence and importance of New England's cultural influence will perhaps suffice. Abraham Lincoln, born in the slave state of Kentucky, began with the mind-set of the then "frontier states" of Indiana and Illinois, northern states with many southern-born inhabitants. But Lincoln, an avid reader of Shakespeare and the Bible, eager to understand and succeed, soon absorbed the more general values of American society. Lincoln believed profoundly in democratic self-government and in the dignity of work. He detested slavery. He hated war. More modestly, he was a teetotaler. Lincoln, then, was a son of the people, a son also of a backwoodsman from Virginia, but a man whose own son was enrolled at Harvard and later became president of a railroad company (the Microsoft of the day). Lincoln was the complete American: an emancipator, who eventually became a fierce and

Jacksonian leader; a Hamiltonian capitalist, but with Boston-based intellectual origins. In brief, he was an avatar of New England's pioneer spirit and providential message. In the words of John Patrick Diggins, Lincoln combined a "Calvinist conscience" regarding the duty of work with a "Lockean commitment to labor, industry, and to the primacy of natural, inalienable rights as universal endowments" as an answer to the corruption of wealth and power."[15] And all the more so when the tragedy and dreadfulness of the Civil War became so clear: then came his vision of an America both benevolent and terrorizing, driven forward by some inscrutable divine purpose. America, triumphant, had liberated a people who should never have been enslaved. But this America, protected though it was by the Lord, also had to atone for its sins—a message that the Calvinist ministers of Boston, watching the massacres and awaiting the death of Metacomet, the last of the Wampanoags, would have understood.

CHAPTER 2
On the Path to Nationhood

We move forward from the 1670s to the 1760s, from a millenarian and even mystical English America—the world of Augustinian thought, of Calvinism, Milton, Cromwell, and the Puritan migration in the mid-seventeenth century—to triumphant, enlightened, Hanoverian Anglo-America, less sure of itself religiously, but now extremely proud of its role in Wolfe's victory over Montcalm at the Plains of Abraham in 1759. England—and Anglo-America's—victory over Quebec, thought the New Englanders, had manifestly been part of the Lord's plan for humankind: Had it not entailed the political disappearance of Canada's "franco-popishness"?

Because of this victory, and for many other reasons also, American society in the 1760s, though still colonial, was nonetheless well on its way to becoming a national entity, even if neither the English nor their American subject/cousins had much of an inkling of what was soon to be. We are inured today, alas, to the sudden appearance of new nationalisms and self-proclaimed republics, ordinarily risible, selfish, and destructive. But late eighteenth-century Europe was more struck by the disappearance of Poland, an ancient commonwealth, from the map of the continent. The eighteenth century did not see what seems obvious to us: with our own twenty-twenty hindsight, it is the rise of a new American consciousness that holds our attention. Contemporaries, by contrast, did not and could not see this clearly.

The siege in 1745 of Louisbourg, on Cape Breton Island in present-day Canada, is a good example of the colonials' changing mood. Great was the joy in the land when a substantial colonial force, 4,000 strong, blessed by the Massachusetts clergy, attacked and captured the French naval base at Louisbourg. For this its leader, William Pepperrell, was knighted by a grateful monarch. Great also was the disappointment in Boston when England in 1748 returned Louisbourg to the French in exchange for the Indian city of Madras. Had they been able to see into the future, His Majesty's ministers would perhaps have made a less wounding choice.

*****

A growing American colonial and patriotic identity, then, but two-sided. On the one hand, these loyal American subjects were more patriotic than a good number of King George's English subjects, who had hardly rushed to help their Protestant, Hanoverian monarch when Bonnie Prince Charlie threatened to usurp his throne in 1745: indeed, the Stuart (and Catholic) Pretender's expedition had managed to march all the way from Scotland to Derby, from which London was not much more than a fortnight's march away. With, on the other hand, a new and countervailing American cultural specificity, a new "pre-democratic" "pre-patriotism" that insisted—vis-à-vis Britain—on the particularities of American culture, which, thought many Americans, was more innocent, better structured socially, and in a word, quite different from its respected English models.

Viewed from London, Anglo-Americans were thought to be amiable primitives, unlettered, unsophisticated, faintly barbarous, but also—like the Native Americans—innocents of a kind, uncorrupted by Europe's luxury and wasteful urban ways. From the British capital, which was the world's most populous city, nearly twenty times larger than Philadelphia, the most populous city in British America, Americans were backwoodsmen, part European, to be sure, but in their habits part Indian as well.

Quakers, whose relations with Indians were wholly atypical, were seen in Europe as typically American. In 1734 Voltaire, who lived in London from 1726 to 1729, sang their praises in his *Lettres philosophiques*. Likewise, in 1792, during the French Revolution, Brissot, who was the most influential of the Girondins, and who had visited America (where he was thrilled to find a copy of Montesquieu's *l'Esprit des Lois* in Harvard College's Library), distinguished himself among his Jacobin friends by wearing all black, as everyone in Paris imagined serious Americans to dress. It all made sense to Parisian eyes: Wasn't Brissot squarely in the footsteps of Benjamin Franklin, a cult hero and a Philadelphian if not a Quaker? In America, Franklin had styled himself in both dress and spirit as a man of science and a British gentleman. But in Paris, in what can be seen as an ironic and precocious nod to the Parisian intelligentsia, then already quite taken with what we would now call the politically correct defense of the "third world," Franklin had sported instead a splendid Indian-style beaver cap. In the New World, republican virtue, Protestant self-respect, and American self-awareness had easily converged. And upon this rather shaky idea an image of Anglo-American innocence emerged that was in turn interiorized by the Americans themselves. (Many prominent Virginians took pride in being descendants of Princess Pocahontas.) It did not seem to matter, either in Williamsburg or in London, that the first concern of the American settlers had been to exterminate their native neighbors.

(It is not too far-fetched perhaps to see in this ancient American yearning for blameless virtue and the simple life one of the origins of modern Americans' concern for the sexual correctness of their leaders. Washington and Lincoln were irreproachable in this respect; Jefferson, John F. Kennedy, and Bill Clinton were not, and their political fame has suffered from its proximity to libidinous excess.)

Alongside innocence, another dimension of America's patriotic, pre-national imagination lay, thought Americans, in their peculiar talent for self-government. The increasing currency of this idea is hardly surprising. Anglo-Americans had indeed practiced self-government even before they felt any need to theorize about this aspect of their political universalism. Tocqueville, always on the lookout for his *idées mères*, would later be struck by this facet of the American character, which the French, he thought, sorely needed.

The lack of a local aristocracy, as well as New England's relative independence from Britain up until the 1660s, had made it impossible to regulate the Massachusetts townships that sprang up as the early frontier moved farther and farther away from Boston and its surrounding villages. Starting in 1632, the General Court had recognized the right of the countryside's inhabitants to participate in the election of all local authorities, including the governor. In 1634 it was decided that no tax could be levied in Massachusetts without the consent, either direct or indirect, of those who would have to pay it. In 1644 the colony's government became bicameral: in the upper house sat the governor and his advisers, but they could not rule without the consent of the elected deputies in the lower chamber.

The other colonies were, to be sure, a bit slower in proceeding to self-rule, but by the eve of the Revolution, all of them, after many ups and downs, had developed political structures that were more or less similar. And those structures in turn more or less resembled Great Britain's, and therefore conformed more or less to the theory of the separation of powers that had been elaborated and defended by Montesquieu, who was widely read by Americans. The great difference, of course, and the one that in the 1760s and the early 1770s would seem more and more relevant to Americans, was that their own balanced governments had not been captured by selfish aristocratic oligarchs as had happened in the mother country.

And alongside (imported) innocence and (actual) self-government was a third identifying factor, again of English origin (but neglected by historians until around 1950), namely, the political ideology of the English Protestant reformers known as the Commonwealth men, derived from the themes of English Radical Whigs. Here was a quasi-populist strand, quite progressive in some ways, which, though not yet republican, did certainly consider the British monarchy with a jaundiced eye.

For many social historians (among them Louis Hartz) the founding principle of American society from its earliest days had always been a pragmatic, Lockean individualism. Later studies, however, made it clear that the political theory that was most present in American minds on the eve of the Revolution of 1776 came from an entirely different ideological background.

For the American cousins of the Radical Whigs (whose principles went back, *inter alia*, to the ideas of refugee Huguenots and Parisian Jansenists like Charles Rollin, a historian of cities in antiquity whose work was well known in Boston, and the Abbé Vertot, another prolific French priest),[1] the core of political life was in the unending rivalry between the British people and their British monarch. On one side—or so this world view posited—was a union of property-owning citizens and independent farmers, some rich, some poor. On the other were their unscrupulous and indefatigable rivals, the servants of a corrupt and corrupting monarchy.

The impact of this doctrine on American colonial minds after 1730 is surprising and revealing as in many ways it made no sense. By 1763, as Bernard Bailyn has judiciously observed, "the great landmarks of European life—the church and the ideas of orthodoxy, the state and the idea of authority; much of the array of institutions and ideas that buttressed the society of the *ancien régime*—had faded in their exposure to the open environment of America. But until the disturbance of the 1760s these changes had not been seized upon as grounds for a reconsideration of society and politics."[2] Indeed: the Commonwealth men's view of a society that had no internal fissures was hopelessly out of place, and so it was that *after* independence it suddenly became divisively critical for Americans to understand precisely how the world view of the Commonwealth men might or might not make sense in America as they lived it day by day. *Before* independence, however, the Commonwealth men's view of life fitted nicely into Americans' life as they liked to imagine it not in the frame of lived reality, but in the "virtual" context of their ambiguous relation to the British crown. Here was an ideological stand that was, at that early point, ideally suited to the colonies' overall cultural situation as it was defined in relationship not to their own society but to the supposed history of their mother country. It made of them loyal members of a British

Commonwealth, but it simultaneously placed them at some distance from the mainstream of (aristocratized) British public life dominated as they imagined it to be by scheming monarchs and great nobles. (The fear of aristocratic conspiracy was a critical part of revolutionary doctrine in colonial America, as it was in Georgian Britain and as it would also be in Revolutionary France.) Why, asked Thomas Hutchinson, the exiled governor of Massachusetts, had the colonies rebelled? To which his answer was that objections to Westminster's decisions were a mere pretense: "If no taxes or duties had been laid on the colonies, other pretenses would have been found for exception to the authority of Parliament."[3] How true, we might add, but where he saw conspiracies afoot, we see instead the swelling chorus of American national feeling.

Innocence, self-government, opposition to corrupt monarchism: these were some of the constituent parts of American pre-national consciousness, with, until the late 1760s, another element that also fed America's pre-national sense of self, namely—and surprisingly—British nationalism.

How could this have been? How could the patriotism of the British have mattered so much as to be a constituent part of an American patriotism whose first concern would be to deny the Britishness of the American colonies?

At first glance, this affinity does seem deeply improbable, if only because, as in the history of all European nationalisms, the primary characteristics of British nationalism were its particularist intransigence, its nasty brutality, and its limitless arrogance: "Look around" an as-yet-unreformed Charles James Fox said to his fellow members of the British House of Commons: "Observe the magnificence of our metropolis—the extreme of our empire—the immensity of our commerce and the opulence of our people."[4] Unsurprisingly, this British self-satisfaction generated a strong current of Anglophobia all over Europe, as best witnessed perhaps by Robespierre's exclamation, in year II of the French Revolution, "I hate the English people," and by Napoleon's aphorism on Britain as a nation of shopkeepers.

And yet, although England's national and religious ideology of exclusion was, to be sure, particularist and offensive to most Europeans as it soon would be to all Americans, English nationalism was also, in its own way, a universalist ideology, and it was understood as such everywhere: Anglophilia was as widespread in Europe as was Anglophobia. Perfidious Albion was seen by some as bizarrely biblical and selfish, but it was also perceived as a land of respect for law and as the homeland of parliamentary liberty. Gaspard Monge, one of the founders of topology, declared in 1797: "The English government and the French Republic cannot co-exist . . . Destroy a government that has corrupted the morality of the entire planet; but preserve a nation to which Europe owes a large part of its Enlightenment: do not oppress a nation that has given Newton to the universe."[5] For many Europeans and until 1765 for all Anglo-Americans, the term "England" was synonymous with the word "liberty": in Mozart's "Abduction from the Seraglio," a bullied young woman exclaims that she is born for freedom because of her English origin: *"Ich bin eine Engländerin, zur Freiheit geboren."* Montesquieu, Voltaire, Madame de Staël, and the Anglophile monarchists of the French Constituent Assembly of 1789 would have understood her indignation.

In 1760 Londoners—and Anglo-Americans also—were sure of the libertarian affinities that bound Britain's fate to world liberty, as well they might have been because their understanding of nationalism was typical of what all Europeans of the time assumed when they thought about nationalism. We think of nationalism as a force of oppression; they thought of it as a force of liberation, as would the French Jacobins in 1789, who thrived on the belief that a perfect overlap existed between their two passions: their love of their *Grande Nation*, and their benevolent interest in humanity as a whole. Revealingly, one of the first gestures of these Jacobins was in 1790 to declare not war but peace to the world. True, war against (foreign) *châteaux* was to become the French and Jacobin order of the day in 1792, but even then, the French continued to declare peace to humble homes, to the cottages of Europe, and, indeed, to those of the entire world, with the possible exceptions of those in their own colonies.

This conjunction of nationalism and universalism, we might add, which seems surprising and even absurd today, was a constant of enlightened and radical thought in both the eighteenth and early nineteenth centuries: Mazzini in the 1830s and 1840s was both a convinced Italian nationalist and a convinced European internationalist. And as late as the 1960s, Charles de Gaulle's calculating acceptance of a United Europe was based on a similar (mis)understanding of what nationalism meant. It is deeply disturbing that many Americans today are still convinced that Americanness and liberty must be complementary even in circumstances when all the evidence indicates that this is not the case.

*****

To understand the influence of the English nation and of British nationalism over mid-eighteenth-century Anglo-American minds, it is useful to go back to the early Puritans and to their perception of the place their colonial society would have, not just in the British realm, but in the Christian world as well.

In 1630 the first colonists to settle in Massachusetts—as has been said—intended to inspire the universalist admiration of all Protestant Europe and ultimately the admiration of a converted humanity that might even include the local Wampanoags. By the end of the seventeenth century, however, after Cromwell's demise and after the Stuart Restoration of 1660, not much was left of this initial enthusiasm. The softening of Bostonian religiosity, the development of local commercial activity (Boston was settled in 1630 and shipbuilding there began in 1631), the demands of mercantilism, and the threat of the French presence in Canada were more than enough to drive New England's inhabitants to seek a rapprochement with England, even though, after 1660, England had once again become Anglican, aristocratic, and, at times, threateningly monarchist.

In 1630 Boston had wished to be a beacon for all humanity, but by 1670 many Bostonians had stopped going to church as often as would have been proper earlier. Indeed, the city's religious zeal was crumbling. As Winfried Siemerling describes it, citing the work of Perry Miller: "The Puritans' 'errand into the wilderness' . . . produced a double sense of betrayal. The end of Cromwell's protectorate in 1660 and the Reformation left the Puritan errand with no place of ideological return." Bostonians now had to face the hard fact that their example would never serve to regenerate a re-monarchized Britain. Sacvan Bercovitch elaborates on that sense of betrayal: "They had been twice betrayed. Not only had the world passed them by, but the colony itself, the city set upon a hill as a beacon to mankind, had degenerated into another Sodom." (Hence, incidentally, the theme of the Puritan and later the American Jeremiad, which laments the gap between America as it is and America as it should be, a frame of reference that has served as the context of many discussions of America's national sense of self.)[6]

By the end of the seventeenth century, then, a more modest Boston began to think of itself as a minor cultural outpost, a prosperous satellite, of Great Britain. In this respect it was comparable to other peripheral areas of the English cultural landscape and (unfavorably) comparable to more important dependencies, Ireland and Scotland especially. Now its cultural inferiority was everywhere to be seen, in painting for example, or again in architecture. By 1750, in both North and South, local designs were no more than regional variations on British models that could be found in books or had been brought over by England-trained artists.

Britain now mattered in every way, aesthetically of course, but also as a political model, and for some decades, as Americans inched toward independence, their imitation of British ways became—paradoxically—more pronounced. British manners, like British freedom, fed an adolescent sense of self. In 1764 the editor of the *New Hampshire Gazette* wrote an advertisement for his newly created journal that nicely expressed the loyalty that Americans felt for the distant homeland that was soon to become their bitter enemy: "By this means," he wrote of his newspaper, "the spirited *Englishman*, the mountainous *Welshman*, the brave *Scotsman*, and *Irishman*, and the loyal *American*, may be firmly united and mutually RESOLVED to guard the glorious Throne of BRITANNIA . . . Thus Harmony may be happily restored, Civil War disappointed, and each agree to embrace, as *British Brothers*, in defending the Common Cause."[7] This was Benjamin Franklin's opinion as well: "Can it reasonably be supposed," he asked in 1760, "that there is any danger of their uniting against their own nation, which it is well known, they all love much more than they love one another? I will venture to say union amongst them for such a purpose is not merely improbable, it is impossible;"[8] But by 1765 these halcyon days were numbered.

*****

Innocence, self-government, British libertarianism and patriotism: these were the ingredients of nascent Americanness, and with that (as had been true for the first colonists, as would likewise be true during America's Civil War, and as is also true today—if in a largely perverted and repellent form), religion. "The absolute centrality of Protestantism to British religious experience in the 1700s and long after is so obvious that it has proved easy to pass over," wrote Linda Colley, but the importance of religion in American life was even stronger.[9]

Calvinist Puritanism, as Bostonians at first practiced it, had been rigorously demanding, but by the end of the seventeenth century it had softened. In institutional and religious terms, New England, though still Congregationalist and close to Presbyterianism, now accepted coexistence with other religious denominations—on one side, Baptists and Quakers, and on the other, neo-Catholic Anglicanism. More important yet, this same Puritan Protestantism was required to adapt itself to new ideological demands.

Softer now in its hegemonic institutional claims, Puritanism was also transformed and revivified in the eighteenth century by a theological shift in its inner purpose. Eighteenth-century France was characterized by the near nonexistence of popular religiosity, but England, and to an even greater degree America, were, by contrast, largely recast in a new millenarian mode that was at once mystical and popular. England experienced a Methodist (or for some, a Methodistical) revolution. And in America the Great Awakening was an even more profound crisis: between 1730 and 1760 it shook the thirteen colonies and laid the ground for the 1776 Revolution. In the wake of this crisis, the strongly communal piety of the Puritans was replaced by the emotiveness of a more individualized, wider-reaching religiosity. Jonathan Edwards, its most celebrated preacher and the author of *The Freedom of the Will*, proclaimed in 1742 that the millennium was near, that kings and princes would soon disappear, that "liberty shall reign throughout the earth."[10] In France a seventeenth-century Jansensist (neo-Calvinist) conversion, whether Pascalian or Racinian, often resulted in a retreat from earthly life. Quite to the contrary, the millenarian Protestant conversion of the Great Awakening fed a hope for the imminent renewal of all things, in religion, society, and politics as well: from individuated emotiveness of each believer, a straight path would soon lead to the political individualism of every citizen.[11]

Of course, the old "denominational" forms of Protestantism continued throughout: Baptists, Anglicans, Quakers, and Congregationalists all remained. (Eighteenth-century America counted as many religions as nineteenth-century Republican France counted political parties!) Nevertheless, the more important point was that the basic spirit of Protestant America would, from now on, be in a hybrid of traditional Calvinism and a new millenarianism, rooted in the new strains of English, German, Dutch, and even French populist religiosity. (*An involved but significant connection links America to exiled French Cévenol fundamentalist preachers and their followers, victims of Louis XIV's persecutions of French Protestantism, who, after a brief stay in England, took refuge in Rhode Island in 1750.*)

Protestantism, millenarianism, then, but anti-Catholicism as well. The new ministers denounced in a single breath papist tyranny and the "ignorance, idolatry, and slavery" of the Bourbon monarchs. In Boston,

Jonathan Mayhew celebrated the symbiosis of England and America and saluted Massachusetts as "little inferior perhaps to the greatest in Europe, and in felicity to none," a place "far greater [in] purity and perfection [than any other land] since the times of the apostles."[12] And from there, across the Charles in Cambridge, Nathaniel Appleton explained to his flock that the Catholic church in Quebec and elsewhere was the tool of the Antichrist.

Here was an important ideological and individuating change in what American religion was about. Moreover, the Great Awakening was also a critical geopolitical change because it now made universally accessible to all Americans, northern and southern, what this New England–based, but now American, religion was about. Tocqueville's *idée mère* had made of Puritan New England America's cultural birthplace, but this French aristocrat was not much concerned with extension of this mother idea. The impact of the Great Awakening helps us to fill in the gaps in his prophetic insight.

Reformed Protestantism, then, and from there to anti-Catholicism, and from there to a deep-seated Francophobia: separated from Britain by a narrow channel, the France of Hogarth's prints was Britain's hereditary enemy, and it was the Anglo-Americans' hereditary enemy as well, only a few short portages from Quebec. England was for the English a virile country, and France, an absolutist, popish, and misery-struck land, ruled by libidinous priests, amoral nuns, seductive women, and vain, effeminate military men who understood nothing about modern liberty. And Francophobia was likewise a strong component of pre-revolutionary American mores.

It was, to begin with, deeply ingrained in the memories of many of its immigrants. The approximately two thousand French Protestant Huguenots in New Rochelle, near New York, are an obvious case in point. The Palatine Germans are another, victims of the tyranny inflicted upon them by the Marquis de Louvois, France's minister of war under Louis XIV. Nineteenth-century German nationalists retained vivid memories of the French pillaging of the Palatinate (it was to maintain this memory that the Heidelberg palace, which had been burned by the *roi soleil*'s troops, was not rebuilt), and these memories were strongly felt in eighteenth-century America as well. Thirteen thousand inhabitants of the Rhineland left the Palatinate for England during the famine of 1708–1709, and three thousand of them went farther yet, all the way to Pennsylvania: one well imagines that they had little love for the French, and by the same token, for New France and its warlike Indian allies. America's Francophilia had deep historical roots, but so does its current Francophobia.

*****

A more emotive Protestant individualism, then, all the stronger because reinforced and spread by another basic ingredient of incipient Americanness, the individuation of economic forms. These mattered for their social imprint, but also for their quasi-miraculous effect.

How could the Puritans in particular and Americans in general be sure that they truly were God's chosen people? This was *the* question that had tortured the Calvinist mind for more than a century, haunted as it was by the metaphysical ubiquity of its uncompromising God, and by the earthly absence of His presence: If God at times appeared to reward the evil-minded, how could those who had been truly saved know that they had indeed been saved? One answer to this question, which gained strength ceaselessly from the mid-seventeenth century onward, was that the faithful should simply use their eyes: America's unexpected wealth and material strength had to be in some way signs of God's protection. New Englanders (now become, in eighteenth-century folklore, penny-pinching Yankees where before they had been fanatical Puritans) gradually realized where they could look for comfort.

One proof of their well-being (and of their forthcoming salvation) was simply that there were ever more of them. Native Americans died, but white (and black) Americans went forth and multiplied. After some initial hardships (America's "starvation times"), the colonial population of European origin grew in an unprecedented manner. Thanks in part to immigration, the population of Massachusetts increased by 5 to 6 percent annually until 1650, and then simply by dint of its birth rate and low death rate by 3 percent thereafter in the eighteenth century. The population of New York City doubled between 1665 and 1775, to reach around 30,000 inhabitants. In 1700 all the colonies together had a population of 250,000 Anglo-Americans (many of them of Scottish, Irish, or German origin, as well as English), and in 1775 of at least 2.5 million. (England and Wales had a population of some 7.5 million at the time.)

A second indicator, just as telling as demographics, was the magnitude of American wealth and its increasing commercial importance for Great Britain. Two causes were determining in this respect: the protective effect of British imperialism (an omen of America's close economic and cultural relation to Britain from the 1820s to our own day), and the sociology of American life, which now became—and after this, remained—a basic aspect of the American national idea.

The dream of late nineteenth-century imperialists had been to make of Europe's overseas colonies a source of raw materials and domestic employment, as well as a captive export market for their major industries. That dream failed lamentably. (In 1913 colonial exports amounted to only 1 percent of Germany's international trade.)

By contrast, eighteenth-century England's mercantilist colonial empire, and with it America's prosperity, was a huge material success. Some few great fortunes were made in eighteenth-century England, as we can see from Jane Austen's novels and from the treasures of English country-house museums today. But in America, tens of thousands of small fortunes were made within this mercantilist system, which may be imagined as a closed circuit, with colonies furnishing raw materials and serving as a market for Britain's finished products. All of Europe's nation states would try to follow this economic model, but it was certainly the British who perfected it, and many diasporas prospered with and within it: Scottish, Huguenot, and even Jewish—all of them acting as intermediaries between the colonies, Britain, and the world. Between 1620 and 1700 the quantity of tobacco shipped from Virginia to London went from nothing to nearly twenty thousand tons. By the beginning of the

Revolution, 20 percent of England's exports and 30 percent of its imports were to and from the American market. American wages were the highest in the world.

The second factor of material change was the individuation of America's economic life. Economically and industrially speaking, the Puritans had not intended to innovate, but American circumstances forced them to do so. In theory, Boston in 1630 was to be, in Christian terminology, "a perfect society," and as such, necessarily based on inherited communitarian tradition and on set religious principles. But circumstances (among them the famed "frontier effect," to which we shall return) decreed that economic individualism—capitalism, in a word—should become the economic law of this most Christian land. This was a profound transformation. The Puritan colonists had hoped to re-create the traditionalist model they had left behind in Europe. They did not wish to create anew, but they were driven to do the reverse of what they had planned.

The old organizing principle of ancient English economic and social structure (indeed, of all feudal western Europe), whether in religious, economic, or social life, was—in theory at least—corporatist. Groups mattered (like butchers, bakers, and candlestick makers). Individuals did not. So could the jurist Jean Bodin write in the sixteenth century that a king was to the families of his realm what the head of a family was to his wife and children. In this context, a father's patriarchal social rights (like a monarch's patriarchal political rights) invariably trumped those of the individual. A younger son from a noble family was, by this logic, sent to serve the church and the daughter of a large family would join a convent, with no consideration whatever for his or her own desires. A young woman friend of Madame de Sévigné, soon to be married, asked who her bridegroom was to be and was told to mind her own business. Economic activity was—in theory at least—governed by the same principle: guilds and their members formed holy alliances governed by tradition and set rules.

But modernity, and especially American modernity, meant that individualism displaced community as the fulcrum of both economic and social life: what the Great Awakening had done for religion, circumstances did for American economic life. How to impose feudal taxes on farmers in America, when most of them could simply pick up and move to "uninhabited," unfettered land on the frontier? How to convince a cabinetmaker to accept working conditions that favored older tradesmen when new cities and new markets were unfolding before his very eyes?

The effect of greater material prosperity born from cheap land, capitalist habit, and British protectionism was to make coastal colonial America a rich place for whites. Its urban centers began to rival those at home. In Britain the poor (as in Hogarth's prints of Gin Lane) were numerous and rowdy: shelters to aid the most destitute had long since become commonplace. But the first establishment of this kind was not opened in Philadelphia until 1732, and in New York there were none until 1760. It was only in the middle decades of the nineteenth century that American cities took on a much darker hue.

The poor in America were fewer than in Europe, and the rich were ever richer and more numerous. A new elite of colonial Americans emerged, many of whose oligarchic members had inherited their wealth or married into it, as was the case with George Washington. The heretofore humble homes of southern slave owners now took on a grander look with porticos and columns as did, in the North, many a wealthy merchant's mansion. (In the 1760s the Quaker bourgeoisie of Philadelphia maintained a volume of trade with England that was greater than that of the five New England colonies combined.) One can readily imagine also that, regardless of its British patriotism, this "new class," though disdained by the British officials posted to the colonies, had little respect for these foreign-born and relatively destitute careerists.

*****

A heightened libertarian patriotism, religion, and triumphant economic individualism: here were the ingredients of a heady brew that crystallized with the making of war.

War has been a constant element in the formation of American consciousness: the Puritans' community was forged in the crucible of a quasi-genocidal struggle against Native Americans; an American nation would emerge from the War of Independence, as would American universalism from the Civil War. And even American social democracy was coterminous with two world wars. It was likewise from some deep instinct that George W. Bush seized on the idea of a "War on Terror" in order to realize his dream of a softly fascistic America. Eighteenth-century Anglo-America, whose mortal enemy was France, was no exception to this rule.

In space, the contest (in America) hinged on who was to control the lands west of the Alleghenies and east of the Mississippi. In time, this rivalry was part of a second hundred years' war between France and Britain, which began in 1689 when William of Orange ascended to the English throne and which would end with the defeat of France at Waterloo in 1815.

The longer-term effect of this conflict in the nineteenth century was Victorian England's domination of the globe. Its immediate impact in the middle decades of the eighteenth century was the emergence of an intracolonial solidarity of English-speaking colonies in opposition to the French.

The losers in what Americans call the French and Indian War were the French state and some thousands of French settlers as well, including the deported Acadians, many of whom died in 1755 on their way to Louisiana. (Advertisements in major American cities announced a "favourable Opportunity" in the sale of land left vacant by the exiled French.)

But far worse were the drastic losses sustained by the Indians. There were hardly any Native Americans left in New England by 1750. All wars are brutal, but here the settlers were surely more brutal than were the Native Americans. It was common in tribal communities to take in the wives and children of defeated enemies. But age and sex did not count for the colonists. In 1666 Virginia's governor stated it succinctly and prophetically: "I think it is necessary to Distroy all these Northerne Indians for . . . twill be a great Terror and Example of Instruction to all other Indians."[13]

Native Americans were forced to choose sides, and many fought alongside Louis XV's outnumbered troops. The Anglo-American land-hungry population was steadily increasing, but the French were relatively few.

For Indians to the east of the Mississippi, the defeat of the French in the French and Indian War was another fateful step in the history of their long torment. Hardly had the treaty of Paris been signed in 1763 before new colonists, from Vermont all the way to Florida, began pushing west, north, and south. In New England alone, 264 new municipalities sprang up between 1760 and 1776.

True enough, after the departure of the French, the British government, as sole guarantor of public order on the North American continent, did try to stem the tide of migrants: it was not in British interest to antagonize the Indian tribes. But nothing could stop the westward flow of settlers, and British regulations only served to anger the colonists.

*****

In 1760 the old duality of British king and British citizen, united by the memory of the Glorious Revolution of 1688, had produced an Anglo-American people keen on liberty and mortally opposed to absolutist France, with its Catholic king, his Canadian army, and his savage Indian allies. By the late 1770s, though, all this would change. Then the American people would be fighting alongside their French allies (*Lafayette oblige!*), and against the tyrannical, corrupting, conniving King George III, abetted as he was by his savage Indian allies. America had been a provincial backwater: it would now be, as it still imagines itself—and as it had imagined itself in its first New England decades—a beacon for the world: "Every spot of the old world," wrote Tom Paine in *Common Sense*, "is overrun with oppression. Freedom hath been hunted round the globe. Asia and Africa have long since expelled her. Europe regards her like a stranger, and England has given her warning to depart. O! receive the fugitive, and prepare in time an asylum for mankind."[14] And behind that shift, as we have endeavored to show, was the gradual formation of a still colonial but already recognizably American consciousness.

CHAPTER 3
An American Republic

In both private and public life, some moments matter a great deal more than others. In the history of the United States, four epochs are of particular consequence: 1620–1660 for the creation in New England of a near-theocracy; 1860–1865 for the creation of a democratic republic of free men; 1932–1940 for the (abortive) creation of an American social democracy; and of course, 1776–1787 for the creation of a representative and Enlightened republic.

Why and how did Anglo-Americans rethink their society between 1765 and 1787? One strategy in this matter, which has been learnedly pursued by many historians, has been to document in great detail the many specific and articulated grievances that Anglo-Americans had against the British.

For example, much can be made of the indisputable fact that Britain, eager to stabilize its North American possessions where Native Americans were still of consequence (as in the Ohio valley), had tried to block the westward paths of Anglo-American settlers and land speculators. Likewise, in a mercantilist age when colonies were seen as natural producers of raw materials and as markets for a more advanced and industrializing home country, Britain had chosen to restrain its colonies' right to produce finished textile or metal goods. The colonists also resented Britain's fiscal encroachments: the maintenance of empire was an expensive proposition, as the Seven Years' War had shown (it had doubled England's national debt), and English landlords were determined that American farmers should pay a larger share of Britain's imperial costs: Were not these Americans the first beneficiaries of the demise of the North American empire of the French?

Ingenious ideological and political arguments were then framed by colonial pamphleteers to justify what they thought—in good faith—were valid responses to British claims. Had not English legislators confused external and internal taxation? Were not the natural rights of Americans inscribed in a common law that was above and beyond the legislated fiat of Britain's (corrupt) legislators?

Besides, Britain, as everyone knew, was a parliamentary monarchy ruled more by Parliament than by the monarch; in England, Parliament exercised many of the nation's sovereign rights, as everyone understood, including King George III. But did that British Parliament at Westminster exercise sovereign rights over Britain's American colonies? Learned colonials argued that it did not. Hadn't most of the colonies been founded, in the seventeenth century, either directly by the crown or by agents empowered by the crown? Parliament had had nothing to do with these settlements at the time, and should have nothing to do with them now. In America, only the monarch had sovereign rights. But was it not also true that, since the Glorious Revolution, British monarchs had been understood to wield power by the grace, not just of God, but of their subjects? It followed, went on the colonial constitutionalists, that in America, neither Parliament nor monarch had much right to regulate, tax, or govern. Q.E.D.

Another historical strategy has focused less on the explicit arguments and grievances of rebellious Americans than on ancient neo-Marxist assumptions about how conflict is generally occasioned in all societies. In this loose Marxist frame, which was first applied to American history in the early decades of the twentieth century, the real issue about American independence—it was then claimed—had less to do with Anglo-America's relation to the home country than with the internal dynamics of American society. Aphoristically, this was to say, in imitation of Ireland's situation in the late nineteenth century, that both in 1776 and in 1787, "home rule" (that is, whether America would be independent) mattered less than "who ruled at home."

For most Americans, the U.S. Constitution is perceived as an immanent document, more or less brought down from heaven onto God's chosen acre. And it was in response to this happy view that many leftist American historians of the 1920s worked hard to show that the enactment of the federal constitution had had less to do with governmental principle than with the speculation of rich bond owners whose wealth was sure to appreciate under a stronger government.[1] Rightist historians, then, determined to make of America an ideologically motivated nation of those whose legal rights are being trampled by a tyrannical state, and leftist historians, in one way or another, since the 1920s, have tried to create a leftist "useable past" that might also serve in contemporary leftist politics.

*****

These interpretations of the American Revolution, whether of the left or of the right, will of course never be fully proved or disproved. They appeal or repel. But a third and perhaps more ecumenical view might be that behind the various political, economic, or ideological claims of the Anglo-Americans was their quickening sense of being part of an American nation (even if, as against the French at that same time, they seldom used that term, and preferred to speak of an "American people").

That they did not see into their own hearts is not surprising: their sense of nationhood was as yet largely invisible to themselves, as it was wholly invisible to the British, who never even began to understand what they had on their hands. In 1776 an exasperated and baffled English pamphleteer concluded that, as far as he could tell, either the Americans were English "or they are fallen out of the clouds or started up in America as mushrooms."[2] Indeed! In the standard British view, Americans had been hyper-patriotic Britishers in 1765. How could they have changed so dramatically from one decade to the next, and after that from year to year? It had to be that they were either deceived or unreasonably petulant. So thought George III and his partisans, which meant, among other things, that because the Americans became more confident and self-assertive year by year, the British tactic of granting this year what would have been acceptable last year was doomed to repeated failure. Having become a people with cultural and economic specificity, Americans then gradually became—to their own great surprise—"one nation, under God." John Adams, who was born in 1735 and became the second president of the United States in 1796, illustrated this epochal transformation by the evolution of his own thinking: in his early manhood he was an English patriot; he then became a "Massachusetts patriot" and in 1774 called that erstwhile province that was on the verge of becoming a state "my country" and referred to its delegation to the Philadelphia Congress as "an embassy." Two years later he became what he would remain for the half century until his death (which like Jefferson's occurred on July 4, 1826): an American nationalist.

In the Habermasian view of contemporary Europe, the willed creation of European institutions will—or so we can hope—eventually generate a new European patriotism, a *Verfassungspatriotismus*. The genesis of the American national idea illustrates the perfectly opposite principle: there, nation came first and institutions second. As Adams was to put it in 1818: "The people of America had been educated in an habitual affection for England. . . . But when they found her a cruel beldam, willing like Lady Macbeth, to 'dash their brains out,' it is no wonder if their filial affections ceased, and were changed to indignation and horror."[3]

(*One should note in passing that Adams's judgment was in some ways flawed: historians estimate today that in 1776 one American in three was hostile or indifferent to American independence. But then again, American nationalism was a habit that took on weight as it went along: nationalism in general is without doubt the most contagious of humankind's public and imagined maladies.*)

Adams's intuition was in fact a genuine stroke of genius. The clue to the unfolding of events was, just as he said, in the American people's new and different sense of what American society should be about *po-*

litically, even if Americans at first had no small difficulty in giving a precise incarnation to their new apprehension of who they were. What kind of revolution did they want? Did they wish to obtain British sanction of their ancient liber*ties*, or more complicatedly, of their newfound liber*ty*? Would they be a republic? Closely related to Britain or not at all? And if they did form a republic, would it be representative or democratic? So many questions that were still in abeyance in 1775 but whose answers became clearer when America's sense of nation sharpened month by month. In brief, as Page Smith wrote some thirty years ago in his *People's History of the American Revolution*, the question that really mattered and to which historians had "given comparatively little attention" was "the formation of a national consciousness between 1765 and 1774."[4] Theodore Roosevelt, who was himself quite an expert on America's sense of self, was similarly minded: for him, the revolutionary decade mattered because it was when Americans established their new federal state, with its unique institutions and system of government, but also because it was when the American national idea took shape: the "crucible in which all the new types are melted into one was shaped from 1776 to 1789, and our nationality was definitely fixed in all its essentials by the men of Washington's day."[5]

It is a common theme, in French literary circles especially, to imagine contemporary America as a "virtual" nation: in 1911 Emile Boutmy, then a recognized Parisian *Américaniste*, put it quite eloquently in ways that still ring true to some in France today: "Listen to the shudders and echo of this name: France. Then, speak the name of the United States. The first comes from the depths of our being: it seems to be a long-repeated voice coming from some mysterious place. The second has a brief and dry sound to it, an outdoor sound, like two flints struck together close by."[6] For Americans, nothing could be further from the truth.

What were, in the 1770s, the deeper foundations of America's nascent consciousness of itself? First, no doubt, in daily life, a new and widely shared feeling of not being really English anymore, of being the inhabitants of a new place (and perhaps even now, of a new country) where people spoke, thought, and socialized in a particular way. Americans' political instincts had changed also: in Britain, thought the Radical Whigs, most people were still deceived by the pomp and circumstance of traditional politics, of "Old Corruption," as it would soon be known. But in America, observed the British publicist "Junius" in 1769, "they equally detest the pageantry of a king, and the supercilious hypocrisy of a bishop."[7]

Then too were the numerous commercial, personal, and ideological links that connected all Americans to one another. Benjamin Franklin, the most famous of Philadelphians, was Boston-born. References in the press of one "province" about events in another province (there were 38 newspapers in Britain's American colonies at the time) quintupled between 1730 and 1770.[8] Collective memories were another link: the fear of the French and their "cruel" Native American allies had run deep. The Seven Years' War of 1756–1763, which had actually begun two years earlier at Pittsburgh, had reminded all the colonies of their common links. (*It was in that war, incidentally, that Washington, as a Virginian-British officer, had acquired his military reputation—which was more favorably understood in Boston and Philadelphia than it was in Paris, where he had been denounced as a war criminal since signing in 1754 a confession of guilt in the death of a French officer, a document drawn up, as he pointed out, in a language that he could not read.*)

Praxis also can serve as a means to understand America's growing national sense of self, where this useful Marxist concept describes the links that run from events to theory and back from theory to events, the one informing the other in a pattern of reciprocal causation. Put more simply, this is to say that politics and events reshaped the political consciousness that had given rise to politics and events.

We can suppose that, in the long run, even a more pliable British response to American grievances would have failed: American national feeling was too strong to be fitted into any transatlantic mold. But the obstinacy of the aristocratic clique that ran the British Empire certainly quickened American resolve. From first to last, the response of Britain's noble peers was to be more firm. (*We have to keep in mind that it took two French revolutions—in 1789 and again in 1830—to convince the British gentry that the winds of change couldn't be resisted.*) Conceivably, firmness, had it been balanced by the granting of internal autonomy, might have sufficed before 1770. But firmness after 1774 invariably failed, as it had to: British resolve to punish merely strengthened American resolve to resist, and it sharpened the Americans' sense of togetherness. Upon hearing of Britain's move against Boston (the "Coercive Acts" of 1774 ordered the city's harbor shut down until tea duties had been paid), the young Virginian Landon Carter wrote in his diary: "This is but a Prelude to destroy the Liberties of America. The other Colonies, cannot look on the affair but as a dangerous alarm."[9] In 1774, Americans were only committed to fitful resistance. By 1776, independence had become their goal.

Armed conflict had a similar effect. In 1815, in an earlier version of his famous judgment on the causes of the Revolution, Adams had downplayed the importance of the war: "What do we mean by the Revolution? The war? That was no part in the Revolution: it was only an effect and consequence of it. The Revolution was in the minds of the people, and this was effected from 1760 to 1775, in the course of fifteen years before a drop of blood was shed at Lexington."[10] Yes and no: war did not create America's revolution or its nationality; but it did dramatically affect ongoing political life and political ideology, as war would always do, for better or for worse, throughout American history. The existence of the Continental Army and George Washington's growing prestige as its commander made a great deal of difference, as did the growing camaraderie of his officers, many of whom were to hold elected office for the next half century. Dr. David Ramsay, "the most distinguished of the early national historians," wrote in 1789 that Americans in 1775 had known little of each other, but that "a continental army and Congress composed of men from all the States, by mixing together, were assimilated into one mass. Individuals . . . disseminated the principle of union among them. Local prejudices abated. By frequent collision asperities were worn off, and a foundation was laid for the establishment of a nation."[11] More than 200,000 men served at one time or another under Washington's command.

Occasional victories, but perhaps even more so, repeated defeats and challenging reversals made for stronger resolve. One cannot say of the War of American Independence, as one can say of war in Europe in 1792, that "it revolutionized the French Revolution," but something of the kind did take place nonetheless.

By 1776, in both fact and perception, wide gaps separated the thirteen colonies from their (step)mother country: a land of freedom, without bishops or aristocrats, from one that seemed to be under the thumb of an aggrandizing monarch abetted by a rich, titled, and arrogant nobility, and after 1765 Americans gradually came to think of themselves as uniquely placed in history to capitalize on, to complete and fulfill, the promises of human existence. "Christian Europe," wrote Tom Paine, "and not England is the parent country of America."[12] The changes that had overtaken their provincial societies, Americans saw, had been good: elements not of deviance and retrogression, but of betterment and progress. "Their rustic blemishes had become the marks of a chosen people."[13] (Philip Deloria has recently described the Boston Tea Party of December 1773, when irate Bostonians disguised as Indians dumped 342 chests of tea into the sea rather than pay a new London-ordered duty, as "a catalytic moment . . . through which Americans redefined themselves as something other than British Colonists.")[14]

*****

A national revolution, then, but also a revolution of universal inclusion: the program of American independence was vast and ambitious. At once biblical and Enlightened, it stood at the intersection of all the currents that had transformed Enlightened Europe.

Most important in the formulation of America's new and national message were the ideas of the Commonwealth men, already described in the context of prerevolutionary Anglo-America, which were not that far removed from the Jacobinical mainsprings of the French Revolution. (It was one of the wonders of this revolutionary age that Tom Paine, who best expressed the sensibility of the Radical Whigs in England and of the Patriots in America, should also have found an echo in Paris, where Paine became a member of the French Convention, as a colleague —and as a dedicated antagonist—of Robespierre and nearly lost his head in the process.)

Of frequent relevance also were the texts of John Locke, especially his *Second Treatise on Civil Government*, which said of men—and of subjects—that they were all equal in their natural rights. (James Otis thus explained to his fellow Bostonians that a law of nature gave Americans the right to refuse to pay taxes levied by an institution that did not represent them. This would have come as a great practical surprise to the overwhelming majority of human beings alive at the time.)[15]

The philosophy of natural rights, in its many forms, was deeply comforting to Americans and easily accessible to them rhetorically. It was a fundamental part of the American national idea that America and Americans were close to nature and to virtue: Montesquieu (and many others) had made of virtue the cornerstone of a republican sensibility, and Americans were certainly more virtuous—they thought—than were their English cousins. Noah Webster in his 1785 *Sketches of American Policy* put it nicely: What was modern virtue? "The great Montesquieu," he answered, had meant by that term "*patriotism*, or disinterested public spirit and love of one's country." (*Webster, we might add, personally doubted such concepts: "With the utmost respect for such authorities," he continued, "I must deny that such a general principle ever did or ever can exist in human society . . . The real principle that is predominant in every individual and directs all his actions is self-interest." And in 1787 he wrote, in an essay entitled "Property": "The system of the great Montesquieu will ever be erroneous, till the words* property *or lands in fee simple* are substituted for *virtue, throughout his* Spirit of Laws.*")*

Virtue, then, and once again—as always before and since—religion, which in Americans' image of nation reinforced their other ideological inclinations. It is useful here to juxtapose the two more or less contemporaneous French and American revolutions, so close in time, so different in their effects.

To be sure, the break in France between revolution and religion was not complete. A pro-revolutionary Christian strand found expression in the neo-Jansenist, Roman Catholic rigor of the Abbé Grégoire, who would later correspond with Thomas Jefferson on the issue of slavery. (As one might expect, Grégoire, who often voted with Robespierre, was on this matter well to the left of Jefferson.)

Nonetheless, by and large, the French Revolution—and Jacobinism, which was its ideological quintessence—was resolutely hostile to the Christian religion, and, for that matter, to Hebraic religious rites as well. In France, revolution thrived by *opposing* the Church; Jacobinism there became a secular religion, many of whose high priests were obsessed by hatred of its traditionalist rival.

The American Revolution, by contrast, realized itself *through* or *next to* religion. (Samuel Adams, a Boston populist, conjured up the idea of America as a "Christian Sparta," simultaneously militarized, virtuous, and religious.)

Paradoxically, the great American statesmen of the day—Jefferson, Madison, Adams, and after them, Monroe and Lincoln—were more deistic than Christian. The name of Jesus Christ does not figure in any of George Washington's public or private writings. Jefferson was even more secular in his thinking; at one point, with a razor, he carefully excised from his copy of the Gospels any explicit reference to the supernatural.[16] But on the whole, these men assumed that their political ideal would be compatible with all forms of Protestantism, however evangelical and millenarian these might be. (Suggestively, in the two decades before 1789, a similar rapprochement had brought together, in France, Enlightenment *philosophes* and Calvinist ministers, the difference between the two countries being of course in the minority status of Protestants in France.) In 1765 John Adams, though not yet an American patriot, already knew that his plans for America were "the opening of a grand scheme and design in Providence for the illumination of the ignorant and the emancipation of the slavish part of mankind all over the earth." In the next decade, with some few exceptions—most of them Anglican—American religious figures sided with the partisans of American nationality, as did most of their parishioners.

This message has an importance that goes beyond the situation at hand, as it points to a constant in the history of American liberty, namely that religion has often overlapped with America's universalist message. It has not always done so. The Puritans, as we have seen, proved to be in rapid succession eager to accept Native Americans as fellow Christians and then, some few years later, eager to exterminate them instead, once again in the name of Christian principle. Similar ambiguities appear throughout American history and in America today: though universalist-minded Christians are by no means unknown in America at the moment, organized American religion today (especially in its dominant and fundamentalist and pentecostal modes) has been largely hijacked by militant right-wing nationalists.

But at other times, for example in 1860, America's Protestant sensibility was—in the northern states at least—resolutely libertarian and won over to the abolition of slavery. The point here is that in 1776 religion was likewise resolutely patriotic. Providence, thought America's Protestants, had a plan for the world, and an independent America was a critical part of that plan.

The background of religion's pro-revolutionary allegiance was varied. Simple conformity was one aspect: by 1776 America had a long Lutheran tradition of collaborationism with whoever was in charge. Whatever the dominant forces of society or the state might want, this would be the modern Lutheran choice, as it had been Luther's when he sided in 1525 with the dominant princes and against the rebellious peasants, many of whom were Lutherans, but weak. When American Lutherans opted for revolution, so did the Lutheran religious establishment.

Far more important, however, was nonconformity, that is, the legacy of the Great Awakening. By weakening the hold of institutionalized religion, and by emphasizing the importance of individuated emotion in religious life, the Great Awakening had laid the groundwork for political change as well.

So it is that we can find numerous instances not just of pro-independence religious statements in the late 1770s but of religious/republican millenarian statements after that, in the 1780s and 1790s, mystical republican statements that recycled a traditional religious vocabulary of redemption. The principles of Lockean individualism (surely) and those of the Commonwealth men may have been part of the immediate experience of many, but what American settler did not know something of the Bible? For those Americans who had learned to read in the Holy Book, as Puritanism had taught them to do, and especially as Puritanism renewed by the Awakening had taught them to do, it was simple enough to move from what they had learned about religion to what they were learning about national politics. Liberty, wrote "Cato" in the *Boston Gazette*, "is divinity that stirs within us . . . 'tis the very principle of self valuation."[17] When Tom Paine asserted that George III was "the royal brute of Britain" and that his monarchy was "popery" made into a "system of government," and that "the King of America . . . reigns above, and doth not make havoc of mankind like the Royal Brute of Britain," many of his readers recognized in these words a new version of what they felt were eternal religious verities.[18]

In any case, between 1765, when the stirrings of American separateness began to find political expression, and 1783, when the War of Independence came to an end, Americans had moved from a largely fantasized British patriotism to their own national consciousness. The national idea now became the focus of American public life, as religion had been in the seventeenth century. Moreover, this new passion was widely shared, and it is suggestive in this context to consider the comparative history of political emigration for revolutionary America and revolutionary France. True, in proportion to overall population, American loyalists who emigrated from the thirteen colonies were far more numerous than the French émigrés (most of whom, incidentally, were *not* nobles).

But in France, most émigrés when they returned carried within themselves a newfound and contagious bitterness about 1789 and republican inclusion. In America, by contrast, where left and right had common roots in both religion and Enlightenment, most émigrés came home, where they quickly and quietly blended in with their former republican antagonists, whose views now became their own.

It is in the same perspective of togetherness and national becoming that we can also consider the next and second phase of America's revolutionary trajectory, from independence internationally recognized in 1783, to the inauguration of George Washington as the first president of the new republic in 1789.

*****

All commentators of this period of postrevolutionary consolidation are careful to see nation building as an important element of their narrative. Still, most of them also have one of two other concerns uppermost in their minds.

A first approach is to see the urge to a strengthened federalism in the mid-1780s as a rightist response to the leftist social and institutional disorder born of revolution. A stronger government, in this view, appealed to Americans who both feared social disorder and looked to a re-created central government that could raise tariffs and guarantee the economic well-being of American producers who were now beyond the protection of the British mercantilist system, which had oppressed their productive abilities but had also guaranteed them rich markets throughout the world.

By contrast, a second frame (more to our liking) insists less on left-versus-right than on the dysfunctions of this first more or less national government, which was so institutionally inefficacious that its first president, John Hancock, did not even bother to accept that office. In this "Confederation," each state explicitly preserved its sovereignty, and South Carolina even reserved the right to declare war, sign treaties with foreign powers, and maintain its own navy.

Something is to be said for both of these interpretive strategies. Inevitably, independence, and the often disruptive and destructive war that had led to it, did indeed imply some material changes, transfers of property, and shifts of social norms as well. Tom Paine explained that when he heard the words "liberty" and "rights," "equality" also came to mind: "The floor of Freedom is as level as water."[19] More Americans were now involved in public life: by 1800 many states had institutionalized universal male suffrage, and some places had also adopted the secret ballot, a practice that became the rule after 1850. Americans were now better informed and far more often members of proselytizing associations for this or that cause: twenty years after independence, in 1810, the country counted—for 7 million Americans—376 newspapers that sold 22 million copies. It is a commonplace to say of the revolution of 1830 in France that it was the work of journalists, but the circulation of French newspapers at that time was nowhere near what it had been for a generation in America.

The condition of women improved: "Remember the Ladies," Abigail Adams had written to her husband John in Philadelphia. Adams, though quite attached to his willful wife, did not do much to follow her advice on this issue, but the Revolution did contribute to raising the moral and civic position of American women by ennobling the theme of republican motherhood—of the republican mother charged with the civic education of children who would soon be republican voters, producers, and officials.

Likewise, the issue of slavery was also brought into question by independence. It is perhaps too optimistic to suggest that after 1776, for African Americans, "a revolution within a revolution had occurred," but "the identification between the cause of the colonies and the cause of the Negroes bound in chattel slavery—an identification built into the very language of politics—became inescapable."[20] Before, almost no one in public life had spoken of it, though in a sense slavery was everywhere: four of America's first five presidents were owners of slaves, who numbered 20 percent of the population. But now the issue was placed on the table: some states abolished the international slave trade, whose temporary abolition was decreed by Congress in April 1776. Likewise, the first American antislavery society—soon to become a model for Wilberforce in England and for the *Société des Amis des noirs* in France—was founded in Philadelphia in 1775. In 1790 St. George Tucker urged students at William and Mary to consider "the inconsistency between our avowed principle and practices [and] whether it is practicable to wipe off that stigma [of slavery] from our nation and government."[21]

African Americans did make real gains during the American Revolution. Paradoxically, some did so because desperate English generals promised freedom to any black who would join their army, an affinity that was criticized by the drafters of the Declaration of Independence—if in politely veiled terms—as proof that the British ignored the property rights of white Americans. Other African Americans became free by serving in the American army: by the final battles of the war, nearly a quarter of the American army was made up of blacks. In 1783 the Virginia Supreme Court ruled that blacks who had been committed to military service by their owners were entitled to be free. Many of these freedmen then moved to the northern states, where in some places slavery had been partially or fully abolished: there were fewer than a thousand free blacks in the North in 1770, but that number rose to 50,000 by 1810.[22]

During the war, Washington invited the black poet Phillis Wheatley to his headquarters. (Jefferson, as Gary Nash points out, had a low opinion of Wheatley: "He diminished her talent with an almost perverse enthusiasm. 'Religion indeed has produced a Phillis Wheatley,' he wrote in his *Notes on the State of Virginia*, published in the year of Wheatley's death, 'but it could not produce a poet.'")[23] Many Hamiltonians felt sympathy of a kind for the Haitian rebels in their struggle against colonial France. John Adams negotiated an agreement with Toussaint l'Ouverture (which Jefferson later annulled). Timothy Pickering, an arch-conservative from New England and not much of a democrat, did, however, hate slavery, and he labeled Jefferson "the Negro President" because the power of this democratic figure rested on the acquiescence of southern slave owners.

Social change there was, then, and socially combative popular movements there also were, and historians in the heady days of the New Deal were not wrong to emphasize the repercussions of two populist anti-taxation insurrections: Shay's Rebellion in Massachusetts in 1786–1787 and the Whiskey Rebellion in Pennsylvania in 1794–1797. It has also been argued—and in all likelihood rightly so—that most Americans in 1787 were opposed to the new constitution, which many prosperous burghers perceived as a way to guarantee public finance and their own holdings of government debt.

(*Ironically, Patrick Henry, "the most ardent of the anti-federalist spokesmen," based his opposition to the new regime on the Commonwealth arguments he had once used against the British. A strong American state would now be the enemy of the American people, he argued, as the strong British state had been before 1776: "Must I give my soul, my lungs to Congress?" he asked in an oration that lasted two days; "Congress must have our souls; the state must have our souls. This is dishonorable and disgraceful."*[24])

The republic's first years, then, were not wholly calm socially, and neither were they particularly calm institutionally. In the American Commonwealth theory of politics, which had underpinned a great deal of revolutionary thinking in 1776, it was commonly assumed that a united people could have but one will: bicameralism may have suited British civil society, as Montesquieu had argued, but for some of the Commonwealth men and their successors, it had no place in the American scheme of things as they imagined it—quite wrongly—to be.

So it was that with the Revolution behind them, many of the former royal provinces that had now become constituent states shrank the prerogatives of their executives, shed their upper houses, and even eliminated their governors, as in Pennsylvania, which for good measure created a board of censors whose task it was to make sure that its unicameral assembly would respect its democratic constitution.

These ideas, incidentally, had a clear international resonance at the time, and it is more than a coincidence that the French Convention of 1792–1795, for not wholly dissimilar reasons, followed a similar trajectory. There, a unicameral legislature (named a "Convention" in imitation of American precedent) ruled without an executive: hence the dictatorial rule in 1793–1794 of two legislative offshoots, the Committee of Public Safety, with Robespierre and Saint-Just, and the Committee of Public Security, which included the painter David.

Likewise, some of the new American states moved their capitals from the seacoast to the interior (as from New York to Albany) in order to give pioneer settlers better access to the seat of government, another institutional change that also had its analog in France during its Revolution, when the unevenly sized royal provinces were transformed into smaller and uniform Republican departments whose administrative centers were situated within a day's walk of their farthest point.

These American institutional and social departures were not without importance. Nonetheless, the larger fact is that these institutional manipulations did not even begin to threaten the established order: thus the critical legality of slavery was everywhere asserted, and the text of the Constitution would make a euphemistic reference to it in its fourth paragraph, which described the inhabitants of the new federal state as free citizens, Indians, and "other persons." Similarly, the slave trade went on unregulated in these years, and 100,000 new slaves were brought into the country in the first two decades of the new nation's existence. (The slave trade was not abolished until 1808.)

In a similar register of social stability, and despite some significant transfers of property since 60,000 loyalists had fled the country, mostly to Canada (though some followed the last loyalist governor of Massachusetts, Thomas Hutchinson, to Britain), property arrangements for the 3 million Americans who had stayed behind were left essentially intact, as was the critically important Common Law, which at that point structured American civil society more than governmental statute.[25]

Indeed, the most critical step that these seemingly unstable assemblies took was to waive whatever vestigial provincial rights individual states may have had to their western territories, thereby making possible the Northwest Ordinance of 1787, a cardinal text of American life, as it not only regulated admissions of new states to the federal Union but mandated local self-government, religious freedom, and education, and decreed—ominously—that "there shall be neither slavery nor involuntary servitude in the said territory." This was certainly a libertarian and typically American and universalist statement, but it can hardly be described as a revolutionary step.

In brief: social unrest and institutional disorder may have prompted Americans to move to the second act of their revolutionary drama, namely the elaboration of their federal constitution. But another and better case can be made for nationality as the driving force behind the making of the Constitution of 1787.

At the dawn of their national consciousness, enamored of economic and religious individualism as they had always been, Americans had also reasoned that a "confederal" (and weak) state was in the genius of their new homeland. But upon reflection, many Americans, some of them war veterans, others legislators in the Congress, concluded from experience in the 1780s that their existing institution fitted neither of their basic national needs: a strong defense of antistate individualism at home and a stronger state vis-à-vis the world (the unfavorable treaty that John Jay negotiated with Spain over the Mississippi was deeply offensive to the new inhabitants of America's western provinces) and also vis-à-vis the constituent states, which had no small tendency to annoy one another largely for fiscal reasons. The state of New York, for example, had decided to levy a tax on vessels transiting through its waters on their way to New Jersey or Connecticut.

The creation of a stronger federal state also corresponded to the new mores of postrevolutionary Americans: in the 1780s between 5 and 10 percent of Americans had already moved from one home to another, half of them from one state to another. Movement from north to south and vice-versa was rare, but movement from east to west was very frequent —and of great consequence.

The American Revolution of 1776 was a libertarian one, to be sure, and its founding Declaration of Independence was written with a concern for the good and liberal opinion of mankind. But in an age when nationalism was on the left and was universally perceived as the antithesis of a hierarchic and corporate Old Regime, the spirit of 1776 could be seen as both libertarian *and* national: "The eighteenth-century founders," observed Oscar and Lilian Handlin, "believed nationalism perfectly compatible with republicanism, that system of government in which virtuous people ruled themselves without a monarchy or an aristocracy, the hope of mankind."[26] And the central idea of the American political structure as it was devised in 1787 was therefore not to abandon 1776 but to reinforce it by creating a new national state that would be, once again, strong vis-à-vis foreigners but weak vis-à-vis its individual citizens.

Hence also, paradoxically, the choice that was made in 1787 to create a presidential rather than a ministerial system: America's imperial presidency has often been—and certainly is today—a threat to Americans' civil liberties, and yet it seemed obvious to the founders in 1787 that the presidential form of the executive was, from a libertarian point of view, preferable to a ministerial arrangement such as then prevailed in England, where the existence of an executive chosen by the legislative branch negated the principle of the separation of powers that Montesquieu had famously presented as the institutional key to modern freedom.

In sum, we can follow here Edmund Morgan's judgment: "Nationalism was the strongest force binding Americans of the Revolutionary generation together. Commitment to the idea of an American nation stabilized disputatious politics and rallied both propertied and philosophical opinion to the creation in 1787 of a stronger national and federal state. Devotion to the nation helped to keep both sides in any conflict on speaking terms, and even made possible the creation of a new and stronger framework in 1787 when the old one proved unsatisfactory."[27]

In the third and next phase of America's early national period, the first years of the federal government also reveal the preeminence of national concerns. Many historians have dwelled on the divisions that opposed urban, moneyed, anglophile, and right-wing Hamiltonians on the one hand, to the left-wing, agricultural, antistate, and pro-French Jeffersonians who suspected banks and loved the land, provided that others were found to till it. "Those who labor in the earth," nobly wrote the universalist and slave-owing third president of the United States, "are the chosen people of God, if ever He had a chosen people."[28] Nonetheless, the most representative and middling stance in these supposedly divisive years was that of President Washington who favored a cautious and neutralist policy vis-à-vis both France and Britain overseas, and, at home, toward the Native Americans of the Old Northwest. Washington did indeed lean toward Hamilton but mainly because it was his belief that only peace and prosperity could ensure the solvency and stability of the new state.

True, when he became president in 1800, Jefferson did (up to a point) act on his leftist principles: he cut down the size of the federal army, whose budget shrank by half; he decided to forgo an American high seas fleet (a particularly incongruous decision given that this dedicated internationalist wondered in 1806 if the United States should not claim the Gulf Stream as part of its territorial waters); he eliminated consumption taxes; he paid back a large part of the federal debt ("a moral canker"); and he managed the protocol of the new republic with conspicuous casualness.

Still, in the end, the transition in 1800 from Hamiltonian and Adamsite Federalists to the more left-wing Republicans (the terms "left" and "right" in this sense were invented in Paris in 1792) did not have that much effect on the ground. Hamilton's national bank and the servicing of the national debt were not abolished. As regards the federal army, ironically, it was under the aegis of the antimilitarist Jefferson that the U.S. Military Academy at West Point was created in 1802. In foreign affairs, the Louisiana Purchase (to which we will return) was as nationalist and statist a statement as could be imagined. Robert Tucker, an astute student of Jefferson's foreign policy, was right to conclude that, in the mind of the Union's third president, "a vision of man's future that was as grand as it was timeless, was joined to a view that seemed not only unwilling but almost unable to transcend, however modestly, the particular interests of the state."[29]

Moreover, it is revealing that after initial quarrels (and a nationally galvanizing war with Britain in 1812), Federalists and Republicans found themselves in broad agreement on nearly all issues. In 1816 James Monroe—America's former minister to Paris—was elected president by a great majority. He was reelected in 1820 by a vote in the electoral college of 231 to 1, with that single vote being cast for John Quincy Adams, who had been elected as a Federalist senator in 1802 and who now became Monroe's secretary of state.

National unanimity, then, about America's purpose, and with this, after 1815, a corresponding indifference to the political life of other nations, whether British monarchic politics, which had been a model for the Hamiltonians, or French revolutionary yearnings, so much admired by the Jeffersonians. In 1793 the democratic society of Charleston, South Carolina (the archetypal slave state as African Americans made up the majority of its population), had written to the Jacobin society of Paris to request an affiliation, and this the Robespierrist assembly had graciously accepted. But after 1800, passions of this kind fell off dramatically, and after 1815 they vanished altogether.

*****

Eric Foner, a brilliant, leftist, and patriotic historian of the United States, notes that the nation has from the first been marked by a "devotion to freedom,"[30] a trait that has always been, he writes, the essence of the American national idea. This is true. But it is also true that the American cult of freedom has consistently shared its preeminence with the idea of the American nation triumphant in its own right, regardless of principle.

At this time the issue of American national self-confidence had two edges. One, very sharp, bore down on the physical enemies of God's elect, be they Native Americans first of all, or Mexicans after that, or eventually in 1861–1865, slave-holding Southerners. The other edge, more innocent, and in fact often naïve, was in the ubiquitous cultural assertion of Americanness.

In the newly independent America, no aesthetic domain was left untouched. Because art and liberty had always traveled together in history from Ancient Greece to republican Florence, and then to the London of the Glorious Revolution and to libertarian Paris, it stood to reason that art would now move to America. Ezra Stiles, the president of Yale and a gifted musician, assumed that, soon, "all the arts may be transported from Europe and Asia, and flourish in America with an augmented Lustre."[31] America—it was widely assumed by its budding and as yet unrecognized painters, writers, and musicians—was surely destined to be the capital of world culture. Philip Freneau, in a poem he called "On the Rising Glory of America," set the tone. After him, Joel Barlow, one of the so-called Connecticut Wits, did his bit with a simultaneously deist, nationalist, and universalist epic poem entitled *Visions of Columbus:*

> See, thro' the whole, the same progressive plan,
> That draws, for mutual succor, man to man
> From friends to tribes, from tribes to realms ascend
> Their powers, their interests and their passions blend;
> Adorn their manners, social virtues spread.[32]

(The *Edinburgh Review* remarked that the intentions of its author were highly laudable but that his situation as an epic writer was desperate.)

The arts were all well represented in America's ambitions here, but so were other less poetic but still intellectual disciplines. In 1784 Jedediah Morse, a native of Massachusetts, brought forward a geography of the new nation: Americans, he thought, deserved to have their own school manuals. Likewise, in 1783 Noah Webster, from neighboring Connecticut, published his *An American Spelling Book*, of which in its lifetime more than one hundred million copies would be printed: only the Bible was better known. It is also to Webster that America owed its first dictionary, published in 1806 with a second edition in 1828, entitled the *American Dictionary of the English Language*, whose aim was to bring back the language's original purity, which, Webster thought, it had lost in England.

Historical writing also bore the mark of America's nascent nationalism, with Mercy Otis Warren, a playwright and historian, publishing in 1805 a history of the American Revolution that was born libertarian and nationalist.

It is also to this epoch that we can trace many of the (apocryphal) anecdotes that have become part of America's historical folklore. Active in this domain was Mason Weems (1759–1825), a cleric who compiled a once-famous biography of George Washington, complete with many (fictional) anecdotes that made George the child the father of Washington the statesman, as when George, the model child, confesses to having cut down the cherry tree, with an accompanying and immortal "I cannot tell a lie," an (imagined) remark well known to every American. (In later years a historically minded artist would portray a young Bill Clinton, complete with a three-cornered Washingtonian hat and holding a chainsaw behind his back, with the caption: "I did not chop down this cherry tree.") Weems published his biography in 1799, and never ceased to improve it through the twenty editions that were published before his death in 1825. Fifty thousand copies were sold in his lifetime alone.

So many well-meaning efforts, whose nationalist character is underscored by the strange gap between the claims and popularity of their authors and the aesthetic quality of the work. A genuine American literature of world quality would indeed soon come into being, but only after 1820, and more particularly with the publication of James Fenimore Cooper's first novels.

(*In the context of both Franco-American relations and the American nation's cultural dependency on European manners, it is worth noting that Cooper—this arch-American novelist—lived for years in Paris; it was there that he wrote* The Prairie, *the third of his five* Leatherstocking Tales. *His fondness for the supportive spirit of the culturally minded French capital, one should add, soon became a model for other archetypically American writers like Mark Twain, Ernest Hemingway, and James Baldwin, who all lived for some years in the City of Light, so aptly named by Walter Benjamin "the Capital of the Nineteenth Century.")*

Readers of Eric Hobsbawm's pages on the "invention of tradition" will be more struck by the intensity than by the quality of these early American exercises. But their aesthetic mediocrity indirectly speaks to the yearnings of Americans for any aesthetic productions that, however lamely, celebrated the glories of their new nation.

*****

National(ist) cultural forms and nationalist passion: these were (on the face of it, it any case) innocent and harmless intellectual exercises. But there was nothing innocent about the fate of the first enemies of the new republic, that is to say, Native Americans, for whom the War of Independence and its sequels were an irremediable catastrophe.

In 1775 the newly assembled Continental Congress at Philadelphia, mindful of its difficult military situation, opened negotiations with the Native American tribes. Very sensibly, given their choice of enemies— American settlers versus British soldiers—the Native Americans rebuffed the offers of the white Americans.

Most involved at first were the Shawnees and the Mingos to the north, and to the south the Cherokees, armed by the British, who struck in Georgia and Virginia. To contain these attacks, these two nascent states raised a militia of 4,500 men, about the same number that Washington had under his orders at the time.

This was a savage and unforgiving conflict. In late 1776 no fewer than 5,000 discouraged American soldiers relented and accepted a British offer of a general amnesty. By contrast, the war against the Native Americans mobilized unforgiving hostility on both sides and created among the Irish, German, and Scotish immigrants a new sense of American unity. Dr. David Ramsay, in his day a noted historian of South Carolina, reminiscing in 1785 on these earlier events, concluded that the Indian raids had

> increased the unanimity of the inhabitants, and invigorated their opposition to Great-Britain. Several who called themselves Tories in 1775 became active Whigs in 1776 and cheerfully took arms in the first instance against the Indians, and in the second against Great Britain as the instigator of their barbarous devastations. Before this event some well-meaning people could not see the justice or propriety of contending with their formerly protective parent state; but Indian cruelties, excited by royal artifices, soon extinguished all their predilection for the country of their forefathers.[33]

General Burgoyne's defeat at Saratoga (which brought the French into the war) reminded the Mohawk leader Joseph Brant and his fellow warriors that Britain was their last best hope. In the summer and fall of 1778, in the Wyoming Valley of Pennsylvania and in the Cherry Valley of New York State, hundreds of white men, as well as women and children, were put to death by Native Americans, who were then slaughtered in turn. Washington ordered General Sullivan to this theater of war with 2,300 soldiers, who were told to pursue "the total destruction and devastation of the (Indian) settlements and the capture of as many prisoners of every age and sex as possible." Sullivan did well: forty towns "besides scattering houses" were burnt, and as he noted in his report to Congress: "The quantity of Corn destroyed must amount to 160,000 Bushels, with a vast quantity of vegetables of every kind . . . Except [for] one Town . . . about 80 miles from Genessee, there is not a single Town left in the Country." Contrary to Washington's orders, no prisoners were taken, or rather, those who were taken were scalped, killed, and even mutilated. In a parallel incursion near Pittsburgh, 600 more Continentals moved up the Allegheny, burning Indian towns with the idea of driving Native Americans off the land forever. Washington did not encourage these barbarisms: mindful of his experience as an aide to British General Edward Braddock, who had been slaughtered along with hundreds of his redcoats by Indian and French fighters in 1755, Washington was ever cautious in his dealings with the Indian nations. But neither was he ready to pass up a unique buying opportunity: he therefore entered into a partnership with the governor of New York and arranged to buy six thousand acres of now uninhabited land. They were, he wrote, "amazingly cheap."[34]

Self-defense and an inherited suspicion of all Native Americans, together with a preponderance of power: these motivations explain a great deal. But alas, we can go further and consider as a cause of renewed strife the very nature of America's universalist republic.

It is a truth universally acknowledged that the principles of American republicanism in 1787 are best described in Madison's legendary contributions to *The Federalist Papers*. Could a republican form of government be successful in a vast republic? Montesquieu had thought not: modern republicanism, he decided, could only thrive in a small state that was inhabited by virtuous and simple yeomen. Rousseau concurred in this judgment. In June 1788, at the Virginia ratifying convention, Patrick Henry likewise and pessimistically opined: "One government cannot reign over so extensive a country as this is without absolute despotism."[35] Madison disagreed: the presence of factions (which English political philosophers had long since identified as a fatal malediction, destructive of the public good) had *seemed* to be a problem, he argued, but in America, factions (soon to become parties) were in fact a blessing in disguise. In a small state, a mean-spirited faction might indeed overwhelm society as a whole. But in a large state (such as the newly independent United States), factions might spring up everywhere, but no one of them could hope to rule in so vast a realm. "Extend the sphere," he wrote, "and you take in a greater variety of parties and interests; you make it less probable that a majority of the whole will have a common motive to invade the rights of other citizens; or if such a common motive exists, it will be more difficult for all who feel it to discover their own strength, and to act in unison with each other."[36]

When the populace did act in unison, however, we can also ask today, to what purpose? What practical and common ends could unite the faction-prone citizens of the new federal republic?

Could the partisans of foreign adventurism prevail? This was unlikely: vis-à-vis Europe, and more particularly vis-à-vis Britain, an independent America was weak, and even Jefferson proved cool when the revolutionary shenanigans of Citizen Genêt, the ambassador of republican France, threatened to involve America in a war with Britain.

But might there be some "other" whose offensive presence could unite all individual citizens in a common purpose?

In the classical definition of republicanism, as Montesquieu had understood it, and as Rousseau had advocated also, virtue, strictly understood, would be the necessary foundation of any republican state. And in that ideological context, no one could have argued that dispossessing or murdering Indians was a properly republican idea.

In the new Madisonian definition of republicanism, however, virtue was no longer the central theme. Consensus was at the center instead, but for the weak, consensus was a siren song. Of course, as a political principle consensus is much to be preferred to its theoretical opposite, namely government by confrontation, or, as in nineteenth-century France, government by ongoing revolution.

But the consensual nature of American government had its costs for two basic reasons. First, it meant that the positive resolution of divisive social conflict through politics became ever more difficult in America, as would be made clear in the 1850s, when the nation's federal structure and the domination of Southerners in the Senate made it impossible to find a new solution to the problem of slavery, and in the 1930s, when an entrenched judiciary enabled vested interests to resist Franklin Roosevelt's New Deal. Where consensus is a necessary prerequisite for change, there often is no change. The need for consensus left the strongest elements of American civil society (namely its propertied white men) in an institutional position to resist whatever claims might be made through politics by the weakest members of the American community, namely Native Americans before 1850, African Americans after that, women, and in more recent times, illegal and markedly foreign-seeming immigrants.

Second, the consensual nature of the government was costly because Madisonian consensus often fostered aggressive stands that were geared to the destruction of "others." Historically, a consequence of the American pattern of divided governance has been that it is very difficult to forge coalitions that have an agenda for change, but that it is quite simple—as many malevolent public figures have understood—to galvanize particular constituencies against some "enemy of the state" whose precise nature has varied from one moment to the next.

It is often through its choice of foreign enemies that a nation defines itself, and America has been no exception: Pilgrims against Indians, the new republic against Britain, democratic America against German and Japanese imperialism, America versus the evil empire, and now America against the Muslim world. It has also often defined itself against *internal* enemies, such as new immigrants, with the passing of the Alien and Sedition acts of 1798; or the Irish, much detested by the Know-Nothing party of the 1850s; or Asians in the 1880s and 1890s; or southern and eastern Europeans in the 1920s; or Hispanics in our own day, or African Americans always.

But more dramatic yet was the even more brutal and quasi-genocidal war against the one enemy whose persecution could in the eighteenth and nineteenth centuries easily unite white Americans of all sizes and shapes. Fred Anderson and Andrew Cayton, gifted historians of this issue, have written:

> Making war against Indians legitimized ambitious passions, controlled factionalism, and created a "sentiment [of] . . . attachment to the federal compact: All must feel the injuries we have received," explained Andrew Jackson about Native Americans

and their allies to the voters of Nashville in 1809, "all must be determined to resist them . . . let us . . . with one heart and hand declare to the world, that firm determination . . . to go to any length with the government of our country in defense and support of the nation's rights and independence."[37]

Once again, as so often in American history, a universalist purpose (in this case the new definition of federal citizenship) could all too easily be twisted to serve a reprehensible and particularist design. As Walter Benjamin sadly observed, "there is no document of culture which is not at the same time a document of barbarism."[38] So it was, for example, that in 1776 Jefferson proposed that the newly created state of Virginia should grant every citizen fifty acres of land, but without mentioning to whom those acres had heretofore belonged.

*****

The war with Britain ended in 1783, but the war in the West went on. Although the Indian tribes had been promised a large part of the Old Northwest, settlers continued to pour across the Alleghenies. There were hardly any whites in Ohio in 1783, but they numbered 45,000 in 1800 and 230,000 in 1810. The Miami and Delaware Indians, led by Little Turtle, rose up once more: in 1790 they defeated federal troops, who fell back by more than a hundred miles. In the autumn of 1791 a second army of 2,000 men was sent out under the command of General Arthur St. Clair: it was cut to pieces by 1,000 Indian warriors under Little Turtle and a Shawnee war chief, Tecumseh. But this outcome could not stand, and in 1792 a third American army, commanded by General Anthony Wayne, was sent forth, this time 3,000 strong. (The entire army of the United States numbered at this point 5,000 men.) On August 20, 1794, whites and Native Americans clashed again. Caught by surprise, the U.S. army fell back at first, but in the face of overwhelming odds the Indian resistance soon collapsed. General Wayne burned everything that he did not destroy. The British who had egged the

Indians on now refused them any kind of help. By 1795 the losers were pushed farther west.

In the South, much the same result was achieved more peaceably: Washington negotiated a secret treaty with a Creek chieftain named Alexander McGillivray, who was by ancestry less Creek than he was Scots and French. The Creeks would be guaranteed some territorial integrity, and McGillivray would also receive a commission and pay as a general in the army of the United States. This dubious arrangement did not last, especially after the annexation of Louisiana in 1802 made the forced displacement of southern and northwestern Indians more feasible: when all was said and done, why not push all of the Native Americans westward to "uninhabited" lands across the Mississippi as Jefferson had suggested?

Native Americans, who before 1776 had largely controlled lands between the Appalachians and the Mississippi, were everywhere pushed back. Now, they gradually resolved to make a last-ditch fight, as Powhatan's successor Opechancanough had tried in 1622 in Virginia, and King Philip in 1675 in New England. Tecumseh, who in 1808 with his brother, the prophet Lalawethika, had founded a new Indian community at Prophetstown, tried to rally what remained of the different tribes: "Brothers, we all belong to one family . . . we must assist each other to bear our burdens . . . The white men despise and cheat the Indians; they abuse and insult them; they do not think the red men sufficiently good to live." When urged by General William Henry Harrison (who would soon become the ninth president of the United States) to sell more territory yet, the Indian warrior replied that he would neither yield nor sell more land: "Sell a country! Why not sell the air, the clouds and the great sea, as well as the earth."[39] But the balance of power was now inexorably tilted against his people: his 600 followers were defeated by 1,100 U.S. soldiers at the battle of Tippecanoe in 1811. Prophetstown was burned to the ground. Indians had routinely executed their prisoners, and Americans now also did so. During the War of 1812, Tecumseh, whose name meant meteor or falling star, allied himself to the British and helped them recapture Detroit and Fort Dearborn, soon to be Chicago. He was killed in October 1813 in Canada, at the battle of the Thames.

*****

The new American republic was nationalistically inclined. It was also decidedly expansionist. Louisiana was at stake here.

Napoleon, by birth a Corsican, by career a militarist, was by choice a racist, a confirmed anti-Semite and very hostile to blacks as well. (In 1802 he restored slavery in what was left of the French colonial empire where it had been, in theory at least, abolished by Robespierre's Jacobins in 1794.) Napoleon was also a confirmed imperialist, hence his expedition in 1798 to Egypt, which he hoped would become a steppingstone for the French conquest—or reconquest—of India. (They had lost their large share of it to the British in 1763.) But once that fantasy had been laid waste, Napoleon turned his attention to the reconstitution of the *ancien régime* French Caribbean empire. Haiti, which had secured de facto independence in the 1790s, would be reconquered: vast profits would again be made from sugar plantations, whose reenslaved workers would be supplied from a reannexed Louisiana, which France had ceded to Spain in 1763.

As it happens—in one of history's silent turning points—Napoleon's plan collapsed. The price of its success would have been to accept Haiti's internal autonomy and the definitive abolition of slavery in France's colonial empire. Then a republican French fleet, based in New Orleans, working with a free black and republican army, based in Haiti, could have swept the Caribbean islands and Louisiana as well. Britain's fate in the region would have been transformed, and America's as well. How could slavery have been upheld in Alabama and Mississippi if it had it been abolished in a contiguous Louisiana? And, in 1820, what Missouri Compromise could then have been enacted?

But Napoleon, whose wife came from an aristocratic French planter family in Martinique, chose quite otherwise. He did his best: Toussaint L'Ouverture, the Haitian commander who had offered to be his ally, was captured by treachery and sent to die of cold and misery in a French alpine prison. A French army was sent to reconquer the island under the command of Napoleon's brother-in-law, General Charles Leclerc.

But soon after he arrived, Leclerc died of yellow fever, as did most of his soldiers. Napoleon's reactionary gamble had failed, and because the prospect of war between France and Britain had meanwhile become stronger, Napoleon reasoned that he had no choice but to cut his losses and sell Louisiana to the United States for 15 million dollars as Britain would in all likelihood capture it shortly.

The Louisiana Purchase was a great event in world history, much more consequential than is usually understood. It is also a suggestive event in the history of American patriotism and American nationalism: domestic reactions to it clearly illustrate how easily any American patriot, however liberal and however brilliant, can move toward nationalistic goals. Jefferson, in the past, had been an antimilitarist pacifist who was suspicious of national authority. In 1798, when Congress passed laws on the press that he thought too strict, this president-to-be of the federal republic had even argued in favor of states' rights and "nullification."

But the acquisition by the French of Louisiana from the Spanish triggered an immediate reversal on his part, as he explained in April 1802 to the head of America's diplomatic mission in France: "The day that France takes possession of New Orleans . . . seals the union of two nations, who, in conjunction, can maintain exclusive possession of the ocean. From that moment we must marry ourselves to the British fleet and nation." France was, thought Jefferson, America's "natural friend." But by possessing New Orleans, France had become the "natural enemy." And a natural enemy that could easily be overcome: "For however greater her force is than ours compared in the abstract, it is nothing in comparison of ours when to be exerted on our soil."[40] It is likewise suggestive that Jefferson now decided to consider further expansion that might also lead to war: first, toward the Pacific in 1805, with an expedition under the command of his former private secretary Meriwether Lewis, a relationship that underlines the importance of this mission, and second, in 1807, toward Mexico, with an expedition that went beyond the Rio Grande into territory that then belonged to Spain and would later be Mexico's.

Wedged in 1776 between the Atlantic and the Alleghenies, never at that time more than three hundred miles from the sea, the American state now found itself in 1803 sovereign over ten times the land that it had claimed a quarter of a century before. One would have to go back to the Arab conquests of the eighth century to find so rapid and so durable a territorial expansion.

It is with much justice that Jefferson has come down in the history of the United States as the founding father whose thought and actions were most prone to self-contradiction, and thus, from the perspective of this essay's emphasis on the proximity in America of inclusion and exclusion, the most typical. Was he not both a slave owner and the first apologist of American freedom? A partisan of states' rights and of federal power? An internationalist and an American nationalist? His duality—along with his talents—makes him the archetypal American president, as Ahab in Melville's *Moby-Dick* is the archetypal hero of American literature, at once, in Richard Slotkin's words, "victim and hero, Quaker and killer, Christian and blood-lusting pagan."[41]

But what Jefferson's political enemies attributed to character faults we can see in another light. With regard to Louisiana, Jefferson's change of mind went beyond the ambiguities of his personality: again, when America's national power and prosperity are at stake, all previous hesitations about the virtues of nationalist conquest seem to lapse.

And also typically, what might have seemed at first to be an American nationalist land-grab was, in very brief time, described as a necessary world-historical step, important for the United States, to be sure, but also critical for world liberty and world peace. John Quincy Adams explained it all in 1811: the New World had faced a choice between remaining "an endless multitude of little insignificant clans and tribes at eternal war with one another for a rock, or a fish pond, the sport and fable of European masters and oppressors" and, on the other hand, becoming "a nation, coextensive with the North American continent, destined by God and nature to be the most populous and most powerful people ever combined under one social compact."[42]

* * * * *

National and cultural expansionism, and with this, once again, war, with its typically decisive role in the evolution of American politics and society. It was not because Americans had proclaimed their independence that they chose to fight a war against Britain in 1775–1776; it was because war had already broken out in 1775 that Americans—with some hesitation—decided to proclaim their independence.

Of the wars in which the United States has been involved (with the possible exception of the recent preemptive invasion of Iraq, but preemptive of what?), none has been more pointless than the War of 1812. By that same token, few have been more revealing. Of course, that war, like all wars, had real and tangible causes. Britain had indeed played fast and loose with many agreements it had made with its former colony: locked as it was in a struggle with Bonapartist France, Britain, as an imperial power, had been rough in its handling of America's claim to the right to trade with the French. The Royal Navy's seizure of American sailors on the high seas was both an injury and an insult to America's national pride.

And yet, the American commercial interests that were most injured by British restrictive practices were also the ones that were least interested in provoking Britain in any way. New England's federalist delegates in Congress voted massively against the war, and even thought in 1814 of seceding from the Union. Inversely, the Jeffersonian democrats who had the least complaint were the most warlike: but Andrew Jackson understood why this did not matter. For him, the war had to do with building national character, as it did for his archenemy-to-be, Calhoun: "The national character" he explained, would acquire "energy" because this conflict would be remembered as collective defense "of the personal rights of its citizens."[43]

This useless and, in the main, ideologically motivated war would have ended with the annexation of Canada, had the Americans been victorious. (As in 1775, French Catholic Canadians did not respond to Protestant America's defiance of their colonial oppressors.) With this conquest, Jefferson explained (he had also dreamt of annexing Cuba), "we should have such an empire for liberty as she has never surveyed since the creation."[44] But as it happened, things turned out differently. Defeating Britain, which had just defeated Napoleon, proved more difficult than had been conveniently assumed by the War Hawks in the U.S. Congress. The Treaty of Ghent, which ended the war, merely restored the status quo and said nothing about America's first grievance, namely Britain's claim to the right to accost neutral vessels at sea.

As regarded the American national idea, however, the war was a great success. First, New England's failure to secede consolidated the idea that America's federal and national unity could never be undone, a verdict that the North's victory in the Civil War would later enshrine forever. Second, Andrew Jackson's decisive victory over 15,000 highly trained British regulars at the battle of New Orleans was a source of great pride. True, as the battle had occurred after the signing of the peace treaty (news traveled slowly before the invention of the telegraph) this victory had no practical consequence, except for the death of 13 Americans and 291 British soldiers including their commanding general, a brother-in-law of the Duke of Wellington. But it did later make a great difference to Jackson, who would become the seventh president of the United States. In the presidential election of 1824, which he lost, and the one of 1828, which he won, Jackson's prestige rested more on his military record than on his democratic instincts, which—insofar as he had any—developed only after he had been elected.

*****

The next great event in America's ever more confident self-assertion after the Louisiana Purchase and the War of 1812 was the elaboration in 1823 of the Monroe Doctrine, which, like many events and individuals in American history, brought together in close-fitting manner our two themes of inclusive universalism and exclusionary nationalism. We owe its promulgation to James Monroe, a Virginian president—and slave owner—and to his secretary of state, John Quincy Adams, a New Englander who would succeed Monroe as president (following in the footsteps of his father, John Adams) and would later become a well-known abolitionist and defender of African Americans.

In some respects, the Monroe Doctrine was a generous document: it was courageous of America to proclaim its opposition to European interference in the affairs of the New World. At issue was Russia, which had established a foothold in Alaska in 1741, and Spain, then under the rule of its most odious monarch, Ferdinand VII, and interested in reconquering its colonies in Latin America.

But the doctrine had another side to it as well: first because the United States, while warning other powers not to interfere in South America, did not renounce its own right to do so. In 1842 it invoked the doctrine to justify its own expansionism in Texas on the grounds that the area was threatened by British ambitions. Moreover, America not only reserved the right to exclude Europeans from the Americas, it also claimed it had the right to restore order in Latin America whenever and wherever it had lapsed. (*In 1904, with his "corollary," Theodore Roosevelt made such incursions a principle of international law: in 1824 the vice president of "Greater Colombia," Francisco Santander, had, it is true, described Monroe's document as "heartening for mankind," but at that same time Simon Bolivar, prophetically and revealingly, sighed that the United States was "destined by Providence to burden Latin America with trouble in the name of freedom.")*[45]

Another aspect of the protective, anticolonialist Monroe Doctrine was that, during the first half of the nineteenth century, at least, it was cost free for America. The doctrine generally suited British as well as American interests: indeed, before Monroe unilaterally proclaimed it, George Canning, Britain's foreign minister at the time, had gone so far as to offer the United States an explicit treaty of cooperation, which

Monroe had declined despite Jefferson's endorsement of it. In subsequent years, where the Royal Navy could not be relied on to enforce the doctrine, it was of no consequence, and where the British fleet was there to enforce it, its application required no additional American effort or expense.

The issue deserves a larger frame. It is customary to speak of America's isolationism as a central aspect of its foreign policy from the origins to 1941, and certainly Americans in those times did define themselves against "the broils of Europe," as Jefferson had put it. America was innocence, rurality, democracy, self-government, and peace, most or all of which, thought most Americans, were beyond the ken of the Old World. But in actual fact, until the 1870s, America's freedom of action depended very closely on Britain's good will and on its support of the United States as a world power. In 1798, for example, John Adams gave serious thought to declaring war on France, but held back because he feared that the British would be unable to contain the French fleet.[46]

For Lord Bryce (who was a friend of Theodore Roosevelt and published in 1888 a famous and still useful book, *The American Commonwealth*), the relationship of Britain and the United States was so close that Washington could have done without any and all of its diplomats, with one exception, its ambassador to London. And the relationship between the two nations remained strong after America became the senior partner, as had begun to be clear when Britain agreed to compensate the United States for the damages to its commerce caused by two Confederate cruisers that had been built in British shipyards during the Civil War. From then on, it was widely assumed that the destinies of the two nations were completely entwined: on the occasion of Queen Victoria's Diamond Jubilee in 1897, the *New York Times* reminded its readers that America "was part, and a great part, of the Greater Britain which seems so plainly destined to dominate the planet." That was also the belief of John Hay, America's secretary of state in London in 1898: for him, the British and American flags were made to fly together, "carrying always in their shadow freedom and civilization." "Whether we will it or not," English-speaking people were fated to labor jointly "by the very nature of things, and no man and no group of men can prevent it"; their new and common venture was "a sanction like that of religion" and "the beneficent work of the world."[47]

And if we look forward to the mid-twentieth century, we can gauge the importance of the British fleet to the Monroe Doctrine and to America's early national ambitions in yet another way. In 1939, America, though immensely powerful, was as yet unmilitarized, and therefore still depended for its security—as it had since 1815—on the strength of the Royal Navy, a state of affairs that would not end decisively until America's first-ever great naval victory at Midway Island in June 1942.

It is in that same context of British naval domination we can also consider Franklin Roosevelt's "Vichy gamble." In 1939, with the help of the French navy (quite considerable at that time), Britain's domination of the seas was unchallengeable. But in May–June 1940, with the collapse of France, all this was suddenly at risk: if Vichy France were to join its fleet to Germany's and Italy's, Britain might well succumb. Hence Roosevelt's determined support for Vichy France. Hence also, in no small part, America's entrance into a war that its elites had concluded could no longer be avoided, to the great relief, and, ironically, to the eventual humbling, of Churchill's imperial Britain at the hands of a newly imperialized America.

*****

Republican idealism on the one hand; nationalist calculations on the other, with the one leading so easily to the other: "*Zwei Seelen wohnen, ach! in meiner Brust,*" wrote Goethe (Two souls, Oh! live within my breast).[48] Libertarian inclusion and violent or even murderous exclusion: the Pilgrims had experienced this dichotomy. Jefferson had understood it existentially. And so would the survivors of Hiroshima and Nagasaki.

PART II: 1825-1912

CHAPTER 4
A Democratic Sense of Self

The middle decades of the nineteenth century are a critical moment in the democratization of the American national idea: its apogee was in the democratic abolition of slavery in 1863 and 1865. Its darker side was manifested, first, in the war of conquest against Mexico in 1847; second, in the eventual rebirth of institutionalized racial discrimination in 1877; and finally, for the length and breadth of the nineteenth century, in the ongoing and quasi-genocidal war of white Americans against Native Americans. Give me liberty or give me death? Yes, and who today could regret the victory of the North over the South in 1865? But how disconcerting it is that libertarian and democratic patriotism was in Jacksonian America so easily transformed into aggressive and oftentimes cruel nationalistic abuse: a proximity so characteristic of American life, from the Puritan fathers to George W. Bush's "crusade" in Iraq.

For Tocqueville, the centrality of democracy to this phase of the American experience was self-evident: "Many important things could be said about the social condition of Anglo-Americans," he wrote in 1832, "but one of them dominates all the others. The social condition of Americans is above all else democratic. It has been that way since the birth of the colonies. It is even more that way today."[1] This judgment was historically inaccurate as regards America's origins. But by his time, it had *become* quite true: as of 1821, twenty-one of the twenty-four states of the Union had abolished their propertied franchise (which had not been set very high in any case), as against France, once again, where voting was severely restricted until 1848, or Britain, where universal manhood suffrage (in cities but not in the countryside) did not become the rule until 1867. In colonial times, the last royal governor of Massachusetts,

Thomas Hutchinson, had complained that "anything with the appearance of a man" thought he had the right to vote. But now, what Hutchinson had apprehended as an aberration had become an established rule: politics in America became a domestic and democratic passion and an ongoing show, ceaselessly renewed and universally understood. (Many of the popular terms that are used even today to describe aspects of American politics—dark horse, lame duck, pork barrel, and so on—date from this period.)

Along with a more democratic franchise came waves of democratic reform, with new public schools, which after 1855 were free and open in Massachusetts to all children of all races and religions, and new jails also. (The ostensible purpose of Tocqueville's visit to the United States in 1831 was to inspect the rejuvenated—and individuated—American prison system with its methods of solitary confinement.)

The aim of the Founding Fathers had been to create a representative republic, but by 1830 America was well on the way to becoming a democratic republic instead. Other nineteenth-century societies were similarly affected by the impulse toward greater democracy, but none, as it were, so democratically. Tocqueville's real purpose in coming to America was set in that context: Why was it that his homeland, France, whose political system was born as America's was from a democratizing revolution, had taken such a bad, Napoleonic, authoritarian turn? And his second purpose—which had been, would be, and still is a goal of many Frenchmen in contemplating American society—was to find out what the democratic future of his own country would be socially and perhaps politically: by 1830 America had become a laboratory for futurist modernity.

Abraham Lincoln may not have read Tocqueville, but he too underscored the foundational nature of America's democratic political culture: respect for democratic public opinion had always been "the central idea" of America's national self-perception. Here was a truth, he thought, which was inscribed in the hearts of men, in God's providential will as well, and in America's entire history. In his unstinting eulogy of Thomas

Jefferson and of the Declaration of Independence, which more than the Constitution was his lodestar, Lincoln explained his faith in greater detail:

> The principles of Jefferson are the definitions and axioms of free society . . . All honor to Jefferson—to the man who, in the concrete pressure of a struggle for national independence by a single people, had the coolness, forecast and capacity to introduce into a merely revolutionary document, an abstract truth, applicable to all men and all times, and so to embalm it there, that today, and in all coming days, it shall be a rebuke and a stumbling-block to the very harbingers of reappearing tyranny and oppression.[2]

To understand America's inclusive democratic patriotism and its exclusionary nationalism as they developed in the middle decades of the nineteenth century is also to understand America's changing sense of self, and once more we are reminded of the extraordinary steadfastness of "the American creed," never the same from generation to generation, but always faithful to its roots. Americans on the eve of the Civil War were no longer Calvinists, but they were still and emphatically so—as seventeenth-century Puritans had been—a religious nation. On the verge of massive industrialization, they were no longer yeomen farmers. But they were still dedicated to the ideal of independent economic actors. And most important, they were still republican citizens, as they had become in the last quarter of the eighteenth century.

By the 1830s Americans imagined themselves as politically mobilized and libertarian Democrats (in 1824, only 27 percent of adult males had bothered to vote, but by 1840 that figure had nearly trebled), divinely chosen to bear a message of civil liberty and free labor, a message sanctioned by public opinion they would apply peaceably (if possible) but that they would forcibly impose as their national will if they had to. But how to understand the causes of this deep-seated and critical change in self-perception?

A critical factor in the democratization of America was quite simply the dramatic rise of its capacity to create wealth: a rising tide that raised even the smallest boats. True, this greater wealth was very unevenly distributed, but the great majority of Protestant Americans in this democratic age had a lively sense that their society worked and prospered because they too worked and therefore prospered. "Cake for some *or* bread for the many." Europeans often understood capitalism in that mode. But these early nineteenth-century Americans thought instead of "cake for some *and* bread for the many."

After a slow start, the seventeenth-century settlers had become respectable yeomen and burghers with handsome houses and solid stone walls that bespoke their respectability. They were not penniless immigrants but settled colonists. In the second and third quarters of the eighteenth century these settled colonists had become rich merchants and slave-owning planters. They were loyal Anglo-Americans but not to be condescended to by impecunious English-born colonial officials.

In similar manner, the war of 1812–1815 marks the beginning of American industrialism, and the great prosperity that followed this shift left its mark on the consciousness of all Americans. The fewer than 3 million settlers of the thirteen colonies had by 1820 become 9 million, an increase of a third in every decade, due in part to immigration, but largely to a very high birth rate and greater longevity. (One can juxtapose America's exuberant progress to France's modest trajectory: in 1500 it was the most populous country in Europe; later, from 27 million in 1789, it rose to only 39 million in 1860 and 41 million in 1939.)

In this period the foundations of New York's twentieth-century glory were also laid—on the heels of Paris, the "capital of the nineteenth century"—thanks to the city's situation as a harbor and as the gateway to the West and the Old Northwest, first with the opening of the Erie Canal in 1825 and again in the 1850s with the creation of a national railway grid. Paradoxically but in America not atypically, a good deal of this prosperity was based not on individual endeavors but on state-sponsored spending for economic infrastructure like the Erie Canal. In the short period of 1824–1828, nearly ninety such projects were funded by the federal government alone.[3]

America had been a rural society in 1776, a commercial one in 1820, and was now on the verge of becoming a predominantly industrial one, as witnessed by its rates of urbanization, which were close to those of Great Britain. In 1860, most of the inhabitants of Massachusetts lived in cities of more than 2,500 inhabitants. It is a related fact that the United States was among the first nations to manage tariff policies so as to favor the growth of particularly important—and politically efficacious—industries: the tariff of 1816, a critical part of Henry Clay's American system, was the first such measure that aimed for the protection of specific industries rather than revenue. It is also symbolic that Friedrich List, whose name is invariably associated with the "infant industry argument" (which holds that for nationalistic and neo-mercantilist reasons, nascent industries need to be protected from mature firms overseas), started his professional life as a young professor at the University of Tübingen, whence, persecuted for his reformist views, he fled to America, became familiar in his new country with Clay's ideas, and only returned to Germany in 1832 as a consul of the United States, thanks to Andrew Jackson's patronage.

Another consequential—and highly visible democratic and symbolic —change was in the heightening tempo of the westward movement, whose significance can be measured by its importance to American politics: Would the West be settled by free democrats, or by planters and their slaves? In France, Proudhon, who was, all things considered, a conservative anarchist but an anarchist nonetheless, dreamed of a society in which every working citizen would have access to the capital that would enable him to become an independent producer. In America, his dream became a social reality thanks to the distribution of land to settlers by the federal government: "Vote yourself a farm" was one of Horace Greeley's favorite aphorisms, as was "Go west, young man, go west!" Of course, one of the effects of these land grants was the incessant wars that ever pushed (supposedly warlike) Native Americans westward, but a highly visible effect was to bring plausibility to the view that American democrats had of their society as democratic and peaceful. Also a sign of America's advancing cultural and democratic maturity was the fluttering, pictorial representation of treasured national landscapes by members of the first genuine school of American painting, the Hudson River School of the 1840s and 1860s, such as Thomas Cole, Asher Durand, Jasper Cropsey, and Albert Bierstadt. To quote one of America's cherished poems, "this land was ours before we knew it."

*****

At the same time, however, a clue to the nature of enrichment and national sentiment in Jacksonian America was that although Americans perceived themselves as rich and democratic—and often were so—many of them were in actual fact democrats to be sure, but desperately poor. Tocqueville himself, many of whose American contacts were Whigs, who were favorable to banks and property, badly underreported the dark sides of American urban life. American history did not travel nonstop from greater wealth to a more equal distribution of wealth, even if a rising tide is said to lift all boats, but Americans then as now were reluctant to recognize the inequalities that marred the egalitarian claims they made for their nation.

A first point was that in the southern states—which were democratic also, if in their own way—civil society was dominated by an elite of 10,000 families of which only 3,000 owned more than 100 slaves, whereas most southern white farmers owned no slaves at all. In Texas— a southern state that pretended to be a western one as well—in 1860, 68 percent of political representatives owned at least one slave at a time when three out of four households owned none.[4] It mattered also that in gold, and therefore in constant dollars, the market value of a slave rose from $300 in 1790 (which coincidentally was about the cost of buying a replacement for an often fatal military service in Napoleonic France) to $2000 in 1860 because of a speculative boom in the value of African Americans during the 1850s.[5] On that scale, few northern factory owners could rival in wealth the owners of a vast plantation whom Tocqueville saw as a parodic version of his own class in France: "The American of the South loves grandeur, luxury, glory, noise, pleasure, idleness above all. [He has] the tastes, the prejudices, the weakness and the grandeur of all aristocracies."[6]

Inequalities, then, abounded in the South, as one might expect, but they were no less frequent in the North, which imagined itself to be more democratic than the South: there, too, a wide gap separated the very rich from the very poor. In New York, between 1828 and 1845, the proportion of total wealth owned by the richest 5 percent of New Yorkers rose from 63 percent to 80 percent. In Philadelphia, similarly, in 1860, more than half of the city's wealth belonged to the top one percent of the population, as against the 3 percent owned by the bottom 80 percent of the city's inhabitants. Overall, we can suppose that the richest 5 percent of the nation's citizens collected about one-third of its national income. At the time of Tocqueville's visit, Boston counted 75 people with fortunes of $100,000, and New York, 100 such. In Boston, it was estimated that, because of "fevers," "the average age of Irish life in Boston does not exceed fourteen years."[7] Unsurprisingly, one of the favorite themes of the southern apologists for slavery was to juxtapose the harsh conditions of life of factory workers, abandoned to their fate by selfish, greedy Yankee employers, with the happy patriarchal relations which, they claimed, governed plantation life.

By the 1830s and 1840s, misery-struck people abounded in America's larger cities. It may be that the very poor in New York were not quite as destitute as the Irish immigrants in Friedrich Engels's Manchester, or in the Saint-Merri district of Louis-Philippe's Paris, but the poorer inhabitants of New York's slums also lived in indescribable conditions, where a hundred people might share a single privy, and where children, homeless and destitute people, prostitutes (there were 10,000 in that city in 1832),[8] criminals, alcoholics, and run-of-the-mill workers and artisans all lived in a context of extreme poverty and violence. America was perceived as a land of social mobility, but in actual social fact, the great majority of workers' children would themselves become industrial workers. To move from one class to the next was rare and painful. Lincoln, who was born very poor, ended by breaking with his own pioneer family, refused to attend his father's funeral, and in no small part rose in society by marrying up into a southern slave-owning family.

Nonetheless, what matters as regards America's national self-image was not the poverty itself but the fact that most American democrats refused to see the deep and deepening fissures that disfigured their society. Why this willful ignorance? When Nicholas Biddle, the governor of the Bank of the United States in Philadelphia and Jackson's "ennemi intime," wanted to deride the president's attack on the bank's prerogatives, he referred by instinct not to a domestic image of class war but to a foreign one: Jackson's message, he said, "has all the fury of a chained panther, biting the bars of his cage. It really is a manifesto of anarchy, such as Marat or Robespierre might have issued to the mob of the Faubourg Saint-Antoine."[9] But this highly dramatic exaggeration carried very little weight in America, even among the very rich. A more common response was to perceive America as a blest democratic society in which hard work rather than class solidarity was the path to salvation.

Why this blindness?

First, no doubt, because there had always been rich and poor in America, especially in cities, since the second half of the eighteenth century. Because some discrepancies in wealth had always existed, the new, more dramatic cleavages did not seem that novel. The style of life favored by the American rich had long since set them apart from the hoi polloi: during his sojourn in France Jefferson had considered with studied attention the nomenclature of Bordeaux and Médoc wines.

A second explanation centers on perception and self-perception. In France, the noble émigré children and grandchildren of once liberal and enlightened aristocrats felt obliged, especially after 1830, to present themselves as uncompromising royalist reactionaries, hostile to modernity in all its forms. But all Americans, including the rich, continued to sing the praises of citizenship and the ancient Greco-

Roman *polis*. Having grown up in a log cabin—or pretending to have done so—became an informal requirement for high office. Daniel Webster, who was close to New England industrialists and a friend of the partisan Bank of the United States, did grant that he had not had "the honor," as had his older brothers, of having been born in a log cabin, but this familial cabin, he pointed out, still stood, and, he added, it was his wont to visit it annually.[10] William Henry Harrison, who was president for one month in 1840, also owned one, but unbeknownst to the voters, his was walnut paneled and book lined, and looked out on his 2,000-acre estate.

In their daily lives, Americans pretended that the rich did not exist. America's sense of its national self was so strong—and so egalitarian— that it concealed, even from its victims, horrendous material inequalities of all sorts: the existence of slavery, of course, but urban slums in the North as well. Georges Duby's judgment about fourteenth-century France is even more relevant to nineteenth-century America: "The attitudes of individuals and groups of individuals to their own situation in society and the conduct these attitudes dictate are determined not so much by actual economic conditions as by images in the minds of individuals and groups."[11] How true! In America, in the jargon of (Marxist) social science, the gap was great between "subjective" feelings of classlessness and "objective" differences of class determination, a difference that perhaps ought not to surprise us as we live in an age when most citizens of western and increasingly oligarchic democracies seem determined to focus on their ability to vote freely and to ignore the widening chasm between themselves and the very rich. Marx, who lived for years in Germany, France, and Britain but had never even visited the United States, did not have it quite right. Nationalism in his view was a sinister weapon that the possessing class manipulated in order to deceive excluded, self-hating proletarians (as in "self-hating Jews") who were victims of "false consciousness" and were, as such, eager to be deceived. And this does often happen; but in America, it often happens also that the informed poor are quite aware of what they are doing, and embrace nationalistic and excluding goals and ideals (as in their detestation of "gay marriage") because they reluctantly gauge these exclusions to be suitable compensation for the adversities they are made to bear in everyday life (as in unaffordable medical insurance).

Myth and reality regarding social class, and regarding law and order as well: Americans lived (or thought they lived) in a society that worshiped law and due process. They imagined themselves to be citizens of a nation that had—thanks to the bold leadership of Chief Justice John Marshall—accepted the idea of the judicial review of legislative acts. The prestige in their country of law and lawmaking was great: Tocqueville was convinced that in America lawyers would soon become a new aristocracy.

But democratic America was in fact a very violent place, as it had always been: seventeenth-century New Englanders had ruthlessly annihilated Native Americans. In the eighteenth century, Appalachia, settled by the Scotch-Irish, had become a dangerous place for everyone, white, black, or red. Brutality was endemic both in American cities and in the countryside: every social group brutalized its inferiors in a ladder of cascading disdain. In a notorious incident in the suburbs of Boston— a relatively tranquil place—an Ursuline convent was set on fire by a mob in 1834.

Immigrants were often considered a fair target, but only from time to time. By contrast, slavery was founded on fear and violence everywhere and always. To be sure, some slaves were—just as Calhoun argued—better off materially than some factory workers. Many were certainly better fed and housed than were Russian serfs at the time or starving Irish peasants in Britain's empire. Slavery itself, like freedom, had many shapes, and in many respects it was less brutal in the United States than slavery in Brazil or the Caribbean. African Americans had managed to create a specific culture of their own and in the South, 250,000 blacks, though constrained in many ways, were no longer enslaved. Nonetheless, exploitation, fear, and punishment were at the heart of American bondage. Revolts like that in Southampton County in Virginia, in 1831, led by an African-American preacher, Nat Turner—which led to the murder of more than fifty whites and to Turner's execution—were rare. But the threat—and fear—of violence was always present.

Based as it was on bondage of the many by the few, and of one "race" by another, southern culture in its length and breadth revolved around the presence of sexual and physical violence. Duels were endemic there. Margaret Mitchell's mendacious *Gone with the Wind*, and the even more odious film of the same name by David O. Selznick, are useful here as carefully drawn *inversions* of life as it really was. Whippings were common. Families were routinely broken up. Between 1830 and 1860, 300,000 slaves were sold, with or without their families, by genteel Virginians who had worn out their lands by the exclusive growing of tobacco, to planters in the new states of the "Old Southwest" (Alabama and Mississippi especially). "The first colonists," wrote Richard Slotkin some decades ago, "saw in America an opportunity to regenerate their fortunes, their spirits, and the power of their church and nation: but the means to that regeneration ultimately became the means of violence, and the myth of regeneration through violence became the structuring metaphor of the American experience."[12] Seldom was this more true than in these early democratic years. Tocqueville was ill-advised to entitle a chapter of his book *"Comment les mœurs s'adoucissent à mesure que les conditions s'égalisent"* (How mores become gentler as social conditions become more equal).[13]

*****

A geographically mobile society, ever transformed by technological and economic change, marked by great differences of wealth, and prone to violence; a land also of unprecedented prosperity and opportunity, with, as always, individualism at its core, now democratized—these were the real and imagined ingredients of the American national idea in the Jacksonian and post-Jacksonian age. How strange that Emerson, that adamant critic of Fourierist, utopian, and communitarian "phalansteries," should have noted in his journal in 1847 that "individualism has never been tried," when all of American culture and society had as its bedrock, in one form or another, a blend of economic and religious individualism.[14] Masculinist individualism was at the center of American life ordinarily, but feminist individualism mattered also. "No American woman," wrote Catherine Beecher, the sister of Harriet Beecher Stowe, who would later write *Uncle Tom's Cabin*, "has any occasion for feeling that hers is an humble or insignificant lot. The value of what an individual accomplishes, is to be estimated by the importance of the enterprise achieved, and not by the particular position of the laborer."[15]

A useful gauge of the extent and depth of America's democratic and individualist creed, and of its place in Americans' idea of their nation, is a comparison of its social impact in Jacksonian America with its scope in Slavic and Germanic Europe, and even in France, regardless of that country's Declaration of the Rights of Man in August 1789 (which was nearly contemporaneous to the American Bill of Rights).

The term "individualism," to be sure, had been coined in Paris by the utopian socialist Saint-Simonians, but what matters here is that they, like other Europeans, were deeply suspicious of it. (To remind themselves of this dislike, they wore blouses that could only be buttoned from the back, by a fellow Saint-Simonian.) Likewise, in Germany in 1848, the defense of ancient and corporate guilds—along with riots against money-lending Jews—was an important aspect of antibourgeois politics. In Russia also, the emancipation of serfs was immediately followed by the enactment of complex legislation that made it very hard for individual peasants to leave their villages and move to the city. (*One could add that French suspicion of individualistic capitalism survives to this day in the Parisian reprobation of the so-called Anglo-Saxon model of individuated economic life, which the French like to contrast to their "French social model," of Catholic and socialist origin, and which they see as more communitarian, more concerned with the stability of the social order, and better regulated by a well-policed lay and administrative state.*)

And how to account, by contrast, for the insistent presence of individualism as a constituent part of the American national creed? One explanation in Tocqueville's work is that individualism was a providential fact: where individualism, he wrote, "is of democratic origin, it is bound to develop as social conditions are leveled."[16] In his view, American democracy furthered individualism, which furthered democratic progress. The spiritual isolation of every sinner had after all been from the first a critical aspect of Calvinism's rejection of clerical authority. The growth of individualism was, he thought, an historical inevitability. (It was a commonplace in post-revolutionary aristocratic France to suppose that Protestantism had been the linear ancestor of the French Revolution.)

Other "usual suspects" that are often cited as foundational texts—and even foundational causes—of American individualism include the writings of Locke, for whom civil society, individualism, and private property antedated the political order, which ought always to be subordinated to civil society by contract. Britain's Radical Whigs have their place here also, with their militant defense of every embattled citizen, perennially at war with the encroaching royal descendants of William the Conqueror and his "Norman banditti." Or again—and of a wholly different causal order—individualism was characteristic of America because of that country's vastness and remoteness, which made of social control a Sisyphean task: in a country where every younger son, every misfit, or every entrepreneur could move westward to an ever-moving frontier, individualism could never be successfully contained.

But however American individualism is to be explained, the simpler fact is that Jacksonian Americans were convinced that their nation was grand and becoming more so because it had made the rights of the individual the cornerstone of its religious and economic structures. It seemed increasingly obvious to most Americans in the 1830s that individualism, American liberty, American prosperity, and America's national sense of self were complementary facts and values that traveled in tandem and that should be a model for the world.

In the eighteenth century, before the American Revolution, many Europeans, notably Buffon and de Pauw, had organized their understanding of colonial America around the theme of decay and decadence. Everything American (plants, caribous, civility, and humans) was by European standards held to be shriveled and pathetic. (To challenge this commonly held idea, Jefferson and Franklin, both more than six feet tall, once stood up at a Parisian dinner party and, towering over their fellow guests, presented themselves as proof positive of America's superiority to Europeans in one respect at least.)

By contrast, Americans in the first half of the nineteenth century were by now convinced of their national superiority. The persistence of individuating progress was for them, incontrovertibly, the essence of modern life, and in no other country was it so plainly the center of social and political life. America was a richer, more just, more noble land than any other, and the symbol of its greatness was the self-reliant pioneer, born, as has been said, in a log cabin that would soon become a mansion. (In later decades, and next to the pioneer, Americans would enthrone the solitary inventor and the individuating, self-enriched, entrepreneur: Old Europe and New North America.)

*****

The prestige of democratic individualism in the United States can be demonstrated by reference to social chapter and economic verse. But it can also be underscored by a look at the feebleness of American social movements that had anti-individualism as their first principle and at the isolation of those thinkers who articulated communitarian principles.

Of such thinkers, a striking instance is that of Orestes Brownson, much influenced by French writers like Pierre Leroux and the Saint-Simonians, who dared to develop in America a communitarian definition of what individualism should ideally be. The man had begun as a strict Calvinist, wrapped up in theological arguments that, in their original forms, no longer held America's attention. From there he moved to Unitarianism, which was theologically more congenial to him but too ecumenical, and he finished—inevitably, one is tempted to say—as a communitarian Roman Catholic. Brownson was also a fervent Democrat who would have liked to change the Democratic Party and make of it, in his own words, "a social democratic party." "Community without individuality," he asserted, "is *tyranny*, the fruits of which are oppression, degradation, and immobility, the synonym of death." But, he went on, "individuality without community is *individualism*, the fruits of which are dissolution, isolation, selfishness, war . . . What we need then is . . . community and individuality harmonized . . . atoned."[17] Brownson also said:

> The men of wealth, the business men, manufacturers and merchants, bankers and brokers, are the men who exert the worst influence on government in every country . . . They act on the beautiful maxim, "Let the government take care of the rich, and the rich will take care of the poor" instead of the far safer maxim, "Let government take care of the weak, the strong can take care of themselves."[18]

No one paid attention.

Catherine Beecher in 1845, likewise, shocked as she was by observation of conditions of work in the new textile mills, expressed similar concerns, albeit in religious terms: a distinction should be made, she argued, between the (antique, European, and Catholic) sacrifice that focused on individual sinners considered one by one, and a healthier Protestant but still communitarian sacrifice geared to the creation of new social solidarities.[19] No one paid attention to her either.

In France, similar theoretical and practical indignation was of lasting effect, and its latest overt assertion by the French state would come during Maréchal Pétain's "Révolution Nationale" in 1940–1944 in Vichy: one for all and all for one. But in America, such communitarian voices had no echo.

Far more notorious than some isolated communitarian thinkers, though related to them indirectly, were the Mormons, whose trajectory also has a message for what the American national idea had to be. This highly regulated sect was created by Joseph Smith, the author, or rather, the popularizer of the *Book of Mormon*, which he presented as a translation made by himself from golden tablets that—guided as he had been by an angel—he had conveniently found in his own garden in Palmyra, New York, in 1823. (These tablets, he later explained, could not be displayed as they had been returned to heaven by the same messenger.) After founding a new city in Illinois, where Joseph Smith was murdered in 1844, the Mormons moved over the Rocky Mountains to Utah, which remains to this day their mighty fortress.

The organization of their agricultural endeavors—the first source of their rapidly expanding wealth—was at once typical and atypical of what democratic America was supposed to be about. On the one hand, each Mormon farmer owned his own land, but on the other hand, unlike most American pioneers, each farmer had strict obligations, especially as regarded the maintenance of a system of canals that were managed by the community's elders.

In many ways, Mormons were typical Americans. It is well known, after all, that vice (as in avarice and pusillanimity) is a virtue (as in frugality and prudence) that has been taken to extremes. Mormons yearned to build a better life for themselves; they were producers and not consumers (as shown by the beehive, which is the symbol of their sect). They were deeply religious and even theocratic. They were also convinced racists: all forms of "miscegenation" were punishable by death. They were prone to violence, and in a spectacular instance of that trait, in 1857, they did not hesitate to murder 120 non-Mormons—men, women, and children—who had stumbled onto their territory.

Mormons were therefore in some sense among the most successful Americans, the proof being that their community is today alive and well, politically influential, and very prosperous. But in a larger, ideological sense, they remained marginal to the America of their time—and ours. In the 1840s they were despised and forced into the wilderness. Their polygamous habits of "plural marriage" repelled most Americans. And in 1857 their community was brought to heel by federal troops. (Prudently, the Mormon leader Brigham Young then chose to accept humiliation as an alternative to destruction.)

*****

Jacksonian and post-Jacksonian America was associationist and democratic, but it rejected communitarianism. Individualism remained its central theme in religion, in politics, and in economic life. The thought of Henry David Thoreau was in some deep way typically American: he was—or claimed to be—an irreconcilable enemy of bourgeois life, whose materialist priorities he rejected for fear that he would at his death suddenly "discover that he had not lived." But Thoreau also thought that the best government was the one that governed least. Public works like roads, bridges, and schools were fine, but any kind of governmental regulation of economic life was of no interest to him, and this in the age of Proudhon, born in 1809, and Marx, born in 1818.

Work, honestly achieved, widely available, and fairly paid, remained for most Americans the be-all and end-all of political and social theory (as the poor in Bill Clinton's America were once again to discover). Revealingly, it is through this avenue of thought that Abraham Lincoln began his pilgrim's progress toward the emancipation of African Americans. Should blacks be free? Should they be accepted as citizens? Lincoln would not be sure of that until 1864. But in the early 1850s Lincoln already claimed, loud and clear, that black laborers were entitled to the fruits of their labor.[20]

In England, and initially in Anglo-America, whose first settlers had hoped to find gold and easy wealth as the Spaniards had in Central and South America, work was still a biblical curse. Benjamin Franklin, once he had achieved material independence, chose to dedicate himself to gentlemanly pursuits like politics and scientific research. John Adams said that merchants worked to raise lawyers whose children would be artists. But in democratic America, work became the highest expression of the self and even a religious act. In the words of Thomas Carlyle (who was, in Britain, a genuine eccentric), "all work, properly understood, was religion." "I was now my own master," wrote a free Frederick Douglass, "a tremendous fact—and the rapturous excitement with which I seized the job may not easily be understood, except by someone with an experience like mine. The thought 'I can work! I can work for a living: I am not afraid of work; I have no Master Hugh to rob me of my earnings' placed me in a state of independence."[21] This nineteenth-century American attitude stands in some contrast to the neo-Marxist slogan of the Parisian "Situationists" in 1968: "Never work!"

"Travail, famille, patrie" (work, family life, homeland) ran the Vichyite slogan in the early 1940s, and the American analog of the 1830s and 1840s might well have been "work, family, nation" with, once again, Abraham Lincoln as the archetypical American who best expressed his nation's deepest aspirations and contradictions. Liberty, he thought, had always been an intrinsic part of American nationhood. It was inscribed in the Revolution of 1776. A house divided against itself on that score could not stand, and it made no sense to argue, as Southerners did, that their right to self-government in their states legitimized the forced servitude of blacks. How could one worship both God and Mammon? To adore the one was to disdain the other: in Lincoln's words, "To deny these things is to deny our national axioms, or dogmas, at least; and it puts an end to all argument." A free society, self-government, and human liberty were all facets of the same principle.[22]

America was about liberty, and it was also about every American individual's right to work in this free country. Or not, if for some higher purpose! "I am glad to see," Lincoln explained

> that a system of labor prevails in New England under which laborers can strike when they want to, where they are not obliged to work under all circumstances . . . I take it that it is best for all to leave each man free to acquire property as fast as he can. Some will get wealthy. I don't believe in a law to prevent a man from getting rich; it would do more harm than good. So while we do not propose any war upon capital, we do wish to allow the hum-

blest man an equal chance to get rich with everybody else. When one starts poor, as do most in the race of life, a free society is such that he can better his condition; he knows there is no fixed condition of labor for his whole life . . . that is the true system.[23]

In France, François Guizot, a Protestant intellectual and Louis-Philippe's prime minister in the 1840s, had been attacked for urging his compatriots: "Enrich yourselves by saving and work." *(Enrichissez vous par l'épargne et par le travail,"* which French anticapitalist critics had derided and reduced to a mere *"enrichissez-vous"*: "Get rich!") In the United States, Lincoln had ennobled this thought and made it a pillar of the American way.

On one side of a Manichean divide, then, America in the 1850s was increasingly perceived as being of two parts: in the South, from a northern point of view, was an enslaving aristocracy, and neither aristocracy nor slavery had any place in a newly democratized America. And in the North, again from a northern point of view, was a rejuvenated, prosperous, republican and now democratic nation that saw no necessary conflict at all between capital and labor.

By 1860 Lincoln, brilliantly intuitive, born in the South and raised in what was then the West, had assembled all of these redefined givens, and by the eve of his nomination, this mid-Westerner had brought together the praise of New England virtues with that of the nation's new productive capacities, a stand that was sure to please the broad public as well as the bankers and manufacturers of New York and Philadelphia, who were by now the first backers of the new Republican Party.

*****

Democracy, individualism, work, and of course, always a critical element of the American national idea, religion: "Upon my arrival in the United States, what struck me most at that time was the religious character of the country . . . At home the spirit of religion and the spirit of liberty are at odds always. Here, they were intimately connected the one to the other:

they ruled the land together."[24] Indeed, and a great deal of Tocqueville's interpretation of American life pivoted around the idea of religion as the organizing principle of individualism and association in that country.

Which means that once again for the 1850s, as for seventeenth-century Massachusetts, as for the time of the Great Awakening, we need to understand the place of religion in American life in order to understand the American sense of nation.

In line with one of the central paradoxes of the American polity, which insisted on the strict separation of church and state, religion was ever more important after 1800: 50,000 churches were built in America between 1776 and 1860. From one clergyman for 1,500 inhabitants in 1775 the nation moved to one for 500 in 1845. Jefferson, lost in his Enlightenment past, opined in 1822 that American Protestantism would gradually transform itself into a kind of mild civic religion, such as that of the enlightened and vaguely republican Theophilantropists in post-Robespierre but still revolutionary France. But that did not happen.

Far from it. Religious fervor was once again reborn after 1800, as it had been half a century before, and as has happened cyclically throughout America's history to our own day. In 1776 America's revolution had depended on the ideological blending of traditional Calvinism and the principles of the western European Enlightenment laid out by Locke, Montesquieu, and Beccaria. But now, American democratization, no longer secularized as it had been, thrived instead as religious revivalism grew.

Emerson remarked at Harvard in 1838: "The Puritans in England and America found in the Christ . . . and in the dogmas inherited from Rome, scope for their austere piety and their longings for civil freedom. But their creed is passing away, and none arises in its room."[25] In a strict sense, this was not untrue: even in Massachusetts, the Puritans' New Jerusalem, Calvinism was little more than a memory by Emerson's time.

But in the larger sense, Emerson was decidedly off the mark: two related faiths were arising in his time, the first a simpler, watered-down Protestantism, and the other the idea of democracy. The two did not just coexist in America: they sustained and fed on each other. Some years later Andrew Johnson, the mediocre vice president who became president after Lincoln's death, was quite right to move from the first of these two registers to the other and back again: "Man can be elevated; man can become more and more endowed with divinity, and as he does, he becomes more Godlike in his character and capable of governing himself. Let us go on elevating our people, perfecting our institutions, until democracy shall reach such a point of perfectibility that we can acclaim with truth that the voice of the people is the voice of God."[26] As Americans renewed their character by coming closer to God, so would they become more capable of self-government.

"Revivalism" is an American term par excellence that has no equivalent in French: its scope is in the religiously conditioned renewal of the self. It brings to mind the American belief in religious becoming from Anne Hutchinson in the seventeenth century to George W. Bush today. In the 1840s it was a determining term. Both revivalism and democracy emphasized the pivotal role of the individual; as in "one man, one vote," religious experience was now fully individuated as well. "In America, religion never intervenes directly in the political governance of society," observed Tocqueville in 1835 (which was then quite true, even if that distinction is unfortunately much less clear today), "but religion must nonetheless be considered to be their premier institution because it enables them to practice liberty even if it is not the cause of their thirst for that value."[27]

Revivalism gathered strength from 1800 onward. At Cane Ridge in Kentucky, in 1801, 25,000 people gathered for a week to preach and pray. Revivalism mutated just as America's representative republic mutated, both of them moving in the same populist direction. Century-old religions now spawned new sects such as the Revivalist Baptists and "New Lights" within both Presbyterianism and Methodism. Alongside these renewals came altogether new religious groups like the Shakers, the Universalists, and the Universal Friends, which were theologically unencumbered and prone to democratic thought.

Though these sects differed, of course, in the nuances of their message, all of them were put forward by new "preachers" who emphasized emotionality and who dwelled on the accessibility of their faith to all, whether rich or poor, from the West (where this movement began) or from the East, learned or unlearned, and above all else, whether male or female: in New England, 70 percent of the new communicants were female. Women preachers were numerous and active: in 1827 one of them, Harriet Livermore, became the first woman to harangue the United States Congress.

The relatedness of American religion and American nationalism comes into sharper focus if we step back from their relationship to see them, not just in their own right, but as parts of a larger national cultural renewal.

The year 1815 is ordinarily considered as the end of the European phase of America's political orientation. After the battle of New Orleans, America saw a rapid development not just of its politics and religion but of its broader cultural traits and habits. At that time many of the characteristics that we have come to think of as typically American also came into focus. Politicized democrats and salvation-minded revivalists there were indeed. But along with them came the "Sabbatarians" whose passion was to enforce respect for the Lord's day. (In this context, properly religious parents would, for example, note their children's Sunday misbehavior but would postpone their just and physical punishment till Monday.) This period was also the high-water mark of interest in phrenology: the movement's official publication, the *American Phrenological Journal*, reached a circulation of over 50,000 copies. Less popular but more consequential was feminism, closely connected as it was to America's religious impulse, which held its first congress in 1848.

(*The importance of the connection between religion and women's rights in America is underscored by the French experience. In France, feminism had been very strong since the late seventeenth century, but since 1789 had found an uncertain harbor in leftist antimonarchism and anticapitalism. It was both loudly applauded and in the main methodically ignored by socialists and com-*

munists, who blithely assumed that the fight for women's rights could be no more than a subcategory of the workers' social struggle against capitalist iniquity. In that French and constraining frame, amicable negotiation rather than resolute confrontation was, sadly, the only real option for women. In America, by contrast, from the 1840s onward, feminism, through religion—and through quasi-religious confrontational indignation—acquired a much more vigorous voice of its own.)

The 1840s also saw the blossoming of whatever communitarianism America was able to sustain, with the creation of (short-lived) communities that followed the precepts of Robert Owen and Fourier. Also active were the prohibitionists, who in 1920 would secure the passage of a constitutional amendment: for them, demon drink (rather than class or economic hardship or social dislocation or unemployment) was the root of all evil, and the extirpation of that evil, which sapped individual energies, would resolve all social problems. By 1834, prohibitionist associations numbered a million members, and Timothy Shay Arthur's *Ten Nights in a Bar Room, and What I Saw There*, published in 1854, was an instant hit. Statistics, it must be said, did give their cause some plausibility: Louisville, Kentucky, which had exported a thousand hectoliters of whiskey in 1810, produced ten times as much ten years later.[28] Per capita consumption of spirits in the nation as a whole trebled between 1790 and 1820. Daniel Webster, Henry Clay, Franklin Pierce, and later Ulysses S. Grant were rumored to be heavy drinkers.

These many concerns, then, with democracy and revivalism, loosely coalesced as the different parts of what has often been called the "Benevolent Empire," an empire that was connected not only to the changing specificities of American political and cultural life, but to American geography as well.

As definitions of the American national idea veered toward a democratic extension of what Americanness was about, the southern states, where the Benevolent Empire did not take hold, found themselves increasingly at odds with the rest of the country. This, however, did not keep Southerners, though ever more estranged from their compatriots, from becoming themselves more "American," in their own way. They too became more religious: although the produce of their plantations was ever more involved in a capitalist world-economic system, planters now pretended to model their behavior on that of the religious patriarchs of biblical yesteryear. And perhaps because of some mimetic effect, their slaves also absorbed a Christian message, but a quite different one of resignation and suffering, righteousness and justice. African-American musical and literary life has borne that imprint ever since.

* * * * *

Democracy, individualism, religion: these now became the first ingredients of the American national idea, but, again, often as a mask for—or at least, in the company of—violence. How to explain this terrible symmetry?

Two types of answers come to mind. The first is that this conjunction of good and bad in democracies has nothing to do with America as such: the origins of all democracies have been violent. Even England had its bloody revolution in the 1640s. And the execution of Charles I in 1649 prefigures that of Louis XVI in 1793. To cite Tocqueville once more, this is to say that democracy was not an aspect of some American exceptionalism. Far from it. As he saw it, the democratization of the western world was a providential fact that merely happened to have occurred first in North America.

Moreover, for Tocqueville, the violent genesis of democracy could not be explained in simple historical terms. It flowed from the facts that men (and women?) naturally yearned for freedom and equality and that violence was often the only way for them to realize their innermost ambition. Democratic violence was in some sense a quasi-religious mystery.

Another type of exonerating explanation of democratic violence emphasizes discrepancies of power. By their nature, strong and rich nations, democratic or not, American or not, often oppress their weaker neighbors. France in 1812 ruled in Madrid and Moscow; Britain in 1900 ruled in Africa from the Cape to Cairo and in many other places also. A racist pleasantly explained that the sun never set on this empire because natives could not be trusted in the dark. The limit of the influence that America was prepared to impose was and had to be the limit of America's strength. And, from its origins, America had become steadily stronger. Its population showed a sharply rising curve: 4 million in 1790, nearly 10 million in 1820, 17 million in 1840, 31 million in 1860. There was no end to it in sight. In this view, democratic, Jacksonian America was violent not because it was democratic, but because it was mighty enough to oppress its neighbors (then as now).

A third type of explanation is, in total contrast, that the relationship of American democracy to violence and abuses of various kinds has a great deal to do with America's essential self. True enough, the powerful do often oppress the weak, and when the weak become strong they often become violent as well. But the Protestant—or better yet, Calvinist— emphasis on material achievement as a clue to the mysteries of God's gracious will gave Americans a sense of superiority that time and again was used to justify aggression. Most Americans, for example, thought their country had a right to the New Southwest because Mexico had not made productive use of it. Much of the disdain that Northerners felt for their southern co-citizens was of the same order: blacks were less productive than southern whites, and all of them were, by northern economic standards, hopelessly incompetent. The sadistic overseer of Uncle Tom's plantation was an import from the North because no Southerner could do even that job properly.

And then again, violence had always been part of American life. It had been there in the nation's distant and monarchic past; it was there now in its democratic present. American history had always been coterminous with *Rassensanierung* (racial cleansing) and the quasi-genocide of Native Americans. Slavery too had been a constant of American life, in many northern states as well as in all of the southern ones, and slavery, as has been said, was a social system that presupposed the constant presence of fear and preventive, exemplary violence. The violence associated with the Scotch-Irish lineage (as in Jackson's case) was archetypically American.

Of these violent and democratic passions, dueling was, for example, one well-known expression. Of course, dueling was not an American specialty: it lay at the intersection of aristocratic honor and modern individualism. (English visitors to early modern Russia were surprised to find that clan-minded Russian nobles did not, at that time, fight duels.) But dueling had a cultural intensity in America, in the southern states especially, that was without parallel in Europe. Relatively infrequent in colonial America, it had become commonplace after 1800. After that date, and for more than half a century, it was broadly assumed, particularly in the South, that only recourse to violence could wipe out the stain of an undeserved insult. In a celebrated episode, which Northerners rightly took to be symbolic of southern barbarism, a South Carolina congressman repeatedly struck with his cane a senator from Massachusetts, whom he accused of having slandered his uncle, a senator from South Carolina.

Along with this tendency toward violence, finally and always, was America's messianic bent. America's God was the God of the Old Testament more than the forgiving Christ of the four gospels. Once aroused, America could not be easily appeased.

Native Americans and Mexicans, though they did not understand this syndrome, would feel its weight. As would southern planters in 1864–1865 at the hands of vengeful New Englanders, who as it happens, twenty years before, had been most unhappy about invading Mexico, in contrast to their southern compatriots who had been at that point the most nationalistic of Americans.

As one historian has written about these legacies:

Throughout the history of the United States, war has been the primary impulse behind the growth and development of the central state. It has been the lever by which presidents and other national officials have bolstered the power of the state in the face of tenacious popular resistance. It has been the well-spring of American nationalism and a spur to political and social change

. . . It is difficult to deny that [America's] government was reared during war.[29]

That is a troubling message, but it did not deter Andrew Jackson, just as today it does not faze George W. Bush, whose war on terror has placed America on a legal footing of undemocratic exclusion that is going to "last for the rest of our lives."[30]

Mythic, Adamic America, with the Abel of democratic inclusion and the Cain of nationalist exclusion. National democracy, then, but "national democratism" also.

CHAPTER 5
National Democratism

"In their relations with strangers," Tocqueville observed,

Americans are impatient of the slightest criticism and insatiable for praise. They are pleased by the mildest praise but seldom quite satisfied even by the most fulsome eulogy. They are at you the whole time to make you praise them and if you do not oblige, they sing their own praise. One might suppose that, doubting their own merits, they want an illustration thereof constantly before their eyes. Their vanity is not only greedy but also restless and jealous. It makes endless demands and gives nothing. It is both mendicant and querulous.[1]

And, one might add, insistent and quarrelsome: Americans like—and liked—to think of themselves as a pacific nation. Woodrow Wilson eloquently described Americans as "a great, peaceful people," but there have been many exceptions to this rule.

We think of America after the War of 1812 as an isolationist power that had turned its back on the world. And yet some (ironic) note should be taken of the many conflicts in which America was involved in those years, starting with an undeclared naval war with France in 1798, with incursions into Haiti (1799, 1800, 1817–1821), Libya and Tripoli (1815), the Marquesas Islands (1813–1814), Spanish Florida (1806–1810, 1812, 1813, 1814, 1816–1818), Santo Domingo (1800), Curaçao (1800), the Galapagos Islands (1813), Algiers (1815), Cuba (1822), Puerto Rico (1824), Argentina (1833, 1851, 1853), and Peru (1835–1836).[2] In the 1960s Senator Everett Dirksen, a conservative politician, counted in

American history 160 military episodes since 1798, with 900 battles from 1775 to 1900 as well as 943 encounters with Native Americans between 1865 and 1898.[3]

* * * * *

Already, America's War of Independence and its sequels had been a dramatic threshold for the Indian nations, who now could no longer use the French to resist the British as they had done before 1763, or the British to resist the Americans as they had tried to do between 1776 and 1783. The War of 1812 further revealed the frailty of their situation, marked as it was in the Old Northwest by the victories of General Harrison, and in the South by the victory of Jackson and his Tennessee militiamen at the battle of Horseshoe Bend in March 1814, which ended with a massacre not just of combatants but of Indian women and children also.

In 1822 a Pawnee chief wrote to President Monroe that the Great Spirit had "made the whites to cultivate the earth, and feed on domestic animals; but he made us, red-skins, to rove through the uncultivated woods and plains; to feed on wild animals and to dress with their skins."[4] But other Native Americans chose to bend with the wind: by 1800, a number of Cherokees had already moved from hunting to sedentary agriculture. Benjamin Hawkins, who had been sent to them as a representative of the United States (the first treaty between the United States and the "Cherokee Nation" dates to 1791) and lived with the Creeks from 1796 to 1818, reported to his supervisors that they had even planted fruit trees, and that he had been served a meal with bread, pork, potatoes, peanuts, and dried peaches. In 1808 the Cherokees drew up a legislative code in English. In 1809 they formed a National Committee. An indigenous linguist named Sequoyah elaborated an 86-character alphabet that made a written language of his dialect. Many Cherokees converted to Christianity. In 1817 the American Board of Commissioners for Foreign Missions set up missions on their territory, the first of which bore the name of John Eliot, the Puritan preacher to the "praying

Indians" of early Massachusetts. Finally, in 1827, the Georgia Cherokees created a government for their tribe that was modeled on the United States Constitution. By that time the Cherokee territories had roads, eighteen schools, 3,000 plows, and a Cherokee-language newspaper, the *Cherokee Phoenix*, created by a graduate of an American Board school who had gone off to New England and had married a young American woman of European origin.[5] Many Americans, Jefferson among them, had at first responded warmly to these changes: true, Jefferson explained in an excluding manner, those Indians who were foolish enough "to take up the hatchet" would be exiled west of the Mississippi and be "an example to others, and a furtherance of our final consolidation." But—in his characteristically ambiguous mode—he also offered his "affectionate attachment" to them. They would, in time, "form one people with us, and we shall all be Americans; [they] will mix with us by marriage, [their] blood will run in our veins, and [they] will spread with us over this great continent"[6]—an extraordinary statement for a Southerner to make even if many of his peers claimed Princess Pocahontas as a distant ancestor.

As ultimate proof of their Americanization and loyalty, the Cherokees—in order to settle their grievance with their white neighbors—went not to war, but to law, and took their case to the United States Supreme Court, then presided over by John Marshall, who ruled in 1832 that the state of Georgia had no constitutional right to declare Indian laws null and void as the Cherokees had placed themselves under the protection of the federal government. "The Cherokee nation," he wrote, "is a distinct community, occupying its own territory, with boundaries accurately described, and which the citizens of Georgia have no right to enter, but with the assent of the Cherokees themselves, or in conformity with treaties and with acts of Congress. The whole intercourse between the United States and this nation is, by our constitution and laws, vested in the government of the United States."[7]

This decision did not please President Andrew Jackson, and it failed to protect the Cherokees from the Georgia legislators, who continued to go about their business of (il)legal expropriation. Ingeniously, they reasoned that the agreements the state of Georgia had signed with the Cherokees were no longer binding because the Cherokees were no longer hunters and gatherers, but farmers. In brief, by becoming sedentary cultivators, the Indians had violated the older treaties. Besides, to deprive them of their cultivated lands, and thus to restore them to their former way of life, was to do them a favor. Senator John King of Georgia, for example, had seen enough "to convince him that the wild Indian of the woods had more nobleness of character than the half-civilized Indians, who, for the most part, contract the vices of the lower class of whites, and become drunken and thievish, and were as unfit for the duties appertaining to civilized life, as they were for that courage and enterprise which distinguished the true Indian."[8]

No good deed goes unpunished, and the Choctaws, who were the most pacific of the southwestern tribes, were the first to be made to leave, being offered in perpetuity the southern half of what is today the state of Oklahoma. About a third of the tribe elected to remain in Mississippi as citizens of that state. But the federal authorities refused to accept their title deeds as valid and instead redistributed their land to white settlers.

In despair, other Choctaws tried to associate themselves with the more important Cherokees, which did them little good as the Cherokees were deported in turn. Their lands and those of the missionaries who had settled among them were seized. A federal army of 7,000 commanded by Winfield Scott, soon to command an American army in Mexico, then escorted the Cherokees to their new abode in Oklahoma. Of the 17,000 migrants on this "Trail of Tears," 4,000 perished. Remakes of this forced exile occurred as new states entered the Union: Native Americans in Missouri were pushed toward Kansas in 1821 and those in Arkansas were forced westward in 1836.

The justification that was offered for these acts is not in itself of great interest: Frederick the Great once predicted on the eve of starting a war of naked aggression that, in due time, some learned professors would surely be able to show that he had been fully justified in doing whatever he had done. Nonetheless, these lame rationalizations concerning productivity, violence, and progress tell us something about the concepts that had resonance for the votaries of the American national idea.[9]

The first was that the Indians had no real right to land because they did not use it productively: nineteenth-century American courts tended to favor plaintiffs who made productive use of their land (those who had built a dam upstream from their neighbors, for example, rather than those whose enjoyment of a pristine stream had been disturbed). And what was gently applied among neighboring owners of registered property was brutally asserted in the West. There, the white race had—as it were—a divine title deed that was, explained Senator Thomas Hart Benton of Missouri, "in line with the intentions of the Creator." The strengths of the conflicting claims of the white and the red man, he went on, were in direct proportion to the wealth that the white and the red man might extract from the same property. General Harrison, then governor of Indiana and soon to be president of the United States, argued likewise that it was unthinkable that natives should block white settlement: "Is one of the fairest portions of the globe to remain in a state of nature, the haunt of a few wretched savages, when it seems destined by the Creator to give support to a large population and to be the seat of civilization, of science, and of true religion?" This was a restatement of a Puritan theme that John Winthrop, the first governor of colonial Massachusetts, had found convincing: the entire earth, he had long ago explained, had been entrusted to Adam and Eve. (Anticonservationists today are quick to invoke the same arguments to justify industrial abuse of the environment.) But for Winthrop, not all men were equally entitled to the fruits of the land:

That which lies common & hath never been replenished or subdued is free to any that will possesse and improve it, for God hath given to the sonnes of men a double right to the earth, there is a naturall right & and a civil right . . . As for the Natives of

New England, they inclose noe land, neither have they any settled habitation nor any tame cattle to improve the land by, & and soe have noe other but a natural right to those countries. Soe as if we leave them sufficient for their use wee may lawfully take the rest, there being more than enough for them & us.[10]

This was a powerful argument, which had been improved over time, in the work of the Swiss legal expert Emerich de Vattel in the eighteenth century, and later by John Quincy Adams, who reasoned that the economic justification of conquest was the best argument that the Americans had, though he warned that it would be imprudent to strike a definitive bargain with the Indians. America's white population was growing so fast that an arrangement that made sense today might not make sense tomorrow.

Others went further yet: for Representative Richard H. Wilde of Georgia, the Indians might soon be extinct: "And if it were possible to perpetuate the race of Indians, what would be the consequence? Why, that a hundred or a thousand fold the number of white men would not be born, because the Indians would roam and possess, without enjoying, the land which must afford the future whites subsistence . . . Jacob will for ever obtain the inheritance of Esau. We cannot alter the laws of Providence, as we read them in the experience of the ages."[11]

Lewis Cass, a senator from Michigan who invented the doctrine of "popular sovereignty," which Lincoln's opponent, Stephen Douglas, would later make famous and which held that the extension of slavery should be decided not by a northern-dominated Congress but by the residents of each territory, had less ecumenical thoughts about Native Americans. It was manifest, he thought, that the Creator had intended for whites to settle the entire American continent and make it thrive and prosper. Indians, "a barbarous people, depending for subsistence upon the scanty and precarious supplies furnished by the chase, cannot live in contact with a civilized community." He did not find it surprising that with the spread of civilization "the aboriginal population should decrease

. . . From an early period, their rapid declension and ultimate extinction were foreseen and lamented." He also did not find it regrettable:

It would be miserable affectation to regret the progress of civilization and improvement, the triumph of industry and art, by which these regions have been reclaimed, and over which freedom, religion, and science are extending their sway. But we may indulge the wish, that these blessings had been attained at a smaller sacrifice; that the aboriginal population had accommodated themselves to the inevitable change of their condition, produced by the access and progress of the new race of men before whom the hunter and his game were destined to disappear. But such a wish is vain.[12]

Cass, we might add, was otherwise a confirmed democrat, who would be the Jacksonian candidate for the presidency in 1848 and in that same year would speak in praise of the new Second French Republic. Some months later, he would also urge the Senate to suspend diplomatic relations with the Austrian empire, which had just crushed the Hungarian national movement. Hungarians, it appears, were one thing, and Cherokees quite another.

Indians not only failed to make productive use of land; they were also too cruel and warlike. Here, the reasoning was rather involved, but efficacious nonetheless: "So convenient a thing it is," wrote Benjamin Franklin, "to be a reasonable creature, since it enables one to find or make a reason for everything one has a mind to do." In any conflict with Indians, according to this argument, white Americans were the ones who were targets of aggression. In a variant on the eighteenth-century theme of injured innocence, which Americans had elaborated in order to distinguish themselves from corrupt Great Britain (and to which many French writers like Voltaire and Michel Crèvecoeur had contributed), Americans were portrayed as peace-loving farmers in contradistinction to the warring aristocrats of Old Europe. Indians might at first glance appear to belong on the innocent side in that dichotomy, being close to nature, but their cruel and warlike habits disqualified them completely. (Lincoln, at a time when the Civil War was a fiercely contested and very bloody conflict, scolded some visiting Indian chiefs on this very score, reminding his "red brothers" that they were much too prone to warlike pursuits.) A particular fear of white Americans was that the "savages" would form a common front, as in a revolt in 1835 of Florida Seminoles allied with runaway black slaves.

*****

Hatred and contempt for unproductive, cruel Indians, compounded by a passion for violence: these factors inevitably bring to mind Andrew Jackson, the father of America's new and more populist democracy, and his unrelenting campaign for the removal of Indians from the United States to the western territories. Sean Wilentz has written that this barbarous policy was much more important to Jackson himself than to his followers—that it was *not* "a cornerstone of Jacksonian democracy, especially among northern Jacksonians."[13] But in the eyes of this warlike president, Native Americans self-evidently had no place in democratic, prosperous America. "What good man," he asked Congress in December 1830, "would prefer a country covered with forests and ranged by a few thousand savages to our extensive Republic, studded with cities, towns, and prosperous farms, embellished with all the improvements which art can devise or industry execute, occupied by more than 12,000,000 happy people, and filled with all the blessings of liberty, civilization, and religion?"[14] Removing the Indians was no violation of human rights, and some years later Joel Poinsett, secretary of war under President Van Buren, looked back on Jackson's last campaign and described the Trail of Tears as a "generous and enlightened policy . . . ably and judiciously carried into effect by the general appointed to conduct their removal. The reluctance of the Indians to relinquish the land of their birth . . . was entirely overcome by the judicious conduct of that office . . . Humanity, no less than sound policy, dictated this course towards these children of the forest."[15]

Jackson's personal trajectory is revealing here. The man was of Scotch-Irish origin, an ethnic group with habits inherited from the age-old Irish war between Catholics and Protestants. The first of his family to be born in the United States, in the Carolina backcountry, Jackson was a posthumous infant, who soon lost his mother (she died while nursing a relative who was being held prisoner by the British on one of their infamous pontoons). A gifted child, he was chosen by his teachers in 1776 at the age of nine to read "to thirty or forty of his fellow citizens" the newly minted Declaration of Independence. As a youth, he later fought for this same independence in the newly organized American army. Captured by the British, he was struck and badly wounded by an officer whose boots he refused to shine, a task that did not fit the young Jackson's idea of the rights of prisoners of war. With one exception, his entire family died during the War of Independence.

Many historians have chosen to make of these givens (Jackson's ethnic origins, his condition as an orphan, along with his view of the struggle of Indians and whites as a war of Good and Evil) the elements of a psychiatric portrait: Would he be able, as the Founding Fathers had been, to protect the just against the unjust? Would he be able to protect his wards, be they private or public? His predecessors had purged America of British corruption: Would he be worthy of them? Purifying violence was the answer that seemed to him the most appropriate solution to most problems, be they those of the white race, those of the Union, or those of his wife, who was maligned by journalists. In his childhood an aunt had taught him a lesson he would never forget when she scolded him for weeping: "Only girls cry. They are made for that." "And what are boys for?" he asked. "To fight" was Aunt Betty's response, and this he never ceased to do.

A practicing lawyer, though he had received no formal education, Jackson was a "self-made man" (a typically American locution that we owe to his contemporary, Henry Clay). He soon moved to Tennessee, with a young slave woman in tow whom he had just purchased for $200. He quickly became famous there, known for his many talents and for his rages, easily triggered by any disparaging remarks and especially, after his marriage, by those that might be made about his (white!) wife's uncertain past (the Jacksons married in 1791 on the mistaken impression that the bride's first husband had divorced her; a few years later, after he did divorce her, they married again). Lawyers ordinarily do not take offense at their colleagues' adversarial pleas, but Jackson did, and at the age of twenty-two, challenged one of his fellow lawyers to a duel with sabers. In 1806, in another such contest, Jackson did kill his opponent. Calumny, which only a duel could efface, was, he thought, much worse than death: the memory of a man who had died in a duel might still be dear to his children, but the children of a slandered man would have to deal with his dishonor all their lives. Opinions of Jackson vary, but not by much: George Bancroft, a Democrat and historian, wrote that this president was "a pupil of the wilderness." In Sean Wilentz's words, "When aroused, [Jackson] was an accomplished and unforgiving killer."[16]

Irascible and forever angry—indeed, enraged—Jackson and his political temperament are the closest approximation of Bonapartism that we can find in American politics.[17] A congressman, then a senator, and later yet a member of the Tennessee supreme court, Jackson was at heart a soldier. In 1812 he led local militias in a war against the Creeks. In 1815 he triumphed at New Orleans. In 1818 he fought the Seminoles in Florida: his incursion there was on his own initiative. Neither the president nor the secretary of war had expected that he would go so far into Spanish territory, but Jackson had his advocates. "When a nation either savage or civilized . . . grossly violates the laws of nations and of humanity," explained a Kentucky congressman who also proudly claimed to have killed Tecumseh, "retaliations, or reprisals, are always justifiable, often useful, and sometimes essentially necessary, to teach offenders to respect the laws of humanity and to save the effusion of blood."[18] Once again a senator in 1823, Jackson failed to be elected president in 1824, but his triumphant election in 1828 marked a new era of populist and patronage politics.

In an age of high and racist nationalism, Jackson was the right man in the right place: he was, to begin with, a military hero. "How could anyone deny the unbelievable hold that military glory has on the spirit of the American people," wrote Tocqueville. "General Jackson . . . is a man of violent character and modest ability [who owed his election] to the victory that he won, twenty years ago, by the walls of New Orleans."[19] He had also found his doctrinal niche as an Indian killer, as a confirmed Unionist who denied the secessionist fantasies of the South Carolinians, and as a backcountry democrat who could take on the rich of the eastern seaboard.

But Jackson himself, far more than the America he claimed to represent, was responsible for the crimes of the Jacksonian era. Once again we return to the close connection between patriotism and exclusionary nationalism in American history and to a president's role in moving the nation from the one to the other. Sharing as they do many common roots (in contradistinction to European experiences), these two currents of patriotic inclusion and nationalist exclusion can at any given moment attract voters who would not ordinarily be drawn to them. So it was, in Jacksonian times, that the sentiment of racial and historical difference between white Americans and Native Americans could either lead to curiosity and compassion (as in Cooper's novels) or be manipulated into fear and detestation. A great deal depended on both context and presidential leadership.

In that ambiguous context, Jackson's responsibility for the removal of the Indians to the West was determining. Typically, his farewell speech at the end of his presidency in 1837 emphasized the hackneyed themes of white innocence, Native American guilt, and patriarchal salvation: "While the safety and comfort of our own citizens have been greatly promoted by [the Indians'] removal, the philanthropist will rejoice that the remnant of that ill-fated race has been at length placed beyond the reach of injury or oppression, and that the paternal care of the General Government will hereafter watch over them and protect them." Removal was good for everyone, and perhaps especially for those who had been removed. Indeed, Jackson said elsewhere:

> I believe that the [Indians, if] left to themselves, would freely make this election [to migrate]. But they appear to be overawed by the council [*sic*] of some white men and half breeds, who are and have been fattening upon the annuities, the labors, and the folly of the native Indian, and who believe that their income would be destroyed by the removal of the Indians. These . . . are like some of our bawling politicians, who loudly exclaim we are the friends of the people, but who when they obtain their views care no more for the happiness or welfare of the people than the Devil does, but each procure influence through the same channel and for the same base purpose, self-aggrandisement.[20]

"Self-aggrandisement": a deplorable state of mind that Jackson was implicitly contrasting with the capacity for "self-government," which he thought so typical of the average democratic American citizen.

Who has not heard of the American officer who asserted that he had had to destroy a Vietnamese village in order to save it? In some ways, this was a deeply meaningful remark about the sanctity of American goals (a dead village was better than a communist one). But—more complicatedly—the officer's naïve statement was also about the purgative power of violence. The Puritan enemies of King Philip would have understood it, as did the Jacksonian advocates of Indian removal, and as Northerners would soon understand about the South during Sherman's march to the sea.

American brutality against Native Americans, which the new republic had practiced with relative discretion in the 1780s, reached its first apogee in the democratic decade of the 1830s. Tocqueville worried about the tyranny of democratic majorities over democratic minorities, but he could have gone much further with this thought if he considered democratic and presidential majorities of whites and minorities of Native Americans.

Given the swelling of the U.S. population, and the nation's developing sense of self, some sort of conflict with Native Americans was bound to surface. At the same time, however, without Jackson's guiding hand, it seems at least possible if not likely that American democrats in their dealing with the Indian tribes might have adopted a stance closer to Jefferson's somewhat devious policies than to the brutalities that Jackson's example had occasioned and allowed.

*****

National democratism's first victims were Native Americans. Then came the war against Mexico.

The Far West and the "New Southwest" were very sparsely settled in the first decades of the nineteenth century. Only one percent of Mexicans lived in California or north of the Rio Grande. Native American populations were also very small. Inevitably, white Americans soon moved into the area, at first with the consent of the Mexican authorities. By 1830, however, relations had begun to sour between Texans and Mexicans, partly because slavery had been made illegal in Mexico the year before. In 1836 some of the newcomers, formerly Americans but now self-proclaimed Texans, declared themselves to be an independent republic. After repelling a Mexican military expedition, the Lone Star Republic requested that it be admitted to the Union as one more slave state.

In Washington, not everyone approved. On the one hand, the annexation of Texas could be seen as an inevitable stage in the majestic unfolding, from sea to sea, from the mountains to the prairies, of America's "manifest destiny," a locution invented in 1839 by a journalist for the *Democratic Review*, John O'Sullivan (whose wife, as it happens, had been born in Cuba, which many Southerners hoped to annex as well).[21] In 1835 Jackson had even tried to purchase the area from the Mexicans, who had declined his offer. In 1836, though, his last full year in the White House, Jackson hesitated about annexation. Adding two slave owners to the Senate would not please the North, a powerful argument that was later ingeniously met by southern politicians. They gave up an American claim against Britain for some of the land north of California, thereby making possible a compromise in which Britain secured Vancouver Island but gave up Oregon and Washington to the United States as free territories that would eventually become free states in balance to new slave states in Texas and beyond. In addition, annexationists in 1844–1845 presented their plan as a legitimate response to hypothetical English interference in the affairs of the new Texan Republic, an argument that appealed to the northern manufacturing interests.

In December 1845 the United States therefore agreed to annex Texas. But to do so was also to espouse Texans' view of where their border with Mexico was set. As the Mexicans once again refused to sell their rights, in January 1846 the United States unilaterally occupied the disputed territory between the Rio Grande and the border of Texas as Mexico had defined it. Wisely, the Mexicans did not take action in response, knowing full well that an unsuccessful war against the United States would lead to their undoing, not just in Texas, but also in New Mexico and California. Disconcerted by this passivity, President James K. Polk then drafted a war message that called on Congress to declare war on Mexico for refusing to respond to his message. To his relief, however, word soon reached him that Mexicans had crossed the Rio Grande and killed sixteen American soldiers. Polk redrafted his message and announced that the two countries were—finally—at war: "War exists," he officially stated, "by the act of Mexico herself."[22] (In this same mode of thinking, General Winfield Scott, after the fall of Vera Cruz where a thousand Mexicans, most of them civilians, were killed, later proclaimed: "We have not a particle of ill-will towards you—we treat you with all civility—we are not in fact your enemies; we do not plunder your people or insult your women or your religion . . . we are here for no earthly purpose except the hope of obtaining peace."[23]) Native Americans had been guilty of resorting to uncivilized violence in response to white encroachment, and Mexicans were now proven guilty of having tried to resist American annexationism.

Inevitably, once the war had begun, Americans rallied around the flag as they had done before and would do so again, and always. Before the war, many northern voices had bitterly rejected Polk's pro-southern, pro-Texan annexationist adventure: "The United States will conquer Mexico," wrote Emerson in 1846, "but it will be as the man who swallows the arsenic which will bring him down."[24] In the length and breadth of American history, no military campaign, with the exception of Vietnam, has been as criticized as harshly as the Mexican war. Defeat at Cerro Gordo or Chapultepec might even have reversed public opinion, just as defeat in Hue and Saigon reversed it in the 1970s, but that did not happen.

Pushed into war by Polk's mendacious machinations, anti-annexationist Northerners now accepted the idea of the war, although the Northeast provided only 9,000 volunteers for 20,000 Southerners and 20,000 Westerners. Media support also became more vocal as the war dragged on, when for some months the Mexicans refused to read the writing on the wall, and many arguments were invoked to justify America's ongoing war effort.

The first was that because America was synonymous with liberty, every American conquest would enlarge liberty's empire. In July 1846, about a decade before the publication of his *Leaves of Grass*, Walt Whitman decided that the annexation of California would lead to "the increase of human happiness and liberty." In an essay entitled "More Stars for the Spangled Banner" (1846), he likewise observed that Yucatan "won't need a long coaxing to join the United States."[25] In New York, a melodrama entitled *The Siege of Monterey*, much praised by the press, played to delighted audiences. Indeed, concluded the editors of the *New Englander* magazine, this war would prove to be a good thing not just for both Mexico and the United States, but for the entire planet, because it would underscore the advantages of "good systems of government and of religion." Might it not even be a good idea to annex all of Mexico? Europe, asserted the historian-diplomat Bancroft, would not oppose such a move.

Freedom, then, but economic necessity as well, and many here re-furbished the judgments that had been used against Native Americans: Had Mexicans cultivated these lands, built railways, or discovered precious metals there? And yet, industrializing America had a pressing need for new bullion, as the *United States Review* noted in 1853: "the painful scarcity of silver which at present afflicts the entire trading and agricultural community, can only be removed, as the scarcity of gold was removed, by the application of American enterprise to the mines of Mexico. Silver coin will never be abundant in the United States, until the boundary of the South includes the mineral fields of central Mexico, now occupied by a people who have no knowledge, or no appreciation of their value."[26] Lincoln himself once casually asked why it was that Americans, having hardly arrived in California, found gold there, when "Mexican greasers" who had been there for centuries had not been able to do it.[27]

Economic necessity, and with it, as from America's Puritan origins, religion, and more particularly the Protestant religion. Feelings in the United States ran high in these years and in the next decade against Catholicism, in large part as a consequence of Irish immigration. In 1855, 63 percent of Massachusetts voters would vote for the anti-immigrant American Party (better known as the Know-Nothing Party for what was supposed to be members' secretive answer when asked what their party was about: "I know nothing"). As Roman Catholics, Mexicans were thought to be predisposed to cruelty: their murder of the garrison at the Alamo was reminiscent of what Native Americans had done with their prisoners from the beginning of time. In addition, it mattered, as the *Illinois State Register* pointed out, that Mexicans were a quasi-negroid people: Lincoln himself remarked that few of them were really white.

So convincing were the arguments for war and conquest that many voices were raised in favor of a U.S. takeover of the entire North American continent, from the Canadian arctic circle to the Panamanian isthmus. The nation's capacity for growth was unlimited. As the New Orleans *Daily Picayune* was to put it, Americans had "that sort of confidence in the vigor and longevity of the principle of liberty, as to believe it would survive an epidemic conquest embracing in its ravages all Christendom."[28] Many Latin Americans have liked to see themselves in the terms of José Enrique Rodó's Ariel forever oppressed by a brutal Caliban, and we can see their point.

The war was short and in the end decisive. In March 1847 American marines easily captured "the Halls of Montezuma." The United States was by now twice as populous as Mexico, and not just much richer but better armed as well: the U.S. Navy was not strong, but Mexico had no fleet at all.

We can say in hindsight that the war was also ominous. First, it was a dry run for America's own Civil War, as so many of the generals on both sides had begun as junior officers against Mexico. But it was also the first war in which the president claimed the right—as the Constitution allows—to act as commander in chief of America's armed forces.

Matters took their inevitable course, and in 1848 John Slidell, one of America's most experienced diplomats, secured a treaty that granted to the victorious United States everything that it had asked for in 1845, for which success he was roundly blamed by those who now hoped to annex a further third of Mexico's remaining territory. But the fear of angering the northern states induced southern politicians to exhibit some caution.

Later on, Polk, through his secretary of state, offered 100 million dollars to Spain (which rejected this offer) for Cuba, and then went on to dream of annexing Yucatan, whose planters were at the time fighting a rebellion of the Maya Indians. Edward Hannegan, a member of the "Young America" movement, warned his fellow senators that Europeans had designs on that selfsame province: only a United States occupation could forestall a European violation of the Monroe Doctrine.[29]

On balance, the war was a sad chapter in the history of the United States, and our discussion of it can be concluded with a statement by Senator Herschel V. Johnson of Georgia, which he meant to apply to

Mexico, but which has a bizarre echo in defenses of America's role in Iraq today:

> I would not force the adoption of our form of Government upon any people by the sword. But if war is forced upon us, as this has been, and the increase of our territory, and consequently the extension of the area of human liberty and happiness, shall be one of the incidents of such a contest, I believe we should be recreant to our noble mission, if we refused acquiescence in the higher purposes of a wise Providence. War has its evils. In all ages it has been the minister of wholesale death and desolation; but however inscrutable to us, it has also been made, by the Allwise Dispenser of events, the instrumentality of accomplishing the great end of human elevation and human happiness . . . It is in this view that I subscribe to the doctrine of "manifest destiny."[30]

The Mexican war was suggestive in its own right, and its nature and the arguments that were used to support it also foreshadowed the civil conflict that would rip America apart a decade or so later. In many respects this unjustified aggression against Mexico was typical of the expansionism implicit in the democratization of American life. But it also looked forward to the ferocity with which democratic America would turn against its southern self.

President Polk, a Jacksonian and a native of Tennessee, never understood that the destructive side of American nationalism, on which he thrived, would soon lead to a universalist reshaping of America's national idea. "Slavery," he insisted, "was one of the questions adjusted in the compromise of the Constitution. It has, and can have no legitimate connection with the War with Mexico." But it did.[31]

CHAPTER 6
God's New Message in Lincoln's America

Jacksonian democracy had set the stage for the exclusionary nationalistic and even genocidal wars of the 1830s against Native Americans and, less ferociously it is true, against Mexico. But that same democracy, now deployed by religious fervor, would soon culminate in the first American and patriotic apotheosis of inclusion, with the triumph of libertarian thought in 1865. (Its next great moment of universalist inclusion would come during the Second World War.) What had begun in the 1830s as democratic nationalism veered in the 1850s toward its universalist democratic and libertarian twin. In 1847 Polk, one of America's blindest and most mendacious presidents, had engineered the Mexican war. After 1860 Lincoln, America's greatest president, guided America's fortune and unity through its most critical moment. Initially resigned to the existence of slavery and convinced of the racial inferiority of blacks, Lincoln would in the end not just free the slaves, but open to them the gates and prospects of citizenship.

As had been true before 1776, America's new national confidence had great material progress behind it. Industrialization and urbanization progressed rapidly during these decades. In 1815, only New York and Philadelphia had more than 100,000 inhabitants; by 1860, eight American cities had more than 150,000 inhabitants, one more than in England, the world's most industrialized society at the time.

Such an embarrassment of riches might have made America more complacent, as would happen in later eras. Greater wealth in the 1890s and 1920s furthered philistinism, and the boom years of the 1990s furthered the smug image of America as "an indispensable nation." But in the 1850s a greater material self-confidence nurtured by religious sensibility fed America's universalist vocation, as had often happened before. In the 1750s religion had given Anglo-America its sense of universalizing libertarianism in distinction to the popish authoritarianism of the Franco-Canadians; in 1776 it had anointed and sanctified the cause of the new republic. And now, in the 1850s, the importance of religious sentiment reached its high point in American history: it was in that decade that religious feeling deployed the politics of antislavery and most dramatically affected America's national sense of self.

It is important to keep in mind that, in America, religion's noblest purpose has always been to infuse secular objectives with its spirit of transcendence. In the hands of its institutionalized professionals, American religion often disappoints, and it repels in the deeds—self-seeking or corrupt—of some fundamentalist, pentacostal, and pedophile Catholic clergy today. But as the hidden force behind America's enlightened universalism, its strength is often powerful and grand.

*****

The 1820s and 1830s were disappointing decades for the revivalists, who had dreamed of changing the face of America by individualized effort. Americans in 1776 had a lively sense of the *collective* nature of their endeavor: Benjamin Franklin half-jokingly endorsed that communitarian sense by urging his rebellious colleagues to hang together lest they hang separately. But Americans in the 1820s and 1830s believed instead in individual conversion, and in the individual efforts of those who had been reborn in Christ. It followed that Christians would not only hold religious convictions in their hearts but would vigorously pursue strictly religious goals in the public realm: as one believer put it of his own pet idea, "re-establishing the Sabbath was as necessary to the health of the state . . . as enforcing laws against murder and polygamy."[1] But direct political action had seemed to these reformers ill advised and perhaps even counterproductive. Institutions and collective action were not critical for these revivalists, who thought that the sum of their newly revitalized and individuated religious longings would suffice. Associationism mattered as much to them as orchestrated public opinion.

Already, in the Great Awakening of the mid-eighteenth century, the hold of established churches and institutions had been vastly injured by the individuation of religious sentiment, and this trend now went one step further: the more formal denominations, Congregationalist (and Calvinist) or Anglican (and neo-Catholic), yielded ground to Methodists and Baptists, especially in the southern states.

But what religion lost institutionally, it gained in individuated intensity. It seeped into the nooks and crannies of American life, and for two or three decades, newly pious Americans (now become the citizens— or, as it were, the latter day saints—of a "Benevolent Empire") assumed that the simple aggregation of their more intense and more individuated spiritualities would change the world. Once again, if in a softer register, this was to place an emphasis on the Augustinian—and Calvinist—notion of grace, which, now dispensed to all, would unite the faithful who would henceforth live not just through God's love, but in it.

In an immediate sense, this religious and *a*political ideal (since not connected to any specific political consciousness) faded after 1840 and definitively stumbled in the 1850s, with the revival of political animosities and the collapse of the second party system. But in a larger sense, and in the long run also, from that time to ours, a societally concerned religiosity, however institutionally unfocused it might be, would be a cardinal aspect of the American national idea. Millions of Americans affiliated with neither party nor religious denomination would bathe in this ambient light, as best shown perhaps in Lincoln's references to Providence, which became ever more pressing as the Civil War went on. Before the war, Lincoln had campaigned as the champion of a secularized common sense, and had even been accused in Illinois in 1846 by a minister named Peter Cartwright of being an "infidel" who did not believe in the existence of God. (Lincoln's defense was that he was not a member of any "Christian Church" but that he "had never denied the truth of any Christian Church" and had "never spoken with intentional disrespect of religion in general, or any denomination of Christians in particular.") In 1863, however, he saw his countrymen as "an almost chosen people."[2] It would be unwise also to forget the celebrated "under God" that Lincoln inserted in his reading of the Gettysburg Address, that Nicene Creed of the American republic.

But in the short run, in the 1840s, what seemed clear was the failure of apolitism, and the hopes of the Benevolent Empire now gave way to a highly politicized and voluntarist version of the American national idea, an echo of the republican will of 1776 and a forerunner of the progressivist/New Deal ethos of the first half of the twentieth century. Between 1830 and 1860, America, which had begun as a representative republic and had become a democracy, now moved toward a new definition of its national self whose first principle was an increasingly politicized detestation of slavery. In 1840 Emerson wrote: "Our culture is the predominance of an idea which draws after it this train of cities and institutions. Let us rise into a new idea, and they will disappear."[3] And that is what happened.

Slavery had not seemed particularly shocking before independence. The American colonies were part of a British empire, and the existence of slavery within the realm of this imperial institution seemed normal enough. But slavery automatically became an anomaly in a republic of free citizens. Logically speaking, one of two things had to be true: that blacks were so inferior to whites that they could never deserve to be free citizens, or, conversely, that African Americans, from their very humanity, should eventually become free and even become citizens.

Discussed episodically at first, and gradually made illegal in many northern states, the presence of slavery on American soil became an ever more problematic issue after 1830. In 1819 the white inhabitants of Missouri, most of them Southerners who had settled the territory with their 6,000 slaves, petitioned to join the Union as a slave state. A laborious compromise was worked out in 1820, but foresighted Americans in both North and South understood that dreadful prospects were now at hand. John Quincy Adams, America's most principled president, noted in his diary: "The present question is a mere preamble—a title page to a great tragic volume . . . If the Union must be dissolved slavery is precisely the question upon which it ought to break." More poetically but just as lucidly, Jefferson wrote: "This momentous question, like a fire-bell in the night, awakened and filled me with terror."[4]

Originally, in 1800, most antislavery societies (there were about a hundred of them) had been located in the South, where slavery was, as it were, a local issue. Now it became a national issue: southern antislavery societies died off and northern ones became ever more numerous.[5] In 1831 a northern abolitionist, William Lloyd Garrison, became instantly famous in the North and instantly detested in the South for the incendiary articles he printed in his newspaper, *The Liberator*. (Before the end of that year, the state of Georgia offered a reward of $5,000 to anyone who would kidnap Garrison and deliver him to Georgia's judicial officials.) "I will be heard" was his slogan, and in truth he was. His was a fanatical zeal that nothing could stamp out. In 1834, 122,000 abolitionist brochures were distributed through the mails and 1.1 million in 1835. (Most southern postmasters refused to accept them. In 1835, Andrew Jackson "called for a national censorship law to silence abolitionists."[6])

Britain's abolition of slavery in 1833 (the French would likewise abolish it in their colonies in 1848) quickened American responses. An umbrella organization, the American Anti-Slavery Society, was created and proclaimed its goals in a Declaration of Sentiments, which Garrison had drafted, a step that seemed logical for him after his ten years as a propagandist for the Benevolent Empire, during which he had militated in favor of prohibition and pacifism and against violence, profanity, vulgar entertainments, and sexual irregularities. (A pious Baptist, Garrison eventually drifted to unconditional pacifism, which he renounced when the Civil War broke out in 1861. In 1840 he was excluded from the Anti-Slavery Society as an anarchist.)

True, the new detestation of slavery was everywhere counterbalanced by a profound and ancient suspicion of blacks. In 1835 in Boston,

Garrison was attacked by a crowd, tied up, and dragged through the streets. In 1837 another abolitionist journalist, William Lovejoy, was murdered in southern Illinois, whose inhabitants were largely proslavery and of southern origin. Though harried by critics and official censors alike, Garrison and his faithful did not yield. Their banner was the Declaration of Independence, infinitely preferable, they thought, to the Constitution of 1787, which by implication accepted the legality of slavery. Garrison's message could not be halted as it spoke to the deeper yearnings of the American psyche as it had recently been reshaped. In other countries terms such as exploitation, selfishness, and injustice are the rhetorical common coin of reformers, but in America slavery is still the metaphor that fits all sizes: as in "wage slavery," or today, "sexual slavery."[7]

In this period, more than ever before and forevermore, the terms "liberty" and "America" became coterminous for millions of Americans, as was argued by the Harvard historian George Bancroft, who published between 1831 and 1874 a ten-volume and extremely popular *History of the United States* that ran from the earliest times to American independence. In 1854 Bancroft offered to the public a suggestive historical/ theological account of what his country was about. The unity of humanity, as he saw it, was in the reciprocal relation that bound God to his entire creation. Was it not obvious that America was the most universal of nations?

> Our land is not more the recipient of the men of all countries than their ideas. Annihilate the past of any one leading nation of the world, and our destiny would have been changed. Italy and Spain, in the persons of Columbus and Isabella, joined together for the great discovery that opened America to emigration and commerce; France contributed to its Independence; the search for the origin of the language we speak carried us to India; our religion is from Palestine; of the hymns sung in our churches, some were first heard in Italy, some in the deserts of

Arabia, some on the banks of the Euphrates; our arts come from Greece; our jurisprudence from Rome; our maritime code from Russia; England taught us the system of Representative Government; the noble Republic of the United Provinces bequeathed to us, in the world of thought, the great idea of the toleration of all opinions; in the world of action, the prolific principle of federal union. Our country stands, therefore, more than any other as the realisation of the unity of the race . . . Finally, as a consequence of the tendency of the race towards unity and universality, the organization of society must more and more conform to the principle of FREEDOM.[8]

Two points should be made about Bancroft's thinking. The first is that Bancroft had "forgotten" to include blacks—unfit, we must suppose he thought them, to be American. (Many Americans, including Clay, Marshall, and Lincoln, hoped to return emancipated slaves to Africa. Liberia, with its capital at Monrovia, founded in 1822, was the pathetic expression of that absurd idea.) Second, abolitionism, though not explicitly situated as the extension of American liberty, was obviously implied in Bancroft's universalist argument. For Bancroft, all those who had contributed to the American idea of nation had also nourished the idea of American freedom, and vice versa. To be sure, once again, African Americans were not part of his nationalist and inclusive calculus, and in 1857 the American Supreme Court, as shall be seen, would concur by arguing that the federal constitution had been made by whites for whites alone. (In that exclusionary view, white women likewise were no more than partial citizens, and Native Americans also had no role: they would not receive rights of citizenship until 1924.) Nonetheless, from the 1840s on, as Bancroft partly understood, the American idea of freedom acquired a logic of inclusion whose realization, however gradual, was also irresistible.

It is also useful to follow the response of Southerners to America's new sense of self. Jacksonian nationalism and democracy had presented no problem for them whatsoever. But religiously sanctified antislavery as the center of the nation's new self-definition was an increasingly intolerable message.

Particularly revealing in this respect were the perverse but lucid reflections of Senator John Caldwell Calhoun of South Carolina—the most radically reactionary of the southern slave states—who was at various times vice president of the United States, secretary of war, and secretary of state, all of this after having graduated from Yale University, where one of the residential colleges bears his name to this day.

Calhoun's first argument was that the servile condition of blacks was perfectly justified because it was inscribed in both nature and history. The central mistake of abolitionism, he argued, was to suggest that all men were equal. Their inequality was for him self-evident. As for the idea that all men were alike: "Nothing can be more unfounded and false. It rests upon the assumption of a fact, which is contrary to universal observation, in whatever light it may be regarded."[9] All Africans, because of their race, were incapable of that cardinal American virtue: self-government.

Calhoun's second contribution was to suggest that planters were not alone. Looking leftward, he tried to show that slavery and democracy were not antithetical but complementary: poor whites, he thought, if they owned slaves, would then be more free to engage in democratic public life. And looking to the right, though he had surely never read a line of Karl Marx, Calhoun explained to the rich in the North that southern landlords and northern manufacturers had a common interest because they had a common enemy: namely, the very poor. Planters and slaves had radically divergent interests, to be sure, but was this not also true of New England manufacturers and their immigrant employees? It followed, he argued, that planters and manufacturers should unite: this was Calhoun's best argument, but in a nation that had just rededicated itself not just to individualistic economics, but to individual freedom as well, his reasoning could not convince. With some reluctance, Calhoun, who had been a "war-hawk" before the War of 1812, and who in the 1820s had become a nationalistic Jacksonian, now understood the painful logic of his situation: if Americanness had come to mean the end of slavery, he would cease to be an American. In his later days, for this ferocious defender of slavery and states' rights, the United States "were" not (and most certainly, "was" not) a nation: "I never use the word 'Nation' in speaking of the United States," he wrote to a friend in 1849. "We are not a nation, but a Union, a Confederacy of equal and sovereign States."[10]

Many Southerners understood their situation in similar terms. In 1850 Robert Barnwell Rhett, Calhoun's successor in the Senate, urged a dissolution of the American Union on his fellow Southerners. Slave owners had but two alternatives, he argued: abolition or secession. (Given the spectacular growth of northern economic power after 1850, it makes some sense to suppose that southern secession, had it taken place at that time rather than ten years later, might well have been successful.) As the Northerners, Rhett added in 1852, had embarked on a "complete revolution," Southerners had but one valid option: to proclaim themselves "a free and independent nation."[11]

Many a journalist, novelist, and budding sociologist rushed into this same fray of national creationism with arguments that described southern life: its grace, its charm, its linguistic particularism, and its social habits—religious, patriarchal, and so different from the mechanistic, soulless modernity of the North. (An amusing witticism on this theme suggests that the city of Washington, D.C., combined the efficiency of the South and the charm of the North.) Most telling here were the lucid but perverse arguments of George Fitzhugh in his *Sociology for the South; or, The Failure of Free Society* (1854) and his *Cannibals All! or, Slaves without Masters* (1857), which argued that northern capitalism was no guarantee of individuality at all, but, to the contrary, the institutionalization of an un-American selfishness. Indeed, for Fitzhugh, slavery was so perfect an institution that he did not hesitate to advocate not only the resumption of the slave trade, which had been abolished for half a century, but the extension of enslavement to include whites as well as blacks.

The southern response to the shift in the northern idea of America's national purpose has often been labeled a "pseudo-nation,"[12] but the Confederacy was in fact a genuinely new "slave nation," whose genesis can be seen as the inevitable nationalizing effect—and also as an indirect proof—of America's own libertarian self–re-creation in the 1840s and 1850s. How else to understand the immense suffering that southern whites were willing to endure for "the cause"? In the eleven Confederate states, 258,000 soldiers died for a white population of about four and half million, a casualty rate that was twice the one the French endured during the First World War, which destroyed the resilience of France for half a century. With a student population twice that of Harvard, the University of Virginia lost 500 dead as against Harvard's 117.[13] Southern nationalism was a deeply felt "imagined community" albeit an unsuccessful one, as Macedonia was in its first effort to reach statehood as well as nationhood, or as the Basques, the Laplanders, and the Corsicans have been in our own time.

Inclusion and exclusion: these two traditions, in their uneasy coexistence, were now more than ever the warring and constituent parts of a mutating America's nationhood. Inevitably, when the partisans of one of these two strands appropriated the American idea of nation, the other had no choice but to invent an altogether new patriotic passion.

* * * * *

There is no need here to follow in any detail the evolution of pro- and antislavery politics in America. Suffice it to say that what began as one issue among many other issues gradually became the be-all and end-all of American politics. The first omen, as has been said, was the Missouri Compromise of 1820. Then in 1832 came a serious regional disagreement: under Calhoun's leadership, South Carolina, where many whites considered their domination of a black majority an issue of life or death, threatened to leave the Union. President Jackson, enraged and intent on the preservation of the nation, threatened South Carolinians with invasion and Calhoun with execution. Abolitionism was as yet too weak, and the strength of Unionist sentiment too strong: in 1833 Calhoun and his stalwarts backed down.

The 1840s saw a clear acceleration of regionalist sentiment, at once sharpened and thwarted by the Southerners' domination of the undemocratic Senate (although New York State then had a population twelve times larger than that of Florida, each state had the same number of senators). The two political parties that had come into being with the demise of the Federalists after 1815, the Whigs and the Democrats—both of them offshoots of Jefferson's Republican Party—were assailed by ever stronger antislavery minorities. In 1840 a new Liberty Party proposed its own presidential candidate but it managed to secure only 2 percent of the vote. Libertarianism, it seemed at first, was proceeding very slowly, and Charles Francis Adams, the son and grandson of American presidents, who, like his father, had been won over to antislavery, concluded in October 1848: "Enough is visible [to see] that the Free States are not yet roused so fully as they should be to the necessity of sustaining their principles."[14]

Movement, however, proved to be much more rapid than Adams anticipated. Antislavery did not just make steady progress; it also became ever more demanding, to the point that the abolitionists divided into two groups. The most intransigent abolitionists, like Garrison, wanted not just to prevent the extension of slavery into the western territories but to abolish it in those places where tradition—and the federal Constitution—had long since recognized its legal existence. (In 1861 Garrison, a pacifist who hated slavery more than he loved the Union, argued at first for letting the newly Confederate states go their way so as to have a northern Union with no slaves and no war.)

Others, like Lincoln, desperately searched for some compromise that would reconcile their new sense of America's national purpose with a slave system sanctioned by tradition and law. For them, to hate slavery was by no means to sympathize with blacks: many, as has been said, hoped to repatriate freed blacks to Africa, a drastic solution that some African Americans in despair decided might be a solution after all.

In 1850, once again, a crisis brought all passions into play. Now that Mexico had been defeated and the New Southwest annexed, where would the line between slave and non-slave states be drawn? Institutionally, Southerners depended on control of the Senate, and the addition of more free states to the Union would tilt the balance against them.

Horrified by this drift of affairs, two nationally prominent politicians who were not fanatically dedicated either to slavery or to its abolition, Henry Clay and Daniel Webster (the former "self-made," the other none too sober or upright in his business affairs) imagined yet another compromise: California would be admitted to the Union as a free state, but New Mexico would remain a territory (the latter, being a bit too Mexican and not quite white enough, was not admitted to the Union as a state until 1912). In exchange, the federal government and its agents in the free states would be required to capture and repatriate runaway slaves without trial. (Many Northerners, such as Emerson, publicly announced that they would refuse to obey this law.)

Here was a compromise that was no compromise at all, as was shown by a series of events, the first of which was the fate of Kansas in 1854. Stephen Douglas, the last American statesman of the first rank who wanted to preserve the Union as it was, secured, with the approval of President Pierce, a bill along the lines proposed earlier by Lewis Cass, which would allow local residents to decide whether they would accept or reject slavery. Northern Whigs voted against the bill, southern Whigs, for it, and the northern Democrats in Congress were also divided. That same year, politicians who opposed the expansion of slavery formed a new Republican Party. The structure of American politics known as the second party system, which had endured for three decades, was breaking down. (In 1858 Douglas would be reelected to the Senate against Lincoln, but that battle won, he would then lose the war. He died in June 1861.)

Matters took an even sharper turn in 1857 with a Supreme Court decision in the *Dred Scott* case to the effect that African Americans could never become U.S. citizens and thus could not sue in court. (Of the first thirty-three men appointed to the Supreme Court, twenty had been Southerners, and at least one of those on the court at that time had fathered a child by an African-American woman.) Scott had sued for his freedom on the grounds that he had traveled with his owner to areas where slavery was prohibited. Slaves being a form of property, ruled the Court, it followed that owners could take their slaves wherever they pleased.

Slavery, which had been almost universally accepted in 1776 and even in 1787, as a practical necessity that it was best not to discuss, had now become the antithesis of the American national idea. "This . . . zeal for the spread of slavery, I can not but hate," said Lincoln in a speech on the Missouri Compromise. "I hate it because of the monstrous injustice of slavery itself. I hate it because it deprives our republican example of its just influence in the world—enables the enemies of free institutions, with plausibility, to taunt us as hypocrites—causes the real friends of freedom to doubt our sincerity, and especially because it forces so many really good men amongst ourselves into an open war with the very fundamental principles of civil liberty." Senator Sumner of Massachusetts went even further: slavery, he said, "degrades our country and prevents its example" from leading the world to the "universal restoration of power to the governed."[15]

In the 1860 presidential election Douglas stood as the Democratic candidate in the North, but John Cabell Breckinridge of Kentucky, a slave owner who was then the nation's vice president under President James Buchanan, was nominated as a southern Democrat. The Whig Party had vanished. In the ensuing void, the Republican nominee, Abraham Lincoln, though he received only 40 percent of the vote, was elected president.

*****

The first cause of the Great War of 1914–1918 was that most Europeans were resigned to thinking that there would some day be such a war.

In the first weeks of 1861, similarly, Americans considered with varying degrees of expectation and resignation the coming of a civil conflict, unaware that this would be the most terrible of all their wars because the most ideological.

It is rare for both sides in a civil war to have distinct national ambitions. In Spain in 1936, "Franquistas" and Republicans were all nationalists, even if the former were more so than the latter. And as regards the Paris Commune of 1871, although Marx (who had been much impressed by the victory of the democratic North in 1865) wrote about it under the title *The Civil War in France*, both Parisians and Versaillais were Frenchmen, all proud of their one country, even if they envisaged its organization differently. Mao Zedong and Chiang Kai-shek both aimed to control the whole of China. But the American Civil War was at once just that—a civil war and a "Bruderkrieg"—but also a parthogenetic war of nations, as the South was fighting to create a new state centered on a different ideological principle while the North moved from a war of reunification to an equally ideological war of conquest and destruction.

Lincoln said in 1865 that some were dying to break the Union and others to save their nation, but this related more to what the war had first been than to what it had become.

In the end, Lincoln proved to be—and very much to his own surprise—mystical and fierce. In his private life he was practical and melancholic. He loved to tell jokes. By instinct a conservative person with a strong desire to please—and to rise in business and politics—he had in the past preferred to put off until tomorrow what did not absolutely have to be done today. He was not his party's most prominent politician. His ungainly appearance was mocked by cartoonists. He did not elicit confidence or admiration.

Quite typically, Lincoln's policy vis-à-vis the secessionist South was at first conciliatory. The North, he decided, would not declare war on the South, although it might equip a few federal garrisons—like that at Fort Sumter, one of two fortresses the North retained in the South.

In the past, by a stroke of his pen, Jefferson had personally deployed the power of a centralized state of which he disapproved in principle. Polk had personally decided to go to war with Mexico, as McKinley would personally decide to do with Spain, as Wilson would do in a libertarian register, and later George W. Bush in an incipiently fascistic one.

Lincoln merely waited. At (many) times, presidents and coteries have propelled a patriotic people to perfervid nationalism, and Lincoln's prudence is proof—by contrast—of their sinister intent. Of course, guided as he was by an "American creed" that had been rejuvenated by three decades by renewed religious fervor, Lincoln, like most Northerners, was resigned to fighting a war. But he did nothing to hasten it.

At some few moments in history, everything depends on agency, or even more strikingly, on contingency and human folly: if Cleopatra's nose had been of a different turn, Pascal once observed, Caesar would not have wooed her, and world history would have changed its course. Bismarck, had he been defeated by the Austrians at the battle of Königrätz in 1866—which unfortunately he was not—had resolved to kill himself. Lenin might never have reached Russia if Kaiser Wilhem, (another W!) and a near imbecile, had not decided to let him travel through Germany to St. Petersburg. And so on. The attack on Fort Sumter in April 1861 was (perhaps!) of the same order. As Lincoln had decided not to attack the South, if the Confederacy had remained pacific there might have been no Civil War at all. But the aristocratic local commanding Confederate officer, General Pierre Gustave Toutant de Beauregard—a fine-sounding cognomen—could not bear to see, from Charleston's harbor, the Union flag merely hundreds of yards from his shores. The bombardment of this fort was, from the southern point of view, an act of extraordinary stupidity, which Jefferson Davis later lamely described as having been a "defensive measure."

*****

The American Civil War began as a fortuitously declared war of national unification, strictly contemporaneous with similarly motivated wars in

Italy and Germany and in Asian societies as well, with the Taiping revolt in China from 1850 to 1864 and the modernizing revolution and
restoration carried out by the Meiji emperor in Japan in 1867.

Inevitably, however, as the American Civil War progressed, its
raison d'être changed drastically: the abolition of slavery did not displace
the salvation of the American nation as the focus of public opinion, but
"nation" was now redefined to mean, in the North, a nation fighting for
abolition. For Southerners, in a parallel manner, slavery had become,
during the 1840s and 1850s, not just "a peculiar institution," but the
cornerstone of the South's sense of its national self. In his first message
to Congress in 1861 Lincoln had used the term "Union" thirty-two
times; and "nation" only three times. At Gettysburg two years later, he
spoke of the nation five times and of the Union not at all.[16]

Matters progressed slowly at first. In August 1861 Congress voted
to declare to be free any slave who had escaped to the North in order to
avoid forced labor in the southern war effort. Significantly, Lincoln—
then still eager to find some moderate solution and no less eager to avoid
antagonizing the border slave states, which had not seceded—did not
endorse this measure. Likewise, at first, northern soldiers received orders not to pillage Confederate farms, and a Union general in early 1862
even authorized a Confederate planter to search his camp for a runaway
slave. The idea, in both North and South, was of a limited war that would
leave civil society—in North and South—intact.

In the spring of 1862, however, lines hardened. Soldiers were now
forbidden to return runaway slaves who had sought refuge behind the
Union lines. Slavery was abolished in the District of Columbia. A Confiscation Act authorized the president to employ former slaves as soldiers.
In the summer of 1862 Lincoln—bizarrely—made a quasi-religious vow
to abolish slavery after the next Union victory, ostensibly because he did
not wish the move to seem to be a gesture of despair, and on September
22, 1862, after the battle of Antietam, he issued a preliminary version
of the emancipation proclamation, declaring that as of January 1, 1863,
"all persons held as slaves within any state, or designated part of a state,

the people whereof shall then be in rebellion against the United States shall be then, thenceforward, and forever free; and the executive government of the United States, including the military and naval authority thereof, will recognize and maintain the freedom of such persons." (The new law would apply only in areas under Confederate control. It would not apply if the Confederacy surrendered before that date, and it would not apply to the four slave states that had remained loyal to the Union.) Lincoln then also decided to arm freed African Americans, and the first black brigades were organized in Louisiana in October 1862. By the war's end they would number 180,000 soldiers, which came to about 12 percent of the northern army. (They served in all-black regiments under white officers, and were paid less well than their white comrades.)

Having become not just a war of national unity but a war of universalist liberation, the Civil War became a kind of religious war as well, as American tradition required.[17] Northern soldiers marched off to war, and to very high casualty rates, to the rhythms of Julia Ward Howe's millenarian "Battle Hymn of the Republic":

> Mine eyes have seen the glory of the coming of the
> Lord;
> He is trampling out the vintage where the grapes of
> wrath are stored;
> He hath loosed the fateful lightning of his terrible
> swift sword;
> His truth is marching on . . .
> In the beauty of the lilies Christ was born across the
> sea,
> With the glory in his bosom that transfigures you and
> me;
> As He died to make men holy, let us die to make men
> free.
> While God is marching on.

141

Christ had saved humanity by dying on the cross; the Union soldiers would die to free the slaves. These were apocalyptic themes, drawn from the book of Revelation with its peculiar version of the death of Christ, at once a mystic figure and a warrior.[18] (Many who sing this hymn today learn a more pacific version of the line: "As He died to make men holy, let us *live* to make men free.")

As William G. McLoughlin has put it, after 1865 most Americans felt that "the Union was preserved because God willed it."[19] From being part of a nation at war with itself, the northern states had become "God's almost chosen people," a nation under God, dedicated to the pursuit of a universalist, libertarian, and enlightened goal, typically presented in religious terms.

And as the ideological purpose of the war changed, so did everything else. The war, which had begun on the mode of eighteenth-century conflicts in which kings made war on one another but not on each other's people, now drifted toward the twentieth-century model of total war in which civilians are fair game.

The war also became a vehicle of social change. Eighteenth-century and to a lesser degree Napoleonic wars had not implied a reorganization of the civil societies that supported the warring state machines. In preparation of his Russian campaign, for example, Napoleon was careful to keep down the price of bread in Paris, and when in Russia, he chose not to decree the abolition of serfdom. Nor for that matter, at that earlier time, did the Russian state and bureaucracy believe that their War of 1812 had made reform and the end of serfdom from above not just useful but inevitable. By contrast to these various precedents, as the American Civil War went on, its impact was felt everywhere, in civilian life and in the field.

For one thing, both the Union and Confederate governments decreed military conscription (which occasioned riots in New York that caused hundreds of deaths: an orphanage for African-American orphans was set afire; dozens of blacks were lynched, many by Irish immigrants). Forty percent of qualified men in the South, and a third of them in the

North, were called up. In response to protests, Lincoln suspended habeas corpus, the right of prisoners to a court hearing, and 13,000 people were detained without trial. Both Union and Confederacy printed paper money, ordered an income tax, and transformed the ordinary relations between government and civil society, as was also to happen in the two world wars of the twentieth century. In the South, army commanders were authorized to requisition whatever they needed. Slaves were commandeered by the Confederate authorities as laborers for the military. By the war's end, half of the labor force at the South's largest metalworks, the Tredegar Iron works, were African American. In Richmond, Virginia, women were employed in government service. In the North, under the Homestead Act of 1862, the United States government promised to distribute free of charge fifty acres to anyone who had resided on the acreage for five years. In the South, in late 1864, Jefferson Davis proposed to purchase slaves and give them freedom, along with their wives and children, after they served in the Confederate army.

As the war was now being fought for a different purpose, it was also fought differently. At first it was fought "normally," as the war against Mexico had been, in which nearly all of the higher officers of both sides had served. (Ulysses S. Grant had been a captain; Robert E. Lee, a colonel on the staff of General Winfield Scott.) They obeyed the rules of war as taught at West Point, in New York State, where Lee had been superintendent from 1852 to 1855. (The tactical lessons they had learned at school had been codified by General Jomini, a Swiss who had served Napoleon until 1813 and his enemies after that. So it was, for example, that in the first important battle of the war, in July 1861, the two opposing commanders tried to maneuver as Jomini had said they should: each tried to attack on the left while maintaining a stable front in the center and on the right. Had both of them succeeded in this plan, the battle would have ended with the victorious Northerners facing north and equally victorious Southerners facing south.)

But industrial circumstances soon dictated new tactics: railway lines became critical prizes. Casualties skyrocketed because (as would also be true during the First World War) weapons had become much deadlier whereas the generals' tactics had not changed. It also mattered that Lincoln was always ready to reward audacious generals, regardless of casualties: Grant was his favorite, and in a series of battles that he directed between May 5 and June 11, 1864 (at Wilderness, Spotsylvania, and Cold Harbor), northern troops suffered 55,000 dead and wounded—to no end, as in retreat Lee showed himself to be a master tactician, if at the cost of 40,000 Confederate dead. These rhythms of casualties serve as an omen of the Somme and Verdun in 1914–1918.

Soldiers died by the tens of thousands, and civilians were routinely mistreated and their possessions looted. To prevent southern cavalrymen from relying on local supply in the fertile agricultural lands of the Shenandoah Valley, General Philip Sheridan (who personally could not stand the sight of blood) ravaged it and proudly claimed that a crow who wanted to cross that place would have to bring his own supplies. And while Grant, not far from Washington, D.C., incurred unprecedented casualties (he was known even to Lincoln's wife as the butcher of his troops), William Tecumseh Sherman and his army devastated the South as they followed railway lines from Tennessee to Atlanta and then to the sea. Everything that was not stolen was destroyed. "War is hell," he famously and rightly said in one of history's most self-fulfilling prophecies. In an area of fifty by three hundred miles, Sherman's troops ravaged everything, or nearly everything—bridges, roads, railways, plantations, factories, public buildings.

The Prussian chief of staff Helmuth von Moltke, whose military culture was also Napoleonic and Jominian, was not much interested in the lessons of the American Civil War, which he described as one vast riot with armed bands roving from one end of a continent to the other. His intent was to underscore the "korrekt" way in which, during this same decade, the Prussian armies under his command had and would perform in Denmark, Austria, and France. But it was also to misunderstand the nature of future wars.

Many inhabitants of Dallas or Atlanta today speak more or less jokingly of the "War of Northern Aggression," an epithet that, alas, makes a great deal of sense, as was pointed out in 1948 by a southern historian in an essay entitled "General William Tecumseh Sherman and Total War."[20] "This is a truth that needs to be repeated," another historian has written more recently: "if the Civil War was not quite total, it missed totality by only a narrow margin."[21] From Atlanta to the coast, Sherman, far from his supply base at Nashville, in some sense had no choice but to live off the land and "to make Georgia howl," as he put it. But the next phase of his devastating journey, northward through South Carolina from a captured Savannah that could be supplied by sea, had no such excuse. Sherman laughed when one of his officers spoke inadvertently of Burnwell for a Carolina town named Barnwell. (It is surely relevant that of the Union generals, Sherman was one of the least interested before 1865 in freeing slaves, and there surely is also food for thought in the fact that the son of this brutal man later chose to become a Jesuit.)

The typically American conjunction of inclusion (for African Americans) and exclusion (for southern civilians), in a context of an ideologized war of purification, has to give us historical pause. We have to think more about the radical shift in the nature of the American Civil War, from a polite conflict carried out within the established rules of war to a ferocious struggle the likes of which Europeans had not seen since the Thirty Years' War of the seventeenth century. The bombing of Hiroshima in 1945 was also explained in terms of immediate military need, but we sense today, with hindsight, that this type of explanation is woefully incomplete.

A middle-range explanation brings us back to nationalism, that most terrifying of all modern public passions. Why did northern civilians militarize their society—and themselves—with such alacrity and applaud the destructive invasion of the South? And why did Southerners persist in the face of immense suffering? Why did their cause seem so sacred to them? A Union officer once asked a Confederate prisoner, manifestly of modest origins, poorly clothed and poorly shod, why he had fought so fiercely. "Because," answered the southern soldier, "because y'all are down here." Once again we return here to the Marxist idea of praxis, which theorizes the relationship of contingency to underlying ideological potentialities: the reciprocal influences and causation between theories and events. In that context of mutual influences, events —ordinarily unforeseen—quicken existing but still latent ideological tendencies, which in turn, when brought to consciousness, quicken subsequent responses to events. Thus, the War of Independence sharpened an underlying yearning for the construction of an American nation. The war against Mexico quickened America's national and democratic sentiment, which in turn made more feasible the argument that slavery had no place in the American system. And so on.

All of which also brings us back once more to an examination of the foundational principles and structure of the American national idea. It leads us again to the proximity in America of religiously motivated themes of inclusion and exclusion, and to the ease with which America can move from the one to the other, as in the move from a struggle against Japanese militarism in December 1941 to August 1945 and the relentlessly cruel use of fearful atomic weapons against unarmed and defenseless civilians at Hiroshima, and then, for good measure, at Nagasaki. By a large majority, Americans approved of that bombing; in 1864 the capture and burning of Atlanta likewise electrified northern opinion. Lincoln had thought during the previous summer that he would lose the next election. General McClellan, the Democratic choice, was widely popular, and the more radical Republicans had decided to run General Frémont once again (as in 1856) against Lincoln. But Atlanta made all the difference: McClellan stumbled and Frémont withdrew.

This brings us back to the role in the American political system of those sanctified magistrates, the presidents of the United States. Why did Lincoln, a humane and peaceful man whose face expressed, as we know from famous photographs, the sufferings and contradictions of his nation, persist in supporting Grant without regard for the frightful, murderous suffering that this determined but not too skilled general inflicted on his troops? And why also, when Sherman ravaged the South northward from Savannah, did Lincoln do nothing to hold him back?

The haunting anxiety we see in Lincoln's photographic portraits moves us deeply, and perhaps that is because these images make so palpable not just America's sufferings, but also the difficulty—indeed, the impossibility—of conciliating the tragically warring impulses that rent its soul, and his own.

That is also one way to read his second inaugural address, this most mystical of all American political pronouncements: it too moves us by its mix of determination and tragic bewilderment. He writes of the North and the South: "Both read the same Bible, and pray to the same God; and each invokes His aid against the other. It may seem strange that any men should dare to ask a just God's assistance in wringing their bread from the sweat of other men's faces; but let us judge not, that we be not judged. The prayers of both could not be answered; that of neither has been answered fully. The Almighty has His own purposes. 'Woe unto the world because of offenses! For it must needs be that offenses come; but woe to that man by whom the offense cometh!'"

*****

On April 9, 1865, General Lee's surrender put an end to the South's organized resistance, though western fighters continued the struggle for a few weeks. The South, blockaded, decimated, exhausted, and demoralized, was yet not wholly defeated: it just gave up. Its soldiers might have gone on fighting, though desertions mounted, but its civilians, women especially, had suffered too much to go on.

Five days later, on Good Friday, Lincoln died, murdered by an actor whose specialty was Shakespearean roles. Hundreds of thousands came to watch the mortuary train that bore to his grave in Illinois a man who, they thought, had seen the Lord. Death made of Lincoln a Christlike figure: "Through his death, an innocent Lincoln became transformed from the prophet of America's civil religion to its messiah."[22] As William C. Harris has put it: "That Lincoln's assassination occurred on the traditional anniversary of Jesus' crucifixion was viewed by Americans in the Union states as more than a coincidence . . . As Jesus had suffered on the cross for humankind, so Lincoln had suffered and died for God's objectives in the Civil War. He had become a martyr to the Providence-ordained purposes of republicanism—liberty, freedom, self-government, and Union."[23]

And at the other side of the United States, in South Carolina, in June 1865 Edmund Ruffin, a fanatical secessionist who had gone out of his way to attend John Brown's hanging and had been chosen in 1861 to fire one of the first cannon shots against Fort Sumter, shot himself in the head. His last words were imprecations against the hated Northerners who had killed one of his sons at war, ravaged his home and country, and freed his black retainers.

America's democratic nationalism—as well as its "national democratism"—had now reached its zenith. In French one still says today, as Americans once did, "*les Etats-Unis sont*" (the United States *are* . . .). But since Lincoln's day, by instinct, Americans now speak of their homeland in the singular: "The United States *is* . . ." The Civil War, said Woodrow Wilson in a Memorial Day address, "created in this country what had never existed before—a national consciousness." That was a much-exaggerated statement. If it had been completely true, if America's view of African Americans had been durably transformed, Wilson, fifty years after the war, would not still have been the racist that he was. But we can see what he meant to say.

CHAPTER 7
A "Reconstructed" Nation

The decades that followed the Civil War are two of the most lamentable—indeed, probably (with our own!) *the* most lamentable—decades of American history. At stake were the selfsame issues: race and the question of what America's national purpose was to be. Before the Civil War, America's national and republican legacy, amplified as so often happens in that country by religious zeal, had soared. But once the war ended, national reunification was used as a pretext to authorize the return in 1877 of the ex-Confederate states to the bosom of the nation in as unreformed a shape as seemed feasible. Freeing the slaves had brought the American national community forward, but humbling the African-American freedmen now became the cornerstone of the new arrangements.

In the main, the issue is plain enough: once African Americans had been freed, whites lost interest in their fate. Symbolically, Garrison suspended the publication of his *Liberator* and told the American Anti-Slavery Society that it might as well dissolve itself. Even Frederick Douglass, the most eloquent of America's black voices of the time, concurred. What to do with the newly freed Americans? "Do nothing with them; mind your business and let them mind theirs. Your *doing* with them is their greatest misfortune. They have been undone by your doings, and all they now ask and really have need of at your hands, is just to let them alone."[1] And of course in some sense Douglass was not altogether wrong: without the mass of prejudice that kept blacks from fitting into white America, his solution of noninterference and of individualism triumphant might have made practical as well as historical sense. But in the context of the times, when African Americans were politically weak and their enemies numerous, this was ominous advice.

Two questions framed the issue.

The first had to do with the Freedmen's Bureau, a smallish Union bureaucracy that tried—with some success—to normalize the life of freed slaves in the coastal Confederate areas that had been captured by Union forces. How to feed and house them? A difficult assignment in itself, but the Bureau also worked to find them employment, assign to them tillable land, teach them to read and write, and train teachers who might help them to do so. General James S. Wadsworth, sent by Lincoln's secretary of war to investigate conditions in the Mississippi Valley, understood the issue perfectly; to abolish slavery but to leave the freedmen defenseless, with low wages and restrictions on their freedom of movement, would leave them at the bottom of the social order, he said, "not as freedmen, but as serfs." James McKaye, a member of the American Freedmen's Inquiry Commission, put it even more plainly: "If the only object to be accomplished [were] simply 'to compel the negro to labor' in a condition of perpetual subordination and subjection," freedom without land might suffice. But this solution was hopeless "if the object [were] to make the coloured man a self-supporting and self-defending member of [the] community."[2] By June 1865, in the Carolinas, 10,000 former slaves had become the free owners of the land they tilled.

What to do with the Bureau? Dissolve it or encourage it?

The second problem had to do with the resurfacing, in some places almost immediately, of former Confederate authorities, who had recycled themselves as loyal, regional elites. What would Lincoln have done had he lived? Would he have accepted this resurgence? "Beware the contempt of the dead" wrote the Brazilian mulatto novelist Machado de Assis; and it is dangerous indeed to speculate on what Lincoln might have done had he lived. His first instincts would surely have been generously to accept former Confederates who had seen the error of their traitorous ways. Ten days before his death, while visiting the newly liberated Richmond, he "declared his disposition to be lenient towards all persons, however prominent, who had taken part in the struggle."[3] And, in February 1865, at the Hampton Roads meeting with Confederate delegates, Lincoln had held out the prospect of a reconciliation without confiscation of land. Likewise, in the border states that had not seceded, not only was land *not* confiscated, but owners were also compensated for the emancipation of their human chattel.

But his second thoughts might have been of a different order. Lincoln might well have gradually resolved not to abandon African Americans to some new but debased status, just as years before he had gradually resolved to make slavery impossible not just in the unpopulated West but in the entire nation. On that same visit to Richmond, many local whites pretended not to see him, but blacks gave him a triumphal welcome. As William C. Harris describes it: "The docks were virtually deserted, but a group of black workers recognized the tall president, touching off a celebration among the newly freed slaves . . . As he walked through the still smoldering city, guarded only by twelve marines and sailors, crowds of former slaves rushed forward to shake and kiss his hand and shout their praise . . . one black woman exclaimed, 'I know that I am free, for I have seen Father Abraham and felt him.'"[4] And it was a squadron of black cavalrymen that escorted the president back to the Union vessel that would return him to Washington. It is difficult to suppose that this melancholic optimist, very conscious of his place in history, would have been indifferent to the fate of these new American citizens.

Here indeed were the rock and the hard place of American history: the individual rights of citizens versus the rights of individual property. How would Lincoln, at once cautious and visionary, have resolved this dilemma? He too might have dreamed of an America that would have become more fraternal.

*****

Put together, these two issues of land for African Americans and of the restoration or annihilation of the old elites constitute a problem familiar to historians of Europe. Antonio Gramsci first among them, and after him, in America, Barrington Moore, showed that new *rural* arrangements—

more so perhaps than new urban politics—were the key to the history of nineteenth-century democratic Europe. Where feudalism was abolished on terms favorable to the peasantry (as it was in France in 1789–1793), postrevolutionary democratic politics thrived because a liberated peasantry, which understood its place in the struggle of the urban left versus the old right, provided a critical audience for libertarian politics. In those countries where the old aristocratic elites benefited from feudalism's dissolution by keeping the land and driving destitute peasants to the cities (as in northern Germany) or where the bourgeoisie merely substituted itself for the discredited aristocracy (as in Italy), liberalism remained weak and frail.

Lincoln might have understood the givens of this situation. But his successor, Andrew Johnson, a Southerner, did not. In early 1866 he vetoed the Freedmen's Bureau Bill, which would have extended the life of the agency and its mission of distributing land to freedmen, providing schools for their children, and setting up military courts to protect their rights. He also vetoed a Civil Rights Bill that nullified the newly minted Black Codes, which the recycled leaders of the Confederacy had established to restrict the freedom of their former slaves. In the name of property rights, Johnson also ordered that land titles be restored to the former slave owners: there could be no question, he asserted, of "Africanizing" the southern half of the United States. Property rights were sacrosanct. In response to a Republican proposal to grant every freedman "forty acres and a mule" a *New York Times* journalist pithily summarized the issue: "An attempt to justify the confiscation of Southern land under the pretense of doing justice to the freedmen strikes at the root of all property rights in both sections. It concerns Massachusetts quite as much as Mississippi."[5] Johnson also ratified the election to office of former high-ranking Confederate officials, as when Georgia sent the former vice president of the Confederacy to Washington as its senator. All of which did not please the northern Republicans, especially as the restored southern personnel immediately migrated to the otherwise ailing Democratic Party.

All this also led to one last northern universalist burst of energy. In 1866 a new amendment to the Constitution—and arguably the most critical since the Bill of Rights—declared every kind of racial discrimination illegal. (South Carolina, for example, had forbidden black persons to become artisans, mechanics, or shopkeepers.) Then in 1867 a Reconstruction Act was passed by Congress over Johnson's veto. Civil authority in the former Confederate states was handed over to the northern military. Whites who had been prominent Confederate officials would be barred from the polls. Electoral lists were scrutinized: blacks would now be empowered to vote—a daring (and in some measure hypocritical) step as, outside New England, most northern states did not allow African Americans to vote.

The effort to reconstruct the South might well have succeeded, and much was actually achieved: the percentage of black children in schools went from approximately zero in 1860 to 40 percent in 1876. Four thousand southern schools now employed nine thousand teachers, half of them black. A southern Republican Party likewise began to take shape, and blacks joined it en masse. (In 1868, had it not been for African-American voters, 500,000 of whom had joined the Republican Party, Grant would not have secured a majority of the popular vote.) Many southern whites joined it also, including some prudent members of the old planter elites, such as the ineffable General Beauregard of Fort Sumter fame.

But for all of this to continue, two things would have had to happen: first, as has been said, the creation of a propertied black peasantry at the expense of an expropriated planter class, and second, that northern Radical Republicans not give up on their project.

In the end, neither of these two things happened. Land was not redivided, and as one consequence the South's economy, relatively speaking, fell into prolonged doldrums that would last for about a century. Another consequence was that blacks—and poor whites—fell into the "crop lien" system, which mortgaged future harvests against contemporary loans, lent out at usurious rates by local country stores, themselves dependent on the good will of their richer landed neighbors.

Driven to plant only cotton in their (futile) effort to clear themselves of debt, these micro-growers exhausted the soil and steadily worsened their own standard of living.

*****

This adverse restructuring of southern economic life—which, for all its faults, had been involved in a modern cash nexus before the war—was one half of the problem; the other half was the fading of interest in the North about what was happening in the South.

Grant, the former bloody-minded commander in chief of the Union armies, who was also a limpid autobiographer and, after 1868, a mediocre president, fitfully tried to restrain the vengeful Ku Klux Klan bands that had sprung up after the war, but he did not really oppose the return of the South to an approximation of the *status quo ante*. The most enlightened of the backward-looking southern elites, the self-styled "Redeemers," who generously preferred intimidation to murder, were accepted as the legitimate representatives of southern opinion, some of them in the early 1870s and the others after the presidential election of 1876 and the shameful but fateful agreement between Democrats and Republicans in 1877.

By this seedy back-room deal, the Republican magnates, who had secured a minority of the popular vote in the presidential election of 1876, and the Democratic leaders came together in what must surely have been a "smoke-filled room." What was said there is not precisely known, but the outline of the agreement was clear enough: Democrats would accept the Republican Rutherford Hayes as president and in exchange he would end the northern military presence in the South. Blacks were to be left to their own devices, while, conversely, an informal welfare system was set up in the North through the granting of pensions to Union soldiers.

In the name of race and of a perverse understanding of America's national purpose, the former Confederates were accepted with open arms by their northern foes. After all, were these southern white Anglo-

Saxon Protestants not descendants also of the Founding Fathers? Innumerable commemorations of aging veterans on innumerable battle sites sealed this race-bound national ingathering.

In 1866 George Washington Julian, a well-known abolitionist and "ever the principled idealist," laid it out plainly for his fellow congressmen: "The real trouble is that we hate the negro. It is not his ignorance that offends us, but his color . . . Of that fact I entertain no doubt whatsoever."[6] Sadly, in 1875, Walt Whitman, whose poem on the death of Lincoln is an American classic, proved him right: "The black domination, but little above the beasts," wrote Whitman, "viewed as a temporary, deserved punishment for [southern whites'] Slavery and Secession sins, may perhaps be admissible; but as a permanency of course is not to be considered for a moment."[7]

Racism runs deep in American life, and it is a sad instance of historical continuity that in the 1960s, when Martin Luther King Jr. proposed another black–white alliance to Lyndon Johnson, he too was to be disappointed. "[King] pointed out that, in the five Southern states that Johnson lost to Goldwater in 1964, fewer than forty per cent of eligible African-Americans were registered to vote. A voting-rights act would produce a coalition of blacks and white moderates, changing the electoral map of the South."[8] But it didn't.

Some three decades after the agreement of 1877, in his moving book *The Souls of Black Folk*, W. E. B. Du Bois, the premier African-American intellectual of his time (and the first African American to earn a Harvard Ph.D.), said of the relation of African Americans to the American nation's sense of self: "We have woven ourselves with the very warp and woof of this nation—we have fought their battles, shared their sorrows, mingled our blood with theirs, and generation after generation have pleaded with a headstrong, careless people to despise not Justice, Mercy, and Truth, lest the nation be smitten with a curse . . . Would America have been America without her Negro people?" The inclusive answer that history has given us is achingly obvious. But it was in 1877 that white Americans came closest to thinking that African Americans could indeed be excluded from their national consensus. In 1903 Thomas Wentworth Higginson, who had been a colonel in the first Negro regiment of the Union army during the Civil War (black regiments were commanded by white officers), published a *Reader's History of American Literature* whose only memorable feature is that no Afro-American text figures in that collection, not even Frederick Douglass's American classic of 1845, the narrative of his life.[9] Blacks were excluded from the American political community: in 1904, 47 percent of Louisiana's inhabitants were African Americans, but of these 660,000 people, only 1,342 had managed to have their names inserted on the local electoral rolls.[10]

Lynchings now became a distinctive southern habit. As far as we can tell (since our first statistics on this issue start in 1882) about one hundred blacks were lynched in the former Confederate states every year, with an average of 187 per year between 1889 and 1899, one-fourth of them on suspicion of rape. Mississippi and Alabama were the center of this populist justice, which was routinely accepted as normative, to the point that schoolchildren were often brought along to witness these communal murders.

As if purposefully to underscore this message of racial exclusion, also dating from this period is the inclusion of all other regional mythologies as constituent parts of America's national consciousnesses. This ingathering was not to make America a pluralist melting pot by any means: indeed, feelings against "new" immigrants from southern and eastern Europe (Jews and Italians most conspicuously) would rise steadily for some decades yet. The myth of the melting pot—an expression derived from a play by Israel Zangwill of 1908—was for decades precisely that: a myth. But in these same years, each subregion of the American nation did take on a particular connotation as a subcategory of a single and organic (and white!) Americanness. It is at this juncture that New England was suddenly reminded of its English roots and that Harvard, Yale, and Columbia decided that their institutions were nearly as elegant as England's older universities. (During his presidency of

Princeton, Woodrow Wilson, whose mother was English by birth, enthusiastically took up cycling in the lake country, so dear to Wordsworth.) It is likewise to this epoch that we owe the idea that English literature should be the cornerstone of a gentleman's general education. It was then also that publicists and authors trumpeted the idea that there were—and should be—unusually close ties between the American *grande bourgeoisie* and England's aristocratized elites, a tandem that in a later time would be best illustrated by the friendship that (supposedly) bound the Harvard-educated Franklin Roosevelt to Winston Churchill, the son of Lord Randolph Churchill, himself a scion of an American mother and an English ducal house.[11]

And what Harvard and Yale did for the eastern set, Mark Twain did nearly single-handedly for the Midwest: for those who thought New England was too close to Europe, the Midwest of Tom Sawyer and Huckleberry Finn now became a useful antidote. The legends of the West, with its manly, self-reliant cowboys and Indians, also took shape at this time in the dime novels of Erastus Beadle and the work of genuinely gifted western artists like Frederic Remington. (We can note here also that the first anti-Chinese riots in California date to 1877, and the first interdiction of Chinese immigration to 1882.)

So many regional fantasies, all of them archetypically American, which—despite their ostensible message—had very little to do with the life as it really was of New Englanders, Midwesterners, or inhabitants of the Far West, but which had by contrast a great deal to do with the unspoken and rejected other: the excluded African Americans who were now made to appear in letter, song, vaudeville, and later film as buffoonish characters, played, to make matters even more lamentable, by whites in blackface.

The outcome of the post-1877 American "*Ausgleich*" or "compromise" was a durable political solution. Had events unfolded differently —if the northern Republicans had stayed determined and had enfranchised a southern African-American yeomanry—a natural alliance might then have developed between southern blacks and northeastern immigrants. Here would have been the durable foundation of American social democracy in the next arc of America's history. But what developed instead was a wholly different cross-class alliance: between midwestern, rock-ribbed, white Protestant Republican farmers and northeastern capitalism. During the first—and contemporary—decades of the Third Republic in France, after 1870, Georges Clemenceau said that France had become a *"démocratie rurale."* So had America in a way, but it had done so by espousing high capitalism at the expense of new immigrants up to a point, and at the expense of African Americans without reserve.

*****

The foreign policy of the newly redefined, materialistically oriented, and exclusionary American republic was in this same image. As an ever more powerful society, the United States began to make its weight felt in the world, and this in a world that was ever more dominated by ideas of race and of the nation state.

So it was, for example, that at the end of the Civil War the United States made it clear to Napoleon III that it looked with extreme democratic disfavor on his desire to make Mexico, under the rule of Emperor Maximilian, a French-protected Catholic and Hispanic state that would block America's southern expansionist goals. (Manet made of Maximilian's execution one of his most celebrated canvases.)

Britain was likewise politely brought to heel and, as has been said, agreed to pay the United States an indemnity for damage to its commerce caused by Confederate cruisers that had been built in England. (*In the long alliance, tacit and explicit, of Britain and the United States, from the proclamation of the Monroe Doctrine in 1823 to Tony Blair's subservient participation in the war on Iraq, 1867 is the point at which America began its upward trajectory to the complete domination of this "special relationship," a locution invented by Winston Churchill that came into common use after 1956 when an irate America forced Anthony Eden to back down over the Anglo-French invasion of Egypt.*[12])

The year 1867 was significant in other ways: the United States purchased Alaska from the Russians and annexed the island of Midway, which would become the site of America's first great naval victory over Japanese militarism in June 1942. In 1870 Americans landed a few hundred men in Korea, near Seoul. Episodic thought was also given to the annexation of Santo Domingo and of the Virgin Islands, then under Danish jurisdiction.

Closer to home, and far more critical, was the continued and seemingly irreversible decline of Native Americans: in the first half of the nineteenth century, "the idea of the Indian as irremediably savage was the commonly accepted basis for thinking and about him," and matters worsened when pseudoscientific anthropology reinforced ancient prejudices, as in Josiah Nott's *Types of Mankind; or, Ethnological researches based upon the ancient monuments, paintings, etc.* (1856), which argued from the evidence of Indian skulls that Native Americans had overdeveloped organs of "animal propensity: and underdeveloped organs of intellect."[13] The end of the Civil War marked the beginning of the end of their saga, marked at times by battles that have remained (in)famous. Prominent among these conflicts was the revolt of the Sioux in September 1862, as an indirect effect of Minnesota's accession to statehood. Shocked by yet another wave of white immigration and its attendant broken promises, these Native Americans under the leadership of Little Crow rose up and murdered 700 white settlers. Retribution was swift. A local militia under the orders of a General Pope, who had been sent to the frontier for having lost a battle to the Confederates, declared the Sioux to be "maniacs" and "wild animals" who deserved to be treated as such. Lincoln chose to consider most of the captured warriors as prisoners of war. But he did sanction the execution of the leading Indian warriors, who were ingeniously executed: the cutting of a single rope propelled all 38 of them into the void. (This appears to be a record for mass executions in the United States, with the simultaneous execution of 35 African Americans as the sequel to the Denmark Vesey conspiracy in South Carolina in 1822 in second place. It bears recounting here that although multiple execution machines were proposed to the Jacobins in France during the Terror of 1793–1794, executions there were always carried out one by one, as if to underline the individual responsibility of the supposed culprits.)

Inexorably, the 400,000 Native Americans who were left in 1860 were pushed farther west. The 156 million acres that had been assigned to them in 1880 had fallen to 78 million by 1900.[14] They were starving now too, as their major source of food—the buffalo—vanished: these numbered 15 million in 1865 and only about one thousand in 1880. In California alone, 5,000 Native Americans were killed between 1850 (the year California gained statehood) and 1870, and the Indian population went from 150,000 to 30,000 in these same years.

Some of the killings were truly egregious: in 1864, for example, a former Methodist minister named J. M. Chivington presided over the slaughter of 133 Cheyenne Indians, 105 of them women and children, by a militia made up of unemployed miners, many of them drunk. Four years later, a congressional investigation concluded that this encounter had been a nearly unequaled example of barbarism: "Men, fleeing women, and infants were tortured in a way which would put to shame the savages of the interior of Africa."[15]

Many Americans moved by Darwinian thought reasoned that Native Americans were a lost cause, "a degraded relic of a decayed race." As a *New York Daily Graphic* editorialist pensively reflected, it wasn't clear that the Indian was "worth civilizing, even if he is capable of civilization . . . Were the money and effort wasted in trying to civilize the Indians wisely expended in reclaiming and educating the savages in our cities the world would be vastly better off in the end. The globe is none too large for the civilized races to occupy, and all others are doomed by a law that is irrevocable and that it is folly to resist."[16]

The victories of Indians over whites have often achieved renown, perhaps because they were so rare. In December 1866, for example, the Sioux Indians headed by Crazy Horse encircled and destroyed 82 soldiers under the command of a Captain Fetterman. Best known is the victory in June 1876 of the Native Americans over General George

Armstrong Custer, an impetuous officer promoted to the rank of brevet general at the age of twenty-three, proud of his two stars and proud also of his gallant curls, known to us by the many photographs for which he liked to pose. (In 1874 he also published a book entitled *My Life on the Plains* in order to justify his actions, which included violations of treaties he had made with Indians once gold had been discovered in the Black Hills.) By their commanding officer's folly, 264 hapless U.S. troops were trapped that day by thousands of Indians. "This is a good day to die," exclaimed one Indian leader to encourage his warriors. More typical, however, was the "battle" of Wounded Knee in December 1890, which was no battle at all, but a straightforward massacre in which 500 soldiers armed with rapid-firing Hotchkiss guns killed 146 Indians, including dozens of women and children, with dozens more dying of cold and misery shortly thereafter.[17]

The image of the frontier made familiar by films has fixed in our imagination a picture of the frontier that fits well with the happy and learned imaginings of Frederick Jackson Turner, a professor of history at Harvard. But we are more tempted today to think of a continuum between the settler expansionism in the West and the subsequent American imperialism in the Caribbean and the Far East.[18] And American imperialists saw the West in that very same light: in 1900 Theodore Roosevelt, in a new preface to his book *The Winning of the West*, defended America's recent acquisition of colonies in the Caribbean and the Pacific as "but a variant . . . of the great western movement." Senator Henry Cabot Lodge, the head of a committee investigating allegations of American war crimes in the Philippines, concurred: "Today, we do but continue the same movement." Thomas Bender has reminded us that in 1899 Buffalo Bill's Wild West Show "replaced its re-creation of Custer's Last Stand with one of the Battle of San Juan Hill in Cuba."[19] (Mention should be made that Buffalo Bill's traveling show and its semicaptive Indians attracted ten million spectators between 1883 and 1891.)

How to understand these imperialistic outbursts? One could, of course, connect them straightforwardly to the widespread racist and premodernist climate of the *late* nineteenth century in the North Atlantic world, a domineering spirit that stood in contradistinction to its near opposite, the rational positivism of parliamentarianism and international free trade of the *middle* of that century. In the later frame, white Americans in the Wild West would not be far removed in their mind-set from the British in India or the French in North Africa. The argument would point to a ubiquitous Eurocentric nationalism that was present everywhere and that in America was directed alternatively against Native Americans in the West and immigrants from southern and eastern Europe in the Northeast.

And yet, as regards the United States, this reasoning would fall short, if only because the most striking aspect of this first phase of America's high imperialism was the relative *uninvolvement* of the American public. Midway or Alaska (then known as Seward's Folly) was a faraway place of which most Americans were largely unaware. Significantly, American imperialists were very careful not to involve the public in their fantasies. Grant did indeed think about annexing Canada, but when it became obvious to him and others that an armed conflict with Britain would ensue, the project became immediately unthinkable. And even if bringing the Indians to heel pleased masses of newspaper readers, Sitting Bull was, if not a culture hero, at least no less a cultural fixture than Buffalo Bill, with whom he went on tour in the Wild West Show of 1885. True enough, Sitting Bull's reluctance to disavow the Indian ghost dance, which proclaimed the forthcoming return of the buffalo and the demise of all whites, did not please the Indian police, who shot him for resisting arrest in 1890. Nonetheless, the relationship of white Americans to Native Americans was much more complicated and intimate than that of the British to Indians in India, or the French to the Senegalese, or the Dutch to the Indonesians, or the Germans to the Herrero people, or the Australians to the Aborigines.

Empire had been a basic element of Britishness since the eighteenth century, and the Paris Colonial Exhibition of 1931 was also intended to make the French public aware of a Greater France beyond the seas.

Americans were far less involved in, and far less dependent for their collective sense of self on, their foreign conquests.

In the end, the most interesting characteristic of American imperialism in this era after the Civil War is the foreshadowing of what would be its distinctive characteristic in the following two decades—namely, that a small coterie of decision makers (or in recent presidential terminology, deciders) in the seats of power, and principally in Washington and New York, could propel the United States toward highly immoral goals about which the greater American public knew very little and which it might well have rejected had it been better informed.

CHAPTER 8
Robber Baron America

America's economic mutation in this age of high capitalism is one of the wonders of modern history: Appomattox in 1865 marked not just Lee's surrender to Grant, but Jefferson's to Hamilton as well. The effect of America's spectacular growth on its national sense of self was hardly surprising. As the United States had become the most economically powerful nation of the world by 1900, was it not inevitable, then—in an age of imperialism—that it should have also acquired an empire? In actual fact, however, American imperialism was far more the handiwork of a very narrow clique of ideologues and politicians in Washington than it was a response to some popular demand. In 1898 America's imperialist vocation was much closer to George W. Bush's duplicitous declaration of war on Iraq than it was to that moral and nationwide indignation against slavery in the 1850s that drove the nation to civil war. True enough, American prosperity in the 1880s and 1890s did create a new sense of national self, but one that in the main turned inward and not outward.

But first, a word about America's spectacular ability to create wealth and the ensuing shift in its sense of self. In 1860 America's manufactured goods had been less valuable than those of Britain, then the foremost industrial power in the world. But American industry at that time was also inferior to that of Germany and France. By 1903, however, its industrial production was greater than that of those three European countries put together. Between 1860 and 1900, in about one half of a human lifetime, the value of goods produced in the United States rose four-fold. Its industrial output quintupled. America had 30,000 miles of railways in 1860, 74,000 miles in 1875, and 200,000 miles in 1900. In

1860 America was still largely rural, but its urban growth after that was nothing less than phenomenal. The population of Paris trebled between 1780 and 1880, but Chicago grew from 30,000 habitants in 1850 to 110,000 in 1860 and 300,000 ten years later. By 1890 it numbered a million. In 1800 four-fifths of Americans were farmers; by 1880 that had already fallen to one-half.

America's industrial might changed, and so did America's ethnic configuration: in 1860 Americans—with the exception of blacks, of course—were still largely northern European in origin. But even before the Civil War, waves of immigrants had begun to pour into this industrializing nation. The Irish (who were Anglophone, to be sure, but Catholic and therefore suspect) came in the late 1840s and early 1850s. After them, by the 1880s, came others of every national and religious origin—Slavs, Latins, Russians, Lebanese—some of them Roman Catholic, some Greek Orthodox, some Jewish. Three million landed between 1860 and 1890, and after that they arrived at the rate of about a million every year. In 1880, 87 percent of the inhabitants of Chicago were either immigrants or the children of immigrants. Of the 62 million Europeans who left the old continent between 1815 and 1929, more than half headed for the United States.[1] In a single year, 1902, half a million of them landed in New York City alone.

Every aspect of American life was affected by these economic and demographic upheavals. More industrialized than ever, America remained at the heart of its popular culture deeply democratic, but it now developed a new hierarchy, social and professional structures that more than ever excluded blacks and most immigrants. At the top were gigantic industrial firms dominated by WASPs (White Anglo-Saxon Protestants), such as U.S. Steel, General Motors, Ford, Chrysler, Standard Oil, and Alcoa. Finding a place on the ladder of success was hard for immigrants and also hard for some members of America's older elites: "He was for sale in the open market," wrote Henry Adams in 1907 of his youthful self, and "so were many of his friends. All the world knew it, and knew too that they were cheap, to be bought for the price of a mechanic . . . The young man was required to impose himself, by the usual business methods, as a necessity on his elders, in order to compel them to buy him as an investment."[2] "Nowhere in the whole world," wrote Engels in 1886, "do they (the capitalists) come out so shamelessly and tyrannically as over there."[3]

The relationship of town to country in the United States was also transformed. What had been more or less self-sustaining townships (socially if not economically) were pulled into the vortex of the transformed nation, and "with the loss of community," writes Michael Sandel, "came an acute sense of dislocation." "We are unsettled to the very roots of our being," wrote Walter Lippmann in 1914.[4]

Innovation was now everywhere. Tocqueville had described the Americans of his day as ingenious tinkerers who were largely uninterested in either philosophy or pure scientific research, but never were these amateur American scientists more adept or more brilliant than in the 1890s and 1900s, when gifted jacks-of-all-trades like Thomas Alva Edison and Alexander Graham Bell took up where earlier inventors like Samuel F. B. Morse had left off. Prominent also in these years were other pragmatic innovators like Frederick Winslow Taylor, whose techniques of scientific management devalued skilled (and politically radical) workers and replaced them with more pliable middle-level managers. This would soon also be the age of Fordism, with industrial assembly lines in 1913 and the vertical integration of production, from iron mines and steel mills to the final product. In 1890 the U.S. patent office approved no fewer than 25,000 new procedures and inventions. Edison Electric, the ancestor of today's General Electric, employed a thousand workers in the early 1880s and ten times that many in 1892. In brief, American industrial might leaped forward, and that leap is a key to an understanding of America's sense of self vis-à-vis both its own past and the rest of the world.

Inevitably, economic and social transformations of this magnitude were difficult and even disastrous for millions of Americans, small producers especially. Economic cycles of booms and busts—which had already fascinated Marx—left millions of casualties by the roadside. In

1873, 1884, and 1893, hundreds of banks went under, as did the savings of millions. In some times and places, urban unemployment soared and reduced one worker in five to destitution. Violent deaths shot up, as it were, from 25 murders per million inhabitants in 1880 to more than 100 per million in 1900. What could small producers do when pitted by circumstance against the one percent of firms that controlled about one-third of the nation's industrial production, or against the celebrated "trusts" or holding companies, which had been invented in the 1880s by lawyers in the pay of the oil magnate John D. Rockefeller and the financier J. Pierpont Morgan? By 1912 the trusts controlled 112 firms of national size, whose aggregate value came to 22 billion dollars, that is to say, to one-fifth of America's national wealth. In 1899 Hazen Pingree, the governor of Michigan, denounced them for their corrupting effect "upon our national life, upon our citizenship, and upon the lives and characters of the men and women who are the real strength of our republic."[5] Many independent producers collapsed and gave up. Millions of farmers had settled on lands the federal government had allocated to them in the Homestead Act of 1862. By 1890, however, two-thirds of these settlers had abandoned their claims.[6]

*****

Critically, however, America's sense of national self, though transformed by these changes, was not shattered by them, as happened in many other countries at that time or since. From the fifteenth century and Henry the Navigator in Portugal, economic globalization had had winners and losers—the Dutch, for instance, were winners in the seventeenth century and losers in the nineteenth. But because America was by now at the heart of this relentless process of tooth and claw (though it still, misleadingly, appeared to be directed by London financiers), the situation of the United States at the end of the nineteenth century was of a very particular sort.

On the one hand, Americans were ill situated to protect themselves from the global economic juggernaut. In France, for example, when world prices declined for both agricultural and industrial goods, Jules Méline and his conservative allies—some of them modernizing republicans and some reactionary obscurantists—agreed to place very high customs duties on everything (hence the ubiquitous Méline tariff). The French were politically divided, some republicans, some royalists, but all agreed on this defensive economic strategy. But how to protect American grain producers from themselves? Regulating the rates charged by railways, which favored large agro-business, would help a bit, but not much.

Every other nation could—and did—have recourse to protectionism, oftentimes against the United States, and each in its own way (by varyingly protecting small farmers, large landlords, inefficient industries, or all of the above). But in the end, the fact was that every nation was forced in some measure to adapt its economic, social, political, and cultural life to a system whose head might be in London but whose heart and muscle were in the United States.

By and large, Germany managed its new globalized situation quite well economically, but at the cost of destabilizing its already precarious political equilibrium. France managed the transition to globalized economics poorly and soon rightly sensed that other countries were leaving it behind. Historians have written of "the German crisis in French thought," and the title of Edmond Demolins's book of 1890, *A quoi tient la supériorité des Anglo-Saxons?* (What explains the superiority of the Anglo-Saxons?) is eloquent as well.

Non-European states, of course, fared much worse. India lost whatever political autonomy it still had. Its industries withered away. China fell into a century of tormented and accelerated revolution and civil war. Mexico had to adjust its struggling economy to that of its triumphant northern neighbor. We can think also of Muslim countries from Morocco to Indonesia and of their catastrophic descent from 1750 to our own day. In the 1650s Muslim states still encompassed very large Christian minorities. But after 1715, decade by decade, Turkey gradually lost control of central Europe, southern Russia, and the Balkans. In 1830 the

French began their conquest of Algeria and in 1881 of Tunisia. In 1882 the British seized control of Egypt. By 1919, after the Treaty of Versailles, all Muslims the world over, with the exception of a much-diminished Turkey and a distant Iran and Afghanistan, would find themselves subjects of colonial empires that were run from London, Paris, Moscow, Rome, or The Hague—an intolerable affront that to this day marks their national and cultural consciousness. In Asia, only Japan managed to survive as a truly independent state: one whose limits, however, would soon be reached with the inhuman desolation of Hiroshima and Nagasaki.

Many Americans also suffered, as has been said, but their nation as a whole did not,[7] protected as it was by its newfound industrial might and by its openness and prosperity, which attracted eager, talented, often desperate immigrants determined to succeed. In Europe, economic dislocation led to the mushrooming of socialist parties; in Asia, to the birth of national movements. In America, by contrast, the hardships of late nineteenth-century life reinforced the nation's imagined sense of self. The contrast is striking between the response of workers in America and workers in France, although the rhythm of industrial change—and dislocation—was much lower in the *Grande Nation* than in the United States. In France, in response to unstoppable capitalistic change, the French working class (and it is quite proper to use that loaded term to describe French working people at this time) rallied to communitarian and even revolutionary ideological solutions. Very little of this occurred in the United States. An American Socialist party did come into being and in 1912 secured 6 percent of the vote. But in America there could not be an alliance of the far left and of the center, such as was symbolized by the partnership in France of Jean Jaurès and Léon Bourgeois in 1900, or in 1936 in the heady days of the Popular Front, of Edouard Daladier (a nationalist), Léon Blum (a socialist), and Maurice Thorez (a communist). In the 1936 American presidential election, the Socialist candidate polled only one percent of the vote.

Students of postcolonial literature have as their starting point the moment when the oral traditions of newly colonialized people either lapse completely or, at best, survive by inserting their arguments and form into European narrations, genres, and categories that are either imposed on or freely accepted by humbled but nonetheless admiring "natives." In a similar manner, the American domination of the planet's industrial narrative from 1900 onward, especially in the second half of the twentieth century—just as it made possible the expansion of America's traditional sense of national self—obliged all European nations to rethink their own traditions. Walter Benjamin reflected that in every era the attempt must be made to wrest tradition from a conformity that threatens to overpower it. He might have added that in every era losers have also had to rescue their national traditions from the conformity that a dominant power seeks to impose upon them.

*****

On the eastern side of the Atlantic, then, Marx, Liebknecht, and Rosa Luxemburg, or Lenin, Stalin, and Trotsky, and on the western shore of that ocean, the novels of Horatio Alger, whose specialty was to relate the successful social and economic lives and times of eager young men, full of good will and remarkably lucky as well. Mention must likewise be made of an ambiguously titled book published in 1900 by Andrew Carnegie, a self-made magnate and philanthropist, at once rapacious and generous: *The Gospel of Wealth*.

Money, then, and ever more money: but money in America as a neo-Calvinist proof of goodness and endeavor, and as a means to civic-minded generosity. Becoming rich was fine; only becoming rich and selfish was to be blamed. In 1804 the erudite and nationalist compiler of dictionaries Noah Webster had bitterly deplored that money as an end in itself had become the ruling passion of Americans. Andrew Jackson in 1837 had included greed with corruption as one of the dark passions that were threatening America. And Theodore Roosevelt thought much the same. America could never become a nation of "well-to-do hucksters."[8] "The commercial classes," he declared, "are only too likely to regard everything merely from the standpoint of 'Does it pay?' And many a merchant does not take part in politics because he is short-sighted enough to think that it will pay him better to attend purely to making money, and too selfish to be willing to undergo any trouble for the sake of abstract duty."[9] (It is a meaningful aspect of America's openness that by and large this frame of mind did not lapse into a sustained, public discourse of anti-Semitism.)

Through these decades of deep and swift social and economic change, the constancy of Americans' religious and economic thinking was striking. At the turn of the nineteenth century, Americans remained convinced that their social values were inscribed in (Protestant) human nature, and should therefore become a model for the entire world. Theodore Roosevelt admired Britain, but he also thought that America was well on its way to replacing Britain as the beacon of mankind. American culture in literature and painting had come to self-consciousness in the 1840s: it now entered a new phase of dominating self-confidence. Henry James's move from New York to London symbolized the antique, neo-aristocratic, irrelevant side of his sensibility.

Politically, the results of this consolidation of America's traditional national consciousness in rapidly changing times were mixed. Many voters, uneasy about the chaos of their lives, but unable to see their way out of private dilemmas through public involvement and public solution, simply dropped out of politics. American participation in presidential elections, which had been on the order of 80 percent in the mid-nineteenth century, fell to 73 percent in 1900 and 59 percent in 1912.[10] James Bryce, the British ambassador to Washington in 1884 and a gifted political commentator, remarked that American politics signified just about nothing: "Neither party has any principles, any distinctive tenets. Both have traditions. Both claim to have tendencies . . . All has been lost, except office or the hope of it."[11] Engels at much the same time (in 1891) put it thusly: "we find (there) two great gangs of political speculators, who alternately take possession of state power and exploit it by the most corrupt means for the most corrupt ends—and the nation is powerless against these two great cartels of politicians, who are ostensibly its servants, but in reality dominate and plunder it."[12]

A second characteristic of this epoch for Americans was the multiplicity of often irrelevant parapolitical solutions, or plainly apolitical and even privatist solutions, to private dilemmas (as in, again, Henry James's admiration for English country houses). The most promising of all opiates as an alternative to civic involvement or civic despair was consumerism, with the first elaborations of developments that have since become wholly familiar: department stores and conspicuous consumption, the wasteful status-driven expenditure made famous by Thorstein Veblen. The stunning vulgarity of the newly rich millionaires of that time with their "cottages" in Newport has remained legendary to our own day. Historians of New York have likewise underscored the number of private and public institutions that were created at this time in the city to support and dignify the local *nouveaux riches*: the Metropolitan Museum in 1880, the Metropolitan Opera in 1883, as well as a host of private clubs: the Union Club, the Union League, the Manhattan Club, the Knickerbocker Club, the Calumet, the Metropolitan, the Tuxedo, the New York Yacht Club, *et tutti quanti*.[13] And for the less favored, one could cite other diversionary pursuits: mass tourism and professional sports. (The first paid baseball team dates back to 1869, the first "World Series" to 1903, with a victory of the Boston Red Sox over the Pittsburgh Pirates, the latter named no doubt for their city fathers.)

Less escapist—but still apolitical—projects also mobilized the spectators of this Gilded Age. Of these the most elitist and therefore the most irrelevant projects focused on the reform of the judiciary and the creation of a professional, highly motivated bureaucracy on the European model. Roscoe Pound, a professor at Harvard Law School, was one of the principal movers of this plan, as was Henry Adams, a sometime professor of history in the same institution, who was much preoccupied by the dilution of the American working class by foreigners who could not be assimilated, burdened as they were by their "racial inertias." His brother, Charles Francis Adams Jr., showed him the way: "Universal Suffrage in plain English can only mean the government of ignorance and vice," he wrote. "It means a European, and especially Celtic, proletariat on the Atlantic coast; an African proletariat on the shores of the Gulf; and a Chinese proletariat on the Pacific."[14]

Others placed their hopes in a vast array of good causes: the moralization of political life, improvements of municipal government, antitrust legislation, slum clearance, sabbatarianism, agricultural cooperatives, eugenics and the biological improvement of the human race, the professionalization of the middle classes (a principle that sadly spilled over into W. E. B. Du Bois's hopes for "the talented tenth"), the Salvation Army, and the interdiction of demon drink and immigration. These last two projects came into their own after the First World War: the constitutional amendment establishing Prohibition took effect in 1920. In 1891 legislation was passed to weed out criminal and unhealthy immigrants; in 1903, anarchist or subversive immigrants; in 1917, illiterate immigrants; and in 1921 and 1924, immigrants in general.

Another serious question was women's suffrage, which was associated by its enemies with promiscuity, divorce, and national decline, but which was made the law of the land by the Nineteenth Amendment to the Constitution in 1920.

Solutions were largely directed to reshaping civil society from the inside, then, and with, them irrelevant parapolitical solutions, with, as a starter, the militarized repression of social unrest and "proletarian violence." In Chicago on May 4, 1886, during a strike by labor unions, a bomb killed seven policemen and wounded sixty-seven more. Authorities and employers predictably responded in kind. Several men were hanged for murder, labor unions were pushed out, and firms hired private detectives to enforce the new rules. In 1892 a pitched battle with guns, dynamite, and burning gasoline at a steel mill owned by Andrew Carnegie resulted in the death of three guards and ten strikers, followed by the mobilization of Pennsylvania's entire 8,000-man National Guard. The 1894 Pullman strike was broken up by 2,000 federal troops on orders from President Grover Cleveland, after the socialistically minded governor of Illinois, John Peter Altgeld, had refused to act.

Apolitical, parapolitical, and incompletely political solutions also. At stake here were populist associations, like the Farmers' Alliance of 1887 with its million members and the corresponding Colored Farmers' Alliance with a membership of 250,000. Populist parties also arose, in the Midwest especially, their adherents indignant at the high capitalism of eastern bankers but also driven by a nostalgia for the rural America of yesteryear with its small independent producers. Their cause does not attract our sympathy, as it did not appeal to the general public at the time: populists were often teetotalist antiurban and anti-Semitic. They were hostile to African Americans, who had courted their alliance. They were also indifferent to the needs of northeastern working people, often of immigrant origin, who in response voted in 1896 for the Republican ticket on the correct assumption that the populist enemies of their own class enemies (the northeastern moneyed establishment) were *not* their friends. Typically, in the impassioned speech that had won him the nomination of the Democratic Party in 1896, William Jennings Bryan, to use William Gladstone's contemporary language, had threatened the "classes" with the wrath of the "masses": "You shall not press down upon the brow of labor this crown of thorns; you shall not crucify mankind upon a cross of gold." But Bryan's invocation of the cross of gold turned out to be a defense of the use of more silver in American currency, a cause dear to western silver miners but with modest relevance to the condition of working people in Manhattan, Boston, Baltimore, or Philadelphia.

*****

In brief, the 1880s and 1890s were a period of rapid material change in which America's new global and economic preponderance could be seen as the necessary and determining cause of an ancient and now feasible drive to acquire an empire. Looking backward, Senator William J. Fulbright, in televised congressional hearings about the Vietnam War in 1966, gave an account of America's course since 1898: "The inconstancy of American foreign policy is not an accident but an expression of two distinct sides of the American character. Both are characterized by a kind of moralism, but one is the morality of decent instincts tempered by the knowledge of human imperfection and the other is the morality of absolute self-assurance fired by the crusading spirit."[15] This was a useful contribution to an understanding of America's imperialist, neo-Wilsonian trajectory after the Second World War, but it is not a particularly useful way to think about the imperialism of President William McKinley, which was a fabrication justified, but emphatically not caused, by perverse moralism.

Contrary to Fulbright's analysis, America in 1898 was not driven to imperial conquest by the morality of a "crusading spirit." It stumbled into it by default. Its imperialism was caused—or at least made possible—by the confusion of America's political debates, which allowed a small clique of politicians, armchair strategists, and unsavory press lords to manufacture a "small successful war" against the weakest and most isolated of Europe's colonial powers, namely Spain. McKinley's election in 1896 had had almost nothing to do with imperialism: the public did not care about that issue. But it had had a great deal to do with an unfocused unease about America's social trajectory.

In Europe, whose most vigorous nation states (Britain, Germany, Russia, France, and Italy) were deeply concerned about their place in the world economic system, and deeply engaged in the diplomatic jockeying that they saw as a life-and-death struggle in which the losers might lose everything, imperialism was an irresistible passion. Britain defined itself—and its capital—through empire. Pan-Germanism, pan-Slavism, and by imitation, pan-Turkism and Zionism were seen as the sine qua non of victory in some Darwinian fight for race survival. Very little of this impulse existed in the United States. In the previous century the extermination of Native Americans, and after some hesitation the annexation of Mexican territory, and the material destruction of the South by northern armies in 1864–1865 had indeed aroused national zeal and enthusiasm. Then, America's renewed national purpose had directly implied popular wars of imperialist conquest, and often in the name of some divinely sanctioned democratizing mission. But in opposition to this precedent, America's most blatant imperialist pursuits between 1898 and 1920 elicited public indifference or even, as shall be seen, resolute and widespread hostility.

The arguments that were used to justify America's imperialist pursuits and to rationalize isolated and locally determined acts of aggression (as in Hawaii) were of a classic sort, and it is useful to rehearse them as evidence of the constancy through the centuries of the American creed. But many found these cultural arguments unconvincing. In the end—and this needs to be constantly emphasized because this phenomenon is still with us—the salient aspect of America's imperialist venture at the turn of the nineteenth century was the ability of a small clique of individuals, centered on the president (in this case, McKinley, and after him, up to a point, Theodore Roosevelt), to hijack American public opinion to further their own sinister and aggressive acts.

CHAPTER 9
America Renewed and Debased

The last decades of the nineteenth century and the first years of the twentieth are the zenith of the *territorial* phase of American imperialism. In some sense, America's overseas expansion was wholly unsurprising: once the westward course of the United States had been completed, the nation was bound to find other outlets for its multiplying energies. Indeed, one can see this acquisition of external territory as the second of three historical phases: first came a westward continental move from colonial times to the 1880s; then this second territorial imperialism; and, in our own time, since Bretton Woods in 1944, the informal colonization of the entire planet's globalized economy.

The list of America's territorial acquisitions from 1880 to 1917 at the expense of its neighbors close and far is impressive. It includes Cuba, the Panama Canal, the Hawaiian islands, the Philippines, Puerto Rico, and, in last place by date and intrinsic importance, the Caribbean Virgin Islands, which were purchased for 20 million dollars from Denmark for fear that Germany might acquire them—purchased in 1917, one year after Woodrow Wilson announced that the United States had no use for any further acquisitions.[1] To be included also are various islands in the Pacific (Guam in 1898, Samoa in 1878 and 1899, in an agreement ratified by Britain and Germany if not by the Samoans, and Wake Island in 1899), which followed numerous earlier micro-conquests (such as the Jarvis, Baker, and Howland islets in 1857, Kingman Reef in 1858, and Midway in 1867). (Other countries—Britain, France, Germany, Italy, Japan—did much the same in this same epoch, but with some exceptions nothing much is left of their acquisitions today.) The continuous growth of the United States Navy also dates from the last decade of the nineteenth century; by 1917 it was the second most powerful fleet on earth. (Briefly, in 1865, with its 671 vessels, 74 of them ironclads, it had been the most powerful navy in the world, but it had fallen to almost nothing in the early 1880s.) Also from these years dates the modernization of America's army command structure, with the creation of an Army Staff College at Fort Leavenworth and an Army War College in Washington, D.C., charged with training its higher officer corps.

The easiest of these conquests was that of Puerto Rico. American soldiers landed there in 1898 without facing any opposition. In 1917 Congress declared the island to be an American territory whose inhabitants would be American citizens, with internal autonomy, but not entitled to vote in the sacrosanct presidential elections. (Puerto Ricans would soon be among the first of the 35 million Hispanics who migrated to the United States between 1960 and 2000, many of them to New York, then the capital of the twentieth century.)

The most scandalous of these conquests was in Panama, where the United States not only defeated yellow fever but also managed to build the canal, which the French engineer Ferdinand de Lesseps had failed to do though he had succeeded at Suez. The issue went back to 1903, when the Colombian senate rejected a treaty that had been negotiated by Colombia's chargé d'affaires in Washington. Theodore Roosevelt, incensed by this insolence, subsidized a Panamanian revolution organized by Philippe Bunau-Varilla, an habitué of Parisian salons. The insurrection was a great success, and Roosevelt immediately recognized the new Panamanian state, which then immediately ratified the treaty the Colombian senators had rejected. A few months before, Roosevelt had hailed the senators as statesmen; now he derided them as "inefficient bandits" and "contemptible little creatures." Roosevelt was adamant about his procedures: "If I had followed the traditional conservative methods," he wrote, "I would have submitted a dignified state paper of probably two hundred pages to Congress and the debates on it would have been going on yet; but I took the Canal Zone and let Congress debate; and while the debate goes on the Canal does also."[2] (The canal was opened in 1914. For some decades, its width regulated the size of American warships.)

The most lamentable of these American conquests was that of the Hawaiian archipelago. Some twenty years before their annexation, in 1869, Fukuzawa Yukichi, the Japanese Montesquieu and the author of a *Theory of Civilization*, which argued that Japan should model itself on European/American lines, wrote in praise of an independent and assimilating Hawaii, a model perhaps for his own homeland: "Their country is small, but independent: it governs an isolated part of the north Pacific. The only market on the islands is at Honolulu, a port of call for whalers. Other vessels come there also from England and the United States, and thanks to its trade with the comings and goings of ships, it is becoming more prosperous."[3]

But not for long.

Hawaii was perceived as a kind of paradise by the first Europeans who arrived there after Captain Cook's visit of 1774. With the Europeans' coming also came disease, which transformed the islands into a charnel house. Within decades, the 500,000 Hawaiians whose ancestors had arrived in the islands more than a millennium before were reduced by three-quarters.

Politically, their fate was no more enviable: the creation of a Hawaiian nation dates to 1810, and the arrival of the first missionaries and American sugar growers to 1830. In 1850 King Kamehameha III delegated his authority to an American prime minister, G. P. Judd, and in 1887 the United States received the right to create a naval base there, at Pearl Harbor, a useful complement to the islands of Midway and Samoa. In 1891, shocked by the importation of Asian laborers by sugar planters (who had been granted tariff exemptions by Congress in 1875), native Hawaiians decided to make one last stand and rallied to a nationalist monarch, Queen Liliuokalani. To no avail: in 1893 the planters organized a rebellion (they had, they thought, no choice: Congress having rescinded their tariff exemption in 1890, their only hope now was annexation of the islands by the United States); and their move succeeded, supported as it was by U.S. Marines, whose landing had been arranged by the American minister to Hawaii. Queen Liliuokalani was deposed. Frederick Douglass commented in 1894 on this event: "The stories afloat to blacken the character of the Queen do not deceive me . . . when we want the lands of other people, such people are guilty of every species of abomination and are not fit to live. In our conduct of today we are but repeating the treatment towards Mexico in the case of Texas."[4]

Texans had proclaimed their independence in 1836 but had had to wait until 1845 for the United States to decide to annex them; similarly, the Hawaiian coup did not reach its final fruition until 1898, when the United States declared Hawaii to be American soil, though not a state.

The most notorious of these conquests was in 1898 in Cuba, which had been in a state of endemic revolt against colonial Spain since 1868. This war occasioned two famous aphorisms. We owe the first to John Hay, who had become secretary of state after having been one of Lincoln's private secretaries. A conflict with decaying Spain would, he thought, be a "splendid little war." The other *bon mot* about this war we owe to the press baron of yellow journalism, William Randolph Hearst, now famous mostly because of *Citizen Kane*, a classic biographical film starring and directed by Orson Wells.

Hearst had received a disappointing letter from the reporter/artist Frederic Remington—known then and now for stylized and ennobling portraits of cowboys and Indians—whom he had sent to the island to provide the *New York Journal* with drawings of the war and its atrocities. (It was during this conflict that concentration camps were first devised, by the Spanish commandant General "Butcher" Weyler in 1895: the location of America's prison that is beyond the law, in Guantánamo, is not without irony as it was ostensibly to free the inmates of these camps in Cuba that the United States went to war with Spain.) Remington wrote that he had been unable to find either atrocities or much war, to which Hearst replied rather grandly that Remington should focus on the drawings, and that he, Hearst, would take care of the rest: "You furnish the pictures, and I'll furnish the war."

Fortunately for the imperialists, however, an American battleship then blew up in Havana harbor, probably because of deficient boilers, and 260 American sailors died. Here was an opportunity that could not be passed up. War with Spain was declared in late April 1899. The antiquated Spanish ships were easily destroyed wherever they dared to challenge the newer and mightier American vessels. On land, 18,000 men, including Colonel Theodore Roosevelt's legendary Rough Riders and some less legendary Hispanic and black troops—who at home had rioted in Tampa against discriminatory measures—did the rest. In truth, the situation was less promising than it seemed from afar, and the commanding American general, with many of his troops sick and disabled, was about to lift the siege of Santiago when suddenly, on August 12, 1898, the Spanish government gave up.

The Cuban rebels, many of whom had found refuge in the United States, especially in New York, had enthusiastically supported America's intervention, which they expected to lead to Cuba's independence: Congress, after all, had passed the "Teller Amendment" (to the declaration of war against Spain), which proclaimed the liberty of the island and renounced any possibility of an American annexation. A universally minded senator explained that American soldiers were not there to die for the sake of conquest. They were there instead "for humanity's sake . . . to aid a people who have suffered every form of tyranny and who have made a desperate struggle to be free."[5]

Political opinion in Washington's top circles soon shifted, however. In the wake of a debate that involved the spread of yellow fever, the American Senate in 1902 voted the "Platt Amendment," which unilaterally authorized the U.S. government to deny any intrusion by any foreign power in Cuba, and which thus made of the island an informal U.S. protectorate. Cubans were then coerced into making the amendment part of their constitution. American forces, which had been withdrawn, were sent back to Cuba in 1902 and again in 1906 and 1912. (For good measure, in 1904 the president proclaimed the "Roosevelt Corollary" to the Monroe Doctrine, which declared the entire Western Hemisphere to be a sphere of U.S. influence, and which Elihu Root in 1914 specifically described as an extension of Polk's messages of 1845 and 1848.)[6]

The bloodiest of America's colonial conquests was in the Philippines. What to do with these islands? The fight against the Spaniards who had been stationed there was very brief, in large part because the American invasion force included the Filipino rebel leader Emilio Aguinaldo, who had been struggling against Spain for some time and thought that the Americans were there to help him.

When that expectation was not fulfilled, Aguinaldo rebelled once more, but this time against his former allies. The ensuing war lasted for four years and was extremely brutal. It involved 200,000 American soldiers, of whom 4,000 died, as against the 2,500 lost in Cuba (only 400 of them from battle deaths). Estimates of the number of local victims in the Philippines vary between 50,000 and 200,000.[7] In 1901 an American general reported that the island of Luzon alone had lost one-fifth of its 600,000 inhabitants.

This war, like all conflicts that oppose regular troops to armed civilian bands, had broad "collateral" effect. The Spanish concentration camps in Cuba had shocked American opinion, but American camps were soon set up to house Filipino prisoners. Entire villages were destroyed. Captured guerrilla fighters were routinely murdered. General Arthur MacArthur (whose son Douglas would outshine his father's fleeting fame) was dismayed by the turn of events: "I have been reluctantly compelled to believe that the Filipino masses are loyal to Aguinaldo and the government which he heads." This epiphany did not keep him from responding to an investigating senator who asked him if the campaign had been a war of slaughter: "No, it has been the most legitimate and humane war ever conducted on the face of the earth."[8]

*****

The arguments used to legitimate annexation, colonial war, and collateral damage were familiar, and it will be useful to rehearse them once again, not because they stand as causes of America's imperialist burst, but, as has been said, because they speak to the extraordinary durability of America's self-image. The arguments that define Frenchness or Britishness today have very little to do with those that were invoked by British or French apologists of empire a century ago, not to mention those that were used to justify the birth of those two nations. But the constancy of American arguments is one of the defining aspects of American history. What was said then is still often said today to justify George W. Bush's war of conquest.

One of the most common arguments then used revolved around the notion of American innocence and of the dire threats that malevolent forces the world over might bring to bear on the fate of God's almost chosen people. In 1775 Benedict Arnold, who would soon betray the cause that had made him famous, reasoned that with "a due regard to our own defense" the rebellious Yankees would have to invade Canada. In 1846 it was to protect Texas that the United States had to invade Mexico, and then had to annex California. And so it was that in 1898 some American pundits assumed that Hawaii was the only forward post that nature had afforded to Americans to protect the California coast, and a congressman named Kirkpatrick concluded therefrom that annexation of the islands was a moral imperative. He then went on in a way that Californians might well have resented: the United States needed Hawaii in 1898 far more than it had needed California in 1845. In Congress's upper chamber, Senator Allen proposed the precautionary annexation of all the Caribbean islands, starting with Cuba.[9] One thing necessarily led to the other, and some imaginative imperialists urged a forward policy on China also: Would not the Philippines provide an ideal base for such a move?

American innocence was ever threatened, though perhaps now more than ever, and amended also to strike a new Darwinian note: the defense of American innocence had now become license to aggress with impunity against nations deemed amoral or immoral. For Admiral Mahan, an imperialist luminary to whom we will return, war was preferable to the passive acceptance of evil: "Not in universal harmony, nor in fond dreams of unbroken peace, rest now the best hopes of the world . . . Rather in the competition of interests, in that reviving sense of nationality . . . in the jealous determination of each people to provide first for its own . . . are to be heard the assurance that decay has not yet touched the majestic fabric erected by so many centuries of courageous battling."[10] (Even after the eruption of the World War in 1914, Mahan still reasoned that wars were no more than "an occasional excess.")[11]

Innocence and darkness, good and evil: such had always been America's situation. And fortunately, for many imperializing observers, America's power in a cruel world was now such that American victories would be nearly cost free: innocent America was so strong, and its neighbors so weak, that its expansion would be a kind of gravitational process. From its own sheer weight, the American planet would attract to itself minor moons and comets: America's geopolitics had their own special logic. America's success would be ensured by "political gravitation," a concept described in 1819 already by John Quincy Adams, who was then secretary of state, in a letter about Cuba—then a Spanish possession—to the American minister in Madrid. Cuba, explained Adams, would from the nature of things eventually and inevitably become American, as would in time all of Europe's provinces in the New World, from Canada to Patagonia.[12] Others, even more ambitious, saw Ireland succumbing to the same gravitational pull.

Racism was yet another imperialist argument, but now two-edged: white over black or brown for most observers, although some deemed it wise to wonder if Americans really wanted to include more nonwhites under their sovereignty. But two annexationist responses then came to mind. First, living under the American flag was not coterminous with the enjoyment of American citizenship: the Constitution did not follow the flag, as the Supreme Court would rule in 1901. Native Americans were not citizens, a useful model that could be easily applied in the Philippines or Cuba.

Second, was it not the responsibility of white and Protestant Americans to take the destinies of colored peoples in hand, and to substitute their own productive rule for the inefficacious rule of oppressive and cruel (Roman Catholic) Spaniards? With great foresight, at this very moment, W. E. B. Du Bois prophesied that as race would be the central issue of the twentieth century, American colonialism had to be understood as part of a much larger problem, namely that of racism in America itself.[13]

In the dominant white and propertied optic of the day, American imperialism was indeed part and parcel of a "Whig" and racist interpretation of history that set America's world expansion in the context of a racial March of Progress. To take "our little brown brothers" in charge was a moral imperative. In 1854 William H. Seward, then a senator, had opined that the extension of America's sovereignty was part of a law "of progress and development" that nature itself had imposed on the United States, where progress, he thought, would incidentally also mean commerce with California (the "Constantinople of American empire"), with "distant islands," and also with Asia. "Whatever nation shall put that commerce into full employment, and shall conduct it steadily with adequate expansion, will become necessarily the greatest of existing states: greater than any that has ever existed."[14] Theodore Roosevelt in 1904 developed this same reasoning with regard to the recognition of the new Panamanian state: America's aim was to bring law, order, and progress to the world:

It is not true that the United States feels any hunger or entertains any project as regards other nations in the Western Hemisphere save such as are for *their* welfare. All that this country desires is to see the neighboring countries stable, orderly, and prosperous. Any country whose people conduct themselves well can count upon our hearty friendship. If a nation shows that it knows how to act with reasonable efficiency and decency in political and social matters, if it keeps order and pays its obligations, it needs fear no interference from the United States.

John Hay agreed, but from an even loftier point of view: "No man, no party, can fight with any chance of final success against a cosmic tendency . . . against the spirit of the age [in a nation] whose object and purpose are the welfare of humanity."[15]

In 1897 Charles Francis Adams, then head of the Massachusetts Historical Society and a self-styled anti-imperialist, drew a parallel between Spain and Turkey, which was then embroiled in a war with Greece: "What is now taking place in Cuba is historical . . . I have been unable to see what either [Spain or Turkey] has contributed to the accumulated possession of the human race, or why both should not be classed among the many instances of arrested civilisation of a race, developing by degrees an irresistible tendency to retrogression."[16] Elihu Root, secretary of war and then of state from 1889 to 1904, and, like one of his successors, Henry Kissinger, a recipient of a Nobel Peace Prize, concurred: "Government does not depend on consent. The immutable laws of justice and humanity require that a people shall have government, that the weak shall be protected, that cruelty and lust shall be restrained, whether there be consent or not . . . There is no Philippine people."[17]

Senator Alfred Beveridge of Indiana, even better informed since he was speaking in January 1900 on his return from a trip to Manila, agreed: America had a responsibility to impose on others a better and fairer government, similar to its own, the likes of which the Filipinos were utterly unable to bring forth for themselves. John Stuart Mill (and Marx) had speculated that the subjection of a backward nation to a modern one, despite the obvious injustices it implied, might be a good thing all around, and Beveridge shared this apprehension: "What alchemy," he asked his colleagues, "will change the Oriental quality of [the Filipinos'] blood and set the self-governing currents of the American pouring through their Malay veins? How shall they, in the twinkling of an eye, be exalted to the heights of self-governing peoples which required a thousand years for us to reach, Anglo-Saxon though we are?"[18] (In the early 1890s, when he had not yet been elected to the Senate, Beveridge had been more worldly: "We will establish trading-posts throughout the world as distributing points for American products. We will cover the ocean with our merchant marine. Great colonies governing themselves, flying our flag and trading with us, will grow about our posts or trade.")[19]

Race-based pride was a motivation for annexation, as was again religion, and in ways that would already have seemed archaic to a more secularized Europe. Alfred Beveridge—again—opined that imperialism "is God's great purpose made manifest."[20] But few outside the United States would have dared to speak in this manner even at that time. Much depended on the theological nature of American Protestantism at the time (as shall later be seen in greater detail). Suffice it to say here that the New Theology dear to mainstream Protestants in 1900 was a synthesis of capitalist argument and eighteenth-century millenarianism.[21] (It is hardly coincidental that John D. Rockefeller was not just a ruthless and modernizing entrepreneur but a pious Baptist as well, and a generous contributor to the spread abroad of America's foreign missionaries, of whom there were approximately 5,000 in 1900 and 9,000 by 1915.)[22]

In that context it seemed self-evident to many that, just as backward nations were incapable of self-government, so were they incapable of understanding the message of the Christian God without some help, and in the case of the Philippines, in spite of the fact (or was it because of the fact?) that they had been wards of Spain for so long. So it was that in a letter to President McKinley Senator Orville Platt (soon to be famous for his Cuban amendment) solemnly warned: "God has placed upon this Government the solemn duty of providing for the people of these islands a government based upon the principle of liberty no matter how many difficulties the problem may present."[23]

*****

These varied, justifying, and typically American statements—on the relevance of self-government, motherhood (Beveridge: "The influence of the American mother has made the American Republic what it is; and it is in her that our national ideals dwell"),[24] divine blessing, race, and religion—are of interest: they show that America's points of ideological reference were remarkably steadfast, even in this period of rapid and worldwide economic transformation.

But culture and even religion in this instance were less a cause than a justification and a mask. What really mattered in 1898, as had been true with Jackson and with Polk, and as is true with George W. Bush today, was the will of the president and his close advisers. America did not go to war with Spain in 1898 because the public wanted it, but because President McKinley and a small group of like-minded advisers had decided on preemptive war. Robert Kagan has written that "The Spanish American War was, in short, an expression of whom the American people were and what they had made of their nation." This is most probably untrue: as Julius Pratt wrote in 1935 when America was in a less belligerent mood, "It seems safe to conclude, from the evidence available, that the only important business interests (other than the business of sensational journalism) that clamored for intervention in Cuba were certain of those directly or indirectly concerned in the Cuban sugar industry; that opposed to intervention were the influence of other parties (including at least one prominent sugar planter) whose business would suffer direct injury from the war and also the overwhelming preponderance of general business opinion."[25]

Of course justifications were always useful. Once war had been declared, Americans—deceived by a gutter press, patriotic as always, and subterraneously fascinated by violence as a solution to private and public ills—did indeed rally to the flag, as the manipulators of public opinion understood they would. Still, the fact was that those who actively pushed for war with Spain in early 1898, and then a few months later for the annexation of the Philippines, were a small group of people, largely apart from the great majority of Americans.

Few they were, but powerful as they included two presidents (McKinley and Roosevelt), press magnates (Hearst and Pulitzer), a handful of diplomats (Richard Oldney), intellectuals (Henry Adams and his brother Brooks), political stars (like one of John Hay's disciples, Henry Cabot Lodge, who would claim—falsely—that the explosion of the battleship Maine was "a gigantic murder" willfully perpetrated by the Spanish authorities),[26] and war theorists (like, once again, Alfred Thayer Mahan, the author in 1897 of a text that fascinated Theodore Roosevelt, *The Interests of America in Sea Power, Present and Future*).

To America's great credit, however, these voices were not unchallenged. In the past, too, during Jackson's paranoiac assault on the Cherokees, many dissenting voices had been raised (including that of Chief Justice John Marshall, a nationalist, but honest-minded man). Likewise, many had opposed Polk's war of conquest in Mexico. But this time the debate on America's war of imperial and territorial conquest, though muted once war began, was more sustained.

Again, the point must be made that it is illusory to suppose (as crude Marxist principle might imply) that America's imperial zeal at the end of the century resulted in a smooth transition from its preceding and newly found industrial might. The genius of American politics has seldom been that its political actions flow seamlessly outward from the *presence* of material or economic change. These appearances are deceiving: even in those instances where material and social forces seem determining for setting America's course as a nation among other nations, the issue of the moment often has at its root as a first and true cause some social dysfunction and an *absence* of change. In George Bush's America, for example, recent interventions in the Middle East have had little to do with to the international needs of American capitalism, but it has a great deal to do with social and economic problems such as fiscal deficits (and Saudi purchases of American bonds) or ecological irresponsibility (and an insatiable consumption of imported oil).

In 1900, popular demand for imperialist pursuits was much more subdued in America than in contemporary Europe, especially in Britain and Germany. Complementarily in America, protesting voices were very sharp: in June 1898, for example, William Jennings Bryan, the Democratic populist, wondered: "Is our national character so weak that we cannot withstand the temptation to appropriate the first piece of land that comes within our reach?"[27] Civil liberties would wane if militarization waxed. In the debate on the Senate floor, the senior senator from Massachusetts, George Hoar, reminded his colleagues: "Under the Declaration of Independence you cannot govern a foreign territory, a foreign people, another people than your own . . . you cannot subjugate them and govern them against their will, because you think it is for their good."[28] In 1898 in Boston and New York, opponents of war and annexation created an anti-imperialist league that assailed the nation's right to behave as McKinley said it could and should. Carl Schurz, a former ambassador of the United States to Spain, concurred, as did Mark Twain and a former president, Grover Cleveland, who during his time in office had refused to countenance the annexation of Hawaii. At Harvard, Charles Eliot Norton said of America: "She has lost her unique position as a leader in the progress of civilization, and has taken up her place simply as one of grasping and selfish nations of the present day."[29] William James, Norton's Harvard colleague, who had been one of Theodore Roosevelt's instructors, scolded his compatriots for worshiping false gods and for placing "bald and hollow abstractions" in the place of "an intensely living and concrete situation" (a political principle that as it happened dovetailed nicely with his own philosophical and pragmatic concerns).[30] James bitterly criticized the deeper roots of imperialism: "We gave the fighting instinct and the passion of mastery their outing . . . because we thought that . . . we could resume our permanent ideals and character when the fighting fit was done . . . God damn the United States for its vile conduct."[31] America, he thought, was "now openly engaged in crushing out the sacredest thing in this great human world—the attempt of a people long enslaved to . . . be free to follow its internal destinies according to its own ideals." McKinley and his satraps were selling the "ancient soul" of America.[32] A philosophically minded Brooklyn-based Unitarian minister wondered why American barbarism had bothered to go all the way to Luzon in order to display its true self: Hadn't it been enough that an Atlanta railway company organized an excursion train to witness the latest lynching in Georgia?[33]

The most interesting aspect of Captain Dreyfus's case, which took place in this same period, was not his condemnation (given the weight of anti-Semitism in European military circles at the time) but his subsequent exoneration by the courts. Similarly, the most important aspect of America's territorial imperialism is not that it existed but that it was in the main a failure. The idea of the American republic, born of a rebellious colony, now annexing some other nation, ran against the grain. Theodore Roosevelt himself was careful to distance himself from land grabs that European powers would have considered quite legitimate.[34]

America's Jeffersonian empire of liberty does often degenerate into an imperialism of liberty, but even that had clear limits for both the business-oriented or Hamiltonian right and the nascent "pre-social democratic" left. America, they argued, did not need an empire. Money could be made and principles be defended quite simply at home. "For a short while," wrote Robert Osgood half a century ago, a group of American realists "captured popular leadership under the banner of a missionary imperialism, but it never succeeded in breaking down isolationism or creating a concern in the general populace for the imperatives of power. Actually, it hindered the achievements of these objectives by associating with them a kind of egoism not in accord with America's basic hierarchy of values and thereby attaching to some valid realistic insights the stigma of a discredited imperialist élan."[35]

In the same mode, it matters that the aspect of McKinley's foreign policy that most pleased the public and is best remembered was John Hay's "open door" policy toward China. To be sure, the United States did take part in the military conquest of Beijing, which had been besieged by the so-called Boxer rebels. Nonetheless, the heart of Hay's argument was that the economic penetration of the Celestial Empire did not presuppose military conquest. (We should note in passing that Hay was a full century ahead of himself, as the China trade accounted for less than 2 percent of America's commerce at the time.)

It is also useful to consider in detail McKinley's own and repellent account of his decision to annex the Philippines. His first, indeed, his only concern was to emphasize that his role had been to carry out God's will (and not the people's will). That he could and should have consulted public opinion or the elected representatives of the American public seems not to have occurred to him. (This modern president of the United States—and ironically, the last one to have taken part in the Civil War—is much admired today by Karl Rove and by George W. Bush, another president who believes himself to have a personal link to his millenarian God.)

At first McKinley was perplexed. History had clearly shown, he assumed, that Spain was incapable of managing its empire, which was now no more than a shadow of its ancient but useless glory, its decay being the perfect historical antithesis to America's trajectory as a republic under God: "If we are to fulfill our destiny as a nation . . . giving them the benefits of a Christian civilization which has reached its highest development under our republican institutions" was a quasi-religious imperative. The Philippines had come to the United States "in the province of God" and by virtue of "his plan and methods for human progress." But was it also part of God's plan that America should keep this archipelago, which was after all already largely Christianized? America had not fought to conquer these islands, but they were now in American hands: "Avowing unreservedly the purpose which has animated all our effort, and still solicitous to adhere to it, we cannot be unmindful that, without any desire or design on our part, the war has brought us new duties and responsibilities which we must meet and discharge as becomes a great nation on whose growth and career from the beginning the Ruler of Nations has plainly written the high command and pledge of civilization." With as an extraordinary coda: "Incidental to our tenure in the Philippines is the commercial opportunity to which American statesmanship cannot be indifferent."[36]

In a celebrated interview with some Methodist clergymen in 1899, McKinley made what, if authentically recounted, is surely one of the most repellent statements ever made by an American president. One of his clerical visitors later recalled that McKinley told the group: "I walked the floor of the White House night after night until mid-night; and I am not ashamed to tell you, gentlemen, that I went down on my knees and prayed to the Almighty God for light and guidance more than one night. And one night late it came to me this way—I don't know how it was, but it came." Could America give the Philippines back to the Spaniards? No. Hand them over to America's commercial rivals, France or Germany? (He did not mention Britain.) No. Abandon the Filipinos to their own devices? And so his conclusion: "There was nothing left for us to do but to take them all and to educate the Filipinos, and uplift and Christianize them [he had seemingly forgotten that they were Roman Catholics], and by God's grace do the very best we could by them, as our fellow-men for whom Christ also died."[37]

PART III: 1912-2006

CHAPTER 10
Premonitions

After moving toward inclusion from the 1820s to the 1860s, the American national idea fell back toward exclusion from the late 1870s to 1900, in an age of spectacular material growth when concerns of equity and justice seemed less pressing. And yet it would be hasty to assume a close connection between America's economic circumstances and its imperialist pursuits: historically what mattered most was not the weight of public opinion, but the ability of a president, abetted by gutter journalists, public intellectuals, and theoreticians of empire, to involve rank-and-file Americans in his own demagogic program of war, conquest, and exclusion.

Of course, many cultural and historical arguments were then brought forward to justify these moves, and many Americans found the arguments convincing because these sinister excuses had been familiar to them and their forebears for over a century. But culture is often more a mask than a true cause: many Americans today, for example, will disguise their true feelings and argue from moral or religious principle although their choice of concerns and issues implies that their innermost feelings actually revolve around race and exclusion. In the words of the seventeenth-century French moralist La Rochefoucault, hypocrisy is the homage that vice pays to virtue. And the best deceivers of others are oftentimes those who have best deceived themselves.

The next period of American history, from 1910 to the 1960s—particularly the 1930s—is, with the 1770s and the 1860s, one of the sadder but also happier eras of American life. America's sense of self mutated once more: after 1900 it moved forward (very slowly) toward social democracy, which in Europe was a variant of socialism, but which, in the American context of shared origins, was more of a variant on widely held principles of common decency.

In the United States, socialism pure and simple (that is, the state ownership and bureaucratic regulation or management of the economy) was an impossible idea. As a doctrine, it ran against the grain of economic individualism that had been an American birthright from frontier times. Even in the headiest days of the New Deal, in 1936–1937, right and left were much closer in Washington than they were in Paris, London, or Madrid. An American Socialist Labor Party did come into existence in 1877, followed by a less doctrinaire Socialist Party founded in Indianapolis in 1901. The Socialist Party's presidential candidate, Eugene V. Debs, garnered 100,000 votes in 1900 and a million in 1912. At that time fifty American cities had socialist mayors. (Debs and about a thousand other people, incidentally, were imprisoned in 1918 under a new Sedition Act that criminalized overt opposition to the war.) Moreover, American socialism, enfeebled at birth, did no better as an adolescent and proved unable to withstand the prosperity of the 1920s. (Franklin Roosevelt once said that if he could place one book in the hands of every Russian communist, it would be the Sears, Roebuck catalog!) Parliamentary socialism had no future on American shores, and neither did one of international socialism's most extreme ideological variants, very popular in Latin countries, namely, revolutionary syndicalism. Big Bill Haywood (who would seek refuge in the Soviet Union) and his "Wobblies" (Industrial Workers of the World), like the French theoretician Georges Sorel, dreamed of a unified labor movement and a general strike that would bring capitalism to its knees, but nothing much came of that either.

If taken in its less doctrinal form to mean not socialism at all, however, but the right of the state seriously to regulate a civil society that remains basically structured on capitalist lines, then social democracy did have an American future. At stake here were strategies that included compulsory arbitration between employers and employees; state-by-state regulation of conditions of production, work, and marketing; the taxation of income; and the regulation and diminution of America's original sin: racism.

Politically, in the early decades of the twentieth century, an American style, modulated social democracy, did secure a wide—and until the First World War—widening audience. In the 1850s the nation's second political party system, born in the 1830s of Whigs and Democrats, had collapsed when the issue of slavery had irremediably divided the northern (inclusive) and southern (exclusive) ideas of America's moral purpose. The advent of social democracy did not have as profound an effect as had the antislavery movement. It did not shatter the third American party system, which since 1865 had opposed Republicans and Democrats, but it did serve to make clearer the outlines of a left and a right. It revivified the old debate between Hamiltonians and Jeffersonians, the new Hamiltonians being, like their predecessors, the partisans of a dynamic capitalism, whereas the new Jeffersonians were more concerned about the defense of "the little man." (One critical difference was that the Jeffersonians of yesteryear, unlike the social democrats of the 1930s, were hostile to a strong state, and took for granted the perpetuation of American's fundamental injustice—slavery—which the more consequential and individualistic Hamiltonians rejected.)

At stake in this long historical wave were the "New Nationalism" of Theodore Roosevelt, the New Freedom of Woodrow Wilson, the New Deal of Franklin Roosevelt (which the French socialist leader Léon Blum admired so much), the Fair Deal of Harry Truman, and the Great Society of Lyndon Johnson, whose failure would be the most critical event in the domestic history of the United States in the second half of the twentieth century.

Before reaching whatever coherence it would have in national politics in 1912, however, America's social democratic impulse first expressed itself, as has been said, through various voices, parapolitical and populist at first, or even wholly apolitical, as in the campaign for temperance. Inevitably, no fundamental changes could emerge from this fragmented subsoil, but "statehouse" progressivism was not wholly inconsequential, and it is fair to suppose that the Progressives "began to hammer out a program that would be realized to a large degree in the New Deal Era of 1932–68."[1] In many states, electoral primaries were instituted; municipal government improved; and even the corrupt city machines of yore sometimes took on a social coloration, as in Kansas City–St. Louis, where the Pendergast machine, for example, promoted the political career of Harry Truman, an honest man. In 1900 child labor was legal in most states, but it was almost unknown in most states by 1914. Progressives, in short, were quite active locally, if sometimes with misplaced or even baroque results. In the West, for example, much of their energy was dedicated to increasing the value of silver extracted from local mines; in the South, one of their objectives was to legalize segregation, which they thought would resolve the locals' urge to lynch African Americans.

*****

On the national scene, progressivism was first developed in a sustained political manner by Theodore Roosevelt, the imperialist and hero of the battle of San Juan Hill, who became a crowd-drawing vice presidential candidate and then president when McKinley was murdered in 1901. (Mark Hanna, the Republican party boss, was shocked: "Now look," he said, "that damned cowboy is president of the United States.")

Roosevelt had a sympathetic side and was a colorful figure. A graduate of Harvard College, this outdoorsman glorified the western landscape and did a great deal for conservation. He was also an avid reader of Zola's naturalist novels, which certainly was more than could have been said of most conservative French politicians of the time. Very keen on history and quite learned, Roosevelt had written two lively biographies, one of them of Gouverneur Morris, another colorful character who had been America's (one-legged) minister in Paris during the Terror and the lover of Madame Flahaut, whom he shared with Talleyrand, who was himself both lame and colorful.

Roosevelt in his life and thoughts carried many clichés to extreme, but he also loved to defy convention, as he did when he invited a (very mild-mannered) African-American leader, Booker T. Washington, to the White House. Among his intimates were Oscar Strauss, the Jewish secretary of commerce and labor; Charles Bonaparte, an American-born and Catholic descendant of Napoleon's brother Jerome Bonaparte (who, at the emperor's behest, had abandoned his Baltimore wife and family to become the king of Westphalia); and Gifford Pinchot, an ecologist, the father of the American natural park system, with whom Roosevelt went on week-long hikes in the California Sierras.

Roosevelt was an activist, but he was not what we would call politically correct. How to tame a mutinous crowd? By shooting ten or twelve of them. What to think of sentimental and unpractical reformers? They were more pernicious than professional criminals. Thomas Paine? "A filthy little atheist." Putting Indians to death? "I don't go so far as to think that the only good Indians are dead Indians, but I believe nine out of every ten are, and I shouldn't like to inquire too closely into the case of the tenth."

His entire career was a fluke: appointed undersecretary of the navy in 1896, he quit this post to organize a cavalry unit (the celebrated Rough Riders, whom he led to journalistic glory at the battle of San Juan Hill, which hill he left, or so he said, covered with "those damned Spanish dead."[2] The man embodied all the contradictions of his times, as he was simultaneously an ardent partisan of capitalism and a determined regulator of railway interests, or again, simultaneously a convinced democrat concerned with the little man and a convinced believer in the superiority of whites over all other races. He was also, of course, an ardent American imperialist, determined to make Latin America into an American preserve. His greatest achievement there was the creation of a subservient Panamanian state. He was much struck by the imperialist and warmongering writings of Alfred Thayer Mahan, to whom he wrote: "You stand head and shoulders above the rest of us!" In 1907, as a symbol of America's newfound might, he sent the "Great White Fleet" of sixteen battleships to show the flag around the world. Its stay in Yokohama Harbor drew special attention.

In deference to an unwritten rule that held that presidents, in imitation of George Washington, ought not to serve more than two terms, Roosevelt decided in 1908 (when he was only fifty years old) that, having had one term as the heir to McKinley and one in his own right, he would not run again. He also feared that the Republican Party stalwarts might block his nomination as their party's candidate. He had become more strident in his demand for reform, more critical of "malefactors of great wealth," and more keen on laws that would protect factory workers; these stands did not endear him to the movers and shakers of his party.[3]

His vice president and successor, William Howard Taft, was a jurist who later became not just chief justice of the Supreme Court but a bon vivant as well (he weighed more than 300 pounds). Matters between the new president and his former patron soon went from bad to worse. In 1910 an enraged Roosevelt (he was often enraged) decided to challenge Taft for the Republican nomination in the next presidential election. When the Republicans again nominated Taft, Roosevelt formed a new Progressive or Bull Moose Party and ran as its nominee. His hope was to destroy the existing party system, and he took himself very seriously, telling his new party's convention: "We stand at Armageddon . . . We battle for the Lord."[4] And indeed, it is one of the great sadnesses of American history that he did not succeed. After his electoral defeat (which was triggered by some wholly contingent and doctrinally irrelevant events), the political restlessness that had been stirring in America for twenty years failed to coalesce. If Roosevelt had won, a new party system would have come into being, and progressives of all hues would have come together; the old and conservative Republican Party led by Taft would presumably have gone its rightist way. Southern (conservative) Democrats and equally conservative Taftists would then have formed a new, united—and losing—coalition.

In his effort to unseat Taft, Roosevelt presented to the American public a new platform that in the main aimed, in Theda Skocpol's phrase, to "bring the state back in" and that, as has been explained by many historians, prefigured the drive toward a welfare state that we identify with the victory in 1932 of Theodore Roosevelt's distant cousin, Franklin Delano Roosevelt.[5] In a famous and the most radical speech of his career, which he gave in August 1910 at Osawatomie (where one of the martyrs of abolitionism, John Brown, had fought against the partisans of slavery in 1856, and which was in the heart of populist Kansas), Theodore Roosevelt laid out what his "New Nationalism" would be all about, much of it inspired by Herbert Croly's book *The Promise of American Life*, published in 1909, which made of the state the guarantor of "a morally [and] socially desirable distribution of wealth."[6] Industrialism and urbanism, Croly explained, had dissolved the older "natural" forms of social order and now needed to be restrained by a self-conscious and methodical policy of social control.[7] For Croly, nationality and community were completely compatible: "[The] nationalizing of American political, economic and social life was an essentially formative and enlightening political transformation. [America would become more of a democracy only as it became] more of a nation . . . in ideas, in institutions, and in spirits."[8]

Roosevelt's essential insight was that the federal government (and not just states or local municipalities) should become the regulator and guarantor of the public good. Libertarian Americans had feared governmental power, but Roosevelt wanted to use it instead: henceforth, the doings of the railway companies and the great industrial corporations of the day would be restrained, not by civic-minded managers, as so many (naïve) progressivists had assumed, but by federal administrators. In Franklin Roosevelt's words of the 1930s, good government was "in plain English" a "changed concept of the duty and responsibility of government toward economic life,"[9] and this was Theodore Roosevelt's point in 1912 as well. A graduated and equalizing income tax was a key element of his proposed system. The banking system was to be reformed and made more democratic, as was labor legislation. Roosevelt undertook to do something for African Americans. He came out in favor of women's suffrage. Of neocolonial imperialism he said very little. At

Osawatomie, Roosevelt dedicated about five minutes of a two-hour speech to foreign affairs. Of course, America would continue to play a role beyond its borders, but in the context of some kind of international policing: "Justice and fair dealing among nations rest upon principles identical with those which control justice and fair dealing among the individuals of which nations are composed, with the vital exception that each nation must do its own part in international police work . . . I should be heartily ashamed to see us wrong a weaker power, and I should hang my head forever if we tamely suffered wrong from a stronger power." And that was all: already, during his second term, Roosevelt had concluded that the Philippines were America's Achilles' heel.

By instinct, then, Roosevelt understood that a reformed domestic national purpose of inclusion implied a convergent foreign policy. He had earlier argued for soft words and a big stick. Now that he had chosen to speak more loudly at home, the use of force abroad could have little place in his system.

With Lyndon Johnson's decision not to run in 1968, the election of 1912 was—by what did *not* happen—the most important and unforeseeable of the presidential contests of the twentieth century. (Franklin Roosevelt's victory of 1932 in the middle of the Depression was hardly a surprise.) Theodore Roosevelt's defeat at the polls (Wilson won only 42 percent of the popular vote but received 82 percent of the votes in the Electoral College) was the turning point in American history at which America, alas, did not turn.

A Roosevelt victory in 1912 would have transformed the American party system and also—or so we can speculate—the course of world history. Roosevelt, at once an American nationalist, a confirmed democrat, and an Anglophile, would have been from the first openly sympathetic to the Allied cause, and might well have brought America into the war earlier, perhaps even in 1915 with the sinking by a German submarine of the unarmed passenger ship the *Lusitania* with its 1,199 victims, of whom 128 were Americans. (It is relevant here, first, that at the international conference at Algeciras in 1906, Roosevelt had strongly supported Britain and

France against the imperial German claims, and second, that Wilson allowed it to be said in the presidential campaign of 1916 that his opponent, Charles Evan Hughes, was the more likely of the two rivals to involve America in the war.) An American intervention in 1915 would surely have entailed an Allied victory in 1916 or 1917, or better yet, a negotiated settlement, as the Central Powers would soon have recognized that they could not win. In brief, the end of this devastating and senseless conflict would not have entailed the destruction of the German, Austro-Hungarian, Russian, and Ottoman empires, whose succession—as regards the last of these in any case—has yet to be settled. Europe would have been spared the Shoah, and the Middle East its current torments.

But Roosevelt failed, and the third American party system, born of the Civil War, unfortunately survived.

*****

The reformist impulse did in some measure continue, however. It did not altogether vanish even from the old Taftist Republican Party, and it made some inroads on the Democratic side as well. William Jennings Bryan, the Democratic champion of 1896, who had then not carried a single northeastern state, now argued for an income tax, taxes on corporations, greater regulation of the stock exchange, and limits on campaign financing (as money was already becoming what it is today, the overarching malediction of America's political life). In 1904 Bryan welcomed the fact that the trust magnates were not for the Democratic Party, but against it.

It is hazardous to say of Bryan's successful successor as Republican candidate, Woodrow Wilson, that he too was a determined precursor of Franklin Roosevelt's social democracy (even though he appointed Roosevelt undersecretary of the navy). And yet there is something to this idea, even if the great blind spot in Wilson's world view was the one that is most critically relevant to social justice in America, namely race.

Born as he was in Virginia in 1856, Wilson was marked by the history and fate of the Old South, and in the main did almost nothing to promote the civil rights of African Americans. (Once war had been declared in 1917, he did point out that lynching blacks in America was an unfortunate custom, especially as the Germans were at that same moment, he said, lynching Allied armies. But he went no further with this curious thought.) In 1919 W. E. B. Du Bois, on his return from Paris, where he had vainly tried to plead the cause of blacks, both American and colonialized, rightly wrote that Wilson at Versailles had "never at any single moment meant to include in his Democracy" black Americans or the nonwhite people of the world. Harold Nicolson in his account of the preparations for the Treaty of Versailles, at which he had been present, ironically commented on the dread felt by the American delegation at "the terrific theory of the equality of the white man with the black."[10] Of D. W. Griffith's 1915 film *Birth of a Nation*, whose hateful political message was that African Americans did not want to be free and that emancipation had been a dangerous disaster, Wilson, who had dismissed most of the government's black employees and imposed rigid segregation in Washington's federal offices, had said: "It is like writing history with lightning, and my only regret is that it is all so terribly true." In a way, this was not all that surprising a judgment as he himself was quoted in the film several times in praise of the Ku Klux Klan and in his judgment of Reconstruction, which had been, he thought, "a veritable overthrow of civilization in the South."[11] In a typically racist manner, Wilson was also quite convinced that American blacks—like all other blacks—were incapable of "self-government," which mattered to him even more than the principle, as he put it, of "national self-determination." Wilson was a reformer who had no difficulty in leaving the unreformed American South as it was.

But in other domains, this (mediocre) historian and former president of Princeton University and governor of New Jersey did put on the books various measures that had long since been on the progressive agenda. As Herbert Croly had provided Theodore Roosevelt with much of his program, Louis Brandeis, a brilliant—and Jewish—graduate of the Harvard Law School, did the same for Wilson and his program of New Freedom, which was a counterpart to Roosevelt's New Nationalism.

Though none too clearly, Wilson did have some awareness at least that the America of his times would have to be governed differently. "Are we even now, in fact, a nation?" he had asked in 1897, and to this he had answered that, yes, the United States was a nation because Americans were attached to their "idea" of a nation, but that they still had to find the principles that would ensure the practical development of their national idea.[12] In an article on what American ideals should be, Wilson even went so far as to wonder—daringly—whether the creation of a true national community did not depend on the existence of some equalization of economic and social life.[13] Roosevelt had wanted state regulation of the trusts that dominated the American economy, but Wilson claimed to be intent on destroying them altogether in order to ensure the more democratic management of capitalism. Wilson also worked to lower tariffs, as he assumed—rightly—that the high tariffs of his day benefited the entrenched rich and made consumer goods more expensive for the poor. It was under his watch also that the Federal Reserve System was set up in December 1913, with the idea of stabilizing the banking system and making it fairer—which it did, but only up to a point, as the buying and selling of stocks was left as it had been, as many Americans would discover to their chagrin or despair in the early 1930s. An income tax was likewise levied by the federal government, with a one percent tax on incomes over $4,000, and 6 percent for the super-rich with incomes over half a million. When set in comparative context, Wilson's program was reminiscent of William Gladstone's (whom Wilson admired and whose photograph was on his desk in the White House). Like the Grand Old Man of British politics, Wilson aimed to put the interest of the "masses" over those of the "classes," and in historical context, this broad aim does stand as a (hazy) prefiguration of twentieth-century social democracy.

It is, however, deeply revealing that, in the end, the essence of Wilson's experiment in state-guided or "state-reformed" capitalism proved to be ephemeral war measures that were justified by the exigencies of the Great War, which the United States entered in April 1917 not as an ally but as "an associate" of the British and the French.

Suddenly the budget of the federal government, which had seldom risen over a billion dollars, shot up: in the few months that followed (the war ended nineteen months later on November 11, 1918), the United States taxed, borrowed, and spent 32 billion dollars. New taxes were levied on income and estates. "War Boards" were set up to manage the railway system. Bernard Baruch was charged with the allocation of raw materials. In April 1918, critically, and of great consequence as a subsequent social democratic model, Baruch was authorized to resolve industrial conflicts between workers and bosses. (From this period dates the spread to private industry of the forty-hour work week, which had long since existed for federal employees.) Most visible and most popular was the regulation of America's food supply. Here, Herbert Hoover did wonders as a director of the American Relief Administration, which was charged to alleviate the misery of displaced and starving Europeans, especially in Belgium. (Both parties would be eager to nominate Hoover as a presidential candidate in 1920. In American folklore, "remembering starving Belgian babies" became an injunction and a warning to American children who disdained their familial food.)

A darker aspect of reformed governmental practice was the humiliation of many American citizens of German origin. A "Committee on Public Information" disseminated 75 million books, articles, and pamphlets encouraging Americans to support U.S. participation in the war. Many German-language newspapers were shut down. Sauerkraut was renamed Liberty Cabbage, as in a later incarnation French fries would (momentarily) become Freedom Fries. The sunny side of this patriotic frenzy was that the exclusion of Germanness allowed the further and countervailing integration of the new non-German immigrants from eastern and southern Europe.

Within this newfound enthusiasm, many of the classic themes of both the Benevolent Empire of the 1830s and the more recent progressive spirit rose to the fore once again: prohibitionism made gains (many brewers were of German origin). More importantly and durably, so did the push for women's rights: in the context of wartime solidarity, Americans gradually came to accept the idea that female suffrage would be enacted as a reward for the patriotic efforts of women workers and women nurses at the front. (Wilson, as it happens, was hostile to this last reform, which Roosevelt had endorsed.) It was ratified in 1920 as the Nineteenth Amendment to the Constitution. Women, we can note in passing, had been voting in state elections in Wyoming since 1890, its first year of statehood.

Another unintended effect of war fever concerned the situation of African Americans. In the short run, nothing seemed to have changed at all. Lynchings went on as before. In one month, May 1918, eleven blacks were lynched in Georgia; in the southern states as a whole, seventy more were savagely put to death in 1919, many of them war veterans.[14] In Chicago, where a white mob stoned to death a young black swimmer who had drifted toward a beach reserved for whites, fifteen whites and twenty-three blacks died in ensuing riots that left a thousand people homeless.

In the longer run, however, what mattered more was the second great *Völkerwanderung* of that age: after the millions of immigrants from southern and central Europe, now the migrants were hundreds of thousands of African Americans. The two migrations were complements of one another: when the Great War kept Europeans from crossing the ocean, blacks found it opportune to cross the Mason-Dixon Line instead. In 1910 no northern state had a black population of more than 5 percent. Forty years later, blacks were no longer a majority of any state (as they had been in South Carolina from the early eighteenth century), but they were now present everywhere, their humiliation and second-class status a living reproach not just to Southerners but to all of America.

*****

Inclusion and exclusion. These two themes have always been closely related in American history, at times in tandem, as with the destruction of Native Americans during the libertarian War of Independence, or again, as in 1863–1865, when the end of slavery coincided with the excluding impulse to destroy southern society and property in what had become a war of aggression. (A central argument of this essay is that it is these varying proximities of policy that give American presidents so much leeway for good or evil.)

One other rule of American history has been that there can be no durable rebirth of America's universalist spirit, especially as regards foreign policy, without some antecedent transformation of America's social and cultural structures. Such changes, of course, Wilson did not achieve. Indeed, on the critical issue of race, he was not only unwilling to foster change, he was in fact determined to oppose it. So it was that his "New Freedom" remained in large part a cruel snare: the balance between state and civil society in America remained basically unaltered, and, simultaneously, much of Wilson's foreign policy turned to ashes. "My dream," he declared on July 4, 1914, "is that as the years go on and the world knows more and more of America it . . . will turn to America for those moral inspirations which lie at the basis of all freedoms . . . that America will come into the full light of day when all shall know that she puts human rights above all other rights and that her flag is the flag not only of America but of humanity."[15] That is what the world certainly thought for a while in 1917–1919. By 1920, however, nothing of this was left at all. "It would be the irony of fate," Wilson had written in 1913, "if my administration had to deal chiefly with foreign affairs."[16] But that is indeed what happened, and not with the results he would have liked.

In Europe, on the eve of the Great War, many political figures—the French socialist Jean Jaurès most prominently—had a tense and lively sense of the dangers inherent in the nationalist passions of every country. The imminence of war in 1913 was understood by those who feared it, by those who were resigned to its coming, and by those who wanted it, as appears from the varying speeches of Lloyd George, of Alfred von Tirpitz, who commanded the German Imperial Fleet, and of Georges Clemenceau, who was to become the French prime minister in 1917.

By contrast, caught up as they were in America's internal situation by the likes of Roosevelt's New Nationalism and Wilson's New Freedom, Americans paid little attention to foreign policy, which was not a critical issue in the 1912 election. The outbreak of the war in Europe came as a surprise to Americans and reinforced their feeling that the most sensible thing they or their forbears had ever done had been to leave the Old Continent, beset as it was by undemocratic tradition and by warring aristocrats. The *Wabash Plain Dealer*, an Indiana newspaper, suggested that never had Americans "appreciated so keenly . . . the foresight exercised by our forefathers in emigrating from Europe."[17] Jefferson had warned of the "broils of Europe" and his countrymen now concurred in that view.

For Wilson, who was mindful of the ravages caused by the Civil War, another total war (the likes of which Europeans had forgotten about by 1914, as they had not experienced such a conflict since the seventeenth century) had also been unthinkable. It had seemed to Wilson and to most Americans that the march of history and the goals that were common to "enlightened humanity" would make war ever more unlikely. The Carnegie Endowment for International Peace, they thought, would surely gain converts. In olden times, peace had depended—uncertainly—on a complex international equilibrium worked out by diplomats and rulers. But henceforth, or so it was assumed before 1914, peace would depend on the experience of men of good will rather than on complex agreements drafted in secret by "sophisticated men." And once again America would show the way: "I do not know," Wilson said a week before the outbreak of war in Europe, "that there will ever be a declaration of independence or of grievances for mankind, but I believe that if any such doctrine is ever drawn it will be drawn in the spirit of the Declaration of Independence, and that America has lifted high the light which will shine unto all generations and guide the feet of mankind to the goal of justice and liberty and peace."[18]

*****

Chronologically speaking, the war in Europe was the greatest diplomatic problem that Wilson had had to face, but the first focus of American national feeling in foreign affairs under his administration had concerned Latin America.

In this domain, Wilson had worked closely with William Jennings Bryan, the populist known as the Great Commoner, and the defeated Democratic presidential candidate in 1896, 1900, and 1908, whom he appointed secretary of state. In this period Bryan had two concerns: after 1914, he aimed to keep America out of the war in Europe, and from 1912 onward, he strove to reverse America's policy of nationalistic domination in Latin America. Theodore Roosevelt's muscular and aggressive policy had repelled him. Bryan had indeed volunteered as a soldier in 1898, once war with Spain had broken out. But he had resigned from the army on the day the war ended, later explaining that his humanitarian reason for having volunteered at all had been to free Cuba from Old Spain's malevolent colonial domination. America should not, he thought, simply substitute its own rule, however beneficial it might be, for that of the defeated colonial power. Force should have no role in the relations of the United States with its neighbors. The United States certainly had an exemplary role to play, but one that might be compared to the beneficent effects of the sun "whose genial rays constantly coax the buried seed into life, and clothe the earth, first with verdure, and afterward with ripened grain; while violence is the occasional tempest, which can ruin, but cannot give life." In 1910 Bryan stated that America should tell the world that it would never use its fleet to bombard even the most insolvent debtor nations.[19]

Nevertheless, in some measure at least, Bryan had to go on with Taft's "dollar diplomacy," which had secured wide support from business. Between American and British capitalism—if these were to be his only options—he would favor the American variety. In July 1913 he resigned himself to forcing on Nicaragua an agreement closely reminiscent of the one that McKinley had imposed on Cuba. Nicaragua now became a de facto American protectorate.

Mexico was an even bigger problem. In the sequel to the tormented politics that had brought down the pro-business, pro-American, and antipeasant policies of General Porfirio Diaz, a military coup led by General Victoriano Huerta successfully overthrew—and murdered—the elected president of the Mexican republic, Francisco Madero. (*Diaz, the reactionary, meanwhile, had fled to Paris, where as it happens, the modernist and Mexican painter Diego Rivera also lived at that time.*) Wilson was utterly opposed to recognizing the legality of Huerta's regime, which, to add insult to injury from an American point of view, had received the support of the British. On some spurious grounds, Wilson ordered American troops to occupy the Mexican port of Vera Cruz.

More tormented Mexican politics ensued, with coups and counter-coups: the exile of Huerta; a raid on an American border town by Pancho Villa, who oscillated uneasily between revolution and banditry; and an (unsuccessful) American military incursion into northern Mexico led by General John Joseph Pershing, who would soon take command of American troops in France. In the words of a French historian of the region, "by wanting at all costs to make Mexico a part of a suitable world order, where she too would elect to be ruled by some 'good men,' Wilson paradoxically became one of the most interventionist and imperialist of all American presidents."[20]

Of great interest in its own right, Wilson's disastrous Mexican policy holds our attention for two reasons: for what it tells us about Wilson's methods, and for what it shows us about his goals. Theodore Roosevelt had hesitated between progressivism and nationalism, and had tried to present these divergent aims as two sides of a single coin. Wilson was ostensibly more intent on a universalist agenda, but he did not lose sight of America's national purpose. Just as Lincoln had aimed to make of the universalist principles of America's Declaration of Independence a charter that would apply to the nation as a whole, Wilson aimed to make it the basic principle of a new world order.

The Mexican episode also shows how willful Wilson (whom the French likened to a Presbyterian minister) was prone to be. Though cautious and deliberate in forming his opinions, Wilson was unreasonably tenacious in holding on to them once they had been formed. He might listen patiently to a variety of advice, but "on crucial issues his seemingly unquestioning acceptance of the views of others was more the pose of impartiality than the reality of acquiescence . . . no President was ever in more complete control of the conduct of the nation's foreign affairs than Woodrow Wilson."[21]

Jackson, Polk, and McKinley twisted American universalism to fit their selfish pursuits; Wilson and Franklin Roosevelt, by contrast, manipulated their nationalist, isolationist opponents to an opposite end. But once again the message must be that the structures of American government give presidents and presidential advisers full control of the ship of state—for worse in 1847, 1898, and 2001, and for better in social democratic and pre-social democratic America.

*****

Wilson's interventionism in the war in Europe was slow in its gestation. Americans in 1914–1915 were either determined to remain aloof or inclined to wait for their hour as mediator, when the European powers, exhausted by war, would turn to them. Wilson at first advised his fellow citizens to be impartial toward the combatant nations in both thought and deed.

But this material and mental neutralism soon became impossible. America and Britain—especially as regarded their upper bourgeoisie—were in many critical ways alike. Personal, familial, financial, and commercial ties between the two countries were very close. Was not the English Magna Carta the fountainhead of American freedom? (When the Kaiser's brother, Prince Henry of Prussia, was given an honorary degree at Harvard in 1902, the university's president, Charles W. Eliot, a Germanophobe Anglophile, had ironically welcomed this "grandson of Queen Victoria, the ruler of a country whose dedication to freedom we much admire.")

Short-run interests mattered also. The blockade of Germany by the British fleet meant that America's trade with Britain was now more important than ever. In 1812 British ships, then blockading France, had accosted American vessels on the high seas. America at that point had made of these breaches of international law a *casus belli*, but it accepted similar acts after 1914. By 1915 the U.S. economy had become a vast supplier for the Allied war effort. When France and Britain had run through their gold reserves, Wall Street, with the president's approval, agreed to extend London and Paris further credit, to the dismay of Bryan, who would soon resign, and who declared: "Money is the worst of all contrabands because it commands everything else."[22] But Wilson moved ever further from Bryan's point of view. Submarine warfare struck him as ever less acceptable.

In May 1915, after the sinking of the *Lusitania*, Germany's ways of waging war—already much tainted by quite accurate reports of atrocities in Belgium—became for many Americans increasingly hard to bear. Wilson protested against Germany's tactics, which ignored the rules of "fair play, reason and justice" that had become categorical imperatives for modern humanity. In 1916, after a German attack on a French passenger ship, the *Sussex*, Wilson became even more firm. Germany then backed off. But matters shifted once again in January 1917, when the German imperial government, at the behest of its military and over the objections of its prime minister, decided, as part of a last-ditch effort, to allow unlimited submarine warfare against all types of ships from all nations. This change in policy came at the very moment when Wilson had concluded that it was incumbent on the United States to establish (but what he really meant was "to impose") a just peace among all of the belligerent nations. (It was also at this juncture that Wilson first made public his plan for a postwar League of Nations that would guarantee world peace in the future by the sheer weight of its role as the expression of—an American-inspired—world public opinion.) German diplomats informed the United States of their plans for extended submarine warfare on January 31, 1917. Three days later Wilson suspended diplomatic relations with Germany. Matters soon escalated further. In March German submarines sank four American cargo ships. Then the British forwarded to Washington an intercepted telegram in which Arthur Zimmerman, the German foreign minister, asked Germany's ambassador to the United States to urge Mexico to join a defensive and offensive alliance against the Americans. At this same time, the fall of the Russian Empire and Russia's withdrawal from the war, though it certainly complicated the Allies' military effort, did wonders for their propaganda machine, which could now, with some modest legitimacy, present their cause as a struggle of parliamentary democracy against the antidemocratic authoritarianism of their enemies (the German, Austro-Hungarian, and Turkish empires). "It is a fearful thing," Wilson told the U.S. Congress, "to lead this great peaceful people into war, into the most terrible and disastrous of all wars, civilization itself seeming to be in the balance. But the right is more precious than peace, and we shall fight for the things which we have always carried nearest our hearts—for democracy, for the right of those who submit to authority to have a voice in their own governments, for the rights and liberties of small nations, for a universal dominion of right by such a concert of free peoples as shall bring peace and safety to all nations and make the world itself at last free." He was applauded and even cheered. In retrospect, this chagrined him: he is reported to have told his secretary: "My message today was of death for our young men. How strange it seems to applaud that."[23]

The European Allies were none too clear as to why they were fighting a dreadful war that was threatening their very survival. To give Alsace and Lorraine back to France? To guarantee the integrity of the British Empire against the powerful German High Seas Fleet? Austrian and German war aims were even more inscrutable: What did Vienna want? To annex more Italian and Serbian territory and thus bring still more disgruntled peoples under Austrian rule?

By contrast, Americans knew then, as they would in 1941 and as George W. Bush's supporters misguidedly think today, that they had been provoked time and again, and that their just aim was to bring (or to impose) democratic American ways on a more or less undeserving world. From the days of the Benevolent Empire, Americans had known that humankind could triumph over its darker, sinful instincts. An American type of democracy would benefit the whole world—as, of course, it might, if its imposition were a feasible idea.

The war once won, Wilson arrived in London and Paris in December. He was welcomed there as no one else had ever been. Bourgeois and democratic crowds in every country greeted him as the bearer of the Good Word, just as socialist and communist crowds, at this same time, saluted Lenin as the other bearer of humanity's perfervid hopes. French, English, and Italian cheers confirmed Wilson in the high opinion he had of himself and of his country. Western European leaders were much less sure. Clemenceau in particular was determined to wage peace as he had waged war, that is to say, relentlessly. He quipped of Wilson's Fourteen Points (his list of premises for a peace treaty) that the Almighty himself had had only ten. The Italians were determined to extend their rule over both shores of the Adriatic. The English had their eye on former German and Turkish colonial possessions. The French yearned to lord it over the left bank of the Rhine, just as the Germans had done in Alsace and Lorraine. By common agreement, Germany was required to sign a humiliating treaty as the sine qua non for the lifting of a blockade that had reduced German civilians to near starvation.

In the end, after undignified and unsavory horse trades, the Treaty of Versailles granted every victorious power something—but not everything—it had asked for. Wilson's advantage was the creation of the League of Nations, for which he had to forgo both a guarantee of the safety of neutral vessels on the high seas and the internationalization of Germany's former colonies. He also had to promise the French a guarantee for their new borders, which were to include Alsace and Lorraine but not the Rhineland. Huge problems were left unresolved: Would Germany be really disarmed or not? Humiliated or not? Welcomed back to the community of nations or not? And how could an exhausted

Germany pay the war reparations, on which the French insisted because, after all, they had had to pay reparations after the Franco-Prussian War?

The last item on Wilson's agenda was to convince the American people—and through them their senators—to accept his treaty. The president's arrogance profoundly irritated his Republican opponents, many of whom, like Taft, the former president, and Charles Evans Hughes, a former Republican candidate for that office, had expressed some interest in the League of Nations. Wilson paid no attention to such potential allies and refused any modification of his proposals. He chose instead to go over the heads of the political class and, as a true American democrat, to speak to the people. "You have no choice, my fellow citizens," he explained. "You cannot give a false gift . . . Men are not going to stand it . . . There is nothing for any nation to lose whose purposes are right and whose cause is just . . . The whole freedom of the world not only, but the whole peace of mind of the world, depends upon the choice of America . . . I can testify to that . . . The world will be absolutely in despair if America deserts it."[24] The world looked to America, and the Almighty was watching also: there would be a time, he warned, if his treaty were rejected, some moment would come when "in the vengeful Providence of God, another struggle in which, not a few hundred thousand fine men from America will have to die, but as many millions as are necessary to accomplish the final freedom of the peoples of the world."[25] The Mexican intervention had been a fiasco. The rejection of the Versailles Treaty, which legitimated America's noninvolvement in Europe in the 1930s and its apathy in the face of fascist gains, was a major catastrophe.

Wilson's liberal and imperial zeal was in its own way a generous restatement of America's national yearnings. But the achievement of his goals in foreign policy depended on two things: first, in the short run, that he would agree on some compromises with centrists who thought of themselves as mildly universalist and who might have been swayed by an astute president, and second, in the long run, that changes occur in America's domestic structures, as Theodore Roosevelt had begun to grasp. But Wilson, locked in his private—and racist—world, failed to see any of this.

After traveling six thousand miles by train and making forty speeches in short order, Wilson suddenly collapsed in September 1919. Now more or less paralyzed and hidden from public view by his wife and his closest advisers, Wilson watched helplessly as the Senate declined to ratify his treaty. He hoped that the presidential election would revive his project, but the reverse happened. The first (and desultory) act in the drama of American social democracy had come to an end.

CHAPTER 11
Missed Opportunities

"FDR: at long last!" That is the way we often think of American history from the Civil War to the middle decades of the twentieth century. In that long frame, after the disappointments of the Gilded Age and the failure of Wilsonian democracy, comes—finally—a renewal of America's extraordinary march through time.

This is America triumphant, with those huge hangars that produced a heavy bomber every hour, and busy shipyards where "Rosie the Riveter" and her fellow workers—white and black, male and female—created daily a "Liberty Ship" that would carry men and matériel from the arsenal of democracy to the four corners of the globe. This is an America that is close to us, but one that also bathes in the glow of Hollywood's Memory Lane and of a Golden Past.

This is a plausible and, in many ways, a true view of America's life and times. In 1936 Franklin D. Roosevelt's libertarian victory was overwhelming, and in December 1941 America's involvement in the war rallied all hearts, including those of the many millions of Americans who had bitterly resisted their country's entry into the conflict.

Nonetheless, this image of an America wholeheartedly aroused to defend its Enlightenment values has to be partly reconfigured. Experience shows that the shape of America's national origins makes possible moments of strong unanimity, but also sudden retrenchments. Waves of either inclusion or exclusion can be very rapidly followed by their opposite: we have Wilson in 1912 after McKinley in 1898, but we also have the compromise of 1877 after the end of slavery in 1865. In that frame, Franklin Roosevelt's New Deal (a locution he first introduced to the nation in one of the radio broadcasts known as his "fireside chats")

223

should be seen less as a turning point than as a libertarian moment in a structurally stable and often unfortunate sequence. Some emphasis has to be placed not just on the many, important, and real achievements of the New Deal, but on its lacunae as well: so much was left undone! It matters, alas, that Roosevelt, the Democratic candidate, was elected because of his charm, without any real program in 1932 and because a Republican president (triumphantly elected in 1928) happened to be in office in 1929 when the economic roof fell in.

In the end, Roosevelt and his electorate in 1932, in the depths of the Depression, were less interested in massive reforms of social inclusion than in repairing the obvious dysfunctions of capitalism. In that context, it is no surprise that so many social issues were hardly touched or even discussed in any sustained manner (such as the situation of African Americans), or that the New Deal's program of inclusion also proved to be a means to national aggrandizement. At the financial conference at Bretton Woods in July 1944 the British delegates discovered (as their prime minister had already found in November 1943 at Teheran, where Roosevelt had favored Stalin over his British ally) that, in the words of a British historian, "the Americans were unalterably convinced that what was good for American capitalism was good for the world."[1]

From the perspective of this essay it is necessary, though it may seem harsh, to start from the frailty and the incompleteness of Roosevelt's social democracy. Here we consider not just the short-run consequences for America in the 1930s, but the long-run effects on the world as well as on the United States. It is not implausible to suggest that some of the darkest developments in postwar America (such as McCarthyism, or the uncontrolled and uncontrollable American war-making machine that Eisenhower criticized as the "military-industrial complex") have their origin in the "nontransformation" of American life in the two antecedent decades, and more particularly, once again as always in American history, to the political "nonrecognition" of African Americans. Race is the skeleton in the closet of American history.

It is also disturbing that so much of what did change in American society was only tangentially connected to that country's enduring universalist traditions: in the end, war was the greater determinant. Wilsonian principle had mattered, but war was a more efficacious cause of change in 1912–1920, just as war was behind both the apotheosis of the Democratic Party in the late 1930s and 1940s and its near demise with America's defeat in Vietnam.

Since 1914, Europe has lived in an awful fear of war, of its degrading social and moral effects. In America, by contrast, which in the twentieth century triumphed in three world wars, conflict in wars hot or cold has been the engine of social and cultural change in ways that have become unthinkable in Europe, Russia, or China, or in Japan, which is so far the only country to have suffered atomic devastation.

*****

We can begin by briefly retracing, in traditional manner, the "non-ideological" circumstances that brought Roosevelt to power, and with this, America's bid to realize a social democratic program. Here, the first message will be of an America during the 1920s that had abandoned the progressive impulse of the 1900s and 1910s. The second will be that we need to nuance that view.

In the 1920s the Great War (which had not yet become the First World War) had boosted America's self-image to unprecedented heights. Americans had had nothing to do with the origins of this conflict, which had brought misery, regret, and shame to all the nations that been involved in it, with one conspicuous exception: their own country.

At first this glow had spilled over into a larger universalizing concern for the well-being of the planet, but Wilson's successors lost no time in "renationalizing" America's foreign policy. After having overextended their reach in assuming that they could bring Europe's victorious powers to heel, Americans veered in reaction toward an unprecedented and pharisaical self-absorption. In the eighteenth century enlightened Americans, in their own particular way, had lived in the shadow, as it were, of the European Enlightenment. In the nineteenth century many cultured Americans, though now much more able to assert the beneficial specificity of American culture, had still looked to British social and political manners, French civilization, German philosophy, and Italian art as models that their own country would do well to heed. After 1920, though some Americans of the "lost generation" did find their way to Paris (where the exchange rate was favorable and prostitution not just cheap but widely accepted), most of their compatriots opted instead for unprecedented economic and cultural self-sufficiency.

From Wilsonian inclusion, the country now moved rapidly to political and social exclusion of all kinds. "The "Reds" were pursued, prosecuted, and at times, deported. The audacity and numbers of the Ku Klux Klan soared. Its membership peaked in 1926 with six million Klansmen who terrorized whatever activists African-American culture was able to bring forward; in 1924 a motion condemning the Klan was rejected by the Democratic Party's convention. To this day, the legal murder of two Italian anarchists, Sacco and Vanzetti, symbolizes the tone of this unhealthy decade.

Economic growth in the 1920s bolstered Americans' sense of their premier place in the family of nations. After a minor postwar economic crisis (5 million Americans momentarily lost their jobs), matters improved rapidly. In 1900 America still exported more raw materials to other industrial nations than it consumed itself; by 1930 this flow had been reversed. From its foundation in the seventeenth century, America, as a developing economy, had steadily imported capital, mostly from Britain but from other European countries as well. (Tocqueville invested money in American railway shares, a decision he came to regret.) With the Great War, as a mature economy, it exported capital instead. (It is an example of George W. Bush's obtuse incompetence that under his watch the United States has once again become a massive borrower on the world capital markets.) In 1914 America owed the world 3.7 billion dollars. By 1918 the world owed it 3.8 billion dollars.

Postwar economic growth ensured the development of new industries, which in turn, by the boost they gave to national wealth, encouraged the growth of consumption, an incidental side effect of which was a number of picturesque business/political scandals. After the railways of the 1880s, now came automobiles, the oil industry, and public works, as millions of new cars needed fuel and made necessary the construction of thousands of miles of roadways. Science began quietly and at first imperceptibly to take over the role of innovation that had heretofore belonged to tinkerers of genius. Significant here were the beginnings of both genetic research and of more powerful numerical calculators: many critical steps were taken at Harvard under Conrad Aiken, and at the Massachusetts Institute of Technology under Vannevar Bush, who would later be a scientific adviser to Franklin Roosevelt and the architect of the Manhattan Project and the atomic bomb. (We should note here the beginnings of a factor that is important to an understanding of contemporary American life and of America's cultural preeminence in the world and of the close relationship in that country between government and universities, a relationship that would come into its own after 1941 in many domains: the atomic bomb, again, as well as such endeavors as decoding, economic planning, and the manufacture of napalm, which was used in aerial bombings against a defenseless Tokyo in March 1945.)

Electrification was generalized and engendered a sharp rise in productivity. Once more, America's national sense of self was refocused around the ideal of economic individualism and the reality of industrial capitalism. It seemed that the frenetic rate of growth that had marked the 1880s and 1890s had resumed. Membership in labor unions fell from 5 to 3 million between 1920 and 1929.

Economic modernization, then, but cultural change and cultural impact as well. Deeply marked as it was by both economic individualism and traditional Protestantism—neither of which had much intrinsic appeal for many traditionalist Catholic or non-Christian nations—America's dominant religious message was not truly suitable for export. Its cultural message, however, was highly exportable: here was the beginning of America's celebrated "soft power," frequently as disliked by elites of other nations as its hard power, but oftentimes quite seductive as well. Henceforth, an important aspect of America's sense of self—a gratifying proof of its cultural superiority, as it were—related to the impact of its artists, writers, and painters, and especially of Hollywood and its "dream machine." American GIs were lionized by the French in August 1944 as liberators after four long years of German occupation, but they were also perceived as purveyors not just of liberty but of nylon stockings, popular jazz tunes, and Hollywood movies, which had been forbidden by both the Germans and the Vichy government.

A new cultural self-confidence, then, with—in typical American manner—new technological forms. Radio (ill-pronounced as "rahdio" by the mocked and unsuccessful presidential candidate Al Smith in 1928) had become widely used by 1930 and had begun its political career with broadcasts of the two national party conventions in 1924. And then, of course, there were the movies, which made American ways of seeing normative for the entire world.

Before 1914, France—where film had been invented—had rivaled America's rising movie industry. The First World War gave Hollywood a free hand. Movie theaters sold 40 million tickets in 1922, and 100 million in 1930. The invention of the "talkies" established America's domination of this industry. Now and forevermore, Americans would imagine themselves and their nation visually as they learned to understand it through film and later television. Movie stars now took on the air and importance that political personages of the nineteenth century had naturally assumed was theirs. It is more than anecdotal that the great political figures of the first half of the twentieth century were strongly drawn to the movies: Franklin Roosevelt, Hitler, Franco, Stalin, and Churchill were avid film watchers and had small theaters constructed in their various residences. (Stalin's favorite was *Volga, Volga*, which he watched dozens of times. In December 1942, on New Year's Eve, a few weeks after the Anglo-American landing in North Africa, Roosevelt proudly showed his guests the film *Casablanca*, in which Humphrey Bogart played the leading role that had been originally intended for Ronald Reagan.)[2]

In the 1840s and 1850s many Americans—like the young Lincoln—still imagined their nation through a reading of the Bible. What American did not know the stories of David and Goliath, of Moses and his people, or of Christ and the multiplication of the loaves and fishes? Shakespeare and a hagiographic literature on the heroes of American life (the Founding Fathers in general, or George Washington in particular) filled whatever cultural space was left over. But now it was from the rather more lowbrow productions of Hollywood studios that many Americans forged much of their sense of their national self.

With many conspicuous and important exceptions, however (because also in these years America's upward trajectory began as the focus of the world's "high culture"), there emerged an altogether new role that had been prefigured by the New York Armory Show of 1913, which had presented modern artists such as Matisse and Picasso to American art lovers. Soon, during the rule of Nazism, the world's artistic energy would move from Paris and Berlin to New York, which for a few months in 1941–1942 became, for example, the capital of surrealism. Retrospective mention should also be made of Freud's visit in 1909 to Worcester, Massachusetts, to give his first lecture cycle in a non–German-speaking country—another sign of America's forthcoming place in world culture.

With consumerized entertainment in the 1920s came consumerism plain and simple: household appliances could now be bought on credit. Twenty-five million people owned telephone connections. Department stores were the most eloquent institutional expression of this new way of living. In the 1930s Walter Benjamin, an eccentrically Marxist-surrealist critic, waxed lyrical about this (Parisian) commercial invention: for the workers, he explained, the department store—which they could visit but where they could not afford to buy (as in "just looking")—allowed the working class to dream of a classless society in which all these goods would be theirs as well. As Eva Peron once said about her mink coat, why should only the rich be allowed to wear them? Millions of Americans flocked to these new emporiums. Charleston-dancing young women with short skirts, close-cropped hair, and cloche hats were symbols of this new wealth and national confidence, as was a countervailing moralistic prohibition on alcoholic beverages, passed by constitutional amendment, which we remember today as an unsuccessful neoreligious effort to drive demon drink and sin from the American scene.

In summary, the 1920s, like the 1880s and 1890s, can certainly be seen as a hopelessly materialist decade. And yet recent historical accounts have been more mixed. As the prestige of the New Deal has waned, as historians have become more sensitive to the incompleteness of Roosevelt's policies, the defects of the 1920s have seemed less severe. Continuity more than discontinuity seems to be the right frame for thinking of both the 1920s and the 1930s. Calvin Coolidge did indeed declare that the business of America was business, and no one was better situated to understand this than his secretary of the treasury, Andrew Mellon, a prudent financier who managed to wind down about half of the national debt that the United States had incurred during the Great War. But Mellon was also one of the great benefactors of the National Gallery of Art in Washington, D.C.

Many American businessmen of the 1920s, we can now see, were sincerely concerned to harmonize relations between employers and employees. Big business—now more frequently organized in accommodating oligopolies than in triumphant monopolies, and more often managed by managers rather than by robber-baron founders—was less aggressive socially. In his old age, the steel and banking magnate J. P. Morgan was far more cautious than he had been: like Marx, Morgan was struck by the importance of economic crises in the history of capitalist economies.

In a related revisionist mode, Herbert Hoover's historical reputation has improved somewhat (just as Roosevelt's has declined somewhat). In his youth Hoover had been attracted by Theodore Roosevelt's progressivism, and he was after all an engineer and a technocrat rather than a conservative politician. His ideological gyroscope was in a way unstable, as he was not an unconditional apologist of a wholly free market. After the stock market crash he convened some 400 leading businessmen at the White House to resolve America's problems. "The very fact that you gentlemen come together for these broad purposes," he told them, "represents an advance in the whole conception of the relationship of business to public welfare . . . This is a far cry from the arbitrary and dog-eat-dog attitude of the business world some thirty or forty years ago."[3] In this vein, Theda Skocpol has even argued: "During the Progressive Era and early 1920s, a nascent maternal welfare state began to come together in the United States, by occupying a space left open by the absence of civil bureaucracies and a strong working-class movement (the forces that were creating a paternalistic welfare state in other nations)."[4]

All of which speaks to two central points: (1) the New Deal was not brought forward by a social democratic tidal wave; and (2) we should not see Herbert Hoover as a troglodyte and FDR as a visionary. If Al Smith had been elected president in 1928 (which he wasn't on account of his Catholic, wet, and Irish roots), and if Hoover had then run against him in 1932, there might have been no New Deal at all. Writ large, this is to say that the American political system is not a juggernaut that steadily drives American society toward more universalist goals, as Franklin Roosevelt's hagiography falsely implies. It is instead a system of complementary yin and yang, of repetitive patterns of exclusion and inclusion, in which a great deal depends on circumstance and on the personalities of American presidents.

*****

The economic crisis of 1929 was in no small measure fortuitous, being a consequence of long-term economic cycles, to be sure, but also of poor postwar financial management before 1929 and deflationary policies afterward. The world over, every government worked hard to make a bad economic situation worse: after the market crash of October 1929, the first instinct of bourgeois politicians (including Roosevelt until April

1938) was to balance the budget and lower government expenses. In the United States, the ensuing shock was very severe. Nine thousand banks folded. In many urban areas, unemployment rose to more than 50 percent. In some southern states, African-American rural unemployment rose even higher. The Gross National Product fell by a quarter between 1929 and 1932. Millions of men and women who had strongly interiorized the Protestant ethic of self-help were driven to seek public relief. The sales of Cadillac automobiles held up quite well, but the sales of Chevrolets plummeted.

It is hardly surprising, in consequence, that the New Deal, which was supposed to right these various wrongs, should have appeared at the time—as it still does from many angles—as a break in the history of the American nation and its sense of self. Now government interference, which had been covert and focused on growth, would be overt and focused on employment and relief. (Some historians—mindful perhaps of French experience—have even labeled the New Deal as a new American republic. Here the sequence would run from a representative First Republic from 1787 to 1828; to a Second Republic, at once democratic and capitalistic, from 1865 to 1929; to a social democratic Third Republic from 1932 to 1968, with Roosevelt as its founder and Lyndon Johnson as its gravedigger. In this same scheme, George W. Bush, with his neoconservative imperial administration might count as the architect of a Fourth Republic, dedicated to imperialist pursuits abroad and unlicensed capitalism at home.)

In 1932 Walter Lippmann, the best-known journalist of his time, wrote: "Nobody seriously regards [the corporate rich] as having any authority."[5] And Richard Hofstadter opined in 1955 that the New Deal had given to American liberalism a social democratic hue that had never before been part of an American reform movement. They were not wholly wrong, but neither by any means were they wholly right.

Could it have happened some other way? Could the New Deal have gone much further? Given the intensity of America's economic crisis, could a more durable avenue of reform have been created in the 1930s?

Had Roosevelt been more determined; had he resolved to rule not just through the Democratic Party—with its southern wing—but on the basis of a more structured labor movement; had he chosen to do more for southern blacks and force political change on the former Confederate states: could he then have created a truly new Third American Republic?

From time to time, thoughts of this sort did cross his mind. For example, struck by the "Turner thesis"—the argument, advanced by the historian Frederick Jackson Turner, that America's egalitarian frontier was a key to the democratization of American society—Roosevelt reflected in 1932: "A glance at the situation today only too clearly indicates that the equality of opportunity as we have known it no longer exists . . . Our last frontier has long since been reached, and there is practically no more free land . . . There is no safety valve in the form of a Western prairie to which those thrown out of work by the Eastern economic machines can go for a new start." Later in the same speech he declared: "All this calls for a re-appraisal of values . . . Our task now is not discovery or exploitation of natural resources, or necessarily producing more goods. It is the soberer, less dramatic business of administering resources . . . of distributing wealth and products more equitably, of adapting existing economic organizations to the service of the people." A laudable paragraph, which however typically concluded on a very modest note: "The day of enlightened administration has come."[6] Likewise, for Hugh Johnson, one of the key members of Roosevelt's team of New Dealers, the problem of America was not the exploitation of the poor by the rich, but the disequilibrium that ensued whenever one class (which he did not name) was too powerful vis-à-vis any other class (which he also left unnamed).[7]

At the end of the day, the New Deal did not transform America, and its failure to do so gives us pause. Its shortcomings lead us to reflect, not just about the interplay of exclusion and inclusion in American life, but about the depths of support that partisans of war, violence, and exclusion can muster.

Why was Theodore Roosevelt not elected in 1912? Because of his personal quarrel with Taft? Because Americans could not understand his message of state-regulated capitalism? And why was Franklin Roosevelt stymied in so many of his moves? The answer may be because America's progressive impulses had not yielded very much actual progression and had not transformed the deep structures of American life. At this potential turning point America did not turn, because this democracy, however vibrant, did not wish to turn.

An anguishing problem, whose latest avatar today is in the wide public support for George W. Bush's mendacious warmongering. And an anguishing question that has now led many historians to see the New Deal not as a revolution (that failed) but as a set of reformist techniques designed to improve rather than to redirect the workings of American society. In this context of an "organizational synthesis,"[8] the New Deal was no more than an economic *aggiornamento* made necessary by the changing nature of capitalism, which in the size and scope of firms had become less entrepreneurial and more managerial. Many measures were enacted, but their first effect was to enable American industry to move beyond the crisis it had brought upon itself with the stock market crash of 1929.

*****

The history of the New Deal can be seen as falling into two parts. In its first phase, in 1934–1935, Roosevelt's goal was to restore public confidence in the nation's institutions: "The only thing we have to fear is fear itself." A critical aspect of this political moment consisted in bringing to Washington the cadres (lawyers, engineers, academics) of a new federal bureaucracy. Much of this centered around the National Recovery Act, which the Supreme Court would eventually nullify as being unconstitutional. The result was a partial—and not always efficacious—reorganization of some key national industries, whose employers and employees were charged with increasing production while also improving working conditions.

The second New Deal, in 1935–1937, was more consequential, and thus generated among American elites a hatred of the president that was comparable to the detestation felt by the French *grande bourgeoisie* for Léon Blum. (Roosevelt's advantage here was that although Blum was perceived by the French right as a Jewish quasi-foreigner, Roosevelt— a class traitor to be sure—had a lineage that was impeccably Anglican and Anglo-Saxon, with a mere touch of a latinate side, as his middle name, "Delano," was derived from the French Delanoix, or perhaps from a more elegant "De la Noye.")

Now reelected on his own program rather than as a mere alternative to a discredited Herbert Hoover, Roosevelt tried to stabilize agricultural prices and to improve the distribution of credit in a way that—typically— was intended to benefit moneyless borrowers but proved to be of more durable use to moneyed lenders. Another significant step was a vast program of government-sponsored infrastructure, which accounted for 600 airports, 100,000 bridges, and many huge dams and hydroelectric projects, which, taken together, stand as a prefiguration of America's unprecedented wartime industrial burst. Industrial work by children was prohibited. The federal government took it upon itself to set a minimum national wage. In a critical move—unfortunately too limited—trade unionism was encouraged, with disruptive but in the long run beneficial waves of strikes, 4,700 of them in 1937 alone. In December 1936 workers even briefly occupied some of the General Motors factories, and in March 1937 the U.S. Steel Company, the nation's leading metallurgical firm, accepted the unionization of its workforce. The cornerstone of the entire edifice was the passing in 1935 of the National Labor Relations Act and of the Social Security Act, which provided for the relief of aged workers, with some measure of help for handicapped people, children, and the unemployed.

(*The variations in the percentage of income that is collected as federal income tax are symbolic of this involvement of the national government in American economic life. The income tax was levied for the first time during the Civil War at a rate of 5 percent for the highest incomes. Abolished after that war, it was revived in 1894, declared unconstitutional by the Supreme Court in the following year, and re-created by constitutional amendment in 1913. It reached a level of 6 percent for most Americans, but rose to 77 percent for income over a million dollars. It fell again in the 1920s, rose through the 1930s when 30 percent of Americans were required to pay it, and in 1942 reached a rate of 91 percent on the highest incomes. It hovers today at about 21 percent of national income.)*

The New Deal focused on the American worker, but it was also an important moment in the cultural life of the American nation, in photography, dance, music, and painting. The Federal Writers' Project and analogous programs for sculptors and painters generated new indigenous artistic forms that were far removed from either antecedent American academic or then-current French surrealist styles. Their efforts do bring to mind today the "socialist realism" that was at the time being imposed on Soviet artists, but the American version came in an infinitely more spontaneous and attractive form. Choreographically, the highest expression of this neopopulist inspiration was Martha Graham's triumphant masterpiece of 1938, *American Document.* Organized sports became an important part of an American way that was open to all. In 1935 Hollywood produced a film, *Fighting Youth,* "about a college football star distracted from his athletic pursuits by his girlfriend," a young woman who proved to be a spy for a political group that aimed to destroy the American Constitution "by breaking up college football."[9]

These varyingly meaningful steps were critical aspects of a renewed national consciousness. Along with the birth of the republic in the 1770s and the Civil War in the 1860s, the New Deal of the 1930s is one of the high points of American universalism. At the same time, it is just as important to remember, in the words of Paul Conkin, that the New Deal was no more than a "halfway revolution." In that frame, as Conkin puts it, "the story of the New Deal is a sad story, the ever recurring story of what might have been."[10]

What was left undone? Many things. First, the whole endeavor was in some sense antique in its perception of what was at issue. Roosevelt did care sincerely about some workers and some industries. Ever a country gentleman, he was also sincerely moved by the plight of landless laborers—noblesse oblige—and yet it is thought that the New Deal probably worsened the situation of the landless. But Roosevelt was removed from many urban problems and only peripherally concerned with many of America's newer industries (oil, energy, high technology), which he did little to regulate.[11] Under his watch, in the 1930s and the 1940s, the southern states were progressively industrialized, but there was no corresponding transformation of southern labor relations or public culture, which remained violent and retrograde. Social security likewise was insufficiently funded, and covered by taxes levied on employers and employees, in contradistinction to the system in most other countries, where social security payments came—and still come, as they should—from general revenue. Women remained a largely ignored constituency, and it is not as unfair as it might seem to highlight in the New Deal legislation a principle that became very dear to Vichy France after 1940, namely the curtailment of women's work. For some few years, it was made illegal in Roosevelt's America for both husband and wife to be employed by the federal government. It is also worth noting that the original social security program did not cover its beneficiaries' survivors, most of whom would have been women.

As regards citizenship and human rights, the most egregious sin of commission, after the Japanese attack on Pearl Harbor, was the deportation and quasi-incarceration of 130,000 American citizens of Japanese origin. One day, in an insiders' practical joke, Roosevelt and some of his close associates decided to tease Francis Biddle, the attorney general, by pretending to be thinking about abrogating all Americans' civil rights for the duration of the war—a pleasantry that today seems more ominous than amusing given George W. Bush's current disregard for due process.

But the most consequential gap in the New Deal was in the neglect of African Americans' civil rights, a domain that has always been the litmus test of American social reform. In the eighteenth century, 1776 was a critical date for blacks because it placed on the table the idea of citizenship for all, a status to which slaves could suddenly aspire. A century later, after emancipation in 1865, the compromise of 1877 mattered for them again—and for the republic's political fate—because it was then that the North decided to ignore the claims of citizenship that African Americans had just acquired. The 1930s mattered once more, not because rights were taken away, but because more were not granted. (Native Americans were better treated, but in these same years the situation of Mexican Americans probably worsened.)

Moreover, here was a lacuna that now mattered, not just abstractly, but practically and geographically for the nation as a whole. What the American republic stood for as an ideal had always been a concern—indeed an obsession—for Americans everywhere, but practically speaking, despite the existence of significant free black communities in the northern states long before the Civil War, the issue of race had been an overwhelming presence only in some few southern states and counties, where blacks often outnumbered whites.

But the rapid industrialization of the North, followed by two world wars and the seemingly insatiable thirst of war-fired industry for labor, caused one of America's great *Völkerwanderungen*, the move of blacks from the rural South to the factories of the North, with, alas, a corresponding spread of racist habits, such as the "covenants" that made it impossible for African Americans to rent or buy property in white residential areas. Segregation became perhaps more ubiquitous in the North than in the South, where the two races, white and black, lived side by side everywhere, if on a footing of total inequality: in the South, at least, the ones knew the others existed.

Ever patient, and dedicated as they were to the memory of Abraham Lincoln, the Great Liberator, African Americans had voted—insofar as they could and did vote—for Republicans, even in 1932. By 1936, however, once the New Deal had opened up for them prospects of real change, 90 percent of African-American voters cast their ballots for Roosevelt.

But not much came of it. For example, the rights conferred by the new social security program were denied to many blacks, not by race, but by the exclusion of professions in which they were heavily involved, such as agricultural and domestic labor. It was only after he had been directly and explicitly threatened with a march of tens of thousands of black people to Washington that Roosevelt decided in July 1941 to order the partial integration of the labor force in defense industries.[12] Nor did Roosevelt decide to make of lynchings—which southern tradition sanctioned, especially when members of white elites were directly or indirectly involved—a federal crime whose punishment would no longer be at the discretion of local southern juries and authorities.

In brief, Roosevelt's stand—or absence thereof—was tantamount to abandoning African Americans to yet another half-century of urban misery.[13] It is infinitely to her credit that Eleanor Roosevelt, the president's more or less estranged wife and cousin, an eminently respectable public person in her own right, repeatedly and outspokenly criticized the segregationist policies of her husband's administration.

Why so many shortfalls? Some of them were bound up in the American idea of what America was about. How to desegregate an America that still believed in or accepted segregation? What is a nation? How does it come together? To these questions, overwhelmingly, Americans answered that the forms of their civil society were inscribed in nature and best left untouched by a largely parasitic state: "Does your father work? No, he is a policeman." Diplomatic posts were seen as plums that idle but well-placed political and literary figures secured in ways that were not too commendable. Public service was not prestigious. "That government is best which governs least," Thoreau had written. And he had added: "It finally amounts to this, which I also believe, 'That government is best which governs not at all.'"[14] (Henry James would later write that Thoreau had been not just provincial but parochial.) All of this added up to an entrenched suspicion of the state, which necessarily limited the appeal of the New Deal and comforted its Republican antagonists. Prominent among these were the justices of the Supreme Court in 1935–1936, who opposed any number of bills that dealt with industrial relations and the management of agriculture.

An inauspicious cultural setting, and a difficult one institutionally as well: the United States has never had the analog of the "French state machine"—an onerous and ponderous bureaucracy, stifling in many ways, but in others efficacious, highly trained, and politically agnostic, ready in 1936 to serve a socialist government headed by a Jew, and just as ready in 1940 to support a reactionary government headed by an anti-Semitic military figure.

Unable to rely on trained administrative elites, the American federal government had no choice but to hand over the implementation of New Deal programs to incompetent or hostile officials, or worse yet, to Democratic Party stalwarts who had been carefully selected for their loyalty regardless of their honesty or good will. So it was that the Federal Emergency Relief funds were distributed not by federal employees but by state and municipal officials, and especially by Democratic Party officials. In the southern states, subsidies were given out in proportion to the needs of landowners for cheap labor: when the harvest was due and laborers needed, payments became scarce. And everywhere, segregation was accepted as a fact of life: in Texas, housing subsidies were given to build three types of residential buildings: white, black, and Mexican.[15] "All politics are local": a horrid maxim and one that Franklin Roosevelt was too eager to make his own, keen as he was on preserving a balance between his natural audience in northern urban America and his racist supporters in the South. As he saw it, this was an alliance he could not do without, and one that was very frail. The success of local populist and racist demagogues like Huey Long in Louisiana and the perhaps even more sinister Father Coughlin in Detroit, a dedicated Roman Catholic anti-Semite, was for Roosevelt a painful reminder that the ethnic and cultural coalition that had brought him to power was not without its deep-seated contradictions.

But great statesmen are those who resolve great problems, and it must be said, once again, that much of the responsibility and the blame for the incompleteness of the New Deal has to do not just with "vast impersonal forces" but with "agency," that is to say, with what specific individuals—the president first among them—decided to do or not to do. And here, Franklin Roosevelt was at once the solution (as the man who sold the New Deal to America) and the problem.

*****

Roosevelt had a deep sympathy for the poor and the weak, perhaps because of his own brave struggle against polio, a dreadful handicap that enabled the poor and downtrodden to identify with him as well: "Polio made an aristocratic Roosevelt into an underdog. For him it replaced the log cabin."[16] He was also a born politician, with a deep and reassuring voice and the smiling, Burkean confidence of the nobly born. Thanks to photographs or newsreels and to the recording of his speeches, we can easily sense the charm he exuded. (Perhaps we should at this point recall that Lincoln, America's greatest president, was unprepossessing, gawky, and often ridiculed.) The elegance and style of this "word magician" were deeply seductive, as were the props and supports of his public persona: his cigarette holder, his cape, his dog Fala, and his compelling ability with words, stories, and pithy anecdotes.[17]

But Roosevelt "dealt with the appearance of issues, not their deepest substance, and he displayed a flexibility towards political principles that often dismayed even his warmest advisers."[18] Roosevelt did not have a genuinely global understanding of the American economy. His grasp of economics was unexceptional, and John Maynard Keynes, invited to the White House in 1934, later remarked that he had "supposed the president was more literate, economically speaking." (This negative reaction was mutual: Roosevelt's judgment of the leading economist of his time was that "he left a whole rigmarole of figures . . . He must be a mathematician rather than a political economist.") In the celebrated words of the then 92-year-old Oliver Wendell Holmes, Roosevelt was "a second-class intellect, but a first class temperament."[19]

Roosevelt by instinct was hostile to inflationary policies and did not distinguish between state-induced inflation during hard times of high unemployment and demand-pushed inflation in good times when an economy might overheat from too much money chasing too few goods or workers. It was only in 1937–1938, when the economy—and the stock market—once again faltered, that Roosevelt finally resolved on a Keynesian policy of massive "pump-priming." It was less the New Deal than the war that pulled America out of its economic doldrums.

The man was also deeply self-centered, uninterested in advice that ran counter to his proposed intent, and very keen on doing well in public opinion polls. In his essence, Roosevelt remained a landed aristocrat, educated at the best schools, an Anglophile and, as it happens, mildly Francophobic. (His dislike of Charles de Gaulle is well known. In 1944 Roosevelt even suggested to a shocked Anthony Eden, then British foreign minister, that after the war it might be a good idea to annex a part of northern France to Belgium.) His dedication to the unfolding of the American creed was sincere, but his determination to secure it was uncertain. Churchill, de Gaulle, Stalin, and Hitler: for good or evil, these four men had clearly stated goals and worked ceaselessly to achieve them. Roosevelt was less resolute.

The man was a sincere democrat and pacifist. ("I hate war.") He was also conversant with Europe's problems. His relentless enthusiasm and his good will gave America the desire and the energy it needed to go forward. These were immense contributions. But his yearnings for easy solutions that would please the public meant that he did not transform the nation as he could have. He did not bring into being a more profoundly structured social democratic America, which would have had a very different future from the present it has today.

George Washington is now the symbol of America as a republican nation. Abraham Lincoln is a symbol of America as a universalizing people. Franklin Roosevelt could have become an enduring symbol of American fairness. But that did not happen.

Having seduced America by his charm and optimism, but having failed—or not even really tried—to transform its social and governmental structures, Roosevelt was for many years unable to bring the country around diplomatically. Indeed, an unfortunate parallel exists between his hesitations on reform and his equivocation on resistance to international fascism: until late 1938 Roosevelt, like Neville Chamberlain, was an appeaser.

During the 1920s Americans, by a 180-degree turn, withdrew from Wilsonian universalism, made immigration to their country very difficult, and pulled in on themselves, quite confident that they no longer needed Europe's help or example to define their own national purpose. They felt, not altogether unjustly, that they had been deceived into going to war by Anglo-French propaganda and by the wiles of armaments manufacturers. They were now content to hold back and rule their recently acquired territorial empire, which they did with some moderation. The militarized imperialism of the early Theodore Roosevelt gave way to a more tranquil domination. The Philippines, for example, were allowed to move quite steadily toward greater autonomy after 1916 and toward nominal independence in 1935. In 1922 the United States proposed the creation of an Anglo-French-Japanese-American agreement to guarantee once again the territorial integrity of China. In 1928 the Kellogg-Briand Pact "outlawed" war, an interesting goal even if the pact's true purpose was to defuse a French request that the United States honor the guarantee of French borders that Wilson had promised to Clemenceau and that the American Senate had rejected.

In 1932 Roosevelt had denounced the Republicans' economic policies without having a clear idea of what he would put in their place. Similarly, his first steps in foreign policy were none too promising. Herbert Hoover, in the waning days of his presidency, had worked to organize an international meeting to consider the world's economic problems. Roosevelt agreed to the meeting, but only to torpedo its agenda. In consequence, Hjalmar Schacht, Hitler's minister of finance, hailed the new American president as a fellow economic nationalist.

More serious was Roosevelt's determination not to deal with the world's drift toward militarism and fascism. Focused as he was on his quarrel with the Supreme Court, the president did not oppose the 1937

Neutrality Act, by which Congress asserted that in case of a European war the United States would treat victim and aggressor states alike—a point of view that would have made sense in the pre-1914 world of rival nations, but that made no sense in the post-1933 Hitlerian world of ideological rivalries.

Within this pattern of noninvolvement, some progress was made, it is true, but again, as in domestic policy, it was insufficient: here as elsewhere, Roosevelt was more interested in governing by charm and seduction than by bold assertion.

As an industrializing power, nineteenth-century America had always favored high tariffs (much to the chagrin of the rural, staple-producing southern states), and under nationalist pressure that propensity had gone even further after 1929. But now American tariffs were lowered, and in 1934 Cordell Hull—Roosevelt's secretary of state and an old Wilsonian—negotiated an accord of "commercial reciprocity" with foreign nations. America's goal was shifted from defensive and irresponsible protectionism to the encouragement of world economic growth. In a similar vein, diplomatic relations were reestablished with the Soviet Union.

Relations between the United States and Latin America also improved: Roosevelt repudiated the "corollary" to the Monroe Doctrine proclaimed by his distant cousin Theodore in 1904, by which the United States had unilaterally awarded itself a right of interference in the affairs of its southern neighbors. In the context of a newly proclaimed Good Neighbor Policy, American troops were withdrawn from Haiti and relations with Mexico were softened: the United States did not react when Mexico nationalized its foreign-owned—that is, American-owned—oil industry. To be sure, some moments did hark back to the bad old days: in 1933, with American help, Fulgencio Batista established his dictatorship in Cuba, which would last until overthrown by Fidel Castro in 1959. And later on, after 1941, whatever moderation was shown by the United States (as in the suspension of its quasi-protectorate over Nicaragua and Panama) was dictated less by a desire to do good than by the need to counteract Nazi propaganda, which attracted German minorities in South American countries.

Overall, then, Roosevelt's foreign policy record in the 1930s was poor and, until 1939, resolutely isolationist. When Cordell Hull reprimanded General Hugh Johnson, the director of the National Recovery Act, for stating in 1934 that Hitler's persecution of the Jews made him physically sick, Roosevelt did not intervene. The American response to Japan's willful sinking of an American riverboat and spy ship, the USS *Panay* in 1937, was strangely mild. In 1938, after Munich, Roosevelt forwarded congratulatory telegrams to the French and British appeasers and to the fascist aggressors as well.

Only after the collapse of France in May-June 1940 did Roosevelt resolve to involve the United States by incremental steps in the war against Nazism and fascism. Revealingly, however, he was even then less concerned with the fate of French democracy than with the threat its collapse posed for Britain's survival as a world power.

(*Churchill's changing relations with de Gaulle can be seen in that same frame: at first Churchill—a Francophile, and a great admirer of the French army—could not imagine Britain's place in Europe without a strong, independent France as an ally. It was in that spirit that Churchill would insist in 1945 that France receive a seat on the security council of the United Nations as well as a zone of occupation in Germany. In the summer of 1940 and the spring of 1941, before Pearl Harbor, Churchill therefore did what he could for de Gaulle—who was at once Anglophile and Anglophobe—in the hope that Free France could rally at least the French colonial empire to Britain's cause. It seemed to him a matter of life and death that France not abandon Britain altogether: hence the unsuccessful Anglo-Free French raid on Dakar in October 1940. But once America was in the war, Churchill's point of view was radically transformed. Now France sank into near-insignificance and only America really mattered, to de Gaulle's dismay and indignation. Churchill, who, de Gaulle thought, had been a great English patriot as he himself was a great French patriot, had become a mere vassal of the United States, and this he could not forgive.*)

After the fall of France and before the presidential election of 1940 (timing that made his efforts unusually bold politically), Roosevelt worked to secure the enactment of a military draft by Congress. He also arranged for a more or less factitious deal to help the British: in exchange for the right to create bases on British territory, the United States agreed to hand over to Britain fifty destroyers of First World War vintage, of which, as it turned out, only nine were actually serviceable. Then, in March 1941, at Roosevelt's prompting, Congress passed the "lend-lease" bill: America would lend weapons to Britain that Britain would eventually return. Roosevelt illustrated the arrangement for the American public with one of his homey aphorisms: If your neighbor's house was on fire, wouldn't you lend him your garden hose, and not ask him for payment if he'd just return the hose after the fire was out? In April 1941 Roosevelt ordered the navy to extend its Atlantic patrols all the way to Iceland. In June Washington froze German assets in the United States and in July placed an embargo on the exportation of iron, rubber, and especially oil to Japan. This last move would finally force the Japanese to choose between war and retrenchment. In August Roosevelt and Churchill met in Newfoundland and drew up an Atlantic Charter, which was a declaration of democratic and universalist principles. Britain and America were not yet allies, but they were nearly so.

The tenor of this meeting also illustrated two critical themes in the history of the United States.

The first had to do with America's sense of being an "English-speaking nation." (Churchill, whose mother was an American beauty, was to write a *History of the English-Speaking Peoples*, which was very well received in the United States.) The Americans and the British, or at least their leaders, felt bound to each other by affinities of race, culture, and class, in ways that today seem strangely irrelevant. Roosevelt had not been particularly moved by the plight of the Jews, the fall of France, or discrimination against African Americans, but the fate of Britain did matter to him.

This echoed a theme that had been popular in Roosevelt's youth, at Harvard College especially, where the historian John Fiske had presented America as the heir of an exhausted Britain. For Fiske, a strong believer in "political gravitation" who was also the author of ceaselessly reprinted works of nationalist history and a popular lecturer on the theme of America's Manifest Destiny, a great chain of progressing historical continuity linked Cromwell's victory over a traditionalist Charles I in 1645 to Wolfe's triumph over Montcalm (progressive Britain over the France of the Old Regime) in 1759, to Cornwallis's surrender at Yorktown and Grant's victory over Lee at Appomattox, which respectively marked the creation and the victory of American liberty: "The work which the English race began when it colonized North America is destined to go on until every land on the earth's surface that is not already the seat of an old civilization shall become English in its language, in its religion, in its political habits and traditions, and to a predominant extent in the blood of its people."[20]

The second message of the Churchill meeting off Newfoundland followed from the first: America's policies—and especially her foreign policies—often depend on presidential preferences. In 1941, Roosevelt, as a private person, felt himself bound to help the British, and in consequence, he did just that. Once again, as in so many moments in American history, the difference between policies of inclusion and those of exclusion depended on the good sense (as in this instance) or the malevolence of presidents and their advisers. Structure and contingency intersect in the history of all nations, but seldom more so than in the history of the United States.

The wording of the Newfoundland accord—the Atlantic Charter— was designed to assuage America's Wilsonian impulse without threatening either America's right to rule or Britain's imperial goals. Both countries proudly announced their universalist resolve to defend national self-determination for all nations, but not too much was said about which nations were truly nations and therefore deserving of national rights. Nothing, for example, was said of the British Empire and the various African and Asian "non-nations" (or so one had to suppose) that it included. In a related vein, nothing was said about the interdictions on Chinese immigration to the United States. The virtues of democratic rule and free trade were, however, extolled. Churchill urged that the charter mention a new international organization that would take the place of the all-but-defunct League of Nations, but, revealingly, Roosevelt held back, his less-than-Wilsonian idea being that the postwar world should be ruled, gently of course, by what he liked to call the "four policemen"— the United States, Russia, which was then allied to the United States, and America's two dependent allies, Britain and Nationalist China.

Roosevelt had already decided to involve America in the war, but his antagonists saved him the trouble. With regard to the United States, Hitler, who had deceived or attacked every nation of consequence in Europe, was for once lucid. In 1940–1941 he hoped at first that America could be kept out of the war; the agreements he signed with Japan were aimed at the Soviet Union, not at the United States. But his Asian allies forced his hand: between a dangerous route of northern expansionism (Japan had been defeated in 1936 by the Soviet Union in an unofficial Siberian war) and a route of southern expansionism that would have secured their supply of raw materials, especially oil, the Japanese in the summer of 1941 chose the latter. And because the Americans had announced their categorical opposition to a Japanese drive southward toward Dutch Indonesia and its oil, Tokyo, faced with a choice between compliance and naked aggression, chose finally to attack the United States. This was a disastrous error, made disastrous for Germany as well by Hitler's turnabout: instead of continuing to try to keep America out of the war, he now, stupidly, decided to declare war on the United States so as to encourage his Japanese allies to fight harder.

War in the history of the United States has always been the nemesis of social democracy. In the short run, it is true, America's wars have often furthered some communitarian goal and involved the nation as a whole in collective effort. But war more frequently has led to a sad or even fatal erosion of social democratic principles.

From 1935 onward, the (partial) radicalization of the New Deal had angered many Americans. By contrast, after December 7, 1941 ("a date which will live in infamy"), opposition to Roosevelt's wishes practically vanished. As if by magic, the social gains of the 1930s now became part of the American way. But this moment was also the end of the New Deal as such. For one thing, Roosevelt now created a government of national defense that included many prominent Republicans, such as Henry Stimson as secretary of war and Frank Knox as secretary of the navy. Did Roosevelt accede to this renunciation of partisan politics for pragmatic reasons in a national emergency, or had he ceased to struggle for other reasons? In his State of the Union address of January 1944, Roosevelt did explain that America had accepted "so to speak, a second Bill of Rights under which a new basis of security and prosperity can be established for all regardless of station, race, or creed."[21] But his more prophetic pronouncement had been in late 1943, when he jokingly said that "Doctor New Deal" had retired and been replaced by "Doctor Win the War."

In Britain the war marked a turning point in the construction of the welfare state, including national health benefits, as urged in the influential "Beveridge Report." By contrast, Sir William Beveridge's trip to the United States in 1943 and his urging of the American adoption of similar measures came to naught: what emerged from it was the GI Bill and an Employment Act that in a preliminary and abandoned version had been labeled A Full Employment Act. Symbolically, Britain's war production was more closely orchestrated by the British state than was America's enormous productive effort.

George W. Bush, having invaded a country far weaker than his own and proclaimed himself a "war president," benefited from the public's natural tendency to rally around its leaders in wartime, and then used that support to further dismantle American social democracy. The effect of war on the fate of Franklin Roosevelt's New Deal was of the same order, although probably to Roosevelt's chagrin: "We Americans," he wistfully noted in January 1945, "have always believed in freedom of opportunity, and equality of opportunity remains one the principal objectives of our national life . . . We have house-cleaning of our own in this regard." But not much would come from that understanding.

Roosevelt's foreign policy in the last months of his presidency oscillated uneasily between universalist inclusion and nationalist domination. (*Alas, we can suppose from his desire to please that, had he lived longer, he too would have authorized the use of the atomic bomb in August 1945, as, in polls taken at the time, 85 percent of Americans said they approved of that step.*)

At Yalta in February 1945, Churchill, Stalin, and Roosevelt had reaffirmed the principles of the Atlantic Charter, but oftentimes quite insincerely: all three did subscribe to the creation of the United Nations, for which Cordell Hull, that old Wilsonian, had secured the approval of both houses of Congress. But Churchill remained at heart a confirmed imperialist, and Stalin was determined to create a glacis of satellite states on his western borders.

Churchill and Stalin knew what they wanted. Roosevelt was less decided, and Yalta in 1945, like the Versailles Treaty of 1919, was too conciliatory in its concessions to Stalin, given what the West really wanted, but also too demanding, if conciliation had been the West's true purpose. At Yalta Roosevelt insisted on the rights of nations to self-determination, but without being willing to confront Stalin, who had most definitely not fought the war in order to restore Polish militarists to power or Hungarian country gentlemen to their rural seats.

Roosevelt would have had to choose, and a possible way out had been suggested to Averell Harriman, one of Roosevelt's closest advisers, by the Czech president-in-exile, Eduard Benes, whereby postwar Czech foreign policy would have been at the discretion of the Soviets, who would in turn have guaranteed the Czechs their internal autonomy, more or less as was to happen in Finland.[22]

But at Yalta Roosevelt's idea of national independence was more intransigent, and yet, at the same time—given Stalin's purpose—unenforceable. In truth, the Soviet-American arrangement at Yalta made no sense, but Roosevelt, who had seduced America, now assumed that he could likewise seduce "Uncle Joe." This was a terrible misapprehension.

George Washington, once he had resolved on independence, was unshakeable in his purpose. Lincoln, once he had found his way, pursued it to the bitter end. Franklin Roosevelt, by contrast, was a Wilsonian in diplomacy as he had been a social democrat in his reformist program, but incompletely so. A great man in his way and one who died in harness. But was he worthy of the immensely brave young men who died on Omaha Beach or at Okinawa? Perhaps. One would never ask that question of those who died under the leadership of Washington or Lincoln. (Or, for that matter, of George W. Bush.)

Two issues, then: first, Roosevelt should have been either more firm or more accommodating, and second, this situation brings us back to the neighboring themes in American history of inclusion and exclusion, of patriotism and nationalism. Was Roosevelt a nationalist or an internationalist? In theory, this president was committed to a broad program of international cooperation. But his internationalism was invariably defined in ways that were compatible with America's world hegemony, particularly as regarded Europe. Though Roosevelt was eager to secure the collaboration—more or less on his terms—of the Chinese and the Soviets, he was at the same time resolved to substitute American power for that of "Old Europe," and more particularly for that of Great Britain, as had been made clear at Bretton Woods the year before, when by general agreement the dollar was substituted for the pound as the world's currency of reference.

Likewise, as regarded the United Nations, the structure that America imposed on its security council, which still stands, would, in Roosevelt's view, guarantee U.S. predominance in that council, for it replicated in a more polite wording his "four policemen" idea. And as often happens in American life, this self-serving idea had in turn a generous dimension in that Roosevelt's hidden purpose was to avoid a repetition of what had happened in the 1930s. Back then, he now thought, a concerted move by the Americans, the Soviets, the British, and the French would have put an end to the Hitlerian menace.

In brief, neither Roosevelt nor his successors ever lost track of America's interests. When Great Britain, out of breath and out of money, announced in February 1947 that it could no longer uphold

British and American interests in Greece and Turkey, George Marshall, the American secretary of state, observed matter-of-factly that this British statement had a clear implication: America would take over.[23] And in fact Britain's withdrawal was followed in the following month by the declaration of the "Truman Doctrine." Henceforth, the United States would defend any nation that was threatened by any other nation or rebellious minority, which was to say, any nation that seemed likely to come under the control of the Soviet Union or a domestic revolutionary Communist party. Then, in May 1947, Congress voted a credit of 500 million dollars to support the Greek royal government: for the first time in history, America in a time of peace was following an activist policy with regard to a state that was not in its hemisphere.

The British Empire was now a thing of the past, or nearly so. In its place rose America's influence, just as America's productivity had risen: in 1940–1944 America's war industries had produced twice as many guns, ships, planes, and tanks as Germany, Japan, and Italy put together. Now an American empire would take Britain's place as the fulcrum of world politics.

To be sure, America would be far kinder to its satellites than the Soviets would be to theirs: the Anglo-French (and highly immoral) decision in 1956 to invade Egypt on the pretext of keeping the Suez Canal open was soon brought to a halt by Eisenhower, but gently so, as against Russia's brutal bringing to heel of the East Germans, Czechs, and Hungarians between 1953 and 1968. Nevertheless, America too would in some way prevail over its client nations.

And last, we should note that it was on his way back from Yalta and the looming rivalries of the Cold War that Roosevelt invited the king of Arabia to meet him on the American cruiser that was taking him home. With this meeting, followed by Truman's precipitous recognition of the state of Israel in 1948, began the second set of America's postwar problems, close as it would be to a democratic but expansionist Israel, while also hungry for cheap oil.

CHAPTER 12
Decline and Fall

Unlike James M. Cain's celebrated postman, history doesn't usually ring twice. Franklin Roosevelt, especially in 1932 and 1936–1937, could have tried to reshape the deep structures of America's economy and society. He could have done more for labor unions and for African Americans. He could have worked harder to enable the state to act on the economy. But, for fear of alienating the southern wing of his party, and for lack of will as well, he came to the banks of the Rubicon and then backed off. A unique opportunity to strengthen America's version of social democracy had come and gone.

And so it is that the history of post-Roosevelt America can be divided into two parts. The first runs from Harry Truman's presidency in 1945–1953 to the years of John Kennedy and Lyndon Johnson, from 1960 to 1968. In this first phase, America's inclusive social democracy made some inertial headway, though in retrospect its greatest achievement of these decades was that it survived. Then, in the second phase, the left gradually fell apart just as the right pulled itself together, until finally, in the 1990s, the left's strategic retreat became something of a rout with the electoral "victory" of George W. Bush in 2000.

Abroad, both phases of this same period were marked by war: cold in the main, but at times quite hot in Korea and Vietnam.

*****

During the Depression years, Franklin Roosevelt could (perhaps) have counted on the public's indigence and indignation to mobilize opinion. After 1945, even the memory of indigence receded, and with it America's inclusive and reformist zeal. It was said of American socialism at the beginning of the twentieth century that it was killed by prosperity: Could a well-paid worker really want to be a socialist? True or not for 1900, this explanation has great relevance to the fate of social democracy after the Second World War.

In 1945, with some Keynesian exceptions, most economists predicted the coming of a new economic crisis whose first cause would be the end of government spending. Rearming for war had pulled America out of the Depression. It made sense in 1945 to suppose correspondingly that the end of government war expenditures would put the economy right back where it had been in the later 1930s. (So widespread was this assumption that the Russian foreign minister Vyacheslav Molotov suggested, as a special favor to the United States, that Washington should extend a loan to the Soviet Union, which would then use these funds to bolster demand for American products.)

But far from sinking, as expected, America's economic fortunes after 1945 rose to unprecedented heights and from a very healthy start: in that year the United States accounted for 84 percent of the world's production of civilian aircraft, 50 percent of its telephones, and 85 percent of its refrigerators and washing machines. (In 1913 Britain, then at the height of its glory, accounted for only 8 percent of the world's industrial production.)[1] With 6 percent of the global population, the United States was producing one-third of the world's wheat and 55 percent of its steel. U.S. power was unprecedented in both absolute and relative terms. In 1939 Britain had foreign holdings that were worth 16 billion dollars; in 1945 Britain owed the United States 12 billion. The U.S. GNP moved up from 91 billion dollars in 1939 to 166 billion in 1945, which is to say that the United States at that point was earning half of the world's total income. (In these same years, the value of all property in France, private and public, fell by half. In Britain, the production of civilian goods and services during the war fell by more than a fifth, while in America, it rose by 12 percent.)

For Europeans, the First World War had been suicidal, and the second one, though less destructive of lives (in the west at least if not in the east), had added shame and remorse to further material loss.

But America emerged from the war richer and infinitely more powerful than ever before. In 1815 Andrew Jackson's victorious army at the battle of New Orleans had been 6,000 strong. At Gettysburg, the victorious Northerners numbered 120,000. In November 1918 more than one million Americans were aligned in European trenches. And now in 1945 the United States, with its monopoly of nuclear weapons, had the ability not only to defeat but literally to demolish any hostile power. Militarily and economically dominant, America also wielded "soft power," finding itself at the heart of a globalized mass culture centered in Hollywood and New York. In the first decades after the Second World War, Victoria de Grazia has written, "to create a successful national cinema meant finding a niche within the Hollywood system."[2]

Of course, these gaps of wealth and power narrowed after the war's end. But progress in Europe was slow: in 1951, rationing was still in force in Britain. And meanwhile the American economy continued to flourish. By 1960, one American in three had settled in the new suburbs, many in prefabricated Levittowns (from which African Americans were excluded), which seem to us today to have been less than perfect, but which were much praised during the Eisenhower years. Television was almost unknown in 1945, but fifteen years later 40 million Americans owned TV sets. Everyone could feel palpably that "the American Dream" was no impossible fantasy. To be sure, the premises of a consumer society had already been visible in the 1920s, but now boundless prosperity, it seemed, was within everyone's grasp, or so Americans were led to believe by film and television.

This well-being fed America's national sense of itself as a promised land. Its national self-confidence rose to an all-time high and became national arrogance. America had been a goal for Europeans who had wanted to remake their lives. But now Americans came to think that theirs should be a globally providential and dominating state; and as its antifascist crusading spirit of the 1930s mutated into anticommunism in the 1950s, social democracy went into a decline. Labor unions had gained 5 million members during the Second World War: they were

255

stronger after 1945 than they had ever been. But their strength would not arrest the country's rightward drift.

This shift toward the right, as one might expect in the American setting of interconnected exclusion and inclusion, was neither sudden nor brutal. Important liberal steps were taken from time to time. In 1947, critically, Truman abolished segregation in the armed forces. He also urged Congress—vainly—to pass federal laws that would have made lynching a federal offense and that would have superseded the local southern laws that made it impossible for many African Americans to vote. Truman, however, did not give up: encouraged by his reelection as president in 1948, he proposed to renew the New Deal as a whole with what he called "the Fair Deal." He aimed to guarantee Americans some kind of universal medical coverage (a right which, shockingly, they have not secured to this day), and to raise the minimum wage. (It remains today at an embarrassingly low level.) He also pushed through a plan for massive public housing and proposed an extension of social security coverage.

On balance, however, the Fair Deal was not a success. Southern Democrats rejected most of Truman's measures, and even joined Republicans to override a presidential veto concerning labor relations, something that would have been unthinkable under Franklin Roosevelt. Besides, after the outbreak of the Korean War in 1950, Truman lost interest in domestic reform.

The 1950s and 1960s saw a further erosion of the social democratic idea in other realms as well. Big business had become even bigger during the war, and its profits grew apace. Money had always been of consequence in American politics, but now, lobbies and corporate money took on a new and cancerous dimension.

Steadily, the United States began to move to the right, and it is a curious aspect of American politics in the 1950s that the decline of the New Deal would have gone even further had it not been for the restraining presence of a moderate Republican president. As regarded domestic policy, Dwight D. Eisenhower's goal was not to dismantle the New Deal at all, but to broaden its scope by improving its efficiency. He hoped, for example, to secure congressional approval for some private/ public arrangement that would give some sort of medical coverage to all Americans, and especially to the 2 million most handicapped citizens. He agreed to sponsor a (Keynesian) program of interstate highways. He wrote to his brother in 1954: "Should any political party attempt to abolish social security, unemployment insurance, and eliminate labor laws and farm programs, you would not hear of that party again in our political history. There is a tiny splinter group, of course, that believes you can do these things. Among them are . . . [a] few Texas oil million-aires, and an occasional politician or business man from other areas. Their number is negligible and they are stupid."[3] That same year he told a news conference: "When it comes down to dealing with the relation-ships between the human in this country and his government, the people in this administration believe in being what I think we would normally call liberal, and when we deal with the economic affairs of this coun-try, we believe in being conservative."[4] William F. Buckley Jr. founded the reactionary *National Review* in 1955 not to support but to oppose Eisenhower's policies. (Buckley later became an ardent Reaganite.) In 1954, the Supreme Court reversed its decision of 1896 and ruled segre-gation unconstitutional. After some hesitation, in 1957, at Little Rock, Eisenhower ordered federal troops to enforce this ruling.

In foreign affairs, Eisenhower's instincts were humane. It matters greatly, for example, that in 1945 he had urged Truman not to bomb Hiroshima and Nagasaki. "I thought," he later wrote, "that our country should avoid shocking world opinion by the use of a weapon whose employment was, I thought, no longer mandatory as a measure to save American lives. It was my belief that Japan was, at that very moment, seeking some way to surrender with a minimum loss of 'face.'"[5] True enough, during his presidency, many American diplomatic moves were based on the idea that the alternative to peace as America understood it would be nuclear war. And yet it is also true that in 1954 he refused to heed the advice of his chief of staff and his secretary of state, John Foster Dulles, who had urged him to accede to an incredible French request, namely that the United States drop an atomic bomb on the Vietnamese forces who were besieging a 10,000-man French armed camp at Dien Bien Phu. It is to be regretted, however, that Eisenhower only got around to criticizing the "military industrial complex" in his farewell address, and that he did so little to thwart it during his presidency.

*****

As regards social reform, contrary to what is commonly assumed, not much emerged from the presidency of Eisenhower's successor, John F. Kennedy, a media-savvy, handsome, young, falsely eloquent heir of an Irish party machine in Boston, and a very rich philanderer (with actresses, society women, and prostitutes). Charles de Gaulle inamicably labeled him "le garçon coiffeur" (the apprentice hairdresser) and saw him as a kind of political Rudolph Valentino. One commentator on Kennedy's foreign policy has uncharitably emphasized "his fear of failure, and his almost childlike admiration for daring and male heroism."[6]

For Kennedy, what mattered was not social redistribution or more civil rights for African Americans. He naively believed instead—in his well-known words—that "a rising tide lifts all boats," meaning that economic measures that helped the rich would, by strengthening the overall economy, benefit poorer Americans as well. At the time of his assassination, his foreign policy record was mixed (America was already very far involved in Vietnam) and his domestic one was no better.

By contrast, Lyndon B. Johnson's accession to the presidency in 1963 after Kennedy's death was a turning point, but alas, a disastrous one, for both the image and the reality of America's national purpose.

Johnson was a dynamic and supremely able parliamentary intriguer, a willfully vulgar man who loved to shock and dominate his close advisers. Power fascinated him. It was said of him that he looked as if he were always moving, even as he was sitting still. And unlike Kennedy, Johnson did have a plan for reshaping America's public self.

The New Deal had been imagined more or less coherently as an answer to the economic crisis of 1929, in which purpose it largely failed, as we have seen: it took the war and its (Keynesian) governmental expenditures to pull America out of the Depression. By contrast, Johnson's plan for a Great Society was undertaken in a period of full prosperity. Its scope was not just to secure more employment. Its point was social justice, and its centerpiece was the Civil Rights Act of 1964.

At last, the awful compromise of 1877 was to be squarely faced. Now racial discrimination against African Americans and Native Americans would be forbidden in matters relating to both employment and housing. This was a critical moment of national inclusion in a country where slavery and its sequels had been America's peculiar form of original and communal sin. Woodrow Wilson, universally applauded as a great democrat, had refused to consider the issue of race. Franklin Roosevelt had not dared to address the problem. Truman had tried to do so, but with mixed success. Kennedy, obsessed by the Cold War and his imaginary and nasty "missile gap," had not had the time or the will to face it. But Johnson finally tried to answer the questions that in August 1963 had brought more than 200,000 latter-day pilgrims to the grounds in front of the Lincoln Memorial in Washington to hear Martin Luther King Jr.'s eloquent "I Have a Dream" speech.

Many social programs that had frightened Roosevelt and stymied his successors were now made into law. The most visible of these was Medicare, which guaranteed medical assistance to all American citizens over the age of 65. It was approved by Congress in 1965, as was its corollary Medicaid in 1966, which extended some of Medicare's benefits to millions of unemployed or indigent Americans. Notice was now taken that the United States Constitution does not guarantee a citizen's right to education, which, being a municipal obligation, is most generously funded in the richest towns, though it is most needed in the poorest ones. The Great Society program attempted to deal with this, if only peripherally. Preschools for poor children (the Head Start program) were on the president's wish list, as was the creation of a Public Broadcasting Corporation. Above all else was a War on Poverty, whose name strikes a religious and even mystical chord of fraternity so different from what most wars are about. In 1964, at Johnson's request, Congress enacted the creation of an Office of Economic Opportunity, which was charged with many social assignments, one of them the continuing reeducation and retraining of American workers. In brief, America's national purpose was to be universalistically redefined.

Tragically, Johnson's War on Poverty was to be a failure, and one that was immensely consequential both for American social democracy and for the trajectory of American nationalism. Franklin Roosevelt had stumbled, as had Harry Truman, and Lyndon Johnson fell.

The first cause of this doubled failure was of course America's involvement in Vietnam.

*****

From 1945 onward, the foreign policy of the American nation—and within that context the rise of an exclusionary American nationalism—revolved around three catastrophes. The first, which was initially understood as a triumph (as in Paul Fussell's ironic "Thank God for the Atom Bomb!"), was Truman's decision to use atomic weapons against the defeated and peace-seeking Japanese. With this began a cycle of nuclear confrontation whose sequel today is the American-Iranian confrontation over Iran's desire to achieve atomic self-defense against the United States and atomic parity with Israel, the tail that in foreign policy inexplicably wags the American dog.

The second catastrophe, which followed from the first, was Truman's decision to confront the Soviet Union in the name of world democracy. Truman's determination to resist Soviet aggression once Stalin himself had decided to adopt a confrontational policy (as in Korea) is much to be admired. But was it necessary to embark on that contestatory road in the first place?

The third catastrophe, which followed from the second, was the war in Vietnam, which killed Lyndon Johnson's hopes for a Great Society.

In 1945 America's sense of national self and of democratic purpose was stronger than it had ever been: "Pride goeth before a fall." Looking forward, we see that although America's sincere goal was to defend "the Free World," the long-term trend of its policies, as they moved from the inclusion of anti-Stalinist Europe to the global exclusion of movements of national liberation, was to shift from patriotism to self-serving nationalism.

Looking backward from our own day, as we consider American foreign policy after 1945, we are reminded that America's trajectory after the war would have been very different if the New Deal had succeeded during the 1930s in transforming American economic and social structures. An incompletely democratic shift in the American nation's domestic purpose before 1941 set the stage for the nationalist drift of American foreign policy after the war.

The horrifying decision to use the atom bomb, which was first successfully tested on July 16, 1945, highlighted the ambiguities of Harry Truman's ways of thinking. In many ways, Truman is an attractive figure. He began his career as a loyal but nonetheless honest member of a none-too-honest Democratic Party machine in St. Louis, Missouri. In 1944 party stalwarts convinced Roosevelt that Truman, whom FDR hardly knew, would be a suitable running mate, not too far to the right (as Truman had argued for the civil rights of "Negroes") and not too far to the left, as the former vice president, Henry Wallace, was said to be.

Of all the great presidents of the United States to date, Jefferson was surely the most contradictory—and therefore the most American, torn as he always was between a yearning for the realization of America's universalist principles and his acceptation of its most shocking vice, torn also between wishing for an American state that would be weak and one that would be strong. Mutatis mutandis, much the same can be said of Truman. The man had the common touch, and, as one of his admiring biographers remarked, Truman was the "son of rural, inland America, raised only a generation removed from the frontier and imbued with the old Jeffersonian ideal of a rural democracy."[7]

Truman had come to power as an unknown and uncertain man who revealingly invoked divine help in his first address to Congress a few days after the death of Franklin Roosevelt. "As I have assumed my heavy duties," he said, "I humbly pray Almighty God, in the words of King Solomon, 'Give therefore thy servant an understanding heart to judge thy people, that I may discern between good and bad; for who is able to judge this thy so great a people?'"

But though unknown, Truman was a feisty politician eager to assert his authority, and all the more inclined to do so by the nature of his character: he was often impulsive, and not much given to reflection on the complexities of the problems he faced. "I can't understand it," he once wrote to his wife," except to attribute it to God. He guides me, I think."[8] In a celebrated episode, after listening for some time to an economist's "on the one hand" and "on the other hand," Truman exclaimed that what he needed was a good one-armed economist.

Until his accession to the presidency, Truman knew nothing about the atom bomb or the Manhattan Project. His cabinet ministers informed him at once. Work on this intensive effort to develop nuclear weapons went forward quickly. Some weeks later, in Germany at Potsdam, where he was meeting with Stalin and Churchill's successor Atlee, Truman was informed of the successful test explosion (an event which, more than incidentally, delighted nearly all of the physicists involved in the project, most of them university professors). Truman then informed Stalin, who seemed unimpressed, if only because spies had already informed Soviet intelligence about the work that was being done at Los Alamos. What now was to be done? Should the first bomb be dropped on an uninhabited site in Japan as a warning? Or should a city be the first target?

Truman's advisers and military chiefs were divided. Eisenhower was against using it, perhaps because he had now seen at first hand the devastating effect of allied bombings in Germany. But Secretary of War Henry Stimson, who would later—vainly—urge Truman to share atomic secrets with the Russians because they would sooner or later discover them on their own, was ready to use the bomb in 1945, his first concern being that there might soon be nothing left to bomb in Japan: "I was a little fearful," he wrote in his diary, "that before we could get ready the

Air Force might have Japan so thoroughly bombed out that the new weapon would not have a fair background to show its strength."[9] As Godfrey Hodgson has explained: "Although from time to time, those with a voice in the consideration of policy, including Stimson, did acknowledge the possibility that the bomb not be dropped, such occasions were grace notes to the main theme, which was that as soon as the bomb was there, it would be used."[10]

Truman was, then as later, aware of the ghastliness of this weapon. When urged in 1948 to allow the military to decide on its future use, he refused, telling the chairman of the Atomic Energy Commission: "I don't think we ought to use this thing unless we absolutely have to. It is a terrible thing to order the use of something that is so terribly destructive, destructive beyond anything we have ever had. You have got to understand that this isn't a military weapon. It is used to wipe out women and children and unarmed people and not for military uses. So we have got to treat this differently from rifles and cannon and ordinary things like that."[11]

But in July 1945 two points were uppermost in Truman's mind. His most immediate concern was not to endanger the lives of American soldiers. In June 1945 the capture of the small island of Okinawa had occasioned 50,000 American casualties. Many Okinawans had preferred suicide to occupation, and this was seen as a measure of the determination that would drive resistance to an American landing in Japan itself. Very little attention was given to an alternate plan, namely to wait for the Japanese to prefer surrender to starvation. Their supply of oil had been completely cut off; their ability to resist American bombers was now negligible.

Truman's longer-term concern was to drop the bomb so as to impress not just the Japanese, but the Soviets. His secretary of state, James Byrnes, was particularly determined to impress Stalin with the new might of the American nation. Contrary to what is often assumed (as by George W. Bush today), it is ordinarily not a good idea to threaten people who are quite able to defend themselves. Predictably, Stalin's response to the Americans' use of the bomb was not to knuckle under but, on the contrary, to move forward with more determination and to accelerate his country's efforts to acquire the bomb as well.

And beneath these layers of the palimpsest may have lain another, more sinister, unacknowledged reason for using the bomb, namely racism. Would Truman have decided that dropping a bomb on a German city with its blond and blue-eyed children was a good thing to do? To be sure, there is no written evidence to support this hypothesis about the importance of race: no trace of it appears even in the correspondence of James Byrnes, a Southerner who had begun in public life as a protégé of Pitchfork Ben Tillman, a fierce South Carolina racist, and who had remained a profoundly convinced partisan of white supremacy. But we do know that racist reflexes often rose to the surface in wartime America. Thus Stimson, a moderate Republican secretary of war, noted in his diary in 1942 that the pressure being exerted by some African Americans to secure civil equality was secretly encouraged by Japanese and communist agents,[12] and the FBI went so far as to place under arrest a dozen black militants who were accused of hoping for a Japanese victory.

The Japanese were seen as members of a hostile and ambitious race. They were both feared and despised. (Some American soldiers had even taken to decapitating and boiling the heads of dead Japanese soldiers and sending their skulls back home as souvenirs.)[13] Americans were struck by the harsh way the Japanese treated prisoners of war. (The way a nation deals with its war prisoners—formerly feared and now helpless—is often taken, the world over, as expressive of the nation's character, a lesson of which experienced soldiers are well aware and which George W. Bush might also have learned had he carried out his own military obligations.) Memories were alive in America of the brutal air bombardment of Chinese civilians by the Japanese air force. One historian of this era is of the mind that the Japanese were hated by Americans as no enemy had been hated since the wars against American Indians.[14]

In any event, in July 1945 Truman decided to drop the bomb on not just one but two Japanese cities.[15] (It is relevant here that Truman is today one of the neoconservatives' most favored references.) And of course,

Truman's decision did have the outcome he desired: the Japanese, after some last-minute hesitation, did indeed surrender a few days after the bombing of Hiroshima and Nagasaki. But using these bombs also guaranteed that, sooner or later, other states would also acquire them. In a predictable manner, a nationalist and nuclear move by the United States engendered nationalist and nuclear responses in the Soviet Union, in western Europe, and eventually in every nation that is involved in confrontational policies and has the means to secure this devastating weapon. Hiroshima and Nagasaki may have hastened Japan's surrender by a few weeks, but they weakened the moral credit of the United States forever.

It is hard to give a convincing explanation of when and why the Terror broke out in Revolutionary France; but one explanation that holds our attention has to do with the execution of the father-king, Louis XVI. Once that line had been crossed, it then became feasible to execute anyone. We can reason by analogy: once Americans had put to death—and in the most ghastly way—tens of thousands of unarmed civilians in a country that was already on its knees, every other abuse became feasible as well: the massacres of civilians in Korea and Vietnam, Agent Orange, Guantánamo.

How is it that law-abiding and decent Americans feel entitled to approve of such things today? A critical question to which there is no answer. Perhaps the origins of these lapses reach back to the seventeenth-century killing of Indians, or to the devastation of the South by the North in 1864–1865, and perhaps also to the horrifying destruction of Hiroshima and Nagasaki.

*****

The Cold War was the most expensive war in history, and one of the longest, running from the blockade of Berlin in 1948 to the disintegration of the Soviet Union in 1989. Tens of thousands of bombs and rockets, hundreds of now useless military bases, trillions of wasted dollars all speak to its intensity. It seemed at the time to oppose two incompatible state systems, one of which would have to die: better dead than red. On the one hand, an atheistic and communistic and aggressive Soviet Union, and on the other, a pacific "free world" bent on a rational policy of containment. Once the Cold War was under way, this view of the conflict seemed self-evidently sensible. Indeed, once it had been launched, the Cold War made perfect sense as perceived by both sides: from a western point of view, the Soviet dictatorship was tyrannous and unnatural. From a Soviet perspective, capitalism was doomed by history.

But today, as has been seen, we can percieve the issue of the origins of the Cold War differently. Here, our two starting points are in personality (and illusions): those of Franklin Roosevelt and also of an inexperienced Harry Truman on the one side, and, on the other, those of Josef Stalin, along with the goals he had set for himself after his long experience of both bourgeois and fascistic responses to the existence of the Soviet Union.

The Soviet regime had nearly died twice, first in 1919–1920 at the hands of white counterrevolutionaries abetted by British, French, American, and Japanese armies, and second in 1941–1942 at the hands of Nazi Germany and its central European allies, the Slovaks, Hungarians, Croats, Lithuanians, Estonians, Rumanians, and Bulgarians. In 1945, for reasons that were partly ideological but principally geopolitical, Stalin was determined to rearrange central and eastern Europe so that this could never happen again, a policy that made a great deal of Soviet ideological sense, and nationalistic Russian sense as well, given the inimical attitudes to Russia of both Imperial Germany after 1890 and Nazi Germany after 1933.

At once prudent and paranoid (but then, as a well-known joke asserts, to live in the Soviet Union and not to be paranoid was to be totally insane), Stalin did not intend to extend Soviet power everywhere. Nineteenth-century Victorian Britain and Bismarckian Germany had been quasi-hegemonic powers that had carefully respected at least some of their neighbors' pride and rights, and Stalin functioned in a similar mode. Finland's fate was a suggestive example of his modus operandi. This country had twice fought the Soviet Union, at first on its own in

1939, and later as an ally of the Nazis. Stalin could certainly have decided that he had good reason to make of this tiny but disputatious neighbor a subservient—and socialist—satellite. But he did not: instead, Finland lost its diplomatic autonomy (as Benes had suggested Czechoslovakia might also do), but it retained the right to manage its internal arrangements as it saw fit. In similar manner, the Soviets withdrew from territories they had occupied in Norway and Iran. Moreover, Stalin decided not to back Italian and especially Greek communists in their plans for upheaval or revolution.

Stalin worked within an established and age-old European pattern that allowed to each great power a sphere of influence that went beyond its borders (as the Monroe Doctrine did for the United States). Stalin also thought in a Marxist frame, and this incited him to prudent expectation: Why challenge the United States immediately and directly, as time and history were on his side? Inevitably, he thought, fissures would appear in the capitalist camp. Wouldn't Great Britain, patriarchal and proud of its world empire, chafe at American hegemony? Could not some opportunities arise therefrom for a Soviet Union that had remained on decent terms with England? Charles de Gaulle in 1941–1942 had understood that Churchill had resigned himself to doing whatever Washington required of him, but Stalin had a higher estimate of Great Britain's enduring resilience, and this incited him to wait and see.

Stalin's goals were therefore limited, but at the same time he was completely determined to achieve them. And if push came to shove, he also thought that he could secure them without too much trouble: the military superiority of the Soviets in Europe was overwhelming.

But Roosevelt misunderstood Stalin's resolve, just as Stalin underestimated how unwilling the American champions of world democracy would be to see Russia's nearest neighbors, from Estonia to Bulgaria, fall under Soviet—and communist—hegemony. America's national myths, its sense of being the carrier of democracy in a corrupted world, were very strong. It could not and would not yield on this issue. But by nature and choice Stalin feared democracy: he had *said*, of course, that democracy should prevail in eastern Europe (diplomats often lie), but he had no more intention of letting this happen in Poland than he did in the Soviet Union itself.

Truman's naïve response was that Stalin had not kept his diplomatic word. He was sincerely shocked that Poland, a country that had sent millions of its people to America, should now fall into an undemocratic and even retrograde Soviet orbit.

In addition, European and American public opinion was shocked by the barbarous behavior of Soviet troops. (It is thought today that during the Second World War at least two million German women were raped by their liberators. When informed of this, Stalin quipped that Russian soldiers—after what they had been through—deserved a bit of fun. Westerners were not amused.)

From 1945 to 1947, every successive misunderstanding widened the gap between the increasingly reluctant allies. The communist coup d'état in Prague in February 1948 and the beginning of the Soviets' blockade of West Berlin in that same year crystallized American resolve. Truman, who was not much given to hesitation and analysis, and who thought that honest men should keep their word, reacted boldly: timidity was not his forte, as General Douglas MacArthur was to discover in 1951 when Truman defiantly relieved this great war hero of his command in Japan and Korea. Containment now became America's official doctrine in foreign policy.

Containment was a self-fulfilling strategy that was laid out in February 1946 (when alternative arrangements would still have been possible) by George F. Kennan, a career diplomat, quite sure of himself, who saw the Soviet Union in the light of what he had learned about Nazi Germany. In his flawed view, Kennan chose to forget that Stalin had done all he could to cohabit peaceably with Hitler—his worst enemy— and might well have chosen to follow an identical course with the United States. Kennan's starting point was instead that an unbridgeable rivalry —and even a mortal enmity—now separated the capitalist and parliamentary West from the dictatorial and communist East. Whether they liked it or not, he explained, peace-loving Americans were now confronted by an alien force; no durable agreement could ever be reached between the United States and Stalin's communist (and as it was subsequently labeled, evil) empire.

The point of containment was not to push the Soviet Union back and out of east central Europe. (For all his faults, Kennan was not an uninformed and primitive mind, as are the neoconservatives of our own times.) Nor was it, after 1949, to overthrow the Chinese communist regime. It was instead to keep the Soviet Union, now indeed become more militant and aggressive, from extending its sphere of influence to newly decolonialized states in Asia and Africa. Anticommunism became America's national purpose abroad, and this development, more than incidentally, allowed the anticommunist demagogue Joseph McCarthy to run rampant in Washington. Irving Kristol, later to be a founding father of neoconservatism, presumably did not thrill to Senator McCarthy's hunt for "pinks, punks, and perverts," but he did opine in 1952: "There is one thing that the American people know about Senator McCarthy: he, like them, is unequivocally anticommunist. About the spokesmen for American liberalism, they feel no such thing. And with some justification."[16]

American public opinion responded to this new crusade against communism as it had after 1941 to the crusade against militarism, Nazism, and fascism. In the name of universalizing democracy (and for many, in the name of religion also), an often nationalistic and increasingly American empire began to take shape in opposition to its detested and godless Soviet rival. American opinion sanctioned this shift, which, in line with American tradition, followed a presidential lead and was developed by a self-regarding group of advisers, in this instance the "foreign policy establishment,"[17] a circumscribed and elitist group that dominated the American state department at the time.

The origin of this very high-flying lobby, exclusively concerned (it thought) with the public good rather than with some particularist ambition, had its origins in the circle of diplomats and politicians that had coalesced around Elihu Root, who had served in the McKinley and

Theodore Roosevelt administrations and in the Senate, and had built a reputation as an expert in the resolution of international disputes through his work with the Carnegie Endowment for International Peace. Most of them by far were drawn from America's eastern, WASP, upper middle class, a milieu that had strong affinities with British ruling circles. (These same affinities, it will be remembered, had brought together Franklin Roosevelt, a liberal American aristocrat, and Winston Churchill, the grandson of a duke and originally a liberal *enfant terrible*.) Among their numbers figured Henry Stimson, the secretary of war in 1944–1945; John Foster Dulles, later Eisenhower's secretary of state, who was the grandson of one secretary of state and the nephew of another; Dean Acheson, Averell Harriman, Kennan (more vocal but less aggressive and from a more modest milieu); Henry Morgenthau Jr., a member of Roosevelt's cabinet; and Walter Lippmann, the best-known journalist of his time. Curiously, this same elite foreign policy establishment also generated the most notorious Soviet spy of the period, Alger Hiss, who, unlike his tormentors (especially Richard Nixon, who would build his career on this case) but very much like his patrons, had been born to the purple.

The Atlantic Charter of Britain and the United States in 1941, the triumph of the Anglo-American democracies in 1945, the creation of the United Nations (often then known jokingly as the United Stations because of the overlap between the wishes of the United States and the decision of the United Nations), marked the triumph of this informal team or lobby, much of whose success depended on the profound indifference of the American public toward all things foreign and diplomatic. "Convergence theory" gave intellectual credibility to this pressure group, and in a way that was calculated to please, as it conveniently updated the context of the American national idea.[18] In the older, Marxist scheme of things, world history was structured around the idea of class war and the eventual triumph of "the working class." For the "convergers," whose theory took on the idea of America as a providential society inscribed in nature, all societies would in the end converge, all of them becoming more or less successful imitations of the American system.

Some might have thought of this theory as another instance of an aggressive and secular American imperialism, but Kennan, his friends, and his allies saw instead a Jeffersonian "empire of liberty" manifested in America's progress from rebellious colony to world hegemon. America's progress could not be doubted, nor could opposition to it be thought surprising: history showed that the American creed had from time immemorial been pitted against the forces of evil, incarnated at various times by monarchic England, Mexican barbarism, southern slavery, fascism, militarism, and now Godless communism.

We understand today that the interests of all capitalist societies will not always be identical, but American leaders in the 1950s were by contrast convinced that—in the name of universal freedom—America's material interests would and should prevail, and to everyone's advantage. In the celebrated words of Charles Wilson, a secretary of defense who had been an automobile executive, what was good for General Motors would be good for the country, and, he might have added, for the planet as a whole. In time, around the world, standards of living, different for the moment, would eventually all improve as the American supertanker ship of state moved through history, dragging every other country in its wake. (It may yet prove to do that very thing.) America's international and national tasks overlapped. Occasional tensions would arise, but they would be resolved. In late 1955 John Foster Dulles, then secretary of state, favored European unity. He explained to Harold Macmillan, soon to be Britain's prime minister: "It may well be that a six-nation [European] community will evolve protectionist tendencies. It may be that it will show a trend toward greater independence. In the long run, however, I cannot but feel that the resultant increased unity would bring . . . greater responsibility and devotion to the common welfare of Western Europe."[19]

For the moment, during the 1950s, which marked the nadir of Europe's influence in the world, the incompatibility between America's national/universal goal and communism meant that Europe needed to align itself in an American-dominated North Atlantic Treaty Organization, a view that most Europeans supinely accepted at the time, with the conspicuous exception of a much-criticized Charles de Gaulle. (Tony Blair, with his ironically labeled "New Labour," is the last major European politician to persist in this antiquated mode of thought.)

As for the Middle East, the convergence view held that Islamism was as irrelevant to contemporary life as Sovietism. Modernization in that region might come from Nasserism and military rule, or by the westernization of local societies (the path followed by the Shah of Iran). But Muslim countries too would eventually fall in line. And in the realm of theory, the last avatar of misguided convergence theory (as it was celebratedly developed by Francis Fukuyama) was that civilization had come to the end of its societal evolution. Because the essence of modern history had been in the rivalry of the outmoded Soviet Union and a triumphant United States, a society whose structure had been inscribed from the first in "nature," it stood to reason that the end of Sovietism also had to be the end of history.

Convinced of the malevolence of the Soviet Union, blind to the origins of Stalin's "sphere of influence" view, and also convinced of the place of anticommunism in their moralized trajectory of their nation, Americans in the late 1940s were at once resolved and strikingly generous. In 1947, moved in part by the ambiguities of America's economic future (how could it sell its exports if there were no markets ready to accept them?), George Marshall, the former chief of staff of the army and now secretary of state, announced the American plan for a renewal of western Europe. (Russia had been offered a place in this system but declined it, being by now deeply suspicious of Americans bearing gifts.)

In 1900 American leaders had reasoned that their diplomacy should be at the service of their nation's trade. Now that the balance of trade and moral international imperative had shifted, the American diplomatic establishment of the 1950s and 1960s took it for granted that American trade should follow America's supposedly universalist diplomacy. On the whole, Cold War U.S. governments followed an example set by Franklin Roosevelt, who in 1938 had refused to do much when the Mexican government decided to nationalize American oil interests in that country.

Every rule has exceptions, to be sure, and the fortunes of the United Fruit Company—which had once retained the legal services of John Foster Dulles—were not unrelated to the CIA-sponsored overthrow of Guatemala's legally elected president, Jacobo Arbenz, in 1954. In fact, very unenviable indeed was the fate of all local reformers who chose to seek the help—direct or indirect—of the Soviet Union, especially when their country was in Latin America, where the ghost of the Monroe Doctrine might still be invoked. In addition to Arbenz, the fates of Rómulo Gallegos in Venezuela, João Goulart in Brazil, and Salvador Allende in Chile were there to prove it, as were tens of thousands of murdered Central American Indians.

Recently George W. Bush has made halfhearted efforts to overthrow Hugo Chavez, the populist president of Venezuela. He would undoubtedly have acted with greater determination if Chavez's major ally had been the Soviet Union rather than a geriatric Cuban communist regime.

*****

There is no point in detailing here the ups and downs of the half-century-long military-diplomatic tourney that followed the decay of the Soviet-American alliance in 1945–1947. The contest ended, as we know, with the collapse of the "evil empire" in 1989, at the end of the costliest of all wars, costly in dollars certainly, and often—as in Vietnam—costly in blood as well.

The most worthy of respect of the postwar American presidents who fought the Cold War may well have been Dwight Eisenhower. He too, like Truman, believed in confronting the Soviet Union, which, by this time, may well have been an unavoidable policy. This meant that Eisenhower embraced Spain's General Francisco Franco as an anticommunist ally, and that France's colonial war in Indochina was praised as a pursuit of "the cause of human liberty." Still, as can never be said too often, Eisenhower dreaded the use of atomic weapons (in contrast, for example, to George H. W. Bush, who would later opine that the United States could "win" a nuclear war).

And one of the least capable of these same presidents was surely, once again, John F. Kennedy, who brought the world to the edge of destruction, first by supporting Cuban counterrevolutionaries, and then by making a poor impression on the Soviet leader, Nikita Khrushchev, who decided first to challenge him, and then, blessedly, to back off. (A public opinion poll in 1976 made of Kennedy one of the great presidents of the United States, although this romanticized figure—handsome, charming, and murdered at a sadly young age—was in fact one of its least distinguished leaders.)

George W. Bush's foreign policy today does have the merit of being all of a piece (if mendacious and consistently brutal), but that of American social democracy in the 1960s was often confused, being simultaneously intent on upholding human rights and pursuing material and political gains.[20] (As Madeleine Albright, Bill Clinton's secretary of state, later ingeniously put it: "Multilateral when we can, unilateral when we have to.")

Vietnam was Kennedy's (and Johnson's) most serious error, a war that Kennan—the great architect of containment—rightly described as the most disastrous mistake in two centuries of American foreign policy.[21] By 1963 Kennedy had tripled American aid to the government run by the Roman Catholic (like himself) and quite corrupt Diem brothers, who had refused to hold elections, which had been promised by the West in 1954, and which would surely have been favorable to the communists. But Kennedy's death could have been a turning point for U.S. policy toward Vietnam. However, the "best and the brightest" (of America's WASPish foreign policy establishment), keen on the doctrine of containment that had been theirs for two decades, urged Kennedy's successor, Lyndon Johnson, to go forward with the war. To stop, they insisted, in an argument that had been used to justify American involvement in Indochina ever since Eisenhower had articulated his "domino theory," would lead to the collapse of all pro-American governments in Southeast Asia. (The specificities of Vietnamese nationalism escaped them completely.) In their Manichaean universe, to abandon Vietnam to its fate would be to guarantee the progress of the Soviet Union.

Personally, Johnson cared very little about Vietnam, but he did care deeply about his program for a Great Society, and in consequence he got everything tragically wrong. His political instincts, his emotional understanding of America's sense of its national self, led him to conclude that American opinion would not accept even a partial defeat in Vietnam, and this at the very moment when Robert Kennedy, the assassinated president's younger brother, began to favor ending the war. To give up in Vietnam would be, thought Johnson, to court defeat in the 1964 presidential election. To secure his domestic goals, therefore, Johnson decided to win John Kennedy's war rather than to end it. The two types of issues, domestic and foreign, were inextricably bound together in his mind. In March 1965, shortly before he delivered his "We Shall Overcome" speech, in which he declared that to enable African Americans to secure equal rights was to work "for the dignity of man and the destiny of democracy," Johnson gave the order to begin a massive bombing campaign against North Vietnam.

Up to a point, soon reached, this brutal and nationalistic strategy worked beautifully. The 1964 election was indeed a Democratic triumph. But rarely was any victory so completely pyrrhic. The war devoured the public funds that Johnson had wanted to dedicate to his social democratic program. The conflict also proved militarily unmanageable, as just about everyone—including even high-ranking officers—understood from 1968 onward. Johnson's war repulsed the leftist and centrist voters who were his natural constituency. Vietnam was Johnson's undoing, as wars—and especially unsuccessful wars—have proved to be for social democracy in so many times and places.

The social and cultural effects of the war in Vietnam touched all Americans in one way or another. For some, what mattered most was the televised evidence of America's military brutality. For others, defeat rankled, as did the cultural upheaval the war had brought into being. In France, the "événements" of May 1968 were an episode more than a turning point. In America, by contrast, the 1960s were the beginning of a new age, and it is impossible to understand the obscurantist passions of so many of George W. Bush's supporters without starting from that vantage point.

Culture was an important element of the new scene. In the 1930s Theodor Adorno, the exiled German Marxist critic, was much taken with the idea of popular culture until he came to America and had to confront the popular films and songs of the 1940s and 1950s, many of which indeed strike us today as both maudlin and irrelevant, an "opiate of the people" as Leninists said of religion. Popular culture, Adorno discovered was not about ordinary people listening to Beethoven's late string quartets.

The advantage of this mediatized cultural pabulum from a conservative point of view was, of course, its soothing irrelevance. But now, after Vietnam, the tone of American mass culture became more strident and critical. Dissent, redoubled by the indignation generated by the war in Vietnam, soon became a flood. The first trickle of dissenting voices had gone largely unnoticed: Allen Ginsberg and Jack Kerouac for the beat generation, and for others the films of James Dean and the rock 'n' roll of Elvis Presley.

But soon these rivulets became a torrent, and in the mid-1960s bourgeois America was confronted by the "free speech movement," soon to become the "filthy speech movement," by draft evasion, by the liberalization of sexual mores, and by feminism—or its contemporary revival—which can be conveniently dated to the publication of Betty Friedan's *The Feminine Mystique* in 1963. These many strands coalesced as a dissident youth culture or even (as it came to be called) a counterculture, oftentimes violent and drug-ridden. Among its political extensions were the civil rights movement, of course, but also arguments in favor of the recognition of gay rights, human rights, and the rights of

Native Americans, this last cause symbolized by the occupation by Native Americans in 1973 of the town of Wounded Knee, which had been the site of a massacre of Indians in 1890.

It seemed after 1968 as if marginal groups that for centuries had been excluded from the national consensus—blacks, the poor, gays, and so on—were rising up, and the effects of these changes were, in the long run, disastrous for the Democratic Party. From the early 1930s to the mid-1950s, most Americans viewed Franklin Roosevelt, his friends, and his Democratic successors as carriers of the American Dream, as a domestically integrating force that, abroad, stood for the great principles of American nationhood: economic individualism and democracy in the struggle against German militarism, fascism, and communistic collectivism.

But when the Vietnam war turned sour, everything was turned around. Now the Republicans, who had been perceived as reactionary and isolationist, suddenly became once more what they had been in the late nineteenth century, namely the party of the American national idea. And by counterpoint, Hubert Humphrey's Democrats, though despised by the far left, were perceived by mainstream America as the party of blacks, uppity women, pacifists, and intellectuals, as well as the party of defeat and national humiliation.

Now and for the next three decades, American social democracy, which Franklin Roosevelt had not really been able to promote and perhaps had not truly wanted, and which his successors Truman and Johnson had been unable to push forward, shrank smaller and smaller from one presidential election to the next. America moved from one Democratic defeat to another, and from one Republican president (Nixon) to a more determined Republican president (Reagan). The stage was now set for the shameful rise to power of George W. Bush in November 2000.

CHAPTER 13
Wars of Religion in Bush's America

How did George W. Bush become the first magistrate of the world's most powerful polity? Our bad luck? His own cunning? Or should we look to more structural causes, such as the uncanny proximity of good and evil, inclusive patriotism and exclusionary nationalism, in America's public life, or the erratic influence of religion in America, sometimes for better, as in the 1750s and 1850s, and sometimes for worse, as in the early nineteenth-century justification of slavery through biblical reference? These are hard questions to answer even with the twenty-twenty hindsight that is the historians' forte. (They are the ones, it must be remembered, who make up the vision charts by which they then test their own skills.)

In the beginning of his political career, Bush was largely uninterested in foreign affairs. From the classic vision of Americans as a chosen people, two divergent consequences can follow. The first is that the only way out is to impose America's imperial will on all those who labor directly or indirectly for the devil. But another is to place America behind an iron curtain that will prevent all contact with this selfsame satanic axis. As Samuel Huntington has put it: "The recurring tendencies in American History [are] either to retreat to minimum relations with the rest of the world and thus avoid the problem of reconciling the pursuit of self-interest with the adherence to principle in a corrupt and hostile environment, or the opposite solution, to set forth on a 'crusade' to purify the world, to bring it into accordance with American principles."[1]

In his first electoral campaign, Bush argued for a more modest American profile in foreign affairs. He disavowed "nation building." All other things being equal, his instinct was not to have any foreign policy

at all, even in the form of joining in admirable international coopera-
tive efforts, as was implied by his renunciation of the Kyoto Protocol
against global warming and the treaty to ban land mines.

But Bush's later choice, as we now know, was to support nationalist interventionism abroad and exclusionary social retrogression at home.
The first enabling context of this violent and reactionary choice was the
long-run evolution of American religious thought and the decline of
social democracy; the second, middle-term cause was the prosperity of
the 1990s, which reinforced the individuating and antistatist economic
atavisms of American culture; and the third, immediate causes were
9/11 and the international anarchy that followed the collapse of the Soviet Union, a void that gave credibility to Bush's claim that America was
the policeman the world badly needed.

How then to understand the place in history of George W. Bush,
and how to understand the place of his nationalist foreign policy in the
context of his presidency? A difficult assignment, and the answer that is
provided here follows from the structure of this essay: we focus on inherited, ingrained, often unconsciously apprehended habits of thought.
First, we consider Bush's very troubling version of the American creed
that for so long has been at the heart of America's sense of national self.
We then consider the background of Bush's most fervent supporters, and
the negative—exclusionary—foreign and domestic elements of his program. Finally, we conclude with thoughts on his character, bearing in
mind as we do this that in the litany of America's false starts, from the
massacre of the Wampanoag and the Trail of Tears to Hiroshima and
Vietnam, contingency and the personality of a president have often been
of consequence in shaping violent solutions that all Americans will later
regret. Who today is proud of Wounded Knee? Who tomorrow will be
proud of Guantánamo?

*****

Religious and economic individualism have always been central to the
American way. Unsurprisingly, George W. Bush has prospered by

hitching his star to both wings of this tradition, and he has done so by subscribing to their darkest forms. For Bush as a private person and for the American nation as a whole, religion was and is a key. Here it will be useful to retrace the historical evolution of the Protestant ethic in American life, at once theologically varied and politically determining, sometimes for inclusive good (as in the 1770s and 1850s) and sometimes for exclusion (as in the 1890s and today).

In 1620, for the first settlers of Calvinist New England, man was a depraved being, who, thanks to divine grace and to the dire sermons of his clergy, might (perhaps) find salvation. Puritans were anxious people who did not prize conversation and who believed in strict discipline and hard work. (H. L. Mencken quipped that the typical Puritan died tormented by the thought that someone, somewhere, might be having a good time.) Though communitarian and familial, Puritans were also resolutely individualist: at the end of the day, they would be alone when they came face to face with the Lord.

Then came the Great Awakening, between 1730 and 1760. Protestantism in this new mode was still Calvinist, but much sweetened. For these Lockean friend-foes of the Enlightenment, divine grace was still an essential aspect of salvation, but personal conversion could be prodded by the exercise of free will. Every Christian could find God, not through churchly fiat or some kind of Cartesian reasoning, but from within, by emotion. On the eve of the American Revolution, the thirteen colonies' conservative religious establishment was much weakened by this resurgent and now more liberal-minded Protestant fervor. Room had now been made to place value on the sincere conversion of blacks, women, and the socially marginal. The scope of the public sphere was widened. Individualism, so essential to the political message of a Jeffersonian revolution, was strengthened as a social value. The gap between the Enlightenment and Protestant religiosity was narrowed.

In the 1790s, perhaps no more than one American in twenty had a church affiliation, but after 1800, the Second Great Awakening—by its failures as well as its successes—furthered the antislavery cause and strengthened the democratic political will of the new nation. (John Adams attributed his defeat in the 1800 presidential election to the vote-getting contribution of Jefferson's running mate, Aaron Burr, a grandson of Jonathan Edwards, who had secured, he thought, "100,000 votes from the single Circumstance of his descent."[2])

This new Awakening mattered by successfully reasserting the place of religious individualism as a core value of Americanness. Now an American Protestant sinner merely had to wish to be saved in order to be, ipso facto, saved. Now every Christian American democrat could, on his own, find the spiritual home of his deepest yearnings. The first apostle of this creed was the young Charles Grandison Finney, who later would become the president of Oberlin College and later still would be a model for the evangelist Billy Graham. Religion, Finney explained, was the work of man. Every man who looked into his heart could "choose God" and—divine grace notwithstanding—renew his spiritual being.

But the failures of this Second Great Awakening mattered also. Initially its emphasis on individual conversion had seemed enough. To the converted believers of the new Benevolent Empire they had created, it seemed plausible to suppose that society could be reformed without recourse to politics. Public morality, they thought, would spontaneously improve. This quasi-religious expectation was soon disappointed, however: if southern planters persisted in defending slavery and even worked to extend its evil sway, where then was America's salvation?

At this juncture Protestant theological change shifted once again and now furthered liberal thinking. It did so directly, on the faithful, but also indirectly, by its influence on Americans who had ceased to be believing Christians and had secularized its core message. To paraphrase Clausewitz, liberal politics in America was at that moment a continuation of religion by other means. Between 1830 and 1850, especially in New England but throughout the other northern states as well, many thoughtful Americans—such as Emerson and Thoreau—moved from Calvinism to Unitarianism (that is, to a religion that was no real religion, for, as its name implied, it rejected Christian Trinitarianism and the divinity of Christ). Here, quasi-religious fervor became the hand-maiden of a politicized, libertarian ambition. Lincoln, who was at once pragmatic and mystical, did not share that Unitarian allegiance directly, but he functioned in the same broad context.

In a subsequent phase, in the later decades of the nineteenth century, American Protestant theology further dropped its contentious, severe, and Augustinian side. Some Christian theologians, such as Walter Rauschenbusch, the author of *Christianity and the Social Crisis* (1907) and *A Theology for the Social Gospel* (1917), did move leftward, but most Protestants moved instead to placid complacency. In the past, many American Protestants had imagined, for example, physical pain and disease to be tests of their Christian fortitude. But they now decided instead that it was a good thing for them to be healthy.[3] Christian Scientists went even further and wondered if disease existed at all. And did it not make sense, asked the mainstream Protestant theologians of the day, to see economic and capitalist progress as the most convincing sign of God's work on earth? (*In a ridiculous version of this selfsame symbiosis, it was by attending revival meetings in Philadelphia in 1875 that John Wanamaker hit upon the happy idea that similar crowds might be lured to his dry goods store. "No event," wrote a biographer of this inventor of the department store, "had a more far-reaching effect upon his business and religious activities [which were] always closely related."*)[4] In the older and now discredited Calvinist scheme of things, self-restraint had been a virtue (and, as it happens, a means to self-financed entrepreneurialism). Henceforth, Augustinian self-denial would be perceived as an obstacle to consumption and economic growth.

From 1910 onward Protestant fundamentalism took on a new and less ecumenical coloration: it renewed an ancient American tradition of individual questioning, but in a novel and inverted manner. The point of advance Protestantism no longer was to attack private or public immorality in the name of religious principle. It was instead to question cultural modernity in all its works, without, however, breaking with America's hallowed traditions of economic individualism. Indeed, Christ, who had often been portrayed as soulful and benign, was now held up not just as an enemy of cultural modernity but as a corporate example of virile efficiency. So it was, for example, that the advertising executive Bruce Barton, in his *The Man Nobody Knows* (1924), portrayed Christ as the founder of modern business and denied that he had ever been a weakling: "Where did they get that idea? Jesus pushed a plane and swung an adze; he was a successful carpenter. He slept outdoors and spent his days walking around his favorite lake. His muscles were so strong that when he drove the money changers out, nobody dared to oppose him!" For the fundamentalists Christ was a virile role model, and so were his ministers: Billy Sunday, one journalist reported, "stands up like a man in the pulpit and out of it. He speaks like a man. He works like a man . . . He is manly with God and with everyone who comes to hear him. No matter how much you disagree with him, he treats you in a manly fashion. He is not an imitation, but a manly man giving all a square deal."[5]

The term "fundamentalism" is associated today with all denominational forms of religious madness: we speak of the Jewish fundamentalism of Bibi Netanyahu, of the Muslim fundamentalism of Osama bin Laden, and of the Christian fundamentalism of George W. Bush. For half a century, however, the term applied only to the American Protestant tradition, which made epistemological sense, as it had begun its course as the title of a California magazine, *The Fundamentals*, funded by two oil millionaires who, shocked by Darwinian teachings on the subject of evolution, decided to reassert the importance of critical Christian—and, therefore, it was argued— "fundamental" principles.

Needless to say, the older Calvinist idea of the depravity of man was not on their agenda: Finney's work was not undone. A basic point of the new Protestant fundamentalism was, however, that salvation implied a return to the idea of the literal truth of the Bible. The miracles of the Old and New Testaments could not be called into question. They were not to be understood metaphorically. The virgin birth had been just that. And so had been the redeeming message of Christ with the actual fact of his resurrection. Most novel and dangerous was their idea of "dispensationalism," a linguistic turn of phrase that has no strict equivalent in other European languages. By this was meant—and still is meant in Bush's America—that God had "dispensed" laws that would govern all aspects of social life. Religion was no longer a matter of individual belief. It now became a guide to legislation of every sort: in brief, a Christian Sharia. Different fundamentalist and Pentecostal groups today, of course, emphasize different aspects of these beliefs, just as today the uniformly declining mainstream denominations (Episcopalians, Lutherans, Presbyterians, and Methodists) still have varying views of salvation, grace, and good works. Not all born-again Christians approve of Pat Robertson, for example. Fundamentalists are more open to the world; Pentecostals tend to turn inward. Their relations to Mormonism likewise are not uniform. Nonetheless, they share an *air de famille*, and their allegiance to contemporary Republicanism is largely unalloyed.

The progress of fundamentalism in American popular culture was at first muted. At a time when social democracy seemed to be a vital force, Protestant fundamentalists focused their thoughts and actions on civil society rather than on politics. In the first half of the twentieth century, these born-again Christians were politically inactive and more interested in building schools and churches than in holding public office.

The Cold War was a turning point for them. Foreign policy, which in the days of Taft's dollar diplomacy had been about American support for often dubious commercial ventures or complex geopolitical arguments, was redirected by the now tentacular and bureaucratized Washington establishment: everything henceforth would turn on the containment of the Soviet Union. And was it not true that the Soviet Union was a godless power par excellence? Fundamentalists took note. Billy Graham's career serves here as a case in point. Born in North Carolina, Graham found God in 1934 during a revival service. After attending the notorious Bob Jones University and the Florida Bible Institute, Graham graduated from Wheaton College in Illinois, "the Harvard of American Evangelism."[6] He discovered radio broadcasting, a crusading skill that he first practiced in 1949 in Los Angeles, much to the delight of an aging William Randolph Hearst, famous for his yellow journalism during the Spanish-American War. What mendacious newspapers had been to the nineteenth century, mendacious radio would be to the twentieth, and Hearst, as a connoisseur of demagoguery, was impressed by the virulence of the young Graham's imprecations. Finney's older message of individual becoming would now be coupled to the principles of fundamental Protestant belief. Graham's mark on American consciousness was telling: as is well known, it is to him that George and Barbara Bush turned when the behavior of their son George W. had become intolerable even to them.

"The atmosphere of our country is unquestionably charged with a threatening cloud of fanaticism, lighter in some parts, denser in others, but too heavy in all."[7] So wrote Thomas Jefferson, who would be appalled to know that today one American in five subscribes to some form of fundamentalist religious ideology whose influence goes far beyond what this modest percentage might imply. Fundamentalism is a highly structured movement, keenly intent on proselytism: 100,000 American missionaries are now at work around the world (they numbered 52,000 in 1970), as are a billion copies of the New Testament, translated into 2,261 languages and dialects in 175 different countries. Mention should also be made of the 62 million copies of Hal Lindsey's novel *The Late Great Planet Earth* (1970) with its apocalyptic message, as well as Tim LaHaye and Jerry Jenkins's "Rapture" novels, which recycle the Parousia (the yearning for a second coming) that mattered so greatly to the early Christians.[8] International communism was never so active in spreading its word!

American evangelizers are also shrewd businessmen and organizers. Billy Graham, who visited Richard Nixon and Bill Clinton in the White House as he does George W. Bush, has wisely "incorporated" himself and is in consequence the chief executive officer of a moneymaking enterprise that has 500 employees, all of them dedicated to spreading his message around the globe.[9] Politically, it is also critical that fundamentalists are "single-issue voters." About one-third of all senators and congressmen score 100 percent in their allegiance to fundamentalist principles as computed by the Christian Coalition.

Fundamentalists matter because one of them is in the White House, but also because their religious message has been used to justify many lamentable policies, foreign and domestic. Originally, white Protestant fundamentalism had focused its animosity on what it held to be the false religions of Catholics and Jews. But in recent years the scope of fundamentalists' fervor has widened, and they now seem more intent on cleansing American society in general from cultural decomposition. Of particular interest to these Christian fundamentalists, as to their counterparts in Muslim countries, are issues that involve sexuality, such as feminism, birth control, abortion, and homosexuality. Fundamentalist conspiratorialism also thrives on the enmities that it fosters: among its enemies today are "elitist" universities in the Northeast, ecologists concerned about global warming, supporters of the Kyoto Accord, lawyers concerned with free speech, and the sponsors of nongovernmental organizations.

In the 1960s it seemed that the cultural revolution of the young would soon herald a turning to the left of American society and politics. But the reverse happened instead, and the most durable effect of that conflict, we can now see, was to accelerate a then-quiescent fundamentalist revival, better organized and financed by far than were its liberal opponents (where "liberal" is taken in the American sense of the word), a dramatic revival whose greatest beneficiary has been George W. Bush.

Which means—once again, as was true with the Great Awakening of the 1740s and with the Benevolent Empire of the 1830s—that Protestant religiosity is now a basic matrix of American politics. Indeed, one could go further and speak not just of Protestantism in general but of Protestant, fundamentalist, end-time theology today.

The current political life of many societies, it is true, is influenced by religious residues: the case of Japan and Shintoism comes to mind, or Bavaria and Catholicism, or many Arab countries and varieties of Islam. But it is rarer that, within that residual religious frame, the politics of a great modern nation—indeed, the most modern of them all—should be affected, not just by religion, but by religious doctrinal dispute. In this domain, Bush's America can be usefully linked to Saudi Arabia, with its concern for sectarian Wahhabite pronouncements within a more general Muslim world. In an essay entitled "On the Concept of History," written shortly before his death in 1940, Walter Benjamin said that materialism's (that is, Marxism's) relation to theology was like an unbeatable Turkish chess-playing machine within which a cleverly hidden and misshapen dwarf (i.e., mendacious Stalinist pseudo-theology) manipulated the strings that governed the winning moves. This chess machine, mused Benjamin, "can easily be a match for anyone if it enlists the services of theology, which today, as we know, is small and ugly and has to keep out of sight."[10] Which was to say that Soviet Communism was percieved by deluded millions as furthering the goals of a universalist and chosen people, although it served Stalin's goals instead. Likewise today, end-time Protestant theology is the dwarf that manipulates Marxism's victorious enemy, American idealism. What Stalinism was to utopian communism, Bushism is to the American Creed.

In today's America, theology and theodicy—which have often been forces of cultural inclusion—have now become justifications of exclusionary zealotry. They speak to us through George W. Bush.

Religion, then, is one of the forces that led millions of Americans to vote *for* Bush, but just as many—and perhaps even more—Americans voted less *for* him than they did *against* his Democratic opponent, whose party is associated in their minds with defeat, tolerance of idleness, and especially the collapse of what are in their view basic American values.

Much of the Republican Party's strength today paradoxically lies in this flawed cultural perception: although the prospering "House of Bush" was very closely connected with the kleptomaniacal "House of Saud" (as George W. Bush also was with the fraudulent Texan managers of the Enron Corporation), many a destitute and sincerely Christian family, concerned with unemployment and lacking medical insurance, but more concerned about abortion and drugs, would vote for Bush and his moneyed allies because they erroneously perceived the enemy of their own cultural enemy as their friend.

It is often suggested—especially on the extreme right—that the cause of Islamicist success lies in the inability of the Muslim world to cope with cultural modernity (especially as regards women) and economic modernity: despite their noble scientific past, in this view, Muslim cultures today are in the main incapable of imitating western technological achievement. In that context, every purchase of every much-desired cell phone is also a kind of humiliation.

And much the same could be said of large numbers of religious-minded Americans: many of them are today culturally at sea. They are afraid of modernity and feel themselves to be losing ground in the "culture wars" that oppose them and their fundamentalist friends to godless feminists; to the east and west coasts; and to postmodern absurdism, characterized by "artists" who use cow dung to portray the Virgin Mary. Patrick Buchanan, whose origins were in a successful Catholic Irish bourgeoisie that was originally hostile to Jews and WASPs but whose reoriented hostility is now focused on postmodern culture, speaks for these losers (or those who imagine themselves to be so) when he writes: "We must take back our cities and take back our culture and take back our country."[11] Here America's religious values are seen as a threatened, sacred trust that must be defended against a global evil among whose constituent parts are perceived to be black adolescent mothers, homosexual marriage, the United Nations, soccer-playing Europeans (especially the French), as well as the many enemies of the state of Israel, America's only dependable and democratic ally in a Muslim Middle East that has inexplicably gone mad.

George W. Bush is the endpoint of this long national and religious trajectory. The genius of America's political culture was in the precarious—one is tempted to say, miraculous—blending of Enlightenment and religious values. It was Bush's self-imposed mission to destroy that equilibrium, and it may well be that he has achieved that fundamental goal.

*****

As a perverse manipulation of American religiosity binds Bush's regime to the underside of America's religious past, so does a perverse version of America's traditional adherence to economic individualism, the second pillar of America's national sense of self, bind the Bush administration to the underside of the nation's economic past.

Capitalist individualism has on balance been a force of inclusion in American history. A large part of the immigrants' American dream was to achieve a level of well-being that was beyond their dreams at home, and these hopes were largely met, not always for them, but for their children and grandchildren. In recent times that national promise was institutionalized in the collective arrangements that were struck in the 1950s by (moderately) Republican big business and (moderately) Democratic big labor. Here the message was that larger profits would be matched by the gradual betterment of the living standards of the workforce. The world would converge toward the American model, and American social and economic life would converge on the middle classes.

In Bush's America, however, capitalism (which is unchallengeable as an idea in the American national scheme of things) has become less a promise of inclusion than a machine of exclusion that works to make the rich richer and that neglects the poor, refuses to retrain them when their jobs vanish from the competition of cheap labor abroad, and promulgates the idea that the American welfare state—such as it was—should be dismantled.

The first principle of Keynesian policy had been the statist harmonization of industrial capitalism, an arrangement that is now satirized by the right—both religious and secular—as the unholy coalition of "Big Business, Big Labor, and Big Government." Ronald Reagan, once a Roosevelt Democrat, was the first president overtly to reject this settlement, in which course he was followed by his Democratic contemporaries: by Jimmy Carter up to a modest point, and more closely by Bill Clinton. The idea of a trickling down of prosperity has now replaced the New Deal idea of redistribution, and in today's America the poor are too discouraged and too deceived to complain. In the 1930s, as Lizabeth Cohen has shown, workers in Chicago did think the government would help them solve their problems.[12] But that hopeful impulse has largely lapsed.

A first consequence of Bush's Republican and neo-Republican economic policies has been the steady increase from the 1990s onward in the proportion of Americans with incomes below the poverty line. One-fifth of Americans today have no medical insurance. The globalization of the world economy along lines favorable to multinationals, and especially mega-multinationals (most of them American), has increased global wealth but widened the gap—in America as elsewhere—between rich and poor. However beneficial globalization has been in its effect on global productivity, it has also proved very hard both for marginal workers in the Third World (as shown by the fate of Mexican growers of corn or producers of cotton in Mali) and for many American industries as well: in 1950 the United States produced three-quarters of the world's automobiles, versus one-fifth today. Moreover, these industrial changes bore down on the least skilled members of the American workforce, many of them black or Hispanic. Manufacturing employed 20 percent of the nation's workers in 1970, but that figure has since fallen by half, a shift that also affected the percentage of unionization, as the newer industries (such as computer software) are less unionized than the older ones (such as steel).

On one side, then, comfy suburbs and cozy exurbs—whose presence, incidentally, guaranteed Bush's more or less fraudulent 2000 election in Florida—and at the other end of the social spectrum, less qualified workers who were sliding into the lumpenproletariat (Marx's "proletariat of rags"). One-third of Americans today own nothing—or less than nothing, as their debts are often larger than their assets.

To be sure, Europe has experienced difficulties that are not dissimilar, but the difference is that most European workers could react (sensibly) by defending their welfare state, or (foolishly) by blaming the construction of a unified Europe for their woes. In America, by contrast, where competition and economic individualism—like religion—were hallowed by hoary national traditions, economic change strengthened the right but without invigorating the left. The dismantling of ancient economic and political models and the decomposition of emotionally charged party loyalties disoriented Democratic voters: in 2004 Richard Gephardt, the labor union candidate, did just as poorly as Howard Dean, whose sensibility was social democratic. Many privileged Americans drifted toward the right, just as, on the left, millions more of America's underprivileged citizens drifted toward discouragement, electoral absenteeism (in 2000, 82 percent of Australians voted versus 47 percent of Americans), drugs, and the cheap fascinations provided by television, the opiate of the people in a mediatized culture that is symbolically focused on special effects and "virtual reality."

Religion created a base for Bush's aggressive nationalism abroad. The myth of trickle-down economics further weakened the base of his Democratic antagonists. With a free hand at home, Bush was able to impose his aggressive nationalism on the world even as his ignorance and his lack of interest in the well-being of the planet became increasingly evident.

*****

Religion and economic individualism: by his exclusionary manipulation of these basic and structuring principles of America's long-held sense of itself, Bush, like so many of his reactionary predecessors, has succeeded in moving America toward his reactionary ends. But within that broad cultural context, other themes and circumstances of contemporary American life have also helped him a great deal. Of these, racism has been one of the most consequential strands.

Of course in America, as in the rest of the western world, it is impossible today to advocate the kind of overt racism that was common at the beginning of the twentieth century, when millions of Americans adhered to or sympathized with the Ku Klux Klan. True, we still want to see D. W. Griffith's *Birth of a Nation*, but only for its aesthetic qualities. (It often happens that artists of genius—Degas, Wagner, Balzac, Dostoevsky—honorable men on the whole, earnestly believe in a political message that we despise.)

In the 1930s Carter Glass, a senator from Virginia and a conditional supporter of Franklin Roosevelt, when accused of supporting discriminatory legislation against blacks, responded, with feigned naiveté, that that was certainly what he was doing: "Discrimination! Why that is precisely what we propose."[13] (We are reminded here of John Stuart Mill, who once opined: "Of all vulgar modes of escaping from the consideration of the effect of social and moral influences on the human mind, the most vulgar is that of attributing the diversities of conduct and character to inherent natural differences.")[14] But no American elected official could speak today as Carter Glass did and survive politically. Trent Lott's tacit endorsement of Strom Thurmond's racism marked the (temporary) end of Lott's rise to greater power. Immense progress has been made on this score in modern America. Critically, legislation of the 1920s that ruled out immigration to America from the Third World has been repealed and, indeed, reversed. In 1980 four out of five Americans were of European ancestry; that figure will decline to less than two-thirds by 2020.

Yet subterranean racist resentment persists: in the 2000 election, 90 percent of African-American voters cast their votes against Bush, just as a large majority of white men voted for him. Race in America recycles class, and vice versa. "Socially conservative" Christianity likewise often serves as a mask for racial venom: an overt call to deny policies that are favorable to African Americans will not fly, but this does not disallow anguished (and coded) statements about the immorality of teenage girls, followed by a refusal to fund or allow the use of contraceptives.

Most white decision makers in Bush's America do genuinely accept the participation of African Americans in the business and leadership of the American polity, but on condition that their own overall and profitable hegemony—economic and political—not be questioned. The presence of African Americans in high offices of Bush's entourage is a highly ambiguous sign, and one has to wonder in dismay about what drove Secretary of State Colin Powell at the United Nations so diligently to echo his master's mendacious voice. We can note, in passing, Thomas Holt's acid comment on how much "Powell's successful, if brief courtship of American public opinion [owes] . . . to his ability to transcend race. [He is] the un-Negro."[15]

Domestic circumstances and contingency have also provided a contextualizing frame for Bush's discouraging success, and so have the circumstances of America's place in the world. In 1792 Jacques Pierre Brissot—the leader of the Girondins—said of the French Revolution that it needed to be betrayed in order to thrive: foreign conspiracies, he thought, would galvanize domestic opinion. (He was executed in 1793.) In a similar vein, we can ask if George W. Bush could have secured any of his malevolent and nationalistic ambitions without 9/11.

We used to speak of an American republic. Then we spoke of an American empire, and now we speak, fearfully, of a threatened and threatening American empire. In 1854 Henry J. Raymond, the founding editor of the *New York Times*, wrote prophetically that empire was "a great ambition, but Freedom is loftier . . . We are the most ambitious people the world has ever seen:—and I greatly fear we shall sacrifice our liberties to our imperial dream."[16] How sadly prescient.

The general context of Bush's political options has been the world crisis of the welfare state and the worldwide rise of religious feeling. But the specific occasion that enabled him to work for his agenda of "constitutional pre-fascism" was the odious attack of Muslim extremists on the Twin Towers and the Pentagon. George W. Bush and Osama bin Laden: here are two religious extremists desperately in need of each other. Samuel Huntington provides us with a quotation that speaks to the climate of our times and to Bush's ability to exploit America's current disarray. He quotes a young woman:

When I was 19, I moved to New York City . . . If you asked me to describe myself then, I would have told you I was a musician, a poet, an artist, and on a somewhat political level, a woman, a lesbian, and a Jew . . . On Sept. 11, all that changed. I realized that I had been taking the freedoms I have here for granted. Now I have an American flag on my backpack, I cheer the fighter jets as they pass overhead and I am calling myself a patriot.[17]

In London, Paris, and Madrid, murderous terrorist attacks certainly did not go unnoticed. But they did not so strongly overwhelm British, French, or Spanish public opinion. The events of September 11, 2001, however, even more deadly than the Japanese attack on Pearl Harbor, did dramatically disturb Americans. George W. Bush, by instinct, understood what could be made of this: in 1989, Arthur Schlesinger Jr. had written of Nixon that his was an "imperial presidency" whose characteristics were "the all-purpose innovation of national security, the insistence on executive secrecy, the withholding of information from Congress, the refusal to spend funds appropriated by Congress, the attempted intimidation of the press, the use of the White House itself as a base for espionage and sabotage directed against the political opposition." George W. Bush would move forward from that model.

*****

So much for the larger domestic and foreign context of Bush's assault on the civil rights of Americans and the rights of the world's nations. But within that historical and larger frame, many subsidiary factors made it possible for Bush to push America from the center to the right, of which the most critical may well be the tentacular presence of the celebrated "military industrial complex"; the deep involvement of the American imagination with an embattled Israel, and behind that, the existence of a strongly structured pro-Israeli lobby; and the influence of the "neoconservatives."

A brilliant historian of the American South, C. Vann Woodward, once noted that America was a warlike but unmilitarized nation. Would that this were still true! The American army numbered under 1,000 in 1800, 9,000 in 1845, and 25,000 in the 1890s. In 1935 its 139,000 enrollees put it on the same footing as Denmark. It numbers millions today. In 1939, 147,188 civilians worked in the defense bureaucracy. In 1995 that workforce had risen to 3,200,000. No precise and publicly available figures tell us how many people are employed by the intelligence agencies alone, but that figure is often estimated at between 70,000 and 80,000. (We can note in passing that these often lamentably inefficacious sleuths are currently and efficiently guarding approximately 15 million documents that are not available to the public.)

The American defense establishment today dwarfs the armies of all other nations. In the United States (as in the absolutist monarchies of the seventeenth and eighteenth centuries, which collapsed in or after 1789), the national debt has essentially resulted from wartime borrowing and is huge, having risen from 40 billion dollars in 1939 to over 5,000 billion today, a sum that requires annual interest payments of 300 billion dollars, about a fifth of which is paid to foreigners.[18] The "conjunction of an immense military establishment and a large arms industry," warned President Eisenhower in 1960, "is new in the American experience. The total influence—economic, political, even spiritual—is felt in every city, every state house, every office of the federal government . . . In the councils of government, we must guard against the acquisition of unwarranted influence, whether sought or unsought, by the military-industrial complex."[19] At least 7 percent of the nation's energies are dedicated to defense, and one has to wonder if "defense" is the *mot juste*. Close and numerous ties also bind legislators to these "merchants of death," and it is commonplace for former officers—like former legislators—to become effective defense lobbyists, to the Republican Party especially, but to the legislature in general. (Kevin Phillips has updated the story of this arms lobby by describing the equally pernicious oil lobby as a parallel "imperium in imperio."[20])

A related factor in the determination of Bush's imperialist policies is the subterranean work of the so-called Jewish lobby. In some respects, its presence is quite ordinary: ethnic lobbies of all kinds (Greek, Armenian, Irish, Polish . . .) have had long and considerable influence on American foreign policy. In a self-consciously and proudly pluralistic polity, the reverse would be surprising.

Still, the anti-Arab and anti-Muslim tilt that the America-Israel Political Action Committee (or AIPAC) exerts on U.S. foreign policy is unusually consequential. American aid to Israel in 2002 was six times larger than the aid directed to the African continent as a whole, and ten times larger than the amount received by Afghanistan, which was in that same year the cornerstone of America's antiterrorist campaign.[21] At the United Nations, the United States has vetoed more than thirty motions critical of Israel since 1982.

AIPAC is a highly organized lobby with large reserves of (electorally useful) cash at its disposal, and it is careful to hedge its bets by subsidizing both political parties, which it does with some discernment. (We must remember here that—to paraphrase Tip O'Neill's aphorism— "money is the [poisoned] mother's milk of [American] politics.") So was it, for example, that when George H. W. Bush delayed an American guarantee of loans made to Soviet Jews who had found refuge in Israel, a large and perhaps compensatory contribution was made to Bill Clinton's campaign. The Clintons, man and wife, took notice here: Hillary Clinton, a political chameleon *sans pareil*, was sympathetic to the Palestinian cause until she decided to run for office in the state of New York.

Yet it is hard to imagine that a single lobby could in and of itself have legitimized the anti-Arab policy that the United States has followed since Harry Truman's recognition of Israel as a Jewish rather than a bi-religious and bi-national state. The point here will be that American sympathy for Israel—which Bush was able to harness to his warmongering purpose—is indeed well organized, but, again, that it is in the history of American culture where we will find the origins of the ordinarily laudable sympathy Americans have traditionally had for this Jewish state.

At issue here of course is the horror that all Americans and all Europeans—left and right—feel about the Shoah, a monstrous event whose memory no illegitimate action of the state of Israel can erase. Together with the race suicide of the First World War, the murder of six million Jews in central and eastern Europe during the Second World War is the determining event in the history of the twentieth century. This holocaust is a particularly sensitive subject in the United States, where Jewish citizens are both understandably marked by the memory of the final solution and also ill at ease about being one of the few national Jewish populations to have been spared direct persecution during the Nazi years.

The numerous complaints that have been directed (especially in Europe) against the Israeli state and in support of the Palestinian people have exacerbated American Jews' anxieties and revivified their interest in AIPAC. In San Francisco in 1985, for example, in response to a questionnaire that asked whether a Jew might be elected to Congress from that city, one-third of the Jewish respondents answered that such an electoral victory was impossible, and this at a time when the city's three electoral districts were so represented, and when two members of the California senate, the mayor of the city, and a number of city councilors were Jewish as well.[22] Jewishness may also matter more to many American Jews than to many of their coreligionists in Europe because the high rate of intermarriage between Jews and non-Jews in the United States raises fears of a near-disappearance of American Jewish culture, an intolerable prospect for believers whose sense of self is marked by this tradition.

But more important and nobler factors are also present here: many ancient cultural ties have linked American and Jewish cultures, for the good, as in the nature of American humor, the course of American psychiatry, the success of the American film industry, and the economic and intellectual life of the country as a whole, but also for the less good—or even for the disastrous—as in the tilting of America's policy in the Middle East, which is today a Sword of Damocles suspended above the soul—and safety!—of America. In this age of religious wars, of all the threats that the United States faces today, ecological, economic, or political, none is more likely to lead to the utter ruination of the American republic than the war that opposes Islam to Christianity and its Judaic mother-religion, or, as some would have it, the war declared on Islam by Judaism and by Christianity, its extraordinarily successful heretical offshoot.

In 1800, to be sure, America was still an overwhelmingly Protestant state: Roman Catholics then accounted for one percent of the population, and Jews for about one-tenth of one percent. Nonetheless, there have always been Jews in America, some of them having arrived in New York in 1654, when it was still Nieuw Amsterdam. By 1880 their number had risen to 250,000 (many of them immigrants from Germany), and by 1930 to more than 3 million.

But beyond these numbers lay a commonality of culture in the emphasis placed by both American Protestants and Jews on the importance of justice, the pursuit of what is right, and the feeling of being a chosen people marked by a divine mission. "In our household," wrote Henry Kallen, an American Zionist who at Harvard had been a pupil of William James and George Santayana (and also a friend of the black writer Alain Locke, a precursor of the Harlem Renaissance),

> the suffering and slavery of Israel were commonplaces of conversation; from Passover to Passover, freedom was an ideal ceremoniously reverenced, religiously aspired to. The textbook story of the Declaration of Independence came upon me, nurtured upon the deliverance from Egypt and the bondage in exile, like the clangor of trumpets, like sudden light. What a resounding battle cry of freedom! And then, what an invincible march of Democracy to triumph over every enemy—over the English king, over the American Indians, over the uncivilized Mexicans, over the American champions of slavery betraying American freedom; over everything, to the very day of the history lesson.[23]

As Robert Bellah has put it: "Europe is Egypt; America, the promised land."[24] Since the United States was born in 1776 to institutionalize tolerance and the rule of law, the presence of an active Jewish community on its soil was of itself proof of the young country's republican vitality. "It is now no more," wrote George Washington to the Hebrew Congregation of Newport in 1790, "that toleration is spoken of, as if it were by the indulgence of one class of people, that another enjoyed the exercise of their inherent natural rights. For, happily, the Government of the United States, which gives to bigotry no sanction, to persecution no assistance, requires only that they who live under its protection should demean themselves as good citizens, in giving it on all occasions their effectual support."[25] America stands for modernity, tolerance, and democracy, and today, for most Americans and Israelis alike, where in the Middle East do democracy and tolerance exist? What Arab nation today, from Morocco to Iraq, can claim to be truly democratic? And also relevant, for those who hold that Europeans are from Venus and Americans from Mars, is the determination of the state of Israel to assert itself and democracy at all costs.

Oliver Cromwell, the Puritan, opened Britain once again to Jews in 1656, and from that time onward, these two Peoples of the Book— English-speaking Calvinist Protestants and Jews—though pulled apart by anti-Semitism, which was quite strong in America, particularly in the late nineteenth century—have also been very close. It is more than a mere historical curiosity that in late 1862, when General Grant expelled "Jews, as a class" for smuggling and black-market trading at the front, President Lincoln chose to rescind this order: "I do not like to hear of class or nationality condemned on account of a few sinners."[26] Or again that, in the 1870s, President Rutherford B. Hayes delegated an American Jew, Eugene Schuyler, to report on the plight of persecuted Jews in newly independent Romania.[27] Today the United States is the only western country where it is commonly assumed that the terms anti-Zionist and anti-Semitic are largely synonymous.

In that general context of shared concerns, pro-Israeli feeling has been especially strong in George W. Bush's favored electoral base, the "born-again Christians," of whom he is one. Fundamentalist Christian feelings had in the past run high against the Jewish settlements in Palestine, if only because of the sympathy that many Christian Americans felt for Palestine's vocal Christian minority. But that is long since gone. True, in 1972 Billy Graham told Richard Nixon: "I'm friendly with Israel. But they don't know how I really feel about what they are doing to this country." (When this taped message was released in 2002, Graham apologized, and Jewish leaders hastened to accept his apology.)[28] But currently, for the fundamentalist preacher Jerry Falwell, as the historian Anatol Lieven puts it, "to oppose Israel is to oppose God," because, in Falwell's view, the prophet Mohammed himself was a terrorist.[29] For Billy Graham's son and successor Franklin Graham—who was, it is true, disavowed on this score by the White House, after having delivered the sermon at George W. Bush's inaugural service in 2001—Islam is "a very evil and wicked religion" because it is dedicated to the worship of a false God. Armageddon and the coming of a new Messiah are beliefs that are common to both Protestant and Jewish fundamentalists.

Bitter ironies of history: that many religious Jews should today be distancing themselves from the western secular and libertarian Enlightenment tradition that emancipated them and of which they were so important a part. And also that many Americans who live in the mightiest nation on earth should have interiorized the feeling, so common in Israel, of being a beleaguered power surrounded by mortal enemies. Here was a prospect that had not been in the minds of the (often anti-Semitic) theoreticians of containment when in 1946–1947 they too developed a confrontational world view that opposed a beleaguered, peaceful, and even victimized power (their own) to a cunning, immoral, and aggressive one (the Soviet Union.)

*****

Because of the numerous cultural links that by nature bind two chosen peoples, the lobbying of AIPAC would matter a great deal in and of itself. But its effect has been magnified by the presence in high governmental circles of the neoconservatives whose sensibility often replicates that of the pro-Israeli lobby.

Often bound by personal and intellectual affinities, the neoconservative cabal reminds us *(mutatis mutandis)* of the imperialist circle of 1898 and the foreign policy establishment of the 1940s and 1950s, which wielded a determining influence on American foreign policy during the Cold War and the disastrous campaign in Vietnam—with nonetheless a critical difference. The Anglophile circle of Elihu Root and the foreign policy establishment had looked abroad to Britain, and to its past especially, as a model, as did also, if in a lesser register, the "Rockefeller Republicans" and the American "new conservatives" of the 1950s. By contrast, the inspiration and anxieties of the neoconservatives were and are domestic. Britain mattered very little to them, as a subservient Tony Blair would soon realize. For them, defeat in Vietnam, America's counterculture, the University of California at Berkeley and its "filthy speech movement": these were the crystallizing events that mattered.

Here again the point must be that, given the nature of America's governance, in a society where exclusionary nationalism and inclusive patriotism share many points of reference, the determined action of a small but influential group that has the ear of the president will often suffice to shift the enormous weight of American power from restraint to adventurism.

Like their predecessors, the neoconservatives come from the northeastern states, but where the friends and colleagues of George Kennan, Dean Acheson, and John Foster Dulles had usually been lawyers and nearly always WASPs, the neoconservatives are drawn from "a small, well-educated elite, mostly northeastern and metropolitan and largely Jewish."[30] Many of them are either children or grandchildren of politically marginal figures, some of whom were communists in their youth. (In the late 1930s and early 1940s, many fascists were likewise turncoat communists and left-socialist like Doriot, Marion, Déat in France; and of course Mussolini in Italy. Many American neoconservatives have followed a similar trajectory, albeit over two rather one generation and in modulated form.) Many of them also—if in varying degrees—locate themselves as disciples, close or far, of Leo Strauss, a German racial refugee and intellectual who taught at the University of Chicago. (This same university was identified with Milton Friedman's "economistic" view of life, which mattered so much to the partisans of Ronald Reagan and Margaret Thatcher.)

Straussian thought was organized around two axes. The first underscored the importance of high philosophical culture and the inability of the masses to understand ways of thinking that were essential to their well-being. (Typically, in the late 1980s, Allan Bloom, a fervent disciple of Strauss, bitterly criticized, in his bestselling *The Closing of the American Mind*, the corrosive effect of the "politically correct" thinking that had further weakened the broad public's shaky ability to understand the message of the Great Thinkers of the western tradition.)

For the Straussians, it seemed self-evident that the larger public of the western democracies would often be unable to understand either democracy's metaphysic or the practical threats that a democracy might have to face, as had happened in 1933 when the Weimar Republic succumbed, and as they thought was true in 2001 with regard to Saddam Hussein's weapons of mass destruction. That the democratic public would from time to time have to be deceived for its own good was, for them, a fact of life.

In some respects, "Straussianism" was in the Wilsonian tradition, for it too aimed to defend democracy in all climes and at all times. But it was a duplicitous Wilsonianism gone mad, hostile to compromise or to world government, and ready to opt for preemptive war. For these neoconservatives, self-styled "American internationalists," and "democratic globalists," military force was not just a last resort in a multipolar world. It was instead America's first and easiest option as the planet's most powerful country.[31] Far from heeding the prudent and technocratic advice of what Halpern and Clarke have called "the rational center" of American governance, derisive neoconservatives have aggressively and arrogantly rejected the advice of cautious professionals in the intelligence and military services, an imperious judgment that, George W. Bush, has in turn, admiringly translated into his own chosen vocabulary: "The liberty we prize is not America's gift to the world. It is God's gift to humanity."[32]

The second Straussian message flowed from its first and deceptive premise. Paradoxically, democratic leaders would not only have to deceive obtuse democratic publics; they would from time to time have to go even further and act undemocratically in order to save democracy from its own dark instincts. "The illegal we do immediately," Henry Kissinger once joked. "The unconstitutional takes a little longer." But the neoconservatives were neither patient nor humorous. Because the democratic masses might want to capitulate to antidemocrats from ignorance or cowardice, it followed that clairvoyant democratic leaders would often have to impose their own more virile message. (For having decided to resist Hitler in May 1940 when most of his compatriots might have wanted to negotiate instead, Winston Churchill was for the neoconservatives the greatest statesman of the twentieth century.)[33]

History mattered to the neoconservatives, as in Churchill for good, and the collapse of the Weimar Republic for evil. This was the event that had brought so many of them to America and that was for them the prelude to the Shoah. It was also their firm belief that the United States was now democracy's last hope. Weimar had failed, but they, in America, would succeed. And their success meant not just the destabilization of the Soviet Union, but the containment and destruction of another enemy of democracy, namely Islamism, Israel's mortal enemy.

In that context of an inevitable conflict between democracy and its foes, the neoconservatives turned, paradoxically, to the thought of the initially Hitlerite sociologist Carl Schmitt for guidance. Politics for Schmitt were not, as they were held to be in Anglo-Saxon countries especially, about discussion. Politics were about force. Political heroes for Schmitt were those who acted, not those who talked and waited. So it was, he explained, that the French Revolutionary Jacobins in 1793–1794 had been right to terrorize their compatriots: their abrogation of civil rights alone had saved their national community—and the Revolution—from destruction at the hand of Europe's Old Regimes. So it was also, thought Schmitt, that the Nazis' rise to power had been legitimate because it alone had saved Germany from deliquescent and discredited left-wing, republican mismanagement. American neoconservatives took note of this forceful and historical message.

At once paradoxically and predictably, the thought of Leo Strauss's neoconservative disciples replicated many of the ideas of its exact opposite, namely the thought of Sayid Qutb, the first theoretician of fervent Islamism: "*Les extrêmes se touchent!*" In both cases, opponents and their ideology were not merely to be neutralized but to be eliminated, and it is striking that the disciples of these two men, ostensibly so far apart, should have fought side by side quite happily in Afghanistan against their common enemy during the Soviet invasion of that country.

Nor was it surprising that the expectation of American neoconservatives, like that of Qutb, was of a war without end. Where would the axis of evil not try to work its ways? Islamist extremism was a first assignment, but in time, democratic America would turn to other enemies. David Frum and Richard Perle, for example, looked forward to the eventual reconsideration of U.S. relations to many other states; for them, France and Saudi Arabia should be considered "not as friends but as rivals and perhaps even as enemies."[34]

Highly loquacious and proud of their governmental preeminence, the neoconservatives have made no bones about their role as the guiding ideological lights of Bush's nationalistic foreign policy. Their principles are, no doubt, opaque—or even offensive—to many moderate Republicans, whose moderate intelligence these gifted neoconservative academics no doubt hold in some contempt. (One definition that has been offered for a neoconservative is a person who has never been conservative.)

But at the same time one can see how this unfortunate school of thought fits into the stream of American life that emphasizes power, violence, and exclusion. Neoconservatism is a quasi-religion that sees the world in Manichaean terms. Its Jacksonian cult of violence and its vision of America as a chosen nation elected to bring order in the place of chaos have ancient roots.

*****

George W. Bush had considerable social and ideological constituencies that could be relied on to support his agenda, and as has been true of most successful political movements in America, he had also managed to cultivate a particular geographic base that would favor his policies.

Definitions of what America's purpose should be have never been uniformly accepted in the country as a whole. In the United States, vast and populous as it is, many regions that have a particular tradition or pattern of settlement have had particular points of view. In 1776 New England was uniformly won over to independence, but the more loyalist South was not. In 1812 the Jacksonian West and South wanted war, but New Englanders did not. In more recent times, after the Civil War, Irish-Americans, for example, some of them nationalist Fenians, were numerous in the Northeast and for generations harbored feelings of extreme hostility to Great Britain. (In 1940 Joseph P. Kennedy, the Bostonian Irish-American, conservative, and ungenerous father of the future president, took pleasure in imagining Britain's forthcoming defeat at the hands of Hitler.)

In this same mode of regional specificity, the South has been the key to Bush's new crusade: it is no coincidence that the eleven former Confederate states have been solidly aligned in support of his program. It is there that fundamentalist religion, latent racism, suspicion of government, and anti-immigrant xenophobia—that is to say, the bundle of historically conditioned reflexes that Bush has manipulated—are most strongly felt. It is there that particularist instincts are strongest and American universalism weakest.

This is also to say that, once again, we see the echoes of the compromise of 1877 as a sad turning point in the history of the South and of the United States as a whole. Had the foundations then been laid of a durable coalition of southern black farmers and northern immigrants, the likes of George W. Bush would be unthinkable today. True enough, for nearly a century the extent of this disastrous choice (or "path determinacy" in current social scientific jargon) was hidden by the bizarre tactical coalition of southern racists and northern liberals, united within the bosom of the Democratic Party by a common enmity to the Republican Party, which in turn represented midwestern farmers and Wall Street interests. But this was an ad hoc democratic coalition that could not endure after the 1950s, when northern Democrats took the interests of southern blacks to heart.

It was the tragedy of Lyndon Johnson's career that his championship of African-American rights did not spark the creation of a new liberal coalition that would have finally reversed what had happened in 1877. And it was in the wake of that failure that George W. Bush came to power.

A first response in 1948 after Truman's desegregationist efforts was for Southerners to abandon the mainstream of the Democratic Party and to run their own candidates for the presidency. Then, with Ronald Reagan, southern Democrats simply folded themselves into a Republican Party that itself had also moved to the right. Their contribution as Southerners was to add traditions of Jacksonian ferocity and fundamentalist religiosity to the more economic concerns of their midwestern and northeastern allies.

Geography was destiny for the right and for the left as well: in today's America, the "blue states" on the two coasts are strikingly more cosmopolitan and less nationalist than the "red states" of their antagonists. After 9/11, New York City was admired for the courage of its firemen, but conditionally so: New York fascinates the American public by its role at the cutting edge of modernity, but for that same reason it is also seen as a Babylonian haunt of unbridled debauchery, as shown in innumerable telenovellas (*NYPD Blue*, *Sex and the City*, and so on). In the minds of America's no-longer-silent majority, New York is no more to be praised than Paris or Stockholm or the Democratic Party.

In 1900 midwestern populists detested the Bostonian and New York managers of high capitalism. They still detest the Northeast, but their ire today focuses on intellectuals, feminists, and the professorial class generally, who have, in their mind's eye, displaced Jews and bankers, those ancient "enemies of the people."

*****

The more extreme forms of American nationalism are as old—and older!—than the American republic. Their basic principles—exclusion, abstraction, a drive to power, the cult of violence, Protestant messianic religiosity, antistatism, and economic individualism—are as ancient as America itself.

It is important to see, however, how extreme and unprecedented in comparison to what has come before are the ideological goals of the neoconservatives, and how real a threat Bush's administration presents both to America's place in the world and to American freedom. "Habeas corpus," runs the joke: "an archaic term that is no longer used." Without American nationalism's respected ancestry, George W. Bush could not be. But he has also gone well beyond what the past had led us to expect and to fear.

Critically, Bush today finds it electorally convenient to claim that America's situation justifies preemptive war, and that the war on terror —this war without end—can justify infringements on Americans' privacy and free speech. This creative constitutionalism, even in the eyes of Henry Kissinger, is a revolutionary doctrine. Both Polk and McKinley had to forge a *casus belli* for invading other countries precisely because they did not dare to act as Bush has done, that is to say, preemptively.

In the long contest that conservatism waged against social democracy in the first six decades of the twentieth century, traditional old-style northeastern Republicans (like Bush's own grandfather, a senator from Connecticut) were oftentimes more cautious than their Democratic and populist antagonists. After Theodore Roosevelt, most Republican statesmen were uninterested in international involvement and basically pacifistic. Among their concerns were the end of the international arms race and the peaceful extension of America's commercial interests, without reference to ideology. Theirs was what Taft crudely, but accurately, labeled "dollar diplomacy," a policy that occasionally implied incursions—into China (five times), into Russia, Guatemala, Panama, and Nicaragua—but always with an eye to a rapid exit.

Nor did Republicans become more warlike after 1941. During the Second World War, under the banner of bipartisanship, they aligned their views with those of Franklin Roosevelt and his immediate successors. Theirs was a fundamentally *a*moral (but only occasionally *im*moral) and Metternichian policy of pragmatic and strategic containment rather than ideological imperialism. In the early 1970s, for example, Kissinger, an ex-refugee, did not do much—if anything—to restrain Latin American dictators in the name of human rights. But neither did he explicitly encourage Pinochet to overthrow Allende in Chile, nor did he approve when Latin American dictators began to murder their political enemies on American soil. (One of them fell victim to a car bomb within blocks of the White House.) The "near absolute condemnation of aggressive war goes back to Woodrow Wilson," wrote two students of American policy in 1992, "and has been subscribed to by administrations ever since."[35] (In France, Raymond Aron represented a cautious sensibility of the same order.) But George W. Bush has gone far beyond these cautious precedents. In the past, the United States by and large obeyed its obligations under international treaties like the Geneva Convention on the treatment of prisoners. Bush seems to take pride in defying them.

*****

In this complex setting of inherited structures, contingent contexts, and human agency, how are we to gauge the place in history of George W. Bush, whose advisers have advocated preemptive war, deceived the public about weapons of mass destruction, and legitimized the use of what appears to many to be plain torture? Abraham Lincoln also single-handedly suspended habeas corpus, but he never denied that Congress would have the last word in the matter.

Not everything can be blamed on "vast, impersonal forces," whether past or present: although 37 percent of Republican voters are born-again Christians, 67 percent are not, and many of these born-again Christians are more interested in combating AIDS or stopping global warming than they are in banning abortion or gay marriage. Most white women and millions of white men did not vote for Bush. Most American Jews are embarrassed by Israel's roguish sponsoring of Jewish colonies in Arab Palestine: 85 percent of Orthodox Jews voted for Bush, but only one-quarter of all Jews did so. Most Americans do not think that using atomic weapons against Iran is a good idea. They understand that Dick Cheney and Donald Rumsfeld are modestly intelligent bullies who see force as the solution to problems of all kinds. Most Americans do not live, geographically or by conviction, in the former Confederate states.

By instinct, then, we feel that here, as in so many antecedent historical situations, much has depended on good or bad luck and on the personality of America's president at a particular time. Many of us underestimated George W. Bush. At first, the man seemed to be a buffoonish figure. His malapropisms were treasured and lovingly recounted: "Families is where our nation finds hope and wings take dreams." We thought him a figure of fun, just as Charlie Chaplin had ridiculed "the Great Dictator." And we did so with some justice: How could we not be struck by the brutalizing nature of his thinking, by his shallow optimism, by his superficiality and his poor judgment that plunged America into a war that seriously worsened the larger problem it was supposed to solve? In watching and listening to Bush, one could readily imagine that the worst clichés of anti-Americanism must somehow have some truth to them after all.

We took for granted that his rise to power had been a matter of luck and connections. As Beaumarchais's Figaro said of nobles on the eve of the French Revolution, what had this man done but take the trouble to be born? Like Kim Il Sung Jr., George W. Bush without his father would not only not have become president of his country, he would never have achieved prominence in any field.

But we underestimated his perverse talents. Even as regards his birth and status, the man had sound instincts: though born, as the Texas Democrat Ann Richards said of his father, with a silver foot in his mouth, George W. Bush took care to improve on his family lineage. Though his grandfather had reached prominence in the age-old alliance of northeastern late-nineteenth-century Republicanism and Wall Street, the genius of George W. Bush was to succeed where George H. W. Bush had failed in Texas. Where Bush *père* was unable to secure a seat as a Texas congressman (he had not yet learned that in Texas, the word "summer" is not a verb but a noun), Bush *fils*, after a slow start, soon became the indisputably indigenous governor of the Lone Star State.

Much can also be said for his talent as a rallying point for America's tradition of exclusion and narrow particularism. "Turn a weakness into a strength," said Chairman Mao, and this too Bush has done. Accustomed to failure, aware of his inferiority, he learned to ignore all criticisms, especially those that were obviously accurate. (Typically, this narcissist does not read the press.) He learned never to admit to having erred, a useful mechanism of self-defense for a man who has erred so often. But he also learned to lean on others: on his wife, strong and patient, to keep his private life on an even keel, and on all those ambitious figures who for the sake of power are eager to manipulate and willing to be manipulated in turn. Shrewdly, he has generally preferred to seem to govern rather than to govern in fact: had he been more gifted, this president might well have steered the ship of state toward disastrous shoals. By drifting with the tide, by understanding (if never admitting) his own considerable shortcomings, Bush became, *mirabile dictu*, a skilled unifier and the common denominator of varying causes with which many voters could identify.

Obtuse? Inarticulate? An embarrassment? Yes, no doubt, but at the same time, the man had a true gift, if of a sadly perverse kind. Moved by a low shrewdness, George W. Bush managed to harness and magnify the exclusionary passions that for centuries have lurked in the recesses of America's sensibility, dark passions that have usually been subjugated by America's democratic and universalist impulses, but dark passions that are stronger and more important today than they have been since the 1850s, when America's existence as a nation was most dangerously brought into question.

EPILOGUE

Americans love their country. Through the centuries, their image of it has been remarkably constant: most Americans most of the time have thought of themselves as a religious nation and, in the words of their greatest president, an "almost chosen people" dedicated to the defense of individual rights in matters civic, religious, and economic. They have long believed—and still believe—in the reinforcing complementarity of democracy, transcendence, and capitalism.

However, through the centuries this enduring self-image has existed in two versions, one of them of inclusion, the other, of exclusion. These versions are obviously different, but they are also similar, and this for two reasons: first, because they share a common religious and Enlightenment origin, and second, because Americans, whether on the left or on the right, commonly assume that nature, history, fate, or God has intended for their version of Americanness to be what it is.

The first version of this American creed is patriotic (or national) and inclusive. The other is nationalistic and exclusionary. Moreover, these two tendencies—at once related in their origin and Manichaean in their purpose—have existed in unusual and troubling proximity throughout American history. All too often egged on by circumstance or by some misguided or malevolent president, America has slid from the more liberal to the more conservative of these two options, so far apart in most polities, so closely bound in American life.

Of course, these two steadfast interpretations of American politics, universalist and particularist, with their common origins and parallel trajectories, have never been set in stone. "Little by little," said Lincoln in 1854, "but steadily as a man's march to the grave, we have been giving up the OLD for the NEW faith."[1] But for him, revealingly, this new faith was an extension, not a denial, of the old one.

In today's America, racism endures, but class often trumps race, and that was not so in 1950; indeed, it was unthinkable in 1800. As American society, ever pragmatic and innovative, moved from commercialized ruralism in the 1790s to capitalistic industrialism in the 1890s, and to postindustrial postmodernism in the 1990s, its self-image has varied accordingly, but only up to a point. We can easily see why: as regards the changing shape of its *economic* forms (but, again, not its political self-image), America holds to the ancient Chinese proverb that the one thing that doesn't change is that everything changes all the time.

And so the first task of this essay has been to define America's ideational continuities and then to describe briefly the economic, social, and cultural foundations of America's durable but divided self-image: national and nationalistic, inclusive and exclusionary, universalizing and particularist. For example, in periods of economic well-being, such as the 1850s, ideological continuities—especially of religion—mattered more as a determinant: in those years, for the northern states, America really was an imagined, and one might add, a libertarian, community. At other times, as in the late 1880s and again in the 1930s, in periods of great economic hardship, social change and discontinuous economic circumstance were more important.

The pattern proceeds through five arcs. The first moves from the individualized religiosity and economics of the early settlers to the universalist Declaration of Independence and the refounding of the republic in 1787, where the War of Independence was at once a national triumph of transcendental becoming for whites and an irremediable exclusion and catastrophe for Native Americans.

The second arc, more complex, deals with the democratization of the new nation-state up to 1865, with wars of conquest and extermination, but also with a glorious civil war of inclusion and liberation (as if any war can ever be said to have been glorious).

The third and, next to our own, the most distressing epoch in American history runs from the 1870s to 1912. Its theme was the materialist and racist reshaping of America's national purpose, with a burst of imperialist passion to which America's stunning material growth was complicatedly and unexpectedly related.

The fourth, which runs from 1912 to 1968, the year when Richard Nixon and George Wallace together secured 57 percent of the popular vote, was America's phase of approximate social democracy, comparable to the democratic age of Jackson and Lincoln, at once immensely laudable, with D-Day, and horrifying, with its devastating and immoral bombings of Hiroshima and Nagasaki.

The fifth, our own epoch, recalls the third period of American history, with tales of political corruption, wanton international aggression, and more or less covert racism, especially as regards immigration. Placed end to end, these five arcs tell a story that is the history of the United States of America.

The aim of this essay has not been to provide a classic historical narrative. It has aimed instead to chart the flow of energy that has so often moved American opinion from the themes of inclusion (Christian, Republican, or social democratic) to those of exclusion (war, conquest, racism). It has also aimed to underscore—repeatedly—the ability of coteries and presidents in the American system of politics and government to propel their nation from openness to reaction.

But there is more to it than that: America's greatest magistrates—Washington, Jefferson, Lincoln, and Franklin Roosevelt—were all patriots who did indeed make nationalist choices, but cautiously so, and only when these nationalist options could not be avoided. They, too, accepted what Theodore Roosevelt dismissed as mere "attendant cruelties," but they did so with some reluctance. Other presidents, however, might perhaps be described as war criminals, if of the "kinder, gentler" sort. These are the leaders—"deciders," in George W. Bush's memorable vocabulary—who, with their satraps, have taken advantage of the proximity of patriotic and nationalistic ways of thinking in American life to pursue goals that were dear to themselves but deleterious to the nation. Theirs were conscious choices, irresponsible, immoral, and oftentimes plainly unconstitutional or even criminal. So it was, up to a point, for Jackson with the Cherokees in 1834; for Polk with the Mexicans in 1847; and, much more criminally, for McKinley with the Philippines in 1898 and today for George W. Bush, whose dishonesty and arrogance weigh down on the planet as a whole.

*****

For Machiavelli, the most eminent chronicler in 1500 of Italy's past and present, history made it possible to predict the future because human nature never changed: "Prudent men say, and not without reason, that he who wants to predict what will be, must know about what was, because events everywhere and always are very much the same. That is because the actions of men are born of unchanging passions, which, of necessity, engender the same effects."[2] In that frame, more is given to those who have much, but conversely, bad situations will get worse. (Rousseau was of a similar pessimistic mind.)

For Charles Rollin in 1700, by contrast, history made no sense at all: he could see no real reason to suppose either that matters would continue as before or that they would not. For this learned cleric, as well known in Boston as he was in Paris, history was no more than a succession of unfathomable mysteries. Some events revolved around Christian mysteries that were part of God's unchanging will, but many events could not be explained at all. Why did it rain on watery oceans rather than on arid deserts? "By his own lights," Rollin wrote, "man knows nothing of what is to come."[3]

In this debate on the nature of historical thought and its relevance to the future, Tocqueville's was an intermediate solution: history served to explain the present, but (contrary to what Marx would later opine) it pointed to but did not determine a predictable future. For Tocqueville in 1831, to understand seventeenth-century New England was a great step toward understanding America, because all societies were organized around some determining "mother ideas" (*idées mères*), which surely if subterraneously persisted through historical time.

And yet, he also thought, the effects of the past could be amended, ignored, or reversed. "I know full well," he wrote on the last page of his work on American society and politics,

> that many of my contemporaries have assumed that on this earth, nations are never master of their own destiny, and that they necessarily defer to some insurmountable and unintelligible force that derives from some anterior force, from race, soil, or climate. These are false and cowardly doctrines that will always bring forth weak men and pusillanimous nations. Humankind as Providence has made it is neither completely free nor completely enslaved. True enough, she draws around each man a fatal circle beyond which he cannot go. But within those vast limits, man is powerful and free; and so are nations. The nations that we know today cannot prevent the equalizing of social rank; but from that point on, it is up to them to choose between freedom and servitude, between Enlightenment and barbarism, between prosperity and misery.

We can speculate on America's future from each of these three perspectives.

In the first, Machiavellian one, nothing improves: matters that are now bad continue to be predictably bad, and sometimes get worse. In this Rousseauean perspective, the dysfunctional cultural and social contexts that allowed George W. Bush's dark interpretations of American life become yet more dysfunctional. The control of an ever-larger military establishment by civilian authorities weakens steadily. The gap between the very rich and everyone else widens ceaselessly. Deepening public indifference to matters of public interest allows the intensification of regional and racist particularisms. Pro-war nationalism reconciles secular-minded Americans to the ambitions of the Christian right.

American politics and culture become as divisive as they were in the 1930s or the 1850s.

In that context, Bush's version of economic individualism, religion, and democracy gathers strength. The proximity in America of patriotic inclusion and nationalistic exclusion gives plausibility to his illegal projects. Voters continue to drift away from political parties that are ever more often led by self-seeking professional politicians whose first concern is to be elected and reelected. Money further corrupts the American democratic process. From opportunistic calculation, Bush, his advisers, and their successors capitalize on a disillusioned public's suspicion of all government to feather their oligarchic nest. The ability of the state to structure civil society's drive toward more universalist social goals wanes. Global warming is ignored. Deficits worsen. Interest rates rise as the dollar falls. Recession gives way to Depression.

In a parallel movement of doom and gloom abroad, Bush's ethic of preemptive war continues to create insoluble problems. Senator Henry Cabot Lodge explained in 1898 that America does not lower the flag in those places where it has raised it,[4] and that proves to be all too true. Americans continue to trample the very international institutions that they created at the end of the Second World War, the United Nations first among them. In a world where Iranians and Israelis are atomic powers, the risk of war becomes ever less manageable and ever more threatening. In world opinion, the distinction that underpins this book, of an America that hesitates always between good and evil, gradually loses credibility. In foreign lands, Amerika and all its ways are uniformly rejected, not only by countries that are directly targeted by Bush's preemptive use of military force, but also by the still-determined European children of the Enlightenment, who, however unfairly, come to identify America as a whole with the decisions of its rogue government.

In the historically agnostic view of Charles Rollin, by contrast, circumstances largely go on as before, neither better nor worse, and we cannot predict or understand any changes that do occur. True enough, America's economic situation continues unenviable and even fragile: because of George Bush's demagogic unwillingness to tax, the United States continues to finance its fiscal shortfall by issuing bonds that end up in the treasuries of foreign powers, some of them, like Japan, subservient, but others, like China and Saudi Arabia, cautious and potentially hostile. And yet this reality, and the diplomatic difficulties that flow from it, somehow do not shake the public's faith in the American economy. The Bush presidency, and the control of the U.S. government by the right wing of the Republican Party, withstand the collapse of Bush's ill-fated occupation of Iraq: Karl Rove and his ilk, experts in the steady and plausible deformation of the truth, successfully explain that America's failure in the Middle East is the fault of its unreliable allies and of American liberals who have stabbed the United States in the back and sabotaged the nation's war effort. In brief, nothing much changes: both economically and in foreign and domestic policy, Supertanker America sails on without changing course.

Finally, in the Tocquevillean perspective, America's situation unexpectedly improves. The promises of this book's preface, "Graduation Day," come into their own. America's liberal tradition of democratic inclusion once again, as it has in the past, becomes stronger than its darker twin, the tradition of nationalistic exclusion.

America often moves from good to bad, from D-Day to Hiroshima. But it can also move from bad to good. Who would have predicted in 1820 that a Republican enemy of slavery would be elected president in 1860, or supposed in 1928 that Franklin Roosevelt would become president in 1933? Overall, America's sense of self is unusually steadfast, but within its range of possibilities, anything can happen. In 1857 Frederick Douglass, once a slave, spoke for the ages when he wrote that no other country seemed to him as likely as the United States to develop ideas that would make for more liberty and humanity. Americans love their country, but many still think as the anti-imperialist Carl Schurz did in 1899: "Our country—when right, to be kept right; when wrong, to be put right."[5] America's nationalist tradition of exclusion is very strong, but its neighboring tradition of patriotic inclusion is also strong: Americans, who were unconcerned with slavery before 1776, discussed it ceaselessly after 1800. Six decades later, four hundred thousand Union soldiers died to abolish it.

The development of a concern for civil rights in the second half of the twentieth century is also to be remembered. In his famous book, *The American Dilemma* (1944), Gunnar Myrdal eloquently described the tragic situation of African Americans caught between a seemingly indestructible American prejudice, and what he celebratedly called the American Creed, a doctrine of inclusion whose origins were in the values of the Enlightenment. But since Myrdal's day America has changed immensely in this respect, and for the better. In 1968 George Wallace ran as a segregationist in the presidential election. He carried four southern states and received close to 10 million votes. Such an event is unthinkable today.

America's sense of self has often depended on cultural transformations that few had foreseen. Waves of emigration transformed American life between 1870 and 1920, and it may well be that today's wave of new immigrants will transform America's attitudes to its Protestant past. The dream of the 34 million immigrants from Europe who settled in America between 1820 and 1924 was to fit themselves into preexisting molds, as implied by the titles of many historical works on this subject, such as *How the Irish Became White*, or, concerning Italian immigrants, *White upon Arrival*. Immigrants were oftentimes more chauvinistically American than the native born: to quote the German-born Carl Schurz again: "However warm their affection for their native land, [German Americans] have never permitted that affection to interfere with their duties as American citizens."[6] It was in the work of an Italian-born film director Frank Capra that Americans during the 1930s discovered an idealized image of their country that really made sense to them, as in *Mr. Deeds Goes to Town*, which is about an ordinary man who becomes rich but chooses to stay poor; *Mr. Smith Goes to Washington*, the history of an honest man, elected senator, who chooses not to become either selfish or corrupt; and, in 1944, *The Negro Soldier*, which portrayed whites and blacks as comrades fighting for democracy. We could also cite, in this same context of naïve and admiring loyalty, Madeleine Albright, a Czech immigrant, who has called America "the indispensable country." So thoroughly did newcomers assimilate to their adopted homeland that, in the late nineteenth century, some theoretically minded writers even speculated on possible genetic mutations in immigrants who had become Americans.[7]

But perhaps all that will change: today's and tomorrow's immigrants, predominantly from Latin America, may be less impressionable than their predecessors about the prejudices of their new country. (Hispanics, who made up only one percent of the American population in 1900, are 20 percent today.) Of the 25 million people who have settled in the United States since 1965, most have their origin in the Third World, and their perspective on America's neo-European culture will surely have a specificity of its own, less focused—or so we can hope—on a vengeful and unrelentingly Augustinian God, and also less focused on the merits of capitalistic globalization, which, paradoxically, many have tried to flee by coming to its epicenter.

Perhaps the new immigrants, closer as many of them are geographically to their former homeland, will persevere in their linguistic and religious particularisms. They too, like their predecessors, will surely espouse the positive values that America derives from its New England heritage, namely associationism, self-government, and respect for individual rights, but perhaps they will do so without chaining themselves by mind-forged manacles to its apocalyptic biblical fundamentalism, to its religious determinism, and to that passion for violence that has disfigured American public life from King Philip's War in 1675 to the destruction of Hiroshima in 1945 and the prisons of Baghdad and Guantánamo in our own time. Such a "de-anglosaxonization" of America might prove thoroughly beneficial. The cultural particularity of the southern states might wane. Some sociological transformation that we cannot foresee might still make for a renewed America. According to Kevin Phillips: "A careful electoral analysis shows that what can be called a Bush coalition is too narrow to govern successfully and was empowered to win only by a succession of odd circumstances in both 2000 and 2004."[8]

That may well be. Once more, as Bismarck jokingly suggested, a special Providence does perhaps protect the American Republic.

Nonetheless, of our three scenarios, the third and most optimistic appears, at this moment, the least likely. Our rational expectation has to be either Machiavelli's lugubrious prospect of further decline, or Rollin's belief that God's will is inscrutable, that nothing makes much sense, and that matters will somehow go on as they always have.

For William Dean Howells, "What the American public always wants is a tragedy with a happy ending." No doubt. But with regard to endings, a more universal message—as Hegel famously aphorized— holds that it is only at the dusk of history that Minerva's owl takes flight. In matters private and public, by the time we understand what we should have done, it is often too late to do it. Reform is difficult. Common sense is frail and in the main, uncommon. Wisdom often comes from suffering, but an evermore hedonistic nation is not well situated to grasp this ancient truth. Besides, historical experience shows— as even Tocqueville recognized—that our prospects are often drastically narrowed and constrained by antecedent choices. "The great European social theorists—Karl Marx first among them," writes Roberto Unger, "identified the internal dynamics of societies—the revelation of inescapable conflicts and missed opportunities—as the proximate cause of their transformation. These thinkers were mistaken. War and economic catastrophe have been the chief levers of change; catastrophe— unforeseen and uncontrolled—has served as the midwife of reform."[9]

And that, alas, may be where we are today. History doesn't repeat itself, but it rhymes.

NOTES

PREFACE: Graduation Day

1. As is described by Garry Wills in his luminous *Lincoln at Gettysburg: The Words That Remade America* (New York: Simon & Schuster, 1992), 194.

INTRODUCTION: Patriotism and Imperialism

1. This theme of contradiction has been ably developed by Michael Kammen in his *People of Paradox* (Ithaca, NY: Cornell University Press, 1990).

2. As in Donald Rumsfeld, who explained in a speech of February 2, 2006, that the Islamicists "will either succeed in changing our way of life, or we will succeed in changing theirs."

3. A topic that has been the subject of innumerable studies: some of the names that come to mind are the Beards (Charles and Mary), Vernon Parrington, Merle Curti, and Denis Brogan.

4. *Letters of Theodore Roosevelt*, ed. Elting Morison (Cambridge, MA: Harvard University Press, 1954), vol. 7, 676.

5. Kevin Phillips, *American Theocracy: The Perils and Politics of Radical Religion, Oil, and Borrowed Money in the Twenty-first Century* (New York: Viking, 2006), 96.

6. Jon Meacham, *American Gospel: God, the Founding Fathers, and the Making of a Nation* (New York: Random House, 2006), 16.

7. Garry Wills, *Under God: Religion and American Politics* (New York: Simon & Schuster, 1990), 25.

8. In his pamphlet, "Bruno Bauer, the Jewish Question," in *Early Political Writings*, ed. Joseph O'Malley and Richard Davis (Cambridge University Press, 1994), 33.

9. I owe this image to Roberto Unger's *What Should the Left Propose?* (New York: Verso, 2005); Arthur Schlesinger, "Biography of a Nation of Joiners," in *The American Historical Review*, vol. 50, October 1944.

10. Cited by Oscar and Mary Handlin in *Commonwealth* (Cambridge, MA: Harvard University Press, 1947), 224.

11. Leo Marx, *The Machine in the Garden: Technology and the Pastoral Ideal in America* (New York: Oxford University Press, 1964), 228. Cited by Stephanie Wooler in her unpublished paper: "Failure of fraternity: revolution, trauma and the rewriting of the family romance in the French revolution."

12. Judith Shklar, *American Citizenship: The Quest for Inclusion* (Cambridge, MA: Harvard University Press, 1991), 10. Shklar refers her readers to Kay Schlozman and Sydney Verba's *Insult to Injury* (Cambridge, MA: Harvard University Press, 1979) "for an account of [the American Dream's] hold even on the unemployed and the working poor" (Shklar, 105, n7).

13. Richard Slotkin, *Regeneration through Violence: The Mythology of the American Frontier, 1600–1860* (Middletown, CT: Wesleyan University Press, 1973), 4–5.

14. Assmann quoted in Eric Santner, "Miracles Happen: Benjamin, Rosenzweig, Freud, and the Matter of the Neighbor," in *The Neighbor: Three Inquiries in Political Theology*, ed. S. Žižek (Chicago: University of Chicago Press, 2005), 79.

15. Walter LaFeber, *The American Age: United States Foreign Policy at Home and Abroad since 1750* (New York: Norton, 1989), 171.

16. Harry S. Stout, *Upon the Altar of the Nation: A Moral History of the American Civil War* (New York: Viking, 2006), 460.

17. Fred Anderson and Andrew Cayton, *The Dominion of War: Empire and Liberty in North America, 1500–2000* (New York: Viking, 2005), 337.

18. Rousseau quoted in Anthony D. Smith, *The Antiquity of Nations* (Cambridge, UK: Polity Press, 2004), 105.

19. As best described in his *Nationalism* (Oxford: Blackwell, 1993), 4th ed., pp. 82–83, 96.

20. Charles Tilly considers in some detail historical, developmental, and functional theories of nation building in his "Theories of Political Transformation," in *The Formation of National States in Western Europe*, ed. Charles Tilly (Princeton, NJ: Princeton University Press, 1975), 602–638.

21. Breuilly cited in Anthony Douglas Smith, *Nationalism* (Cambridge, UK: Polity Press, 2001), 76.

22. Hans Kohn pointed out decades ago that Central and Eastern European nationalisms "were created often out of the myths of the past and the dreams of the

future, an ideal fatherland, closely linked with the past, devoid of any immediate connection with the present, and expected to become sometime a political reality." Western nationalisms, he went on, were by contrast involved in the building of a political reality. American nationalism might serve as his best example: its genesis was coterminous with political change, and its mythical dimension came after rather than before its birth date. Hans Kohn, *The Idea of Nationalism: A Study of Its Origins and Background* (New York: Macmillan, 1944), 330.

23. Bernard Bailyn, "The Central Themes of the American Revolution: An Interpretation," in *Essays on the American Revolution*, ed. Stephen Kurtz and James Hutson (Chapel Hill: University of North Carolina Press, 1973), 27.

24. Walt Whitman, *Leaves of Grass*, ed. Justin Kaplan (New York: Library Classics of the United States, 1982), 5.

25. The 1979 Middletown Area Study was part of a series of sociological studies of Muncie that began in the 1920s. Virginia Woolf, "Mr. Bennet and Mrs. Brown," in *Collected Essays* (New York: Harcourt, Brace, 1953), 320–321.

26. Octavio Paz, *The Labyrinth of Solitude* (New York: Grove, 1961), 22.

27. Ibid.

28. Scott A. Sandage, *Born Losers: A History of Failure in America* (Cambridge, MA: Harvard University Press, 2005), 277 (quoting Stevens), 278.

29. Cited in David M. Potter, *People of Plenty: Economic Abundance and the American Character* (Chicago: University of Chicago Press, 1962), 92.

30. Unger, *What Should the Left Propose?*, 99.

31. Michael Adas, *Dominance by Design: Technological Imperatives and America's Civilizing Mission* (Cambridge, MA: Harvard University Press, 2005), 130.

32. Edmund Morgan, *American Slavery, American Freedom* (New York: Norton, 1975), 376.

33. Thomas Bender, *A Nation among Nations: America's Place in World History* (New York: Hill and Wang, 2006), 7.

34. John Lukacs, *Democracy and Populism: Fear and Hatred* (New Haven, CT: Yale University Press, 2005), 36.

35. Alain Touraine, *Un Nouveau paradigme pour comprendre le monde aujourd'hui* (Paris: Fayard, 2005), 246. Ian Angus, *A Border Within: National Identity, Cultural Plurality, and Wilderness* (Montreal: McGill-Queen's University Press, 1997), cited

in Winfried Siemerling, *The New North American Studies: Culture, Writing and the Politics of Re/cognition* (New York: Routledge, 2005), 145.

36. Anders Stephanson, *Manifest Destiny: America's Expansionism and the Empire of Right* (Hill and Wang, 1995), xiii.

37. Lynn Hunt, *The Family Romance of the French Revolution* (Berkeley: University of California Press, 1993), 199–200.

38. Slavoj Žižek, "Neighbors and Other Monsters: A Plea for Ethical Violence," in *The Neighbor*, ed. S. Žižek, 186–187.

39. Robert Osgood, *Ideals and Self-Interest in America's Foreign Relations* (Chicago: University of Chicago Press, 1953), 56.

40. John Foster Dulles, "Challenges and Response in United States Policy," in *America's Foreign Policy*, ed. Harold K. Jacobson (New York: Random House, 1960), 327.

41. Randolph Bourne, "Trans-National America," quoted in *The American Intellectual Tradition*, ed. David A. Hollinger (New York: Oxford University Press, 1989), vol. 2, 197.

42. As in Felix Gilbert, *To the Farewell Address: Ideas of Early American Foreign Policy* (New York: Harper Torchbooks, 1965).

43. Norris, again, supported Roosevelt's desire to lift the embargo on arms to the Allies in 1939, but Robert La Follette Jr. opposed it, on the sensible grounds that the French and English colonial empires were not precisely democratic enterprises. See Ronald Feinman, *Twilight of Progressivism: The Western Republican Senators and the New Deal* (Baltimore, MD: Johns Hopkins University Press, 1981), 182–184.

44. Peter Schuck, *Diversity in America: Keeping Government at a Safe Distance* (Cambridge, MA: Harvard University Press, 2003), 310.

45. Roosevelt cited in Meacham, *American Gospel*, 145.

46. "Civil religion" is a term made familiar by Robert Bellah in his "Civil Religion in America" (1967), reprinted in *Beyond Belief: Essays on Religion in a Post-Traditional World* (New York: Harper & Row, 1970). In this context, America's civil religion is a faith at once secular and mystical, with sacred texts (the Declaration of Independence, the Constitution), dogmas (the sanctity of democracy and America's mission in the world), sacred sites (Liberty Hall, the Arlington National Cemetery, Ground Zero), high holy days (the Fourth of July, Memorial Day, Thanksgiving); *ex votos* (the Liberty Bell, the Statue of Liberty); and so on. Jean-

François Colosimo's *Dieu est-il Américain: de la théocratie aux Etats-Unis* (Paris: Fayard, 2006) is an eloquent guide to this aspect of American life.

47. Adams quoted in Zoltan Haraszti, *John Adams and the Prophets of Progress* (Cambridge, MA: Harvard University Press, 1952), 85.

48. *The Works of Herman Melville* (New York: Russell and Russell, 1963), vol. 6, ch. 36, 189.

49. As described by Hunt in *The Family Romance of the French Revolution*, 71, citing Wesley Frank Craven, *The Legend of the Founding Fathers* (New York, New York University Press, 1956).

50. Tocqueville, *Democracy in America*, book II, part 1. (In the Mayer edition, p. 280.)

51. Sean Wilentz, "History and Democracy," *Harvard Magazine*, September–October 2006, 39.

52. Lincoln, *Speeches and Writings, 1859–1865*, ed. Don E. Fehrenbach (New York: Library of America, 1989), 209.

53. Recent research has modified that estimate to one American in five opposed to independence, many of them poor, backcountry people hostile to patriot landlords.

CHAPTER 1: An Almost Chosen People

1. William Stoughton, "New England's True Interest," in *The American Puritans: Their Prose and Poetry*, ed. Perry Miller (Garden City, NY: Anchor, 1956), 113–114.

2. Eliot quoted in Alden T. Vaughan, *New England Encounters* (Boston: Northeastern University Press, 1999), 260.

3. Cited in Deana Rankin, *Between Spenser and Swift: English Writing in Seventeenth-Century Ireland* (Cambridge, UK: Cambridge University Press, 2005), 52.

4. William Bradford, *Of Plymouth Plantation*, ed. Samuel Morison (New York: Knopf, 1952), 296.

5. William T. Hagan, *American Indians* (Chicago: University of Chicago Press, 1993), 189.

6. Mather quoted in Hugh Brogan, *The Penguin History of the United States of America* (London: Penguin, 1990), 63.

7. Bradford, *Of Plymouth Plantation*, 25–26.

8. Hans-Ulrich Wehler, *Nationalismus: Geschichte-Formen-Folgen* (Munich: C. H. Beck, 2001), 62.

9. Walter Russell Mead, *Special Providence: American Foreign Policy and How It Changed the World* (New York: Knopf, 2001), 219.

10. As presented in the *Sourcebook of Criminal Justice Statistics* of 2001, which relied on data provided by Harris Interactive Inc. There figures ranged from 43 percent in the South to 34 percent in the East. It was estimated by Philip J. Cook and Jens Ludwig in their *National Survey on Firearms Ownership and Use* of 1997 that 65 million of 192 million privately owned firearms were handguns. On any given day, 3 million Americans carry a gun on their person or in their car.

11. Bernard Bailyn et al., *The Great Republic* (Lexington, MA: D. C. Heath, 1981), 52.

12. Jon Butler et al., *Religion in American Life: A Short History* (Oxford, UK: Oxford University Press, 2003), 58.

13. Bernard Bailyn, *Atlantic History* (Cambridge, MA: Harvard University Press, 2005), 65.

14. Tocqueville, *Democracy in America*, book I, part 1, ch. 1.

15. John Patrick Diggins, *On Hallowed Ground: Abraham Lincoln and the Foundations of American History* (New Haven, CT: Yale University Press, 2000), 13–14.

CHAPTER 2: On the Path to Nationhood

1. The author of *Histoire des révolutions arrivés dans le gouvernement de la République romaine par M. l'abbé de Vertot.*

2. Bernard Bailyn, *The Ideological Origins of the American Revolution* (Cambridge, MA: Harvard University Press, 1992), 28–29.

3. Ibid., 155.

4. Fox quoted in Linda Colley, *Britons* (New Haven, CT: Yale University Press, 2005), 101.

5. François Perrault, *Gaspard Monge* (Paris: Tallandier, 2004), 271.

6. Winfried Siemerling, *The New North American Studies: Culture, Writing, and the Politics of Re/cognition* (New York: Routledge, 2005), 21, citing Perry Miller, *Errand into the Wilderness* (Cambridge, MA: Belknap Press of Harvard University Press, 1956), 11, and quoting Sacvan Bercovitch, *The American Jeremiad* (Madison: University of Wisconsin Press, 1978), 5.

7. Quoted in T. H. Breen, "Ideology and Nationalism on the Eve of the American Revolution: Revisions Once More in Need of Revising," in *German and American Nationalism*, ed. Hartmut Lehmann and Hermann Wellenreuther (Oxford, UK: Berg, 1999), 53.

8. Quoted in Francis Parkman, *Montcalm and Wolfe: France and England in North America*, Part Seventh, in 3 volumes (Boston, MA: Little, Brown and Company, 1898), vol. III, 251.

9. Colley, *Britons*, 18.

10. Edwards quoted in Ruth H. Bloch, *Visionary Republic* (Cambridge, UK: Cambridge University Press, 1985), 43.

11. I follow here the arguments presented by Alan Heimert in *Religion and the American Mind: From the Great Awakening to the Revolution* (Cambridge, MA: Harvard University Press, 1966).

12. Bloch, *Visionary Republic*, 43.

13. Quoted in Eric Foner, *The New American History* (Philadelphia: Temple University Press, 1997), 13.

14. Thomas Paine, *Common Sense and Related Writings*, ed. Thomas P. Slaughter (Boston: Bedford, 2001), 99.

CHAPTER 3: An American Republic

1. See Charles Beard, *Economic Interpretation of the Constitution of the United States* (New York: Macmillan, 1913).

2. Quoted in Dror Wahrman, *The Making of the Modern Self: Identity and Culture in Eighteenth-Century England* (New Haven, CT: Yale University Press, 2004), 224.

3. In a letter to Hezekiah Niles of February 13, 1818. *The Selected Writings of John and John Quincy Adams*, ed. Adrienne Koch (New York: Knopf, 1946), 203.

4. Page Smith, *A New Age Now Begins: A People's History of the American Revolution* (New York: McGraw Hill, 1976), vol. 1, 412.

5. Roosevelt quoted in Samuel Huntington, *Who Are We? The Challenges to America's National Identity* (New York: Simon & Schuster, 2004), 132, citing Edward Saveth, *American Historians and European Immigrants, 1875–1925* (New York: Columbia University Press, 1948), 121.

6. Emile Boutmy, *Éléments d'une psychologie politique du peuple américain* (Paris: Armand Colin, 1911), 77.

7. Junius quoted in Hugh Brogan, *The Penguin History of the United States of America* (London: Penguin, 1990), 155.

8. Huntington, *Who Are We?*, 111, citing Richard L. Merritt, *Symbols of American Community, 1735–1775* (New Haven, CT: Yale University Press, 1966), 174, 180.

9. *The Diary of Landon Carter of Sabine Hall, 1752–1778*, ed. Jack Greene (Richmond: Virginia Historical Society, 1987), 818 (June 3, 1774).

10. Adams quoted in Bernard Bailyn, *The Ideological Origins of the American Revolution* (Cambridge, MA: Harvard University Press, 1992), 1.

11. David Ramsay, *The History of the American Revolution*, cited in Esmond Wright, *An Empire for Liberty: From Washington to Lincoln* (Cambridge, UK: Blackwell, 1995), 32–33.

12. Paine quoted in Rogers M. Smith, *Civic Ideals: Conflicting Visions of Citizenship in U.S. History* (New Haven, CT: Yale University Press, 1997), 77.

13. Bailyn, *Ideological Origins of the American Revolution*, 20.

14. P. J. Deloria, *Playing Indian* (New Haven, CT: Yale University Press, 1998), 2.

15. Albert Katz Weinberg, *Manifest Destiny: A Study of Nationalist Expansionism in American History* (New York: AMS Press, 1979), 15.

16. Jon Meacham, *American Gospel: God, the Founding Fathers, and the Making of a Nation* (New York: Random House, 2006).

17. Quoted in Ruth H. Bloch, *Visionary Republic* (Cambridge, UK: Cambridge University Press, 1985), 62.

18. Thomas Paine, *Common Sense and Related Writings*, ed. Thomas P. Slaughter (Boston: Bedford, 2001), 98.

19. Paine quoted in Eric Foner, *The Story of American Freedom* (New York: Norton, 1998), 16.

20. Bailyn, *Ideological Origins of the American Revolution*, 235.

21. Gary B. Nash, *The Forgotten Fifth: African Americans in the Age of Revolution* (Cambridge, MA: Harvard University Press, 2006), 97.

22. New York and New Jersey, which had substantial slave populations, passed legislation for gradual emancipation in 1799 and 1804, respectively.

23. Nash, *Forgotten Fifth*, 113.

24. Henry cited in Bailyn, *Ideological Origins of the American Revolution*, 345.

25. See Gary Nash, *The Unknown American Revolution: The Unruly Birth of Democracy and the Struggle to Create America* (New York: Viking, 2005).

26. Oscar and Lilian Handlin, *Liberty in America: 1600 to the Present* (New York: Harper & Row, 1986), 143.

27. Edmund Morgan, "Conflict and Consensus in the American Revolution," in *Essays on the American Revolution*, ed. Stephen Kurtz and James Hutson (Chapel Hill: University of North Carolina Press, 1973), 303.

28. Jefferson cited in Arthur M. Schlesinger Jr., *The Age of Jackson* (Boston: Little, Brown, 1950), 8.

29. Robert Tucker and David Hendrikson, *Empire of Liberty: The Statecraft of Thomas Jefferson* (Oxford, UK: Oxford University Press, 1990), 249.

30. Foner, *American Freedom*, 16.

31. Gordon S. Wood, *The American Revolution: A History* (New York: Random House, 2003), 97.

32. Barlow cited in Kenneth Silverman, *A Cultural History of the American Revolution: Painting, Music, Literature, and the Theater in the Colonies and the United States from the Treaty of Paris to the Inauguration of George Washington, 1763–1789* (New York: Columbia University Press, 1987), 513.

33. Quoted in Fred Anderson and Andrew Cayton, *The Dominion of War* (New York: Viking, 2005), 171.

34. Ibid., 174–175, 177.

35. Wright, *An Empire for Liberty*, 146.

36. Madison, *The Federalist Papers*, #10.

37. Anderson and Cayton, *Dominion of War*, 222.

38. Walter Benjamin, "On the Concept of History," trans. Harry Zohn, in Walter Benjamin, *Selected Writings* (Belknap Press of the Harvard University Press, 2003), vol. 4, 392.

39. Cited in Sidney Lens, *The Forging of the American Empire: From the Revolution to Vietnam: A History of U.S. Imperialism* (Chicago: Haymarket, 2003), 54–55. See

also Angie Debo, *A History of the Indians of the United States* (Norman: University of Oklahoma Press, 1970), 91.

40. As Jefferson wrote in a letter of April 18, 1802, cited in Tucker and Hendrickson, *Empire of Liberty*, 109.

41. Richard Slotkin, *Regeneration through Violence* (Middletown, CT: Wesleyan University Press, 1973), 545.

42. In a letter to Abigail Adams cited in John Lewis Gaddis, *Surprise, Security, and the American Experience* (Cambridge, MA: Harvard University Press, 2004), 26.

43. Anderson and Cayton, *Dominion of War*, 229.

44. Jefferson to James Madison, April 27, 1809, in *The Writings of Thomas Jefferson*, ed. Andrew A. Lipscomb and Albert Ellery Bergh (Washington: Thomas Jefferson Memorial Association of the United States, 1903–04), vol. 12, 277.

45. Santander quoted in Carlos Rangel, *The Latin Americans: Their Love–Hate Relationship with the United States* (New York: Harcourt, 1976), 31. Bolivar, *Cartas del Liberator* (Caracas: Banco de Venezuela, 1964), vol. 7, 260.

46. Richard Buel Jr., *America on the Brink: How the Political Struggle over the War of 1812 Almost Destroyed the Young Republic* (New York: Palgrave, 2005), 17.

47. *New York Times* quoted in Walter Russell Mead, *Special Providence: American Foreign Policy and How It Changed the World* (New York: Knopf, 2001), 5. Hay quoted in Paul C. Nagel, *This Sacred Trust: American Nationality, 1798–1898* (New York: Oxford University Press, 1971), 292–293.

48. Goethe, *Faust*, line 1112, quoted in Anatol Lieven, *America Right or Wrong: An Anatomy of American Nationalism* (Oxford, UK: Oxford University Press, 2004), vi.

CHAPTER 4: A Democratic Sense of Self

1. Tocqueville, *Democracy in America*, book I, ch. 3 (my translation).

2. Lincoln cited in Garry Wills, *Lincoln at Gettysburg: The Words That Remade America* (New York: Touchstone, 1992), 85.

3. Richard John, "Affairs of Office: The Executive Departments, the Election of 1828, and the Making of the Democratic Party," in *The Democratic Experiment: New Directions in American Political History*, ed. Meg Jacobs et al. (Princeton, NJ: Princeton University Press, 2003), 57.

4. Adam Rothman, "The 'Slave Power' in the United States, 1782–1865," in *Rul-*

ing America: A History of Wealth and Power in a Democracy, ed. Steve Fraser and Gary Gerstle (Cambridge, MA: Harvard University Press, 2005).

5. Walter Johnson, *Soul by Soul: Life Inside the Antebellum Slave Market* (Cambridge, MA: Harvard University Press, 1999), 6.

6. Tocqueville cited in Matthew Maguire, *The Conversion of the Imagination* (Cambridge, MA: Harvard University Press, 2006), 203.

7. Maldwyn A. Jones, *The Limits of Liberty: American History, 1607–1992* (London: Oxford University Press, 1995), 131.

8. Carol Smith-Rosenberg, "Beauty, the Beast, and the Militant Woman: A Case Study in Sex Roles and Social Stress in Jacksonian America," in *Women and Power in American History*, ed. Kathryn Sklar (Upper Saddle River, NJ: Prentice Hall, 2002), 189.

9. Cited in Arthur M. Schlesinger, *The Age of Jackson* (Boston: Little, Brown, 1950), 91.

10. David Donald, *Liberty and Union* (Boston: Little, Brown, 1978), 22.

11. Duby quoted in *The Collected Essays of Asa Briggs*, vol. 2: *Images, Problems, Standpoints, Forecasts* (Brighton, UK: Harvester, 1985). See also Colley, *Britons*, 43.

12. Richard Slotkin, *Regeneration through Violence* (Middletown, CT: Wesleyan University Press, 1973), 5.

13. *Democracy in America*, book II, part 3, ch. 1.

14. Emerson quoted in Yehoshua Arieli, *Individualism and Nationalism in American Ideology* (Cambridge, MA: Harvard University Press, 1964), 277; see also Eric Foner, *The Story of American Freedom*, 57.

15. Beecher, "A Treatise on Domestic Economy," quoted in *The American Intellectual Tradition*, ed. David A. Hollinger (Oxford, UK: Oxford University Press, 1989), 234.

16. *Democracy in America*, book II, part 2, ch. 2.

17. Brownson quoted at www.billbrock.net/fch04.htm.

18. Brownson quoted in Arthur Schlesinger Jr., *The Cycles of American History* (Boston: Houghton Mifflin, 1986), 244–245.

19. Kathryn Kish Sklar, "Catherine Beecher Promotes Women's Entrance into the Teaching Profession," in Sklar, *Women and Power in American History*, 204–205.

20. Lincoln had tapped here into a very durable strand of American thinking: in the early 1950s, 39 percent of white Americans did not want a black person to work alongside them, but 87 percent of them nonetheless believed that blacks and whites should receive the same pay for the same work. See Herbert McClosky and John Zaller, *The American Ethos: Public Attitudes toward Capitalism and Democracy* (Cambridge, MA: Harvard University Press, 1984), 84–85.

21. Frederick Douglass, *My Bondage and My Freedom* (New York: Arno, 1968), 349.

22. Lincoln quoted in Arieli, *Individualism and Nationalism*, 307.

23. Ibid., 317.

24. *Democracy in America*, book I, part 2, ch. 9.

25. Emerson quoted in Andrew Delbanco, *The Real American Dream* (Cambridge, MA: Harvard University Press, 1999), 43.

26. *The Literary History of the United States*, 4th ed, ed. Robert Spiller et al. (New York: Macmillan, 1974), 931.

27. *Democracy in America*, book I, part 2, ch. 9; Mark A. Knoll, *The Old Religion in a New World: The History of North American Christianity* (Grand Rapids, MI: Eerdmans, 2002), 63.

28. Walter McDougall, *Promised Land, Crusader State: The American Encounter with the World since 1776* (Boston: Houghton Mifflin, 1997), 80.

29. Bruce D. Porter, cited in Richard Stillman II, *Creating the American State: The Moral Reformers and the Modern Administrative World They Made* (Tuscaloosa: University of Alabama Press, 1998), 10.

30. Al Gore, January 16, 2006, quoting members of the Bush administration in his transcript "Bush Administration Policies on Domestic Surveillance," posted on www.algore.org

CHAPTER 5: National Democratism

1. Tocqueville, *Democracy in America*, book II, part 3, ch. 16.

2. Walter Russell Mead, *Special Providence: American Foreign Policy and How It Changed the World* (New York: Knopf, 2001), 24.

3. Sidney Lens, *The Forging of the American Empire* (1971; London: Pluto, 2003), 7.

4. Quoted in Albert Katz Weinberg, *Manifest Destiny: A Study of Nationalist Expansionism in American History* (New York: AMS Press, 1979), 75–76.

5. Lens, *Forging of the American Empire*, 45.

6. Jefferson quoted in Anderson and Cayton, *The Dominion of War*, 220. See also William G. McLoughlin, *Cherokee Renascence in the New Republic* (Princeton, NJ: Princeton University Press, 1986), 37; and Anthony F. C. Wallace, *Jefferson and the Indians: The Tragic Fate of the First Americans* (Cambridge, MA: Harvard University Press, 1999).

7. Angie Debo, *A History of the Indians of the United States* (Norman: University of Oklahoma Press, 1970), 105–106.

8. King quoted in Weinberg, *Manifest Destiny*, 87–88.

9. In this discussion I follow Weinberg, *Manifest Destiny*, 73–76.

10. John Winthrop, *Reasons for the Plantation in New England* (ca. 1628).

11. Wilde quoted in Weinberg, *Manifest Destiny*, 84.

12. Cass quoted in Scott L. Pratt, *Native Pragmatism: Rethinking the Roots of American Philosophy* (Bloomington: Indiana University Press, 2002), 69. See also Weinberg, *Manifest Destiny*, 85.

13. Sean Wilentz, *The Rise of American Democracy: Jefferson to Lincoln* (New York: Norton, 2005), 325.

14. Jackson quoted in Ira Katznelson and Martin Shefter, *Shaped by War and Trade: International Influences on American Political Development* (Princeton, NJ: Princeton University Press, 2002), 69.

15. Quoted in Michael Paul Rogin, "Indian Removal," in *The Underside of American History*, ed. Thomas R. Frazier (New York: Harcourt Brace Jovanovich, 1971), 225.

16. Bancroft quoted in Michael S. Kimmel, *Manhood in America: A Cultural History* (New York: Oxford University Press, 2006), 24. Wilentz, *Rise of American Democracy*, 172.

17. See Loren Goldner, *Herman Melville* (New York: Queequeg Publications, 2005), 85.

18. Quoted in Anderson and Cayton, *Dominion of War*, 241–243.

19. *Democracy in America*, book I, part 2, ch. 9.

20. Jackson quoted in Rogin, "Indian Removal," 182.

21. O'Sullivan's prose was highly charged: "The far reaching, the boundless future will be the era of American greatness. In its magnificent domain of space and time, the nation of nations is destined to manifest to mankind the excellence of divine principles; to establish on earth the noblest temple ever dedicated to the worship of the Most High—the Sacred and the True. For this blessed mission to the nations of the world, which are shut out from the life-giving light of truth, has America been chosen." Quoted in Warren Zimmerman, *The First Great Triumph: How Five Americans Made Their Country a World Power* (New York: Farrar, Straus & Giroux, 2002), 33. In May 1848 O'Sullivan, accompanied by Stephen Douglas, Lincoln's future rival, went together to the White House and urged Polk to "take early measures with a view to the purchase of the island of Cuba from Spain." Polk confided to his diary that he was "decidedly in favour of purchasing Cuba," as a slave state, of course. *Polk: The Diary of a President, 1845–1849*, ed. Alan Nevins (New York: Longmans, 1929), 321.

22. Polk quoted in Weinberg, *Manifest Destiny*, 167–169.

23. Scott quoted in Howard Zinn, *A People's History of the United States* (New York: HarperCollins, 2003), 166.

24. Joel Porte, *Emerson in His Journals* (Cambridge, MA: Belknap Press of Harvard University Press, 1982), 358.

25. Daniel Boorstin, *The Americans: The National Experience* (New York: Random House, 1965), 273.

26. Quoted in Weinberg, *Manifest Destiny*, 90.

27. Michael Lind, *What Lincoln Believed: The Values and Convictions of America's Greatest President* (New York: Doubleday, 2005), 113.

28. Quoted in Weinberg, *Manifest Destiny*, 178.

29. Frederick Merk, *Manifest Destiny and Mission in American History: A Reinterpretation* (Cambridge, MA: Harvard University Press, 1995), 220.

30. Johnson quoted in Weinberg, *Manifest Destiny*, 178–179.

31. Polk quoted in Arthur M. Schlesinger Jr., *The Age of Jackson* (Boston: Little, Brown, 1950), 452.

CHAPTER 6: God's New Message in Lincoln's America

1. Quoted in Wilentz, *The Rise of American Democracy*, 271.

2. Mark A. Noll, *The Old Religion in a New World: The History of North American Christianity* (Grand Rapids, MI: Eerdmans, 2002), 14.

3. Emerson, "Circles," quoted in Andrew Delbanco, *The Real American Dream* (Cambridge, MA: Harvard University Press, 1999), 10.

4. David Brion Davis, "Expanding the Republic, 1820–1860," in Bernard Bailyn et al., *The Great Republic*, 3rd ed. (Lexington, MA: D. C. Heath, 1985), 367; Adams, March 1820, quoted in Samuel Flagg Bemis, *John Quincy Adams and the Foundations of American Foreign Policy* (Westport, CT: Greenwood, 1949), 421; and in Lynn Hudson Parsons, *John Quincy Adams* (Madison, WI.: Madison House, 1998), 161.

5. David Donald, *Liberty and Union* (Boston: Little, Brown, 1978), 15.

6. Johann Neem, *The Tocqueville Review/La Revue Tocqueville*, vol. xxvii, no. 1 (2006), 108.

7. Eric Foner, *The Story of American Freedom* (New York: Norton, 1998), 46.

8. Bancroft quoted in Boorstin, *The Americans: The National Experience*, 371.

9. Calhoun, "Disquisition on Government," quoted in David Hollinger, *The American Intellectual Tradition* (New York: Oxford University Press, 1989), 347.

10. Calhoun to Liver Dyer, January 1, 1849, quoted in Samuel Huntington, *Who Are We? The Challenges to America's National Identity* (New York: Simon & Schuster, 2004), 115.

11. Rhett quoted in Wilentz, *Rise of American Democracy*, 734.

12. Hugh Brogan, *The Penguin History of the United States of America* (London: Penguin, 1990), 310.

13. Esmond Wright, *An Empire for Liberty: From Washington to Lincoln* (Oxford, UK: Blackwell, 1995), 608.

14. Adams quoted in Wilentz, *Rise of American Democracy*, 629.

15. Sumner cited in Thomas Bender, *A Nation among Nations: America's Place in World History* (New York: Hill and Wang, 2006), 121.

16. William Pfaff, *The Wrath of Nations: Civilizations and the Furies of Nationalism* (New York: Simon & Schuster, 1993), 172.

17. Noll, *Old Religion in a New World*, 109. See also Charles R. Wilson, *Religion and the American Civil War* (New York: Oxford University Press, 1998).

18. See Ernest Tuveson, *Redeemer Nation: The Idea of America's Millennial Role* (Chicago: University of Chicago Press, 1968), 212.

19. McLoughlin quoted in Richard J. Stillman, *Creating the American State* (Tuscaloosa: University of Alabama Press, 1998), 50.

20. John B. Walters, "General William Tecumseh Sherman and Total War," *Journal of Southern History* 14 (November 1948): 447–480.

21. T. Harry Williams, *Americans at War: The Development of the American Military System*, cited in Mark E. Neely, "Was the Civil War a Total War?" in *On the Road to Total War: The American Civil War and the German Wars of Unification, 1861–1871*, ed. Stig Förster and Jorg Nagler (Cambridge, UK: Cambridge University Press, 1997), 36.

22. Harry Stout, *Upon the Altar of the Nation* (New York: Viking, 2006), 455. Not everyone agreed. H. L. Mencken wrote of Lincoln that he was "a plaster saint" and an amalgamation of John Wesley and the Holy Spirit. But that view has not prevailed. Michael Lind, *What Lincoln Believed: The Values and Convictions of America's Greatest President* (New York: Doubleday, 2005), 8.

23. William C. Harris, *Lincoln's Last Months* (Cambridge, MA: Harvard University Press, 2003), 219.

CHAPTER 7: A "Reconstructed" Nation

1. Douglass quoted in David Donald, "Uniting the Republic," in Bernard Bailyn et al., *The Great Republic* (Lexington, MA: D. C. Heath, 1981), 532.

2. Wadsworth and McKaye quoted in Ira Berlin et al., *Slaves No More: Three Essays on Emancipation and the Civil War* (Cambridge, UK: Cambridge University Press, 2006), 150.

3. Memorandum of Gustavus A. Myers, April 1865, quoted in William C. Harris, *Lincoln's Last Months* (Cambridge, MA: Harvard University Press, 2003), 206.

4. Harris, *Lincoln's Last Months*, 204–205.

5. Donald, "Uniting the Republic," 533.

6. See William Richter, *The Historical Dictionary of the Civil War and Reconstruction* (New York: Scarecrow Press, 2004), 327. Julian quoted in David Donald, "Reconstruction," in Bailyn et al., *Great Republic*, 545.

7. Whitman quoted in Kevin Phillips, *American Theocracy: The Peril and Politics of Radical Religion, Oil and Borrowed Money in the Twenty-First Century* (New York: Viking, 2006), 147.

8. David Levering Lewis, review of Taylor Branch's *At Canaan's Edge*, in *The New Yorker* (January 23 & 30, 2006), 86.

9. See Werner Sollors, "A Critique of Pure Pluralism," in *Reconstructing American Literary History*, ed. Sacvan Bercovitch (Cambridge, MA: Harvard University Press, 1986), 252.

10. Tony Smith, *Foreign Attachments* (Cambridge, MA: Harvard University Press, 2000), 34.

11. The darker side of these elective affinities, as will be seen, was in the creation of an imperialist Anglo-American circle around Elihu Root, whose avatars were in the foreign policy lobbies that we associate with Dean Acheson (who favored impeccable Bond Street suits) and John Foster Dulles in the 1950s, and after this, in our own day, between American neoconservatives and the British "new left."

12. Gregor Dallas, *1945: The War That Never Ended* (New Haven, CT: Yale University Press, 2005), 633.

13. Russel Blaine Nye, *Society and Culture in America, 1830–1860* (New York: Harper & Row, 1974), 214–215.

14. Fred Anderson and Andrew Cayton, *The Dominion of War* (New York: Viking, 2005), 321.

15. Quoted in Sidney Lens, *The Forging of the American Empire* (1971; London: Pluto, 2003), 143.

16. Quoted in Michael S. Kimmel, *Manhood in America: A Cultural History* (New York: Oxford University Press, 2006), 65.

17. Anderson and Cayton, *Dominion of War*, 321.

18. Walter LaFeber, *The American Age: United States Foreign Policy at Home and Abroad since 1750* (New York: Norton, 1989), 171.

19. Quotations from Thomas Bender, *A Nation among Nations: America's Place in World History* (New York: Hill and Wang, 2006), 219.

CHAPTER 8: Robber Baron America

1. Peter Skerry, "The Racialization of Immigration Policy," in *Taking Stock: American Government in the Twentieth Century*, ed. Morton Keller (New York: Cambridge University Press, 1999), 85.

2. Henry Adams, *The Education of Henry Adams* (New York: Modern Library, 1931), 241, 247, quoted in Michael S. Kimmel, *Manhood in America: A Cultural History* (New York: Oxford University Press, 2006), 59.

3. In a letter of November 29, 1886, in *Marx and Engels on the United States* (Moscow 1979), 312, cited in Lisa McGirr, "The Passion of Sacco and Vanzetti: A Global History," in the *American Historical Review* (forthcoming, March 2007).

4. Michael J. Sandel, *Democracy's Discontent: America in Search of a Public Philosophy* (Cambridge, MA: Harvard University Press, 1998), 205 (quoting Lippmann).

5. Pingree quoted ibid., 233.

6. David Donald, *Liberty and Union* (Boston: Little, Brown, 1978), 224.

7. I am following the argument of Christopher Hill in *National History and the World of Nations: Japan, France, and the United States in the Second Imperial Wave* (Durham, NC: Duke University Press, forthcoming).

8. Roosevelt quoted in Paul C. Nagel, *This Sacred Trust: American Nationality, 1798–1898* (New York: Oxford University Press, 1971), 38.

9. Roosevelt, "Machine Politics in New York," *Century*, November 1886: see www.theodoreroosevelt.org.

10. Alan Brinkley, *The Unfinished Nation: A Concise History of the American People* (Boston: McGraw-Hill, 2004), 570.

11. Bryce quoted in John L. Thomas, "Nationalizing the Republic, 1877–1920," in Bernard Bailyn et al., *The Great Republic* (Lexington, MA: D. C. Heath, 1981), 627.

12. In his introduction to Marx's Civil War in France, in Robert C. Tucker, *The Marx-Engels Reader* (New York: W. W. Norton, 1972), 536.

13. Sven Beckert, "Democracy in the Age of Capital: Contesting Suffrage Rights in Gilded Age New York," in *The Democratic Experiment*, ed. Meg Jacobs et al. (Princeton, NJ: Princeton University Press, 2003), 155–156.

14. Adams quoted in Alexander Keyssar, *The Right to Vote: The Contested History of Democracy in the United States* (New York: Basic Books, 2000), 122.

15. Fulbright, *The Arrogance of Power*, quoted in Walter McDougall, *Promised Land, Crusader State: The American Encounter with the World since 1776* (Boston: Houghton Mifflin, 1997), 206.

CHAPTER 9: America Renewed and Debased

1. Albert Katz Weinberg, *Manifest Destiny: A Study of Nationalist Expansionism in American History* (New York: AMS Press, 1979), 382.

2. Roosevelt quoted in Bernard Bailyn et al., *The Great Republic* (Lexington, MA: D. C. Heath, 1981), 719.

3. Fukuzawa quoted in Hill, *National history and the world of nations: Japan, France, and the United States in the second imperial wave*, 13 (manuscript page).

4. In a letter of March 1894, quoted in Stephen Wertheim, "The Foreign Policy of Frederick Douglass," *Tempus: The Harvard College History Review* 7, no. 2 (summer 2006), 21.

5. Quoted in Bailyn et al., *Great Republic*, 710.

6. Benjamin Zimmer, "Texas Annexation and the Roosevelt Corollary of the Monroe Doctrine," *Tempus* 7, no. 2, 45.

7. Claude Buss, *The United States and the Philippines: Background for Policy* (Washington, DC: American Enterprise Institute for Public Research, 1977), 3, cited in "The Logic of War, in the Nation at War: The Logic of Colonial Violence," in *German and American Nationalism*, ed. Hartmut Lehman and Hermann Wellenreuther (Oxford, UK: Berg, 1999), 218–219.

8. MacArthur quoted in Fred Anderson and Andrew Cayton, *The Dominion of War* (New York: Viking, 2005), 337, citing Walter Williams, "United States Indian Policy and the Debate over Philippine Annexation: Implications for the Origins of American Imperialism," *Journal of American History* 66 (1980): 826–827.

9. Weinberg, *Manifest Destiny*, 228, 393.

10. Mahan quoted in Bailyn et al., *Great Republic*, 706.

11. Mahan quoted in Walter LaFeber, *The American Age: United States Foreign Policy at Home and Abroad since 1750* (New York: Norton, 1989), 285.

12. Weinberg, *Manifest Destiny*, 228.

13. Alan Dawley, "The Abortive Rule of Big Money," in *Ruling America: A History of Wealth and Power in a Democracy*, ed. Steve Fraser and Gary Gerstle (Cambridge, MA: Harvard University Press, 2005), 163.

14. Seward quoted in Jeremy Lawrence, "William Henry Seward and the Alaska Purchase," *Tempus* 7, no. 2, 51.

15. Roosevelt and Hay quoted in Weinberg, *Manifest Destiny*, 428 (emphasis added), 272.

16. Adams quoted in Maria DeGuzman, *Spain's Long Shadow: The Black Legend, Off-whiteness, and Anglo-American Empire* (Minneapolis, MN: University of Minnesota Press, 2005), 171.

17. Root quoted in William Pfaff, *The Wrath of Nations: Civilization and the Furies of Nationalism* (New York: Touchstone, 1994), 179.

18. Albert J. Beveridge, "Our Philippine Policy," in Beveridge, *The Meaning of the Times and Other Speeches* (Indianapolis: Bobbs-Merrill, 1908), 71.

19. Beveridge quoted in Frederick Merk, *Manifest Destiny and Mission in American History: A Reinterpretation* (Cambridge, MA: Harvard University Press, 1995), 232.

20. John L. Thomas, "Nationalizing the Republic, 1787–1920," in Bailyn et al., *Great Republic*, 713.

21. See Winthrop Still Hudson and John Corrigan, *Religion in America: An Account of the Development of American Religious Life* (London: Prentice Hall, 1999), 265.

22. Walter Russell Mead, *Special Providence: American Foreign Policy and How It Changed the World* (New York: Knopf, 2001), 142.

23. Platt quoted in Weinberg, *Manifest Destiny*, 290.

24. Albert Beveridge, *The Young Man and the World* (Buffalo, NY: Corlis, 1907), 364.

25. Julius Pratt, "American Business and the Spanish-American War, " in *Hispanic American Historical Review*, 14 (1934), 178; Robert Kagan, *Dangerous Nation* (New York: Knopf, 2006), 416.

26. Thomas, "Nationalizing the Republic," 709.

27. Bryan quoted in Paul C. Nagel, *This Sacred Trust: American Nationality, 1798–1898* (New York: Oxford University Press, 1971), 317.

28. Thomas, "Nationalizing the Republic," 711.

29. Norton quoted in Bailyn et al., *Great Republic*, 712.

30. William James, "Letter to *Boston Evening Transcript*," March 1, 1899.

31. James quoted in Warren Zimmermann, *First Great Triumph: How Five Americans Made Their Country a World Power* (New York: Farrar, Straus & Giroux, 2002), 14, 342.

32. James, "Letter to *Boston Evening Transcript*," March 1, 1899, quoted in Anderson and Cayton, *Dominion of War*, 334–335. See also Richard E. Welch Jr., *Response to Imperialism: The United States and the Philippine-American War, 1899–1902* (Chapel Hill: University of North Carolina Press, 1979).

33. Anders Stephanson, *Manifest Destiny: America's Expansionism and the Empire of Right* (New York: Hill and Wang, 1995), 104.

34. David Burton, *Theodore Roosevelt: Confident Imperialist* (Philadelphia: University of Pennsylvania Press, 1968), 35.

35. Robert Endicott Osgood, *Ideals and Self-Interest in America's Foreign Relations: The Great Transformation of the Twentieth Century* (Chicago: University of Chicago Press, 1953), 28.

36. McKinley quoted in Weinberg, *Manifest Destiny*, 292.

37. Merk, *Manifest Destiny*, 253, citing Charles Olcott, *The Life of William McKinley* (Boston: Houghton Mifflin, 1916), vol. 2, 110–111.

CHAPTER 10: Premonitions

1. Ted Halstead and Michael Lind, *The Radical Center: The Future of American Politics* (New York: Doubleday, 2001), 213.

2. Roosevelt quoted in Edmund Morris, *The Rise of Theodore Roosevelt* (New York: Coward, McCann, and Geoghegan, 1979), 656.

3. R. Hal Williams, *America Past and Present* (London: Scott, Foresman/Little, Brown, 1990), 388.

4. Roosevelt, speech at Progressive Party Convention, 1912.

5. Jackson Lears, "The Managerial Revitalization of the Rich," in *Ruling America: A History of Wealth and Power in a Democracy*, ed. Steve Fraser and Gary Gerstle (Cambridge, MA: Harvard University Press, 2005), 188; For Skocpol, see *Bringing the State Back In*, ed. Theda Skocpol et al. (New York: Cambridge University Press, 1985).

6. Eric Foner, *The Story of American Freedom* (New York: Norton, 1998), 153.

7. As summarized by Thomas Bender in *A Nation among Nations: America's Place in World History* (New York: Hill and Wang, 2006), 252.

8. Croly quoted in Michael J. Sandel, *Democracy's Discontent: America in Search of a Public Philosophy* (Cambridge, MA: Harvard University Press, 1996), 340.

9. Roosevelt quoted by Fred Siegel in *The Reader's Companion to American History*, ed. Eric Foner and John Garraty (Boston: Houghton Mifflin, 1991), 654.

10. Harold Nicolson, *Peacemaking 1919* (New York: Universal Library, 1965), 145.

11. Wilson quoted in Eric Foner, *Forever Free: The Story of Emancipation and Reconstruction* (New York: Knopf, 2005), xxii–xxiii.

12. Wilson, "The Making of the Nation," *Atlantic Monthly*, July 1897.

13. Jonathan Hansen, *The Lost Promise of Patriotism: Debating American Identity, 1890–1920* (Chicago: University of Chicago Press, 2003), 29.

14. Foner, *American Freedom*, 174.

15. Wilson quoted in Bernard Bailyn et al., *The Great Republic* (Lexington, MA: D. C. Heath, 1981), 721.

16. Wilson quoted in Hugh Brogan, *The Penguin History of the United States of America* (London: Penguin, 1990), 467.

17. Cited ibid., 67.

18. Wilson quoted in Bailyn et al., *Great Republic*, 722.

19. Bryan quoted in John L. Thomas, "Nationalizing the Republic, 1877–1920," in Bailyn et al., *Great Republic*, 649. See also Edward S. Kaplan, *U.S. Imperialism in Latin America: Bryan's Challenges and Contributions, 1900–1920* (Westport, CT: Greenwood, 1998).

20. Isabelle Vagnoux, *Les Etats-Unis et le Mexique: Histoire d'une Relation Tumultueuse* (Paris: Harmattan, 2003), 100.

21. Robert Osgood, *Ideals and Self-Interest in America's Foreign Relations* (Chicago: University of Chicago Press, 1953), 172.

22. Bryan quoted in Brogan, *Penguin History of the United States*, 470.

23. Wilson quoted ibid., 477.

24. Wilson quoted in Thomas, "Nationalizing the Republic," 755.

25. Anders Stephanson, *Manifest Destiny: America's Expansionism and the Empire of Right* (New York: Hill and Wang, 1995), 118.

CHAPTER 11: Missed Opportunities

1. Hugh Brogan, *The Penguin History of the United States of America* (Penguin: London, 1990), 582.

2. Rick Atkinson, *An Army at Dawn* (New York: Holt, 2002), 266.

3. Hoover quoted in Alan Dawley, "The Abortive Rule of Big Money," in *Ruling America: A History of Wealth and Power in a Democracy*, ed. Steve Fraser and Gary Gerstle (Cambridge, MA: Harvard University Press, 2005), 177.

4. Skocpol quoted in Richard Stillman II, *Creating the American State* (Tuscaloosa: University of Alabama Press, 1998), 96.

5. Lippmann quoted in Dawley, "Abortive Rule of Big Money," 179.

6. Roosevelt, address to the Commonwealth Club, San Francisco, September 23, 1932.

7. Raymond Moley, *The First New Deal* (New York: Harcourt, Brace, and World, 1966), 227.

8. This interpretation was developed in the work of William Chandler Jr. and Robert Wiebe during the 1960s, and more recently in that of Louis Galambos.

9. Barbara J. Keys, *Globalizing Sport: National Rivalry and International Community in the 1930s* (Cambridge, MA: Harvard University Press, 2006), 80.

10. Paul K. Conkin, *The New Deal* (Arlington Heights, IL.: Harlan Davidson, 1967), 73.

11. Ted Halstead and Michael Lind, *The Radical Center: The Future of American Politics* (New York: Doubleday, 2001), 219.

12. Lizabeth Cohen, *A Consumers' Republic: The Politics of Mass Consumption in Postwar America* (New York: Knopf, 2003), 88.

13. Philip Rubio, in *History of Affirmative Action 1619–2000* (Jackson: University Press of Mississippi, 2001), and Ira Katznelson, in *When Affirmative Action Was White: An Untold History of Racial Inequality in Twentieth-Century America* (New York: Norton, 2005), have argued that the gap between black and white workers actually widened during FDR's presidency.

14. Henry David Thoreau, "Civil Disobedience" (1849), cited in David Hollinger, *The American Intellectual Tradition*, vol. 1 (New York: Oxford University Press, 1989), 307.

15. Eric Foner, *The Story of American Freedom* (New York: Norton, 1998), 210.

16. Paul Conkin, *The New Deal* (Wheeling, IL: Harlan Davidson, 1992), 7.

17. John Keegan, *The Second World War* (New York: Viking, 1990), 538.

18. Robert Divine, *America Past and Present* (London: Scott, Foresman/Little, Brown, 1990), 442.

19. Roosevelt and Holmes quoted in Michael J. Sandel, *Democracy's Discontent: America in Search of a Public Philosophy* (Cambridge, MA: Harvard University Press, 1998), 259–260.

20. Warren Zimmermann, *First Great Triumph: How Five Americans Made Their Country a World Power* (New York: Farrar, Straus & Giroux, 2002), 33–34.

21. On January 11, 1944, in *The Public Papers and Addresses of Franklin D. Roosevelt* (New York: Harper and Brothers, 1950), 41.

22. John Lewis Gaddis, *We Now Know: Rethinking Cold War History* (Oxford, UK: Clarendon Press, 1997), 17.

23. S. E. Ambrose and Douglas Brinkley, *Rise to Globalism: American Foreign Policy since 1938* (London: Allen Lane, Penguin, 1971), 79.

CHAPTER 12: Decline and Fall

1. According to Niall Ferguson, cited in James Patterson, *Restless Giant: The United States from Watergate to Bush vs. Gore* (Oxford, UK: Oxford University Press, 2005), 357.

2. Victoria de Grazia, *Irresistible Empire: America's Advance through Twentieth-Century Europe* (Cambridge, MA: Harvard University Press, 2005), 335.

3. Eisenhower to Edgar Newton Eisenhower, November 8, 1954, available at www.eisenhowermemorial.org.

4. Eisenhower quoted in Robert Donovan, *Eisenhower: The Inside Story* (New York: Harper, 1956), 133.

5. Dwight Eisenhower, *Mandate for Change, 1953–1956* (New York: Doubleday, 1963), 312–313.

6. Philip Darby, *Three Faces of Imperialism: British and American Approaches to Asia and Africa, 1870–1970* (New Haven, CT: Yale University Press, 1987), 157.

7. David McCullough, *Truman* (New York: Simon & Schuster, 1992), 991.

8. Truman quoted in Gregor Dallas, *1945: The War That Never Ended* (New Haven, CT: Yale University Press, 2005), 514–515.

9. Stimson, diary, June 6, 1945, describing a meeting with Truman.

10. Godfrey Hodgson, *The Colonel: The Life and Wars of Henry Stimson, 1867–1950* (New York: Knopf, 1990), 279.

11. David Lilienthal, quoting Truman, quoted in McCullough, *Truman*, 393, 650.

12. John Dower, *War without Mercy: Race and Power in the Pacific War* (New York: Pantheon, 1986), 173, 175.

13. See Grady McWhiney, "Ethnic Roots of Southern Violence," in *A Master's Due: Essays in Honor of David Herbert Donald*, ed. William J. Cooper, Michael F. Holt, and John McCardell (Baton Rouge: Louisiana State University Press, 1985), 124.

14. John Dower cited in Walter LaFeber, *The American Age: United States Foreign Policy at Home and Abroad since 1750* (New York: Norton, 1989), 448.

15. See Tsuyoshi Hasegawa, *Racing the Enemy: Stalin, Truman, and the Surrender of Japan* (Cambridge, MA: Harvard University Press, 2005).

16. Kristol quoted in Justin Vaïsse, "Le mouvement néo-conservateur aux Etats-Unis," doctoral dissertation, Paris, 2005, 72.

17. Godfrey Hodgson, "The Foreign Policy Establishment," in *Ruling America: A History of Wealth and Power in a Democracy*, ed. Steve Fraser and Gary Gerstle (Cambridge, MA: Harvard University Press, 2005), 219.

18. Walter Russell Mead, *Power, Terror, Peace, and War: America's Grand Strategy in a World at Risk* (New York: Knopf, 2004), 49.

19. John Lewis Gaddis, *We Now Know: Rethinking Cold War History* (Oxford, UK: Clarendon Press, 1997), 203.

20. Stanley Hoffmann has underscored some of these contradictions in *World Disorders: Troubled Peace in the Post-Cold War Era* (Lanham, MD: Rowman and Littlefield, 1998).

21. Kennan cited in Alan Brinkley, *The Unfinished Nation: A Concise History of the American People* (Boston: McGraw-Hill, 2004), 827.

CHAPTER 13: Wars of Religion in Bush's America

1. Samuel P. Huntington, *American Politics: The Promise of Disharmony* (Cambridge, MA: Harvard University Press, 1981), 240.

2. Adams quoted by Robert A. Ferguson in *Reconstructing American Literary History*, ed. Sacvan Bercovitch (Cambridge, MA: Harvard University Press, 1986), 21.

3. This is one of the themes of Heather Curtis's excellent unpublished manuscript, "The Lord for the body: suffering and divine healing in American vulture, 1860–1900."

4. Cited in Philip Fisher, "Appearing and Disappearing in Public," in Bercovitch, *Reconstructing American Literary History*, 157.

5. Barton and journalist quoted in Michael S. Kimmel, *Manhood in America: A Cultural History* (New York: Oxford University Press, 2006), 130, 119.

6. Kevin Phillips, *American Theocracy: The Peril and Politics of Radical Religion, Oil and Borrowed Money in the Twenty-First Century* (New York: Viking, 2006), 115.

7. Jefferson quoted in Jon Meacham, *American Gospel: God, the Founding Fathers, and the Making of a Nation* (New York: Random House, 2006), 16.

8. Anatol Lieven, *America Right or Wrong: An Anatomy of American Nationalism* (Oxford, UK: Oxford University Press, 2004), 145.

9. Walter Russell Mead, *Special Providence: American Foreign Policy and How It Changed the World* (New York: Knopf, 2001), 143.

10. Walter Benjamin, "On the Concept of History," in *Walter Benjamin's Selected Writings* (Cambridge, MA: Harvard University Press, 2003), 389.

11. Buchanan quoted in Lieven, *America Right or Wrong*, 92.

12. Lizabeth Cohen, *Making a New Deal: Industrial Workers in Chicago* (Cambridge, UK: Cambridge University Press, 1990), 289.

13. Glass quoted in Alexander Keyssar, *The Right to Vote: The Contested History of Democracy in the United States* (New York: Basic Books, 2000), 112.

14. Mill quoted in David M. Potter, *People of Plenty: Economic Abundance and the American Character* (Chicago: University of Chicago Press, 1962), 26.

15. Thomas Holt, *The Problem of Race in the Twenty-first Century* (Cambridge, MA: Harvard University Press, 2000), 112.

16. Raymond quoted in Thomas Bender, *A Nation among Nations: America's Place in World History* (New York: Hill and Wang, 2006), 189.

17. Samuel P. Huntington, *Who Are We? The Challenges to America's National Identity* (New York: Simon & Schuster, 2004), 4.

18. Mead, *Special Providence*, 188–189.

19. Eisenhower's farewell speech, January 17, 1961.

20. Phillips, *American Theocracy*.

21. Lieven, *America Right or Wrong*, 185.

22. Tony Smith, *Foreign Attachments* (Cambridge, MA: Harvard University Press, 2000), 158.

23. Kallen quoted in Werner Sollors, "Critique of Pure Pluralism," in *Reconstructing American Literary History*, ed. Bercovitch, 264.

24. Robert Bellah, "Civil Religion in America," *Daedalus* 96, no. 1 (Winter 1967), 1.

25. Washington quoted in Meacham, *American Gospel*, 261.

26. Ibid., 131.

27. Mead, *Special Providence*, 150.

28. As described in Meacham, *American Gospel*, 214.

29. Lieven, *America Right or Wrong*, 144, 182.

30. Michael Lind, "Neo-conservatives and the Counterrevolution against the New Deal," in *Ruling America: A History of Wealth and Power in a Democracy*, ed. Steve Fraser and Gary Gerstle (Cambridge, MA: Harvard University Press, 2005), 279.

31. Stefan Halpern and Jonathan Clarke, *America Alone: The Neo-Conservatives and the Global Order* (Cambridge, UK: Cambridge University Press, 2004), 4.

32. Stefan Halpern and Jonathan Clarke, *The Silence of the Rational Center: Why American Foreign Policy Is Failing* (New York: Basic Books, 2007), 9.

33. James Mann, *The Rise of the Vulcans: The History of Bush's War Cabinet* (New York: Viking, 2004), 27.

34. Frum and Perle quoted in Anne Norton, *Leo Strauss and the Politics of American Empire* (New Haven, CT: Yale University Press, 2004), 212.

35. Robert Tucker and David Henrickson, *The Imperial Temptation: The New Order and America's Purpose* (New York: Council on Foreign Relations Press, 1992), 44.

EPILOGUE

1. Lincoln quoted in Yehoshua Arieli, *Individualism and Nationalism in American Ideology* (Cambridge, MA: Harvard University Press, 1964), 307.

2. Machiavelli, *Discours sur les premier dix livres de Tite Live* in *Opere complete* di Niccolo Machiavelli (Milan, 1850), 520 (my translation).

3. Charles Rollin, *Abrégé de l'Histoire Ancienne de Monsieur Rollin* (Lyon, 1813), I, xliij.

4. Sidney Lens, *The Forging of the American Empire: From the Revolution to Vietnam: A History of U.S. Imperialism* (Chicago: Haymarket, 2003), 178.

5. Schurz quoted in Ted Halstead and Michael Lind, *The Radical Center: The Future of American Politics* (New York: Doubleday, 2001), 206.

6. Schurz quoted in R. H. Wiebe, *Who Are We? A History of Popular Nationalism* (Princeton, NJ: Princeton University Press, 2002), 86.

7. Wiebe, *Who Are We?*, 96.

8. Kevin Phillips, *American Theocracy: The Perils and Politics of Radical Religion, Oil and Borrowed Money in the Twenty-first Century* (New York: Viking, 2006), 399.

9. Roberto Unger, *What Should the Left Propose?* (London: Verso, 2005), 3.

INDEX

slavery in, 137, 146
of South *vs.* rest of country, 101–102
national identities, 171
national identity, American
    African Americans' exclusion from,
        155–156
    components of, 28, 96, 107, 126, 165–
        167, 300
    conquests not needed for, 163, 165
    constancy of, 313
    expansion of, 165, 171
    two sides of character, 176
National Labor Relations Act, 235
national movements, in Asia, 170
National Recovery Act, 234
nationalism, 19
    British, 24
    dangers of, 212
    Eurocentric, 162
    expansion of, 71–72
    German, 30–31
    patriotism and, 302, 315
    Russian, 266
    universalism *vs.*, 25–26, 49
    uses of, 25, 70, 87–88
    Vietnamese, 275
nationalism, American
    Bush's, 280, 292
    in Civil War, 145–146
    democratic, 125, 148
    as exclusionary, 74, 81, 117, 125, 313
    patriotism *vs.*, 117, 261
    regional differences in, 134, 307
    relation to War of Independence,
        42–43
    religion and, 100, 292
    Roosevelt's, 215, 250–251
    traits of, 57, 124, 308
    universalism *vs.*, 74, 251
    uses of, 57, 269
nationhood
    America's, 41–42, 209, 277
    Atlantic Charter not defining, 247–248
    Union *vs.*, 133, 140, 148

Native Americans
    American public's involvement with,
        21, 162–163
    Britain and, 36, 39, 62–63
    brutality against, 11–12, 79, 103–104,
        118–119, 159–161
    colonists and, 15–16, 62
    discrimination against, 131, 186, 238,
        259
    effects of wars on, 62–64, 108
    effects of westward expansion on, 83–
        84
    efforts to convert, 9–10
    influence on Americans, 20–21, 21, 35
    Jackson's campaign against, 114–115,
        117, 125, 191
    justifications for taking land of, 111–
        113
    loss of European allies, 35–36, 108
    population of, 31–32, 112–113
    Puritans and, 11–13, 49
    pushed westward, 110, 114, 117–118,
        160
    relations with Bostonians, 8–9
    rights movement for, 276–277
    unity of, 68, 114
    whites' battles with, 35, 62–63, 67–68,
        108
    whites' feelings about, 12–15, 44, 66–
        67, 112–113
nature, 47
navy, British, 74–76, 217, 219
navy, Spanish, 183
navy, US, 58, 181, 203, 246
    growth of, 179–180
    US depending on British, 74–76
Nazis, 11–12, 245, 266, 268, 305
neo-Calvinism, 171
neo-Marxism, 96
neoconservatives, 269, 305
    backgrounds of, 302–303
    defense of democracy at all costs,
        303–304
    influence of, 295, 302, 305